PIUS XII, THE HOLOCAUST, AND THE COLD WAR

PIUS XII,
THE HOLOCAUST, AND
THE COLD WAR

Michael Phayer

INDIANA UNIVERSITY PRESS
Bloomington and Indianapolis

Publication of this book is made possible in part with the assistance of a Challenge Grant from the National Endowment for the Humanities, a federal agency that supports research, education, and public programming in the humanities. Any views, findings, conclusions, or recommendations expressed in this publication do not necessarily reflect those of the National Endowment for the Humanities.

This book is a publication of

Indiana University Press
601 North Morton Street
Bloomington, IN 47404-3797 USA

http://iupress.indiana.edu

Telephone orders   800-842-6796
Fax orders   812-855-7931
Orders by e-mail   iuporder@indiana.edu

The paper used in this publication meets the minimum requirements of American National Standard for Information Sciences—Permanence of Paper for Printed Library Materials, ANSI Z39.48-1984.

Manufactured in the United States of America

Library of Congress Cataloging-in-Publication Data

Phayer, Michael, 1935–
   Pius XII, the Holocaust, and the Cold War / Michael Phayer.
      p.   cm.
   Includes bibliographical references and index.
   ISBN-13: 978-0-253-34930-9 (cloth : alk. paper)
   1. Pius XII, Pope, 1876–1958—Relations with Jews. 2. Judaism—Relations—Christianity. 3. Catholic Church—Relations—Judaism. 4. Christianity and anti-semitism—History—20th century. 5. Catholic Church—Foreign relations—Communist countries. 6. Communist countries—Foreign relations—Catholic Church. 7. Communism and Christianity—Catholic Church. 8. Cold War—Religious aspects—Catholic Church. I. Title.
   BX1378.P525 2007
   282.092—dc22
                                                          2007028153

1   2   3   4   5   13   12   11   10   09   08

TO

Pat, caring partner, and Dick, gentle brother.

In fond memory of Karl Bosl.

God did not make death,
and he does not delight in the death of the living.
(Book of Wisdom 1:13)

CONTENTS

PREFACE

When President Jimmy Carter met John Paul II in 1979 at the White House, he asked the pope if they should speak to each other as heads of state or as fellow Christians. Carter recognized that popes wear two hats—one political, as the head of Vatican State, and the other religious, as head of the Catholic Church. John Paul answered President Carter's question by saying they should speak as brothers. It had never before occurred to a statesman or diplomat to ask Pius XII whether they should converse as officials of the state or as fellow Christians.

My purpose is to study the political Pius XII, the pope of World War II, the Holocaust, and the early Cold War. Pius pursued a political career. His theological specialty was in church law, and he once taught international law. He had no pastoral experience to speak of, but he had broad schooling in diplomacy. At an early age he became nuncio to the German state of Bavaria during World War I and after that to Germany itself, perhaps the most important of all of the Vatican's diplomatic postings at that time. Eugenio Pacelli became the cardinal secretary of state of the Vatican in 1930 and retained that position, in effect, for the rest of his life, even after ascending the papal throne. Pius felt comfortable wearing the political hat.

A number of Pope Pius's colleagues and diplomats who were close observers have commented on Pius XII's personality and disposition, largely agreeing that he was very spiritual and very political but disagreeing about which trait predominated and how the two sides of his persona reacted to and interacted with specific wartime and Holocaust events. The French ambassador to the Vatican, Jacques Maritain, felt that Pius was too comfortable with his political role. Yet his colleagues sometimes noted that he wasn't well suited for politics. Those qualities that convinced Domenico Cardinal Tardini, contemporary and colleague of Pius, of the latter's holiness did not work as well for him in the political sphere, in the cardinal's opinion. "Pius XII was by temperament," Tardini wrote, "mild and rather shy. He was not made to be a fighter."[1]

Pope John Paul wore both political and religious hats with aplomb. Upon his death he was widely acclaimed for having contributed to the collapse of communism and widely acclaimed as a holy, perhaps saintly, man. Was Pius XII saintly? The memoir Cardinal Tardini wrote of him suggests that he was. Pius, Tardini recalled, internalized the suffering of all those caught up in the maelstrom of the war and the Holocaust. He gave his food to others; at five feet eleven, he weighed just 125 pounds by the war's end. "Very possibly," wrote the American Protestant diplomat Harold Tittmann, who was posted to the Vatican during the war, "the future will rate him a saint."[2]

Whether Pope Pius was a saint or should soon be declared a saint is not a question that I take up in these pages. Those favoring his canonization need not feel compelled to step forward with the incense defense, nor should those who disfavor it feel exonerated. Historians must not be acolytes lighting the path for Pius XII's canonization, nor should they play devil's advocates who try to derail it. Detractors and defenders of Pope Pius are alike in their rush to judgment, in their inflexible final verdicts. Clio, the muse of history, must remain free to change her mind or nuance her interpretation as new evidence becomes available or as thoughtful reconsideration prompts her.

Finding areas of reasonable common agreement about Pius XII while at the same time leaving the door open for the new interpretations that will surely come when new documents are released or discovered requires one to tread lightly and not expect to reach the end of the path. I write knowing that I will no longer be enjoyably "doing history" when the Vatican finally gets around to opening its archives up to the year 1950. But there is, after all, nothing exceptional about this situation, because the past has always been and will always be dug up anew and understood anew.

Historian Michael Marrus has observed that the eleven-volume record of the Church during World War II presents a pope who was committed to otherworldly concerns. Yet the extensive documents bearing on the Vatican in the national archives of Argentina, Great Britain, and the United States present a pope who was concerned with this-worldly affairs. These impressions are actually two sides of the same coin; saving the church of this world for its other-worldly mission was essential. By the nature of things, national archives mirror the political side of Pius XII. Because of this bias, together with the innumerable omissions from the Vatican's published papers of the World War II years, I address in this book the political Pope Pius, not the spiritual Pope Pius.

INTRODUCTION

Readers will naturally wonder how this book differs in content from my previous book, *The Catholic Church and the Holocaust, 1930–1965.* It does so in two regards. The last seven chapters cover almost entirely new material. Previous chapters overlap with content that I have earlier dealt with but contain valuable new information that was not available at my last writing. There would be no reason to write this book were it not for President Bill Clinton's 1997 order for all branches of the federal government to release their wartime and postwar documents. As a result, millions of pages of new documents became available, many of which bear on the Vatican during and after the war. The face of Pope Pius that we see in these documents is not the same face we see in the eleven volumes the Vatican published of World War II documents, a collection which, though valuable, is nonetheless critically flawed because of its many omissions.

How exactly has the Clinton directive changed the historical landscape? Without a doubt, it has changed it both in breadth and depth. New documents tell us much more about Archbishop Alojzije Stepinać of Croatia and allow us to contradict in the first chapter the label "notorious" that Tony Judt has pinned on him. They afford in chapter 2 a much greater understanding of the genocides of Polish Catholics and Polish Jews than I could delineate in my previous book. More than anything else, the documents open up a vista on Vatican investments during the war that is remarkable because of the new information in chapter 5. Here I must add a word of thanks to historian Charles Gallagher, who very generously allowed me to use material from the diary of Bishop Joseph Patrick Hurley that affords biting and unforgettable glimpses of a money culture in Vatican City.

Pius XII's postwar diplomacy can be described as dangerous because in an atomic age he was willing to risk war. I could not have made this argument in chapter 6 without the benefit of new documents in the National Archives and Records Administration. The same must be said of the book's final chapters on the Vatican "ratlines." Holocaust perpetrators ran to Italy and Spain to use the Vatican's "ratlines" to escape to South America. "Ratline" was the jargon postwar U.S. intelligence agents used to refer to the escape by sea of Nazi and other fascist murderers. In the days of tall sailing vessels, rats ran up the masts' lines to avoid drowning if the ship began to sink; war criminals boarded ships for South America after the Nazi regime began to sink. In chapter 7, I track the jumbled and bizarre path that led to the ratlines. The value in exploring this twisted course lies in the fact that we are led to see that historical outcomes are not predetermined. What turned out to be a Nazi escape route could also have been an escape route for European Catholics had the war ended differently. Recently declassified documents allowed me to unravel the truly surprising origin of the ratlines. The history of the ratlines remains, nevertheless, a work in progress. New documents from Argentina and the British Foreign Office complement those in the United States made available by the president's executive order. Yet to come are studies based on documents from Italian and Spanish archives, which I expect will someday soon complete the historical record. The new U.S. records I have seen disclose fascinating details about American espionage work as agents figured out how the Italian ratline functioned and about American diplomatic correspondence that exposed the Spanish ratline. As might be expected, none of the information about the early history of the ratlines during World War II is to be found in the Vatican's collection of documents.

Chapter 3 dealing with Pope Pius in 1942 is the exception to the rule of new documentation in this volume. No new Vatican documents bear on these years. Yet those familiar with *The Catholic Church and the Holocaust* will notice that I have departed from my earlier position. I now argue that Pius XII denounced genocide in the 1942 Christmas radio address. It is still not clear *whose* genocide or *which* genocide he was referring to, and we can do no more than speculate as to *why* he spoke out. In revising my thinking about the 1942 address, I owe a debt of gratitude to Michael Marrus, whose invitation to participate in a Toronto University conference on the Holocaust and the Netherlands and to discuss the Vatican in that regard led me to rethink the importance of the Christmas address. The Catholic Church's confrontation with the Nazis in the Netherlands makes clear that the Dutch understood Pope Pius to have denounced genocide.

1943 turned out to be the most momentous year of the war—the year when the offensive shifted decisively to the Allies. It was also the most trying and stressful year for Pius XII, the year that the Holocaust came to his home city of Rome. I find the complexities of the situation the pope faced at that time to be the most challenging of any of the prewar, wartime, or postwar episodes he had to deal with. In chapter 4, new documentation, especially decryptions of German messages, shed a more intense light on events in Rome than in the past. I try to explain the factors surrounding the October seizure of Roman Jews as Pius saw them, which means that I deal with the Jewish catastrophe as only one of five circumstances worrying the pope (and the Jews were not necessarily the most important issue on the pope's list). But because the Holocaust is what it is, the Jewish calamity has turned out to be the most important of the various elements that Pope Pius was contending with that year, and how he dealt with it has become the litmus test of his reputation. In this matter I have again shifted somewhat from my previous evaluation. While still presenting the German diplomats in Rome as the initiators of the effort to save the city's Jews, I now believe that the Vatican cooperated in this attempt at rescue. This was possible, I have come to think, while still acknowledging historian Susan Zuccotti's research, which demonstrated that the pope did not give orders for Roman Catholic institutions to open their doors to the Jews.

I have mentioned how this book differs in content from my last study. How does it differ thematically? For the most part it is a matter of emphasis, not a new thematic approach. The focus is on Pius XII and the undiluted fear of communism that drove him. The extraordinary extent to which fear of communism shaped Vatican actions before, during, and after the war is astounding, and it astounded President Roosevelt's (and later Truman's) envoy to the Vatican, Myron Taylor, when he heard Pope Pius tell of the imminence of a Communist invasion of Italy. The only concern overriding but by no means replacing his fear of communism came during a two-year span of his papacy, 1942–1944, when outright physical destruction threatened Rome and the Vatican. There is no other way, other than fear of communism, to explain the pope's audacious ratline venture.

In spite of the abundance of new documents that have become available in the United States, Great Britain, and Argentina, we continue to see through a glass darkly. The wealth of detail and innumerable surprises resulting from the opening of the Vatican's interwar archives mean that until the in-house records of the Vatican for the period of the war and the Cold War become available to historians, historical accuracy will be wanting. The Vatican's published documents in the eleven-volume collection *Actes et Documents du Saint Siège Relatifs á la Seconde Guerre Mondiale* are an indispensable yet vastly incomplete source. None of the Vatican's financial records, which could very well shed light on the disposition of looted gold Ustaša fascists took to Rome at the end of the war (see chapter 8), are contained in *Actes et Documents*. Records that document the close contact of Pope Pius and other top Vatican officials during and after the war with various continental and South American fascists are also not to be found in *Actes et Documents*. These are the sources that would detail the Vatican's ratline operation.

After the war Robert Graham, S.J., one of the editors of the Vatican's documents, collected additional source material from outside the Holy See and interviewed individuals who were knowledgeable about European and Vatican affairs. When he retired, he took these records with him to California. His stash of material was open to the public, although few knew about it. At some point after Graham's death, the Vatican insisted that all of his papers be sealed and returned to Rome.[1] The Holy See, obviously, has a problem with the conduct of its affairs during the war, a problem it wishes to conceal. The gaps in *Actes et Documents* notwithstanding, the new documents available in several national archives allow us to peek under the curtain, even if we cannot draw it fully back.

History at its best is a collaborative effort. I have benefited greatly from a number of excellent studies that have appeared since the turn of the century and the publication of my last book. For prewar Vatican affairs, the two books by David Kertzer, *Prisoner of the Vatican* and *The Popes Against the Jews*, Peter Godman's *Hitler and the Vatican*, Gerhard Besier's *Der Heilige Stuhl und Hitler-Deutschland. Die Faszination des Totalitären*, David Alvarez's *Spies in the Vatican*, and John Pollard's *Money and the Rise of the Modern Papacy* are indispensable.[2] These studies provide astonishing views of great depth and complexity that portray how the Vatican dealt with worldly concerns and problems. We are still waiting for an inquiry into the spiritual world of the Vatican's popes during the first half of the twentieth century.

For the war and the Holocaust years, I have relied especially on Susan Zuccotti's impeccably researched *Under His Very Windows*, Robert Katz's *The Battle for Rome*, and Paul Damian O'Shea's marvelous doctoral dissertation, "Confiteor. Eugenio Pacelli, the Catholic Church and the Jews. An Examination of the Responsibility of Pope Pius XII and the Holocaust, 1917–1943." Gerald D. Feldman's minutely and expansively researched *Allianz and the German Insurance Business, 1930–1945* allowed me to grasp the significance of the Vatican's wartime purchase of shares in an insurance corporation. Attempts to understand Pope Pius during the Holocaust without a clear perception of Germany's process of murdering Poles and Jews inevitably fail. In this respect I relied on

Christopher R. Browning's works, especially the masterful *Origins of the Final Solution*.[3] Also indispensable for the war years is *U.S. Intelligence and the Nazis*, the work of Richard Breitman and three of his colleagues at the Interagency Working Group of the U.S. National Archives and the Japanese Imperial Government Records.[4]

For the postwar years—the early years of the Cold War—Uki Goñi's extremely well-researched *The Real Odessa* was critical.[5] The Argentine and British records Goñi exploited complemented my own research in the U.S. national archives, allowing me to piece together the origin and operation of the Vatican's ratline in a manner much more complete than otherwise would have been the case. A second essential help for the postwar era is the study by the Interagency Working Group, *U.S. Intelligence and the Nazis*. The Interagency Working Group readied the documents for general use that were made available by President Clinton's executive order.

My research of documents in the national archives and at the Center for Advanced Holocaust Studies (of the U.S. Holocaust Memorial Museum) began in 2001 when I was a fellow at the Center. Without the Center's fellowship, my work would have been delayed by years. My research, which I took up again in 2003, was enormously benefited by archivist Greg Bradsher, whose *Holocaust-Era Assets: A Finding Aid to Records at the National Archives at College Park* (National Archives and Records Administration, 1999) was indispensable. Along the way, Greg was invariably ready to help with my questions.

A few disclaimers. First, the pros and cons of the cause for sainthood of Pius XII may be debated as readers see fit, but I do not debate them in this book. Second, I am not qualified to discuss Eugenio Pacelli's formative years; as a consequence, I refrain from drawing on psychological insights to explain his actions or inactions. In the final chapter, I limit myself to reporting on contemporaries' views of Pope Pius and commenting on these impressions and perceptions. Third, because history is by nature unfinished business, I have chosen to ignore single-minded debaters. Much of the literature of the so-called Pius wars does not meet the standard of open-minded historical discourse. Fourth, what we know today from archival records is likely much less than we will someday know. (Before reading Godman's and Besier's books, based on the newly released Vatican documents of the interwar period, I would not have said this.) Conclusions must therefore be considered tentative. I am mindful that historians should never claim to have spoken the final word.

To those who have helped along the way I very much wish to extend words of gratitude. Professors Charles Gallagher and Jonathan Petropoulis reviewed parts of the manuscript and made valuable corrections and observations. Susan Zuccotti performed the same service for an article to be published in *Holocaust and Genocide Studies* in which I developed the thoughts found in chapter 4 dealing with Pius XII's change of course in 1943. Father John Pawlikowski, O.S.M., provided me with a copy of an important Vatican document from the archives of Argentina which I otherwise would not have known about. Paul Damian O'Shea verified a key Italian phrase and provided me with several important references. In London, Nicola Mitchell retrieved some vital documents from the Public Record Office. Mr. Edward O. Barnes at the National Archives in College Park, Maryland, was invariably attentive and helpful when I had difficulties tracking down boxes. I am most grateful to Uki Goñi, who gave me valuable leads and answered questions I had with regard to his references to papers at the British Public Record Office and the papers of Bishop Hudal in Rome. Sherry Hyman, director of archives and records department of the American Joint Distribution Committee, was most helpful by sending me copies of important documents. By her meticulous editing, Kate Babbitt made this book more readable and understandable than I could have imagined. Robert Sloan, editorial director at the Indiana University Press, provided help all along the way both for this and my previous book. To all, my sincere thanks.

PIUS XII, THE HOLOCAUST, AND THE COLD WAR

1
EUGENIO PACELLI
1900 TO 1942

Why the years 1900 to 1942? The turn of the nineteenth century was the time of the first genocides about which Pacelli, as a recently ordained priest, would have read or heard about, and 1942 was the year Pacelli, as Pope Pius XII, denounced genocide. The aim of this chapter is to review briefly the episodes of genocide Pacelli experienced from the turn of the twentieth century to December 1942. Pope Pius, an extremely cautious person and a seasoned diplomat, would not have made a pronouncement about genocide in 1942 without consulting the Vatican record on past atrocities. For this reason it seems important to review them.

African Genocides

Two brutal genocides had occurred in Africa at the turn of the twentieth century. African tribes known as the Herero and Nama rebelled against German colonizers in 1904. The Germans took military action against the tribes: German officers had the authority to shoot any tribesman, no questions asked. If they were not shot, the Herero were put on trial by a military court on the spot.[1] Over the next four years, the Germans rounded up the two tribes and put them in concentration camps. There they received little to eat and declined to the point of complete listlessness, acquiring the blank stare Jews would later exhibit in Nazi concentration camps where they were derogatorily dubbed Müsselmänner (meaning something like "blank-faced Muslims"). At times, the death rate in the camps soared well over 50 percent. Most died of scurvy or typhus.[2] Eventually most Herero and Nama survivors were driven into desert territory where there was no possibility of their sustaining life, a scene that present-day images from Darfur call to mind.[3] In the desert, they wandered from water hole to water hole, but these were scarce and the Germans poisoned some of them.[4] A contemporary military report tells with chilling matter-of-factness what happened to those who were not yet dead or in camps:

> Like half dead wild animals they wandered from water hole to water hole until at last they became a victim of nature in their own homeland. . . . The dry Omaheke [Desert] finished off what German guns began: the execution of the Herero people.[5]

The genocide in German Southwest Africa seems remote to us in the twenty-first century, but only forty years separate it from the Holocaust. Historians see the genocide of the Herero as a warm-up for the genocide of Jews. The murder of the Africans broke a taboo that later found its most radical expression in the Holocaust.[6] The war against the Herero and Nama was a racial war which set a precedent for the Nazi racial wars. It is not known how the Vatican reacted, but Catholics in Germany were encouraged to support the effort in order to "bring order" to Africa. Missionaries on the scene objected to the cruelty of the colonizers to no effect. What the Holy See or the priest Eugenio Pacelli thought of the German cruelty is not known.

Concurrent with genocide in South West Africa was an even more brutal atrocity in the Belgian Congo. An estimated 6 to 10 million natives of the colony were murdered—what one historian has called "a holocaust before Hitler's Holocaust."[7] In exploiting the Congo for rubber, King Leopold II of Belgium enslaved, murdered, flogged, worked to death, and maimed black Africans (cutting off hands was not uncommon).[8] In the first decade of the new century, the Vatican became directly involved in an international debate about whether atrocities were being perpetrated on the Africans. Strong international criticism of King Leopold II arose, expressed by belletrists, Protestant missionaries, and a British consul posted in Africa. In England, a Congo Reform Association was formed which became instrumental in bringing these accusations to the British Parliament.

In the midst of the furor, the Vatican supported the cause of Belgium, a Catholic country. An American prelate, James Cardinal Gibbons of Baltimore, led the counterattack against the king's critics. Gibbons was considered the most outstanding Catholic leader of the American Church up to that time and had contacts among mighty American capitalists such as Nelson Aldrich, the Guggenheims, and John D. Rockefeller, some of whom Leopold had granted mineral rights in the Congo.[9] Gibbons claimed that King Leopold had high-minded ideals and talked about the "splendid results achieved through his humane policy."[10] Year after year, Gibbons defended the Belgian king, neglecting all the while to cultivate a disciplined investigation of how the Belgians were governing the Congolese. John Tracy Ellis, the biographer of Gibbons and dean of American Catholic history during his lifetime, acknowledged that the cardinal's "normally keen judgment went astray."[11]

The Vatican went astray with it. Pope Pius X backed Cardinal Gibbons's defense of the Catholic king through his influential secretary of state, Cardinal Rafael Merry del Val. It appears that instead of being debated on its own right, the Congo affair became snarled in the politics of Protestant loathing of Catholicism. The Vatican encouraged Gibbons to rally other American bishops to oppose the accusations of Protestant missionaries, which it characterized as false.[12] It is not likely that Eugenio Pacelli had any voice in the Holy See's involvement with King Leopold's enterprise, as he had just begun working on a new codification of church law under the tutelage of Cardinal Gasparri, a high-ranking Vatican insider. Yet Pacelli would certainly have been aware of the Holy See's involvement in the multiyear debate over the Congo, and as a student of international law, he would naturally have been interested in legal aspects of colonial matters. We may be certain that Pacelli was a close observer of the pope and the conduct of the Holy See's affairs; after he became Pope Pius XII, he canonized Pius X in 1954.

World War I

It is often said that Pacelli, as Pius XII, patterned himself after Pope Benedict XV. Benedict, elected at the beginning of World War I during a highly politicized conclave that saw cardinals from Central and Entente powers casting barbs at each other, tried but failed to sponsor peace negotiations. Neither of the belligerents heralded the conclave's choice of Benedict. During the war, German money, albeit private money, kept the Vatican afloat, as a result of which Entente powers concluded that Benedict was in Berlin's pocket. Pacelli, whom Benedict posted to Munich as nuncio, was directly involved in sending out feelers about peace. This too raised suspicion that the Holy See favored the Central Powers, since it was not involved with negotiations with France or England.[13] During the war, the Vatican did nothing to advance its reputation when it failed to speak out about protecting Eastern European Jews. Pacelli would certainly have known about this affair, although it is doubtful that he was personally involved in any way.

On the other hand, Benedict attempted to halt the Armenian geno-cide at the hands of the Turks in the middle of the war. In a letter to Sultan Mehmed V, Benedict, without naming the perpetrators, asked the sultan to put an end to the killing and rescue the survivors.[14] The role Eugenio Pacelli played in the wartime Armenian affair contrasts sharply with his role in the African genocides. The future pope had risen rapidly in the bureaucracy of the Holy See; he had been appointed undersecre-tary of state in 1912. He remained in that position until he was sent to Bavaria as nuncio in 1917. Thus, he most likely was involved to some extent with the letter to the sultan. At the very least we can say with as-surance that he would have been very much aware of Benedict's effort to stop the massacre of the Armenians.

During and after World War I, Pope Benedict, in the words of histo-rian Paul O'Shea, "undertook a significant program of assistance for vic-tims of [the] war without reference to nationality, ethnicity or religion."[15] Papal relief, some of which represented the Holy See's own money, came to approximately 20 million dollars, a quite estimable amount for those days. Vatican relief was extensive, ranging to Poland, Russia, Syria, and Lebanon, among other countries.[16] Historian John Pollard wrote that Benedict's support for children was so generous that he may be consid-ered one of the founders of the Save the Children Fund.[17] Pacelli did not leave Rome for Munich until the spring of 1917, and he would certainly have been very aware of Benedict's war relief efforts.

Italian Interwar Aggression

In 1935, Italy declared war on Ethiopia in northeast Africa. Although this probably cannot be considered a racial war, it had racial connota-tions as a colonial venture. It bears importance for our study of Pius XII because as the secretary of state, Cardinal Pacelli would have been closely involved. Pope Pius XI did not want Mussolini's project to fail because he thought it would set back missionary work in the colonies all over Africa. Ironically, there was more religious freedom in Haile Selassie's Ethiopia than there was in Italy.[18] By the time of the war, the Holy See had become so deeply invested in Italian industrial production that it was in no small measure responsible for the war matériel the country produced. Although historian John Pollard argues that the pope did not actually finance the war with a loan to Mussolini, he certainly was loyal to his country.[19] Losing the war would have been costly for the Vatican for obvious reasons, and it would have had serious political repercussions. If Pius XI was complicit in racist materialism associated with the Italian aggression, he was not a racist. He saw to it that Ethiopians were ordained priests and bishops.[20]

Before the war began, Pope Pius XI seemed to take a position against the Italian government. *L'Osservatore Romano* reported that the pope said that "the need to expand is not a right per se, but simply a fact of which note must be taken. Self-defense, on the other hand, constitutes a right, but the exercise of this right may be harmful if it does not observe certain limits and a certain moderation."[21] Although obtuse, the statement, taken together with the pope's refusal to bless Italian soldiers slated for the invasion, made it appear that the pope opposed it. Under pressure from Mussolini, Pius backed away from this position just a week later in an address given at the basilica of St. Paul's Outside the Walls. The pope said he was praying for peace. But he added that the "hopes, the demands, the needs of a great and good people, who are [my] people . . . will be recognized and satisfied . . . but with justice and peace."[22] During the exchanges between the Italian government, which was anxious for the pope's endorsement, and the Vatican, Cardinal Pacelli naturally took an active role.

Pius XI's conduct before the war may be characterized as feckless. His positions, never clearly stated, flip-flopped spinelessly. He prayed, he said, for peace before the war, but he did nothing to support the League of Nations or individual states in their efforts to resolve contested issues between Italy and Ethiopia. At no time before or during the conflict did Pius XI condemn Italy's aggression.[23] Cardinal Pacelli, as Pius XII, would also fail to condemn Germany's aggression against Poland that triggered World War II.

World War II: Catholic Ethnic Atrocities in Poland

Soon after becoming Pius XII in March 1939, the new pope had to deal with atrocities in Poland perpetrated by Catholics against Catholics. When the Treaty of Versailles made Poland a sovereign state, many Germans changed abruptly from being citizens of Germany to being members of a minority group of Germans subject to a Polish government. At the beginning of World War II, relations between Poles and ethnic Germans in Poland, the Volksdeutsch, became bitter, even vicious. The situation proved dreadful for the Vatican and for the new pope, who witnessed atrocities between members of his church.

When Germany occupied and annexed northwestern Poland (the

provinces of Warthegau, Danzig–West Prussia, and Zeichenau) to the Greater Reich, the Vatican had to deal with the question of how to reorganize church administration without aggravating the raw nerve of ethnic feelings that characterized the two groups. The problem proved insurmountable. The Germans aimed to strangle Polish culture in the newly acquired area and insisted that all religious services use the German language (wherever Latin was not obligatory). If Pius had acceded to the reality of this situation and created a German church administration for the newly incorporated territories in question, Poles would have seen it as a double betrayal. First Pius refused to censure Germany's invasion, then he gave implicit recognition to the breaking up of Poland. Betrayal was exactly what Poles felt when Pius appointed the German Franciscan Hilarius Breitinger the apostolic administrator for the Wartheland in May 1942.

Catholic documents disagree about relations between the two ethnic groups. One observer reported that "finally in the interests of the truth I have to say that most of the Volksdeutsch living here in Poland condemn what the Germans are doing" to the Poles. But a second document asserts quite the opposite. "The attitude of the [Volksdeutsch] Catholics toward what the Germans are doing to the Poles varies. Many take an active hand in the persecution of the [Polish] Church. Such Catholics hold rigorously to the complete upheaval of the Church in Poland." The key to unraveling this contradiction may lie in the person of Hilarius Breitinger, the Franciscan who assisted Bishop Dymek in Gnesen-Posen after Cardinal August Hlond fled the country. Breitinger was a Volksdeutscher who, at Hlond's invitation, had been administering to ethnic Germans in Posen since well before the war began. Poles, Breitinger wrote in a letter to Pope Pius, "did not like" his pastoral work, although he was careful not to involve himself in politics.[24] When the war began, Breitinger found out just how much the Polish people did not like him.

Immediately after Germany invaded Poland, Breitinger was arrested and told to report to the local police. He need not take any provisions, he was told, as this was just a formality. The "formality" turned out to be a three-week life-threatening ordeal. Polish vigilantes led Breitinger and other mostly lay Volksdeutschers around the countryside endlessly. All the while Poles heaped abuse on them and beat them with whatever was at hand. Breitinger was struck in the head by a brick which, he thought, would have killed him had it not struck the arm of his glasses. This treatment continued day and night. The captives were given little if anything to eat or to drink. At night they were given no place to sleep. Exposed to the elements, the sick and elderly perished. When some of the captives weakened and were not able to keep up, they were murdered. "It was clear to us what the purpose of all this was," Breitinger later wrote. "We were open game."[25] Finally, as the group of tortured Volksdeutschers found itself between the retreating Polish army and the advancing German army, its tormentors abandoned them. When the German army came upon them, they all sang "Deutschland, Deutschland über Alles," the German national anthem.

Six Volksdeutsch priests sent Cardinal Michael Faulhaber in Munich a letter that, like Breitinger's letter, told of brutal treatment administered to other groups of ethnic Germans. August Rauhut was traveling with another group of Volksdeutschers that was terribly mistreated between the second and eleventh of September 1940. As they attempted to make their way to Gnesen, they were stopped en route and stripped of all their belongings. The police tried to stir up Poles to attack them with some success. While they waited in Wreschen for the train to Gnesen, they witnessed a group of about 100 Volksdeutschers being attacked by angry Poles. When the train came it was full of Polish refugees. Rauhut's group knew that if they boarded it they would be killed.

The next day, more Volksdeutschers arrived in Wreschen just after a German bombing raid. Furious Poles attacked them, throwing rocks and debris at them. Rauhut was called a spy and a traitor; people spat on him. He pulled his jacket over his head so the crowd would not see that he was a Volksdeutsch priest. Unable to take a train safely, the group made its way on foot toward Gnesen. But so many Polish refugees crowded the road that they knew better than to use that route and made their way through forests and fields. They spent three nights in the forest without food or water, thinking that the German army would soon overtake them. The starving group decided to send a delegation of three into the closest town to try to get authorities to authorize their journey to Gnesen. Rauhut was one of the three. This strategy worked temporarily. They got official authorization and were received kindly by Polish priests who put them up overnight. But on their way back to the forest to rescue their group, Polish vigilantes seized them. This time they were taken to an unfriendly official who told them they would be shot. "I was terrified," Rauhut later wrote. At this point, Rauhut was separated from the other German priests and rescued by the local church authority, a Polish vicar general. "I later learned that my fellow delegate was shot at the cemetery after digging his own grave."[26] On the ninth, the German army reached Gnesen. Rauhut referred to this as the "liberation" of the city.

The similar accounts of Rauhut and Breitinger told what must have happened to many—perhaps thousands—of Volksdeutsch. They were a population of about 1.5 million living scattered among 6 million Poles. No doubt the parents and grandparents of ethnic Germans in Poland had passed down to the World War II generation patriotic stories from the era before World War I when Poland was still partitioned among Germany, Austria, and Russia. Breitinger's group proudly greeted the German army with the national anthem and Rauhut reported that Gnesen had been "liberated." For the next four years, life in the Greater Reich was good for the onetime Volksdeutschers, who could often literally cash in on the cruelties that German occupational authorities heaped upon their Polish neighbors who were dispossessed of house and home. But prosperity ended abruptly for the Volksdeutschers in the last year of the war when Poles and Russians killed, maimed, and despoiled many—perhaps most—of them as the German army retreated.

In the interim, the "good" four years for the ethnic Germans, how had they treated Poles when the shoe was on the other foot? In many instances, they treated them badly. In certain areas, the Volksdeutsch refused to attend Mass in a Polish church or take the sacraments from Polish priests. Rather, they attended churches for military or civilian Germans. Often these churches had military chaplains whom the Volksdeutschers called "parachuting priests."[27] What was at play here was a cultural war. It does not seem that the former Volksdeutschers physically abused Poles during the German occupation of Poland. But there was no need for that; the German army killed, beat, and despoiled the Poles living in Greater Reich. The former Volksdeutchers, like the Nazis, wanted to eliminate Polish cultural influence from their vicinity and return to the "good old days" prior to World War I, when the Polish nation was partitioned off the map of Europe.

It is significant that the letters of Breitinger and Rauhut originated from Posen and that negative reports on the Volksdeutsch mentioned Silesia as a particularly troublesome area. It can hardly be accidental that these two provinces are the ones for which documents have survived that deal with troubled Polish-German ethnic relations. Both areas, situated today in western Poland, had pockets of large majorities and large minorities of both ethnic groups that had been rubbing up against each other for hundreds of years. It was precisely these areas—West Prussia, Posen, and Upper Silesia—that had been taken from Germany and given to Poland by the Treaty of Versailles. It was then that the Germans became the minority—Volksdeutschers subject to what they naturally perceived as a foreign government. We would expect that the ethnic conflicts peculiar to these areas would be more pronounced than in other areas of Poland. But even in these areas there were exceptions to the rule of Polish hostility. The letters of the two priests, Breitinger and Rauhut, mention that some Poles tried to come to the rescue of the Catholic Volksdeutschers as they were being tormented. "It must be said," Breitinger wrote, "that many Polish priests tried to come to our assistance and to tell the people to becalm themselves."[28]

Nevertheless, Breitinger was shocked at the treatment dealt to him and his Volksdeutsch followers at the hands of co-religionists. "That all this was possible in a Catholic country, is for me naturally especially bitter."[29] How could it be explained? Breitinger thought that the Polish people had been lied to by civil authorities and were made furious by the press and radio. He also speculated that Polish Catholicism was too superficial.

For both the Volksdeutsch and Poles, nationalism overwhelmed religious consciousness during the war. Many Poles were inspired to lash out at the Volksdeutsch when the hated German invaders penetrated their homeland with overwhelming force, and many took their revenge at the end of the war. It is understandable then, that once the Volksdeutsch became the privileged group, as they had been prior to World War I, they shunned Catholic Poles in those areas where they had been abused by them. But overheated mutual hostility does not seem to have been common to all of Poland. As we will see in the following chapter, it was Breitinger who pleaded with Pius XII to intervene on behalf of the Church in Poland.

Pius XII found out about the atrocities perpetrated by Catholics on Catholics soon after they occurred. Not trusting the Berlin nuncio, Cesare Orsenigo, to dispatch his descriptive letter to the pope, Breitinger gave a copy of it to Cardinal Faulhaber, who sent it on its way. The letter saddened the new pope beyond words. After the war, the area of Poland the Germans had annexed to the Reich was given back to the Poles together with a large area east of the Oder and Neisse rivers that was formerly German and was heavily populated with ethnic Germans. When Pope Pius learned that after the war Cardinal Hlond had banned the use of German in liturgical services in areas where ethnic Germans lived, he wept.[30]

Catholic Genocide in Croatia

The new relatively young pope was confronted with two genocides during the early years of the war, one in Poland, which we take up in the next chapter, and the second in the renegade state of Croatia, formerly a province of Yugoslavia. The two genocides occurred concurrently. I have described the origin of the Nazi puppet state of Croatia and its outcome in *The Catholic Church and the Holocaust*. To recapitulate briefly, a convicted assassin, Ante Pavelić, established Croatia in 1941 with Hitler's backing after the German military campaign in Greece and the collapse of the Yugoslav government. Toward the end of the war, Marshal Josip Tito overpowered Pavelić's Ustaša dictatorship and restored Yugoslav rule under his own power. During the four years of Pavelić's rule, the Ustaša government, whose members were ethnically Croat and religiously Catholic, perpetrated a grotesque atrocity on Serbs who had held power in the Yugoslav government established by the Treaty of Versailles. The Ustaša murdered an estimated 300,000 to 400,000 Serbs, who were Orthodox Christians, and about 50,000 Jews. Of interest here because of new documentation that has recently been declassified is the role that Archbishop Alojzije Stepinać played during the years of genocide. The question of his innocence bears investigating because of the 1946 trial under Tito's rule that found him guilty.

Stepinać, who was named the bishop of Zagreb in 1934, took possession of his diocese as the youngest Catholic prelate in the world. Made an archbishop a few years later while still in his thirties, Stepinać became the highest-ranking church leader in Yugoslavia. Despite the fact that the Vatican had signed a concordat with Yugoslavia in 1935, Stepinać was a strong Croat nationalist who referred to the Yugoslav state as "the jail of the Croatian nation." Stepinać, a ruggedly handsome man, looked stubborn and strong willed with his jutting jaw. As soon as Ante Pavelić came to power, the archbishop arranged to have Pius XII receive him for the purpose of solidifying the dictator's power among Catholic Croatians. Pius granted him an audience but only as a private citizen, not as a head of state, and sent his representative to Croatia but not with the title of nuncio. The Vatican had recognized Yugoslavia with its concordat; now it would use a wait-and-see policy with the new state.

It soon became clear to Stepinać that he got more than he bargained for with the dictator Pavelić. After the German military left Croatia in June 1941 to join the assault on the Soviet Union, Pavelić's Ustaša began slaughtering Serbs by the thousands in the summer and fall. For the next several years until the end of the war, Stepinać and Pius XII were confronted with a genocidal Catholic dictator. To this day, it is impossible to discern how the archbishop and his pope went about discussing how to deal with the dilemma. The editors of *Actes et Documents*, the Vatican's World War II records, included no protocols of the innumerable meetings the pope had with many of the historical figures mentioned

FIGURE 1. Adolf Hitler greets Ante Pavelić, leader of the Croatian puppet state,
upon his arrival at the Berghof in the Bavarian Alps, June 9, 1941.
Courtesy of the United States Holocaust Memorial Museum.

in this book, nor is there a record denoting with whom he met. These omissions apply in the case of Archbishop Stepinać. In the spring of 1942, Stepinać traveled to Rome to give the pope a nine-page report on the situation in Croatia. (The editors of *Actes et Documents* omitted the report.) What is known is that both the pope and the archbishop knew about the Ustaša-perpetrated genocide. We do not need papal records to be certain of this.

But we do know that both Stepinać and the pope thought in terms of either an independent Croatia or a largely independent country in a federated state. In 1941 and 1942, it did not appear to them that Germany would lose the war. Pius XII envisioned a postwar Eastern Europe anchored by a bloc of countries—a constellation like that of the Austro-Hungarian Empire, which earlier in the century had embraced Croatia. Hungarians, Austrians, and Croats had once been the bulwark of Europe that held off the infidel Muslim. Might not they now form a bulwark against the new infidel—the atheist Soviets? In this mindset, the archbishop and the pope looked forward, not toward what genocide might portend in the coming months but toward a Catholic Croatia that would play its part in the constellation of European states of the future. They were willing to countenance what both knew to be a moral outrage for the short term in the hope of a favorable political landscape in the future. The bottom line is that neither Stepinać nor Pius XII publicly condemned the Ustaša government. To do so might have precipitated the end of the regime—and the end of a geopolitical dream.

But Stepinać did condemn the murderous excesses of Pavelić. New documents amplify the extent to which he did this. The following report, dated May 1942, reflects not only Stepinać's reaction but also those of other Catholic leaders:

> According to reports . . . obtained [in New York by a Yugoslav official], there are 600,000 refugees in Serbia from Bosnia and in addition there are two hundred thousand Slovenian refugees in Serbian territory! Now these refugees came because of the outrages of the Ustashi . . . all over Croatia and Bosnia. The Croats did not do much to appease the situation. The archbishop of Sarajevo, Saritch [Sarić] praised the revolutionaries [the Ustaša]—the archbishop of Zagreb [Stepinać] condemned the outrages against the Serbs and Jews, but did not raise his voice against Pavelic.[31]

In October 1942, on a major liturgical feast day, the archbishops said, "We affirm then that all peoples and races descend from God. In fact, there exists but one race."[32] It is clear that other clergy refused to accept Stepinać's leadership. Archbishop Sarić was by no means the only prelate or clergyman in Croatia who wholeheartedly backed Pavelić's murderous regime while saying nothing about its atrocities. Indeed, many clergymen backed the genocide of the Serbs in word or deed or both. The Vatican knew very well that many of the clergy had joined in the slaughter, as Cardinal Eugene Tisserant admitted to a Yugoslav envoy in 1946: "You may have my full assurance that we have the list of all the clergymen who participated in these atrocities and we shall punish them at the right time to cleanse our conscience of the stain with which they spotted us."[33] Therein lay precisely the Vatican's misjudgment—"the right time" never came.

While many of the clergy supported Pavelić's bloody "crusade," Archbishop Stepinać persevered in criticizing Ustaša crimes. In May 1943, U.S. intelligence reported that "archbishop Stepinac protested to [the] Croatian government against persecutions of Jews and Serbians. [He] strongly criticized racial discrimination and murder of innocent victims and atrocities."[34] The information does not make it clear whether Stepinać's criticism was made publicly or privately to Pavelić. The latter is certainly possible, since the U.S. Office of Strategic Services (OSS) had contacts within the Ustaša regime who would have had access to private information. However, a Swiss news agency reported that Stepinać had indeed protested, both publicly and directly to the government:

> In March 1943 the archbishop of Zagreb intervened in favor of Jews victimized by racial laws of Nuremberg by sending a strong and immediate protest to the chief of state, Pavelic. The following Sunday in his homily, the archbishop raised his voice against the racial laws, saying. . . . "no temporal power, no political organization has the right to persecute a man because of his race."[35]

In July, the *New York Times* reported that Vatican radio had broadcast Stepinać's protest against the Ustaša government's adoption of the Nuremberg Laws. (Neither Pius XI nor Pius XII ever specifically denounced the Nuremberg decrees.)[36] This report establishes definitively that Stepinać's criticism of the Ustaša regime was public.

Most important among newly declassified documents are those originating from Switzerland in the person of Monsignor Augustin Juretić.[37] This Croat priest went into voluntary exile, at Stepinać's urging, in the fall of 1942. As a supporter of Pavelić's rival, Vlatko Maček of the Croatian Peasant Party, Juretić took exception to the Ustaša's genocidal actions. In Switzerland, Juretić received information leaked from Croatia on an ongoing basis that he fed to the Yugoslav Government in Exile in London and, at times, to the OSS. With Pavelić disgracing the country, Catholics fed up with the Ustaša would certainly have seen the possibility of a moderate democratic Croatia under Maček but within a federal Yugoslav state. The fact that Archbishop Stepinać fed Juretić a steady stream of information critical of the Pavelić regime after urging his clerical colleague to leave the country strongly suggests that he would have welcomed a Maček government. An officer of the Royal Yugoslav army, Stanislav Rapoteć, sneaked into Croatia in April 1942 with the help of a British submarine. After hearing praises of Stepinać from Jewish and Serbian underground personnel, Rapoteć met with the archbishop. "In their meetings, Stepinać spoke wistfully of a new federated postwar Yugoslav state as advocated by Maček's followers."[38]

In June 1943, Juretić wrote a lengthy report defending Stepinać and sent it to Allen Dulles, chief of the OSS, for his consideration. "The report," historian Norman Goda wrote, "contains short and long excerpts from a number of Stepinać's sermons and as well as letters from Stepinać to Croatian government officials from 1941 to 1943, all of which question and attack the regime's persecution of other races, religions, and nationalities."[39] Because of the length and detail of the excerpts, it must be concluded that Juretić was receiving Stepinać's documents from the archbishop himself. It must also be concluded that Stepinać knew that his information would be shared with the Yugoslav Government in Exile and with the OSS and, in fact, intended this when he sent dispatches to Switzerland.

Juretić concluded his favorable memorial on Stepinać by saying that the words of the archbishop "have dug an insuperable ditch between him and the Quisling government and German authorities."[40] Although this was an overly inflated conclusion, the documents released in the past few years substantiate without any doubt Stepinać's condemnation of Ustaša mistreatment of Jews and Serbs and of the regime's genocide. Yet while Stepinać condemned the government's deeds, he did not condemn the government itself. Stepinać, a Croat nationalist, was willing to suffer the Pavelić regime until something better—a Maček regime—was a viable alternative. Although he had criticized the former Yugoslav government, when faced with the Ustaša's wanton slaughter, Stepinać would have second-guessed himself and favored an independent Croatia within a federated Yugoslav state.[41] In no way is Stepinać deserving of the label "notorious" pinned on him by historian Tony Judt.[42] No other Catholic church leader in Europe spoke out against atrocities as clearly as Stepinać, with the single exception of Johannes de Jong in the Netherlands. Among the Catholic leaders of the various national churches in Eastern Europe, Stepinać was without parallel in his outspoken opposition to genocide.

Before addressing the world about genocide at Christmas 1942, Pope Pius would naturally have looked back over his life and the genocides that had periodically arisen. What did he see? What did he make of what he saw? The turn-of-the-century genocides probably had little relevance in his mind to the contemporary scene in Europe. That genocide involved Christians murdering non-Christian, non-Western African natives. Even if Pius XII accepted uncritically Pius X's claim that King Leopold's agents in the Congo were not guilty of genocide, he was still left with the fact that Christians had slaughtered innocent people in South West Africa.

The Armenian genocide during World War I must have given Pius greater pause for thought. The killing took place in a European context, not in far-off Africa. In this instance, the tables were reversed. The Ottoman Turks, Muslims, killed Christians, although they were Orthodox Christians who were not subject to Rome. Even so, Pope Benedict attempted to intervene to stop the massacre. Since Benedict had mentored Pacelli, promoting him in the Vatican secretariat and posting him to

Munich as nuncio in the middle of the war, there is good reason to speculate that Benedict's letter to the sultan influenced Pope Pius's decision to
speak out in 1942.

By that year, Pius could see that war and genocide went hand in
hand. Pius XI, Pacelli's second mentor and predecessor, did not see fit
to speak out against Italy's invasion of Ethiopia. Following Pius XI, the
new pope did not speak out against the German invasion of Poland.
Instead, he sought to undermine Hitler through secret negotiations. But
no sooner had the war begun than atrocities began to be committed
by Polish Catholics on Catholic ethnic Germans, and soon thereafter
by Catholic ethnic Germans on the Polish Catholics. This was unprecedented and deplorable. We cannot help but wonder what went through
Pius's mind as he read the letter of Franciscan Hilarius Breitinger (which
also was omitted in the Vatican's documentary collection). But there was
nothing that Pius XII could do about it because almost immediately the
Catholic infighting was submerged in the German genocide of Polish
Catholics. Here, again, the situation was deplorable. Germans, Catholic
and Protestant Christians, carried out Nazi orders to kill and plunder
fellow Christians.

Simultaneously, Catholic Croats set upon Serbian Orthodox Christians in dismembered Yugoslavia. The slaughter took on the form of a
rampage that bore little resemblance to the businesslike killing of Jews
by Himmler's SS, and it went far beyond the limited atrocities Catholics in Poland committed against ethnic Germans. This was a genocide,
and it was perpetrated by Catholics. The pope knew that he could do
little to halt Nazi genocide in Poland, but Croatia was another matter.
Pavelić was Catholic; he had been received by the pope. The Ustaša link
with Rome gave it a measure of credibility among Catholic Croatians.
In contrast to Hitler, Pope Pius was in a position to assert some control
over Pavelić, and thus in Croatia. But he left it to Archbishop Stepinać
to berate the Ustaši for their crimes against humanity. Whether the pope
urged the archbishop in this regard we cannot say for lack of documents.
In weighing what he should do, Pius hoped—chanced would be a better
word—that the war would conclude in a way that favored the emergence
of a bloc of Catholic countries in East Central Europe. Croatia would
be part of the geopolitical map the pope dreamed of. On the other hand,
attempting to rein in Pavelić's regime could doom the Croatian Church
to schism. Pius knew very well that a number of bishops, like Archbishop
Sarić, and many of the lower clergy, especially members of the Franciscan
order, backed Pavelić wholeheartedly, even to the extent of encouraging
the massacre of the Serbs or, worse, participating in it.[43] Thus, the hope

for a future Catholic entity in place of Yugoslavia and the concern over renegade Croat clerics prompted Pius to do nothing diplomatically that would undermine Pavelić's position. The Roman pontiff did not challenge the first genocide perpetrated by Catholics.

To be sure, Pius XII was confronted with a more difficult situation than those of his predecessors, including his model, Pope Benedict. The genocide that had been taking place since the beginning of the war was not happening in faraway places such as Africa and the Middle East but in Europe itself. The German, Croatian, and Austrian perpetrators included many Catholics. Furthermore, many of the victims up to that time, mid-1942, were Catholic or Orthodox Christians. So although the situation was complex compared to previous cases, there were papal precedents both for speaking out and, as with the Belgian Congo, looking the other way. Pius chose to look the other way until the end of 1942.

2

THE GENOCIDES OF
POLISH CATHOLICS AND
POLISH JEWS

When Eugenio Pacelli became Pope Pius XII less than a year before World War II began, the Polish Catholic press rejoiced. "A political pontificate!" The curia has elected the most tested, most vigorous person to lead the Church. "Will Pius make his mark on our times?" the Poles asked confidently.[1] Within two years this brimming-over optimism had turned into great disenchantment with the new pope.

It is widely known that Pope Pius XII had to concern himself with the murder of Jews in occupied Poland during World War II. Not so widely known is the fact that the pope first had to deal with the genocide of Polish Catholics even before the Germans began killing Jews in death camps. And, until recently, no one understood how the destiny of these two populations crossed paths in the middle of the war, leading to the immediate and outright murder of the Jews and a respite for the Catholics that was only intended to be temporary.

To understand how Pius XII reacted to the killing of European Jews we must first take into account his reaction to the killing of Polish Catholics. This relationship can be explored by analyzing how and when the decision to murder European Jews and especially Polish Jews came about. Scholars have been studying this process for decades, and with the publication of Christopher Browning's *The Origins of the Final Solution* in 2004, we have a detailed exploration of the Holocaust about which there is now widespread agreement. When the editors of the Vatican's World War II documents did their work in the 1960s, the Holocaust was known to be a historical event, of course, but at that time, no body of knowledge about it existed. The editors, in a word, did not understand how the genocide of Polish Jews affected Polish Catholics. It is important to search this relationship out, because how Pope Pius reacted to the catastrophe of Polish Catholics conditioned his reaction to the murder of the Jews—the Holocaust itself.

Since the time of World War I, the Vatican had deferred to Germany at the expense of Poland. The Vatican had not liked the Versailles Treaty that gave birth to modern-day Poland and had not thought that the country's chances for independence were good.[2] Most of the Vatican's deference to Germany can be traced directly to Eugenio Pacelli, first as nuncio to Germany, then as the Vatican's secretary of state, and finally as Pius XII.[3] Neither Pius XI (who had earlier had a rocky time as nuncio to Poland) nor Pius XII felt that Poland was the key in the Vatican's dream of rebuilding a large Catholic presence in Central Europe after World War I.

As we will see, Pius XII was reluctant to speak out about genocide in Poland until the end of 1942. It would be speculative to assert that this reluctance resulted from the Holy See's political mindset about Poland. But it was not just the murder of Poles that confronted Pius XII. What the Germans did to the Catholic Church in Poland and to Polish Catholics ranks as one of the greatest persecutions in the Church's centuries-long history. Genocide and persecution were the result of two forces: the madcap schemes of German demographers that culminated in the Nazi land grab known as its Lebensraum program and the pitiless hatred of Nazis of the Catholic religion. Although Hitler's lieutenants were restrained in Germany because of the need to keep the home front united during the war, they had a free hand to cut as wide a swath as they wished through the Polish Church. What they accomplished there was brutal. For whatever reason, it was difficult for Pope Pius XII to come to terms with the fact that Germany, the country he believed could be central in reestablishing Catholicism in Central Europe, was in fact depriving Poles of the Church's sacraments and massacring them.

"All Poles Will Disappear from the World"

To say that German plans for expansion into Eastern Europe prior to the war were inchoate considerably understates the historical reality. Hitler's ultimate intention was that Poland should cease to exist. Top army officers knew that Hitler intended to "destroy and exterminate the Polish people."[4] On a number of occasions Reichsführer Heinrich Himmler made explicit statements regarding Poland's extinction such as his statement that "all Poles will disappear from the world."[5] Nazi Germany's intentions for occupied Poland were fourfold: the elimination of Jews, the murder of the Polish intelligentsia, the eventual elimination of "primitive Poles" either by forced emigration or forced labor under genocidal conditions, and the resettling of many hundreds of thousands of ethnic Germans from Northern, Southern, and Eastern Europe into the Reich portion of Poland—bringing them "home to the Reich." The Germans had a two-stage plan to eliminate gentile Poles. Reinhard Heydrich, head of the Reich Security Main Office that oversaw resettlement, said that first the Polish elite were "to be taken care" of in concentration camps. Then "primitive Poles" were to be "incorporated into the labor force while deporting them at the same time." They were to become "permanent seasonal and migrant laborers."[6]

Moving and relocating millions of people many hundreds of miles would constitute a monumental task under optimal conditions. But because the Germans were stealing the property of Poles they had overrun late in 1939, this elimination-resettlement program had to be undertaken under wartime conditions. The complexity of the Nazi plan together with the complications of war and the ineptitude of those overseeing the operation doomed hundreds of thousands of Polish Jews and gentiles to death or unimaginable misery. The ethnic German settlers who were brought "home to the Reich" received equally harsh treatment a few years later at the end of the war at the hands of Poles and Russians— death, merciless beating, rape, and confiscation of their newly acquired properties. Seldom in history have the decisions of a government led to the ghastly end of so many, be they friend or foe, as those of the Nazi regime regarding Poland.

The population of what Christopher Browning calls Germany's "laboratory of racial policy" included 22 million Poles, of whom 20 million were gentiles and 2 million Jews. All of them lived in the western half of occupied Poland after the Soviet Union and Germany divided the country in two in 1939.[7] The German portion was further divided into a northwestern sector called the Greater Reich, which was annexed outright to Germany, and a central sector, called the General Government (see map, p. 34). In the early years of the war, the Germans drove about 12 million Poles from the annexed sector into the central area, approximately 10 million gentiles and 2 million Jews.[8] The misery visited on these people as they were uprooted from house and home, often in winter weather, led to the deaths of many of them. Their deaths cannot be considered unforeseen accidents; they were foreseen and intended.[9] The hundreds of thousands of uprooted Poles were allowed to carry with them only one blanket apiece and only enough food for a few days. Adolf Eichmann carried out the forced emigration of these individuals. Virtually all of the transplanted Jews eventually perished. It is not possible to establish a reasonable estimate of the death toll among the gentiles, but it was certainly considerable. Of the 3 million Catholics who died during the occupation, only approximately 600,000 died in combat at the onset of World War II.[10]

Two years after the beginning of the war, Adolf Hitler publicly repeated what he had said in January 1939: that the war would mean the destruction of European Jews. There is no doubt that the elimination of Jews topped the list of the fourfold Nazi program of 1939 in Poland. But theory and practice often got turned on their heads because of bureaucratic mismanagement, such as bringing thousands of settlers "home to the Reich" before homes were available. Although their early emigration schedules usually zeroed in on Jews, the Nazis found that to accommodate immigrating settlers it was gentiles who had to be moved out. It happened this way because the properties of the deported Jews did not match the expectations of the immigrating ethnic Germans being brought "home to the Reich" from their widely scattered European enclaves. The Nazis had promised the settlers a better standard of living, but many of the Jews were marginal shopkeepers or poor tradesmen. Giving the settlers the possessions of such Jews would decrease, not improve, their standing of living. Few of the Jews who were being evicted were farmers, but most of the settlers were. The small number of Jewish farmers did not usually work enough land to accommodate the "Aryan" settler. Since the Germans had not yet decided to eliminate Jews by murder, that portion of Poland's population became a managerial headache for their resettlement program instead of a convenient piece of what Hitler gloriously referred to as the reordering of the "ethnographic relationships" of Europe.[11]

"Laboratory" aptly describes German resettlement measures in Poland. Resettlement of ethnic Germans may best be described as a hit-or-miss experiment. The polycratic bureaucracy that administered Germany's resettlement program operated clumsily, haltingly, sometimes backwardly. Himmler's "plans for extensive demographic engineering through massive expulsions proved easier to imagine than to carry out."[12] Finally, more than two years after the program began, Reinhard Heydrich realized that gentiles, much more than Jews, would constitute the uprooted. At a meeting in January 1941, Heydrich estimated that to bring 167,450 settlers "home to the Reich," 444,000 Poles (meaning non-Jews) would have to be driven from their homes. An additional

327,000 Poles would have to be uprooted for other reasons.[13] The deportation figures for the first year and a half of the war bear Heydrich out: 503,000 gentile Poles were forced from their homes, as compared to only 63,000 Jews.[14] Most of the latter, more than likely, were driven into the General Government on principle rather than as part of the resettlement operation. Thus, although elimination of Jews topped Nazi priorities, the reality of resettlement made the deportation of gentiles more urgent and the Jewish question less urgent.

Nazi resettlement agents working in the field recognized that they were not following the script when they dealt with Polish gentiles instead of Jews. "The resettlement and evacuation must be accomplished on a different basis [than] Himmler had initially intended," several of his agents noted.[15] At a January 1940 meeting, Eichmann mentioned Himmler's intention, namely, the "immediate evacuation of Jews." But less than a week later, contrary to Eichmann's announcement, resettlement authorities targeted 400,000 gentiles for removal.[16] The realities of the resettlement program called for "a ruthless decimation of the Polish population."[17] By the spring, Himmler had accepted the reality of this situation.

However, the idea of a "ruthless decimation of the Polish population" ran into snags of its own. In March, Hermann Göring, as head of the Main Trusteeship Office East, abruptly ordered deportation of Poles to stop.[18] The trusteeship office, actually an institution that oversaw exploitation of both Polish Jews and gentiles, insisted that Polish gentile farm laborers and skilled laborers could not be disturbed because such actions might endanger support for the German military. Göring had no objection to deporting Jews, but that did not work for Himmler's "home to the Reich" effort. Hans Frank, governor-general of the deportation dumping ground the Germans called the General Government, backed Göring on the matter of uprooting Polish gentiles, but he did not want any more Jews either.[19] These contradictions eventually worked themselves out, as Christopher Browning has noted, in the field or at regional meetings. Sometimes they would be "solved" by surpassing events (such as the decision to ghettoize all Jews) or would be resolved by Hitler one way or another, depending on which of his top lieutenants got to him at an opportune moment, as Himmler did late in May 1940.[20]

The organizing principle of resettlement, which dislodged Hitler's and Himmler's initial goals of eliminating the Jews, rested on the backs of the uprooted gentile Poles. They were just as unhappy to be thrown out of house and home as any other group would be, and they sought to thwart Nazi intentions. One way to do this was to anticipate the deportation order by selling off one's house and farm. This, no doubt, garnered gentile Poles only a fraction of what their property was worth, but it left them with something. To whom would they sell? One or other of the ethnic Germans of Poland, the Volksdeutsch, could be counted on to exploit the misfortune of his Polish neighbor. Other Poles evaded, or attempted to evade, the Nazi resettlement scheme by anticipating the evacuation order and hiding nearby in the woods or "getting lost" in a regional city. Later they could hope to win the sympathy of the settler who occupied their property or survive by poaching from their own farms.[21] If the settler was a Galician or Volhynian farmer, the chance of some kind of secret arrangement between settler and runaway Pole improved because settlers from those areas spoke fluent Polish.

The Germans, who were aware of the sympathetic sensibilities of these settlers and wanted to ward off collusion, tried to arrange matters so that the new settlers would not actually see the Polish family being run out of its house and off its land.[22] In the end, it does not seem likely that many Poles were able to save themselves in this manner. The evasive actions some Poles took forced Germans to spend manpower hunting them down in forests and succeeded in the short term by decreasing the number of deportees, but in the long run they would inexorably become victims in one way or another. It is estimated that by June 1943, Göring's Main Trusteeship Office East had stolen close to 400 million Reichsmarks' worth of property from deported Jewish and gentile Poles, the preponderance from the latter.[23]

The Nazis could agree on at least two priorities: exterminating the Polish intelligentsia and forcing (gentile) Poles to do hard labor in the Old Reich. In October 1940, Hitler spelled this out: "Polish leaders and intelligentsia were to be killed and the people kept at such a low standard of living that they would have to export migrant labor to the Reich to survive."[24] Heydrich estimated that by 1940, Germany, the Old Reich, needed about 1 million forced laborers in addition to the POWs already there. Himmler of course wanted only "racially acceptable" Poles for the Old Reich, but how and from where were they to be selected? Agreement up and down the line existed at least on the need to satisfy Germany's labor shortage. Any fit-looking Pole, regardless of "racial characteristics," was liable to be pulled from a group of the uprooted unfortunates and sent off to the Old Reich.[25] In fact, they were not all so fit. According to a contemporary non-German report from occupied Poland, "Many die on the way to their destination [in the Old Reich] and the Germans throw their corpses in the ditch by the road."[26] Eventually, a system emerged for differentiating between Poles who were racially fit for labor in Germany, Poles who were to be left in the Greater Reich for agriculture, and Poles—the least fit—who were to be deported to the General Government. This hierarchy, like all Nazi racial nonsense, broke down when the labor shortage in the Old Reich became so constricted that even Jews were forced to do labor there.[27] By the time the war ended, somewhere in the vicinity of 2 million Polish men and women had been taken to Germany to satisfy its labor shortage.[28]

Killing the Polish intelligentsia was the most easily achievable of the Nazi genocidal goals. These murders did not complicate "home to the Reich" measures; in fact, the release of better homes and more substantial businesses suited the settlers well, if only a relative few. And of course the murders did not require that people be moved en masse to another part of the country, thereby burdening a railroad system already stressed by the war. The Nazis knew that because Polish nationalism was so closely intertwined with religion, the Catholic Church would play a central role in any resistance movement. Therefore, they targeted the clergy, both bishops and priests, for murder. But they also included the nobility, industrialists, entrepreneurs, lawyers, some doctors, university professors, politicians, newspaper owners and editors, large retailers, and others who fell to Nazi caprice in the targeted portion of the population. Reinhard Heydrich estimated that these groups accounted for about 3 percent of the population, or about 1 million people in German-occupied Poland.[29]

Mobile killing squads, which the Nazis called Einzatzgruppen, committed most of the murders. The squads were special units of the Security Police whose personnel came from various law enforcement backgrounds. Their leaders, hand-picked by Reinhard Heydrich, were Waffen-SS officers—members of the military branch of the SS. As a rule, they were highly educated; the majority held doctoral degrees, many in law.[30] Before the war ended, the forces these men commanded would be responsible for the murder of between 1 and 1.5 million people, mostly Jews. But they began their work by wiping out the mostly Catholic intelligentsia in Poland soon after the war began.

Two documents originating in Poland from Polish sources provide glimpses of the work of the mobile killing squad as it affected church personnel. One document originated in the spring of 1940, the other in the fall of 1942. The 1940 document carries the gentiles' sense that they were in the middle of an ongoing disaster—"deteriorating daily."[31] By the time the second document was written, it may be assumed that the killing squads had pretty well wiped out the intelligentsia. As we will see, the middle of 1942 was a key turning point for the fortunes of Polish Catholics and Polish Jews.

As early as the spring of 1940, hundreds of church personnel had

been detained, imprisoned, or deported or were just plain missing. Many
of those missing were probably executed and disposed of randomly in
forests. In occupied northwestern Poland, the Greater Reich, many
priests were murdered, and many others were hauled off to the General
Government. One hundred priests were in jail in Lublin, thirty in Warsaw, twenty-six in Cracow, and thirty in Silesia. The location of many
others was simply unknown. Bishops Fulman, Goral, and Wetmanski
and Auxiliary Bishop Tomczak of Lodz were arrested and tortured in
jail. The director of Catholic Action, Abbé Stanislas Nowicki, was beaten
so badly about the head that he needed an operation. In Radom, four
priests had their teeth knocked out during interrogations. Bishop Fulman
in Lublin was arrested and charged with having a machine gun mounted
in his garden, which, of course the Germans had smuggled in and planted
there. "This was a most absurd charge—75 year old man who has never
seen a machine gun and hasn't the slightest idea how they work!"[32] Fulman, his auxiliary bishop, and the other priests arrested with him were
taken to the Oranienburg concentration camp, where they were given
little to eat and had to stand for hours in frigid cold for roll calls. Fulman
was sentenced to death and the rest were sentenced to life imprisonment
at hard labor. (Fulman's sentence was also later commuted to life.)[33]
In Bydgoszcz, the mobile killing squad reported it had exterminated or
otherwise disposed of all but seventeen of the city's seventy-five priests,
after which "it was assumed that the survivors were either sufficiently
shaken or weak-hearted and apolitical that no further difficulties from
the church were expected."[34] In the same city, 10,000 of the lay and clerical intelligentsia were murdered during the first months of the war.[35]

By 1942, the number of Polish priests had been drastically reduced
from its prewar total of 14,000.[36] In Pelplin, 291 of the diocese's 646
priests were missing. In Lublin, 150 priests were in prison and many
others were missing.[37] A number of persecuted priests found refuge in
Cracow. For no apparent reason, other than the moody capriciousness
of Hans Frank, the Church did not suffer the same degree of persecution
in Cracow as elsewhere. Frank maintained his lavish headquarters in
Cracow while overseeing the deaths of millions of Jews and "Gypsies."
What happened to the priests that did not find refuge in Cracow? Many
of them perished in concentration camps such as Oranienburg, Mauthausen, and Dachau. The Vatican reported that of the 2,800 priests
incarcerated at Dachau between 1940 and 1945, only 816 survived.[38]
Priests were sent to concentration camps in wholesale numbers—144
alone in one transport to Dachau.

Three of the four Nazi objectives in Poland were fulfilled. To some considerable extent, the intelligentsia was murdered or put in concentration camps. Gentile Poles forced into slave labor were exiled en masse to the Old Reich. During the early years of the war, many Jews starved to death, and those who survived the early years were exterminated after the previous two objectives had been achieved—in other words, late in the time period under consideration, 1939 to 1943.

"We Intend to Dam Up Church Life in Poland"

The Nazis intended to follow one church policy for Volksdeutsch Christians and a different one for Polish gentiles, who were overwhelmingly Catholic. They used a policy of radical disestablishment of religion for Voksdeutschers.[39] This meant cutting off state support for churches and banning contact between pastors and the people outside the walls of the church. Thus, confessional schools, social ministry, ancillary organizations, and publications would no longer be possible. When Hanns Kerrl, the Reich minister for church affairs in Germany, objected to this policy, Reinhard Heydrich went over his head to win approval for his actions.[40] As far as the Nazis were concerned, the Volksdeutsch churches simply had no rights. As legal entities, they ceased to exist. The regional Gauleiter controlled the churches' budgets, even though the state contributed no financial support.[41] In addition to losing the state support of the Polish government, the churches had to pay taxes which were to be collected retroactively to the date of the beginning of the war.[42] That was not all. The Nazis secularized church property and seized transportable valuables as booty.

After only a few months of this treatment, the Volksdeutsch churches were brought low. "The church is not just being crippled, but actually destroyed," reported a churchman in a complaint inadvisably sent to the SS.[43] The clergy, the Volksdeutscher said, could no longer even feed themselves but had to live off the good will of friends. "Not just crippled but destroyed" accurately depicts what the Nazis intended for Christianity; they could act on their intentions in the Greater Reich in a way they could not in the Old Reich. For the Nazis, although the Volksdeutsch people living in the Greater Reich were demographically and ethnically valuable, they required lessons in Nazi ideology.

Even though it seemed that the Church of the Volksdeutsch Christians was doomed, religious life, if it was confined to within church walls, could continue. Drastic as conditions were for these churches, they pale in comparison to what the Nazis had in store for the Polish Church. Whereas the Nazis were prepared to tolerate limited religious practice among the Volksdeutsch, their aim for Polish Catholics was to disrupt religious life altogether. In November of the first year of the war, a Polish Franciscan of the Greater Reich reported that Poles felt they were "catacomb Christians."[44] Thus, the attack on religion began immediately after Poland's surrender. By October 1941, a little more than half of the 828 priests in the diocese of Posen (Greater Reich area) were either in jail, in concentration camps, deported to the General Government, or dead.[45] Before long these conditions would spread throughout the country and intensify.

Murdering or jailing priests put religious practice in disarray, but the Nazis did not stop at that. Knowing Catholicism to be a sacramental and hierarchical religion, they attacked the Church at these levels. The bishops of thirty-nine of the country's forty-six dioceses in western Poland were deported (or were already in exile), imprisoned, or psychologically disabled by stress. One bishop was still at his post, "although menaced often with the threat of deportation or jail" to such an extent that he could hardly function. By closing the churches, either entirely or sporadically, Nazis denied the people the sacraments. They converted the cathedral of the diocese of Pelplin into a garage and used other churches as warehouses or barracks. In the Greater Reich, sacramental marriage was violated when the Germans annulled all unions of Poles with ethnic Germans that had taken place after 1918. Elsewhere in the Greater Reich, priests were forbidden to preach or give religious instruction. By terrorizing the priests and vandalizing churches, the Germans hoped to disorient and dumbfound the people. As they attacked the clergy and restricted the sacraments, the Germans also violated Polish morality. In some areas they used X-rays on the reproductive organs of young men and women, rendering them infertile. Given the Nazis' domestic euthanasia program, it is not surprising that they exterminated the mentally disabled: in Chelm, they shot 428 children housed in a mental institution.[46] The practice of murdering mental patients in Polish institutions in the Greater Reich became common. Asserting that religious conditions in German-occupied Poland were much worse than those in Soviet-occupied Poland, the author of the 1941 report said that there was no parallel to what the Germans were doing.[47]

Matters got worse, not better, at least until the latter half of 1942. The summary of conditions of that year provide a long list of curtailments:

closing most churches

closing all seminaries

banning preaching

restricting sacraments

    no confessions

    no First Communion preparation for children

    no marriages for men under 28 years of age or for women under 25

    no ordinations to the priesthood and suppression of religious

    orders[48]

All the restrictions placed on the Volksdeutsch churches affected Polish Catholics as well. Closing churches and eliminating most liturgies had a psychological impact. Only ten churches remained open in the diocese of Gnesen, which had a Catholic population of 359,000. In Pelplin, less than half of the churches were still functioning.[49] The closures and the elimination of some of the Sunday liturgies in churches that remained opened meant that the churches overflowed and worshipers had to stand outside during Mass. In some places, Catholics actually had to rent buildings in order to have liturgical functions. All in all, the picture of religious conditions in Poland in 1942 resembles the 1941 picture, but a marked deterioration had taken place.

In sum, there is no reason to disagree with the conclusion of the 1942 document that the persecution of the Church in Poland was one of the worst in the Church's long history.

"Et Papa Tacet"—and the Pope Keeps Silent

The German invasion of Poland in September 1939 ended four weeks later. Poland had to lay down its arms and surrender. Immediately thereafter, the Nazis placed the first part of the planned genocide in operation. The murderous onslaught and the uprooting and deportation of Poles began.

The Vatican reacted forthrightly and in a timely manner. Before the year was out, Pius addressed the College of Cardinals, decrying the atrocities perpetrated against the elderly and women and children. The Holy See expressed its deep anguish and disapproval outside the Vatican as well. Demonstrating that it was well informed, Vatican radio broadcast in January 1940 that a large section of Poland had been formed into a General Government, into which Poles were being forced from their homes "in the depth of one of Europe's severest winters, on principles and by methods that can be described only as brutal." The broadcast referred, of course, to the people who had been ejected from the Greater Reich in northwestern Poland and driven south. The Vatican reported that once they reached their destination, "Jews and Poles [were] herded into separate ghettos, hermetically sealed where they [faced] starvation while Polish grain [was] shipped to Germany."[50] This was the last time the Vatican spoke as pointedly and explicitly during the war. This is extremely curious, since, as historian Gerhard Besier has written, a "church which concentrates on the administration of the sacraments, must be watchful to protect this function under all circumstances."[51]

Why did the pope keep silent? After clearly setting off along a path of assertiveness in a moral aspect of the war, why did Pope Pius desist? The evidence suggests that Hitler cowed the Vatican into silence. He threatened the Vatican with physical destruction if it spoke out against the "battle of the German Volk." This threat came to the Holy See second hand, not directly from Germany. Hitler could only have meant his "home to the Reich" program, because at the political rather than the moral level, the pope had not singled out Germany for blame for starting the war of aggression. There is additional evidence that the Vatican was cowed into silence by German threats of physical retaliation.[52] Such threats would have been a devastating blow to Pope Pius. As we will see in chapter 4, saving the Eternal City from harm carried momentous religious implications in the mind of the pope.

The Poles were dumbfounded by Pius's retreat to silence. Beginning in January 1940, Polish church leaders peppered Pius XII with letters telling him about the atrocities that they—the Catholics, not the Jews—were being subjected to. Hardly a month passed without a new appeal (Bishop Splett wrote in January, Bishop Dymek in February, Bishop Radonski in July, Bishop Preysing in October), and there were likely other letters that were not included in the Vatican's documentation.[53] At the end of the year, Pius answered the outcries of wrongs committed against the Polish people and Church by telling them it was their lot to suffer for the greater glory of God. Poland was Job.

Rather than speak out, Pope Pius engaged in diplomacy. Since Germany did not allow the Vatican to place a nuncio in Poland, that country's religious business had to be carried on through Monsignor Cesare Orsenigo, the nuncio to Germany. In August 1940, Orsenigo protested privately to the German government, but began weakly by saying it was necessary to bring a "painful matter" to their attention. He listed the abuses against the Church (but not those against the Polish people).[54] These and other protests Orsenigo filed had no effect. In November, Bishop Sapieha of Cracow wrote the nuncio telling him that a protest by the pope was "indispensable."[55]

It is doubtful that Nuncio Orsenigo sent Sapieha's request on to the Holy See. The Poles believed that Orsenigo purposefully minimized their situation in his reports to Rome and that he lacked determination when he approached the Nazi regime regarding its actions in Poland. The following telling incident supports this criticism. Hilarius Breitinger, the Franciscan apostolic administrator of the Warthegau region of occupied Poland, carried a letter that was critical of the pope's silence to Berlin and gave it to Nuncio Orsenigo to send to Rome by diplomatic pouch. Orsenigo remonstrated with him, saying that in such trying times one should always try to be supportive of the pope. From Berlin, Breitinger traveled to Munich, where he gave a copy of the letter to Cardinal Faulhaber. The cardinal assured Breitinger that he would have a soldier carry the letter to Rome secretly. When Breitinger returned to Berlin, Orsenigo asked him if he had changed his mind about the letter. Orsenigo had sat on the letter for a week![56]

Whether Nuncio Orsenigo sent Bishop Sapieha's request on or not, the pope did not protest Germany's atrocities in Poland, and Vatican-Polish relations came under greater strain in 1942. Early in the year, Bishop Sapieha wrote Rome saying that the persecution of the Poles and the Church had become tragic in the extreme—they were deprived of human rights, treated as animals, imprisoned without trial or recourse; they lacked the necessities of life; they were deported; they were put in concentration camps; they were killed. From Sapieha's perspective in central Poland, German atrocities had reached their apogee. Sapieha wrote that in these circumstances, he had to admit that some of the faithful had lost respect for and confidence in the pope.[57]

At midyear, Hilarius Breitinger contacted the Vatican for a second time, providing the pope with another detailed picture of the horrendous conditions of the Church. Volksdeutsch Catholics found the practice of their faith jeopardized at every turn. Some churches were closed because there were no longer any priests to staff them; others were closed at the caprice of the local German authorities. Catholics were told to drop their affiliation with the church if they wanted jobs or advancement. All kinds of anti-church propaganda rained down on them every day. As a result, some Catholics dropped out of the Church; others became lackadaisical in practice. It was obvious, Breitinger wrote, that the objective was to root out Christianity altogether.[58]

The situation was even more bleak for Polish Catholics. Germans treated them as a *minderwertig,* subhuman race. They were denied their natural rights, their churches were often shut down, they were forbidden to attend nearby churches, and they were subjected to demeaning propaganda. Under the circumstances, some Polish people began to be attracted to communism. Those who formerly practiced their faith began to ask "if there was a God" and whether the pope "had completely forgotten about the Poles."[59] In order to submit an objective picture, Breitinger wrote, he had to say these things, and he did so, he added, at the express wish of the Polish vicar general Blericq and the Polish auxiliary bishop Dymek. Then, to demonstrate the virtual impossibility of providing for the religious needs of the people, Breitinger furnished statistical data.

Pope Pius got more news from outside Poland that was sure to depress him. From exile, Cardinal Hlond pressured the pope several times to speak out. When his promptings had no effect, he curtly told the pope he doubted that "it was the will of God that the atrocities and anti-Christian programs [of the Nazis] be passed over in silence."[60] Kazimierz Papée, the Polish ambassador to the Holy See, beat a well-traveled path to the door of Secretary of State Maglione. In May 1942, he asked why the Vatican had not protested the latest atrocity in Poland. The cardinal replied that it was not possible for the Vatican to document each and every atrocity. Papée retorted that verification was unnecessary when the atrocities were so numerous, ongoing, and notorious.[61]

It is strange, to say the least, that the Vatican believed the reports in 1939 about German atrocities and reacted to them forthrightly but refused to credit the reports of 1941 and 1942. The two documents we have discussed above that detail German atrocities were both sent to the Holy See (although both were omitted from *Actes et Documents*), so there can be no doubt about Pius XII's awareness of the tragic situation of the Poles. Thus, Maglione's reply to the Polish ambassador rings hollow. In May, Harold Tittmann of the U.S. mission to the Holy See reported that "in Poland the attitude of the population toward the Holy See is reported to be reserved, even openly hostile. . . . The Polish people apparently have no patience with arguments to the effect that intervention by the Holy See would only worsen their plight."[62]

But worse was yet to come. In September 1942, the exiled Bishop Radonski wrote two letters to the Holy See which the editors of *Actes et Documents* called "fierce."[63] Radonski was infuriated by the appointment in May of Hilarius Breitinger, a German national, as the apostolic administrator to the Warthegau, a clear violation of the Vatican's concordat with Poland.[64] Beyond this breach, Radonski no doubt feared that the appointment of a German signaled the Vatican's willingness to let Hitler have the northwestern sector of Poland that he had incorporated into his Greater Reich. In a September letter to the Vatican, Radonski listed the atrocities toward and deprivations of the Polish people—a litany well known by this time in Rome—and pointed an accusatory finger directly at Pius: "et Papa tacet, tamquamsi nihil eum interesset de ovibus [and the pope keeps quiet as though these matters are of no interest to him]."[65]

In February 1943, Radonski wrote another hot letter to the Vatican, saying that although he realized that the pope had made a few statements favorable to the Poles and that the Vatican had attempted to do works of mercy for the people, that was not enough in the present circumstances. The exiled bishop recalled that Pope Pius XI had encouraged Spanish and Mexican Catholics when they were being persecuted and asked pointedly and defiantly if Poles counted less than Jews. This marked the first time Jews were mentioned in a letter pleading for the pope to protest the treatment of Catholics and the Church. Why did Jews figure in Radonski's thinking at this time? In November 1942, Jan Karski, the daring rescuer who had witnessed murdered Jews at Belzec, had carried a message from Polish Jewish leaders to Wladislav Raczkiewicz, president of the Polish Government in Exile in London, asking him to call upon the Vatican to enforce "religious sanctions, excommunication included" for those who participated in genocide.[66] Raczkiewicz complied and also asked the pope to condemn crimes against Jews in Poland.[67] The following month, Pope Pius actually did address genocide in his Christmas address, as we will see in the following chapter. It appears, then, that Radonski, also in residence in London, assumed that Karski's message had had an effect on the pope; he was incensed that Pius would speak out when asked to do so by Jews when he had not done so when asked by Catholics.

It is not possible to say with certainty why Radonski brought up the Jews. But what clearly emerges from the Polish ordeal is that the accusation of silence leveled at Pius XII during World War II did not first come from outside the Church with reference to Jews but from inside the Church with reference to Catholics.

Exiled bishop Radonski's bitter complaints to the Holy Father occurred in the fall of 1942 and early 1943. In comparison to the letters of the previous two and a half years since the beginning of the war, the letters coming to the Vatican from within Poland during the second half of 1942 and the first half of 1943 say little about German atrocities. Breitinger, it is true, wrote negatively again in November 1942. He told Pope Pius that people always were asking "if the pope could not help out and why he keeps silent."[68] But then in March 1943, Breitinger again wrote to the pope, this time with something positive to say. The people now, he reported, understood that Pius's silence had been "an heroic silence."[69] Bishop Adamski, writing from a very different location in occupied Poland, reported similarly that the people were no longer swayed by the strong propaganda against the Church. That same spring Pius XII, encouraged by Bishop Sapieha, wrote to Polish Catholics telling them all that he had done and tried to do for them, both those under occupation and those in concentration camps outside Poland. Pius concluded by saying that he had never forgotten the Poles, and he praised their "heroic silence" in the midst of all their suffering.[70] Of course, they had not been silent at all, but his compliments found their mark. Church leaders wrote back to Pius telling him that the Poles would never forget his noble and saintly words.

What had happened? What accounts for the abrupt about-face in Polish-Vatican relations during the winter of 1942–1943? The editors of the massive Vatican documentary collection, knowing nothing of the history of the Holocaust which had not yet been written, struggled to account for the turn from negative to positive. The evidence, it seemed to the editors, who completely overlooked the initial critical remarks of the pope and Vatican radio regarding German atrocities, pointed to a firm papal policy and the reaction to it by Polish church leaders. Singling out the letters of bishops Sapieha and Radonski, the editors sought in the introduction to volume three of *Actes et Documents* to build a drama around Pope Pius in which he would emerge from disrespect to respect. After noting various congratulatory messages sent to the pope after his praise of the Poles' "heroic silence," the editors, wanting to make Radonski look petty, pointed out that he refused to write to Pius in a complimentary manner. "Nothing was found among the documents on the reaction of Radonski," they noted.[71]

Actually, the exchange of letters between the Vatican and the bishops cannot explain the abrupt change in the attitude of the Poles toward Pope Pius around the fall of 1942. The explanation lies, rather, in the evolution of two genocidal processes, one against Polish Catholics, the other against Polish Jews. Recent Holocaust scholarship allows us to follow these evolutions in a way that solves the puzzle of the about-face in relations between the pope and Polish Catholics in the middle of World War II.

The Holocaust

By the middle of 1942, the Polish intelligentsia were out of the picture and the Germans were left with what they called a population of "primitive Poles" and Jews. The latter had been destined for elimination since the beginning of the war, whereas the former had been relegated to forced labor in the Greater Reich, the General Government, or the Old Reich. Of these two populations, Polish Catholics always fared better than the Jews as far as the food chain was concerned, since their lot was to work for the German economy. In contrast, an estimated 600,000 Jews died of starvation during the occupation of Poland, although Jewish mortality did not increase everywhere in the occupied country. Although the Germans had muddled through with their "home to the Reich" program and consequential uprooting of Catholic gentile Poles, the question of what was to be done with the Jewish population confounded them. Shoving them all into some area as far east as possible was impractical, and their plan to deport them to the island of Madagascar off the east coast of Africa, which they hoped to control after defeating England, proved impossible. The Jews were stuck in Poland.[72] In general, this was the situation of the remaining gentile Poles and Polish Jews when Germany declared war on the Soviet Union toward the end of June 1941, an event that temporarily offered a solution for the question of what to do with the Jews of Poland.

Prior to Germany's invasion of Russia, a process of ghettoization of Jews arose out of local circumstances, not policy set by Berlin. The brutal SS general Arthur Greiser, an administrator of a Nazi district in occupied Poland (a Gau), was one of those who took the initiative and established the Lodz ghetto in the fall of 1939. Greiser meant to trap the Jews in the ghetto. In the cockeyed thinking of Gauleiter Greiser, they would be forced to surrender all the wealth they had hoarded before they could be expelled to he knew not where.[73] The Warsaw ghetto, in contrast, was established at the insistence of German health authorities who wanted to control the spread of contagious diseases. The two 1940 ghettos, Lodz and Warsaw, which accounted for about a third of all Jews in western occupied Poland, presented the Germans with yet another problem—how to pay for keeping the Jews alive, if only barely so, until their deportation to wherever. The solution—employing them—meant integrating them with the economy, even though that would violate eliminationist Nazi ideology.

Hitler's war against the Bolshevist Jews of the Soviet Union, Operation Barbarossa, had the temporary effect of increasing the economic integration of the ghettoized Jews in Germany's war effort. Blitzkrieg against Soviet soldiers foundered, and German troops, ill clad for the Russian cold, were forced to retreat. The Germany army realized that Hitler's prediction that Jewish corruption would cause Bolshevist Russia to "collapse like a house of cards" was way off the mark, and it prepared itself for an extended war. Productivity for the war effort became the

Courtesy of the United States Holocaust Memorial Museum.

order of the day. Impressed with the quality of textiles ghetto Jews had been able to produce, the army "was soon ordering military supplies of all kinds" from the ghetto industries.[74] In the Nazi bureaucratic struggle between the "productionists," who emphasized the priority of winning the war, and the "attritionists," who emphasized the priority of eliminating the Jews, the former gained the upper hand early in 1942.

But that was in occupied Poland; Hitler was in Berlin. As Operation Barbarossa began, genocide was in the air. The Nazis gave no thought to ghettoizing the Jews in areas under Soviet occupation or Soviet Jews themselves, as had been the lot of Jews in western Poland. Rather, they would be shot or, perhaps more likely, driven into "hunger areas" and left there to starve. Nazis reckoned that 20 to 30 million Slavs and Jews would die due to these policies.[75] The mortality projections soon became actual body counts. By the end of 1941, the death toll among noncombatants was devastating. Between 500,000 and 800,000 Jews, including women and children, had been murdered—on the average of 2,700 to 4,200 per day—and entire regions were reported "free of Jews."[76] The Nazis clearly had crossed a line with Operation Barbarossa. Before, isolated groups such as the intelligentsia or the mentally handicapped had been killed, but now people were being murdered en masse, and this was becoming known among Germans, civilians and party members alike.

FIGURE 2. Arthur Greiser, the *Gauleiter* of the Warthegau in northwest Poland, deprived
Catholics of the sacraments, killed thousands of Catholics and Jews, and forced additional
thousands off their lands and out of their homes. Captured after the war, he was hung
by the Poles in July 1946 despite Pope Pius XII's plea for clemency.
Courtesy of the United States Holocaust Memorial Museum.

The military successes of Operation Barbarossa in the summer and
fall of 1941 excited Hitler. In a heady mood, he spoke of creating a "Garden of Eden" in the east whose current inhabitants would be finished
off.[77] Nazis everywhere in German-controlled Europe who yearned to
be rid of the Jews in their areas also became excited once they became
aware of the policy of genocide. Christopher Browning has concluded
that "victory euphoria in mid-July marked not only the conclusion of the
decision-making process leading to the mass murder of Soviet Jewry, but
also the point at which Hitler inaugurated the decision-making process
that led to the extension of the Final Solution to European Jewry."[78]
Knowing Hitler's mind and what they thought he intended, Nazis took
it upon themselves to began to experiment with gas, either in mobile
vans or small buildings, as a means of wholesale murder. Personnel of
the "T-4" euthanasia program in the Old Reich found their way east,
where a limited number of Jews and Russians fell victim to poisoning
by either carbon monoxide or Zyklon B on an experimental basis. The

prospect of mass murder by gas excited Himmler because it could reduce the number of men needed for the mobile killing squads or at least reduce the psychological strain that murdering young children, women, and the elderly by gunshot at close range was having on the shooters. By October 1941, Himmler and Heydrich had satisfied themselves that gas could be the medium for "effective mass killing."[79]

With both the means for mass genocide and the mentality of genocide in place far and wide among Nazis—in Paris, Belgrade, and Lodz as well as in Berlin—all European Jews, not only those in the Greater Reich and General Government, were in imminent danger. Nazis had thought all along of deporting Jews to the east. Consistent with this mindset, in the fall of 1941 they coined jargon about deporting people "over the Bug," a major waterway in eastern Europe, but what they really meant by the geographical phrase was outright murder. Even as "over the Bug" jargon made the rounds, the Germans built the first gas chamber at Belzec in the General Government.[80]

Although there is some question about when the decision was made to implement the murder of all European Jews, it is certain that at least the murder by gas of some Jews began late in 1941. It may be assumed, furthermore, that full implementation was only a question of time. In January 1942, the Nazis held a meeting to organize murder by gassing at Wannsee, a posh Berlin suburb. By that time Jews from the Greater Reich were already being murdered truckload by truckload in gas vans at the Chelmno death camp in northern Poland. Construction of buildings to be used as gas chambers was simultaneously under way at the Belzec camp in the General Government. By the middle of March 1942, mass murders were under way there; the first victims were Jews from Galicia in southern Poland. At the same time, a converted peasant's hut became an operational gas chamber at the Birkenau camp in southern Poland. Jews from Silesia in western Poland were the first victims in that experiment.[81] Murders were under way at Sobibor by June at the latest; then came Treblinka near Warsaw. Majdanek's gas chamber was functioning by July, and that same month the new gas chamber–crematorium complex was built at Birkenau to replace the earlier crude facility. The other three massive facilities at Birkenau were not completed until the spring of 1943. What this construction schedule tells us is that relatively few Jews (relative to the eventual total number of victims) had perished in the death camps before mid-1942.

What then were Jews doing during the first two years of the war? They were working. In spite of widespread starvation, the mortality rate of Polish Jews did not decline everywhere during these two years.[82] At

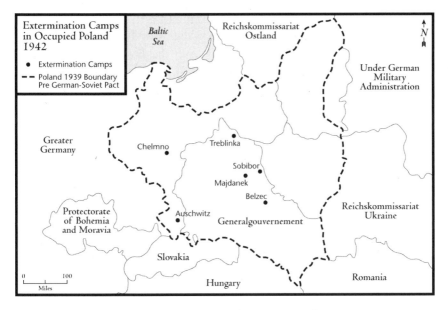

Courtesy of the United States Holocaust Memorial Museum.

the war's outset, Nazis had planned to kill off Jews with a combination of malnutrition and work—the attritionists' combination. But the initial failure of Operation Barbarossa in the winter of 1941 necessitated increased production of war matériel. Consequently, a shift in emphasis took place—Jewish production over Jewish attrition. By 1942, Germany was experiencing a severe labor shortage. In this situation, Nazi "productionists," especially the army officer corps, thought Jewish work in Poland indispensable. But Hitler did not. Nazi ideology prevailed, perhaps abetted by a food shortage in 1942. On July 19, Himmler proclaimed Aktion Reinhard (in honor of the assassinated Heydrich), the murder of all Jews in the General Government area of occupied Poland, where most Jews had been herded. During the ensuing six months, the Jews of the Warsaw ghetto, over 400,000, were taken to the nearby Treblinka death camp and gassed. The same fate befell other ghettoized Jews. It was, in Christopher Browning's words, not death through labor (attrition) but the death of labor.[83]

Who would take the place of the Jews? There was but one alternative—Polish Catholics. Their genocide, it will be recalled, was to be a two-tiered operation; first, the intelligentsia would be decimated and then "primitive Poles" whenever there was a labor surplus. By mid-1942, the intelligentsia had been taken care of, but Germany was in dire need of Poles, hundreds of thousands of whom had already been dispatched to the Old Reich as forced laborers. Had Operation Barbarossa been successful, the Nazis could have killed off both the Jews and a substantial number of Catholics, but it was unsuccessful, and Catholics had to stand in for Jews in the labor force. In February 1943, Arthur Greiser looked forward to the day when he could run Catholic Poles out of the Danzig and West Prussian areas of the Greater Reich to make it a haven for soldiers. He wanted to make the "country of the Warthegau," a country of and for front soldiers.[84] That day, of course, would never come, but the fact that he was dreaming of a day when only Germans would live there reveals that Poles continued to work in the Greater Reich. Because of the stress Operation Barbarossa placed on German resources, the second tier of the genocidal plan for Polish Catholics had to be postponed. In September 1942, the German Armed Forces High Command "ordered that Jewish workers were now to be replaced with Poles."[85]

An Italian businessman, Count Malvezzi, who had just returned from Poland in September 1942, brought information back to Italy that confirmed Hitler's orders to kill the ghettoized Jews and the command to the army to replace them in the workforce with Poles. "It seems that by the middle of October [the Nazis] want to empty entire ghettos of hundreds of thousands of languishing unfortunates to make room for the Poles, who are being moved from their own homes," which were, in turn, being turned over to Germans whose homes had been bombed out.[86] Malvezzi gave this information to Monsignor Giovanni Battista Montini of the Vatican secretariat of state.[87]

Thus, the destinies of Polish Jews and Polish Catholics crossed paths when the Holocaust was implemented in the second half of 1942 in the middle of World War II. The Germans, who had intended to reduce Poles to helot status, now sought their support. "Forgetting their pompous pretensions to racial purity," the Germans wanted to harness the Poles for the struggle against bolshevism.[88] When the Nazis captured Cardinal Hlond as he attempted to make his way back to his diocese in 1943, they promised to free him if he would inspire Catholics to join in the struggle against their "common enemy." (He refused.) The German loss at Stalingrad soon thereafter in the spring of 1943 made the suspension of the plans to eliminate Polish Catholics permanent.[89]

Hitler's order to liquidate the ghettos spelled the end for Polish Jews. They, along with every Jew the Germans could find in Europe, suffered unspeakable deaths in the newly constructed gas chambers. Before the war ended, more than 700 hundred trains from every corner of the continent would roll toward Auschwitz and the other five death camps.[90]

According to genocide historian Raul Hilberg, altogether about 3 million Jews were murdered in the death camps, of which Auschwitz and Treblinka claimed most of the victims.[91]

Historian Christopher Browning's analysis of the Holocaust in *Nazi Policy, Jewish Workers, German Killers* allows us to understand the unexpected about-face in the relations between Pope Pius and the Polish Church late in 1942 and early 1943. There was, of course, some lag time between the army command for Poles to replace Jews in the workforce and the implementation of that order. In November 1942, Breitinger still had reason to complain to Pius about why he "kept silent." But in March 1943, he wrote the pope again to say that now Catholics understood that his was a "heroic silence." This surprisingly abrupt turnaround may be taken as typical of the change of mind of all Polish church leaders in occupied Poland. Radonski, who was still complaining bitterly in the spring of 1943, wrote Pope Pius from exile. He was unaware of the changed circumstances of Polish Catholics and, as we have seen, wanted to keep the pope from making an appeal on behalf of Polish Jews.

Before 1943, the Polish hierarchy could not induce Pius XII to denounce German atrocities. But when Jews went to the death camps and Catholics took their places in the labor force, Polish bishops did no better than the pope. They did not denounce the German murder of the Jews, who were citizens and their fellow countrymen. For this the Polish hierarchy apologized in 1995 on the fiftieth anniversary of World War II.

Pius XII never apologized. The pope followed a political strategy during the war that was based on the Vatican's prewar analysis of Nazi racism and Communist atheism which determined that the latter constituted the greater danger for the future of the Catholic Church. Monsignor Domenico Tardini explained this to Harold Tittmann, who represented President Roosevelt when Myron Taylor was away from Rome.[92] Pius was much more concerned with Russian persecutions in eastern occupied Poland than with German persecutions in the west, Tardini said. Europe was faced with two great dangers, Nazism and communism. If the war should end with both of these powers defeated, there would be peace, but if communism prevailed, there would be disaster. At the end of the war, Communists would take advantage of the upheaval because communism was committed to aggression. Tardini said, "Communism cannot renounce its struggle against religion and Christian civilization because it has as its fundamental principle that capitalism must be destroyed and that religion is but the opium with which capitalism has drugged the proletariat."[93]

Tardini patiently explained the Vatican's view to Tittmann to try to thwart the U.S. lend-lease policy of sending war matériel to Soviet Russia. The Holy See did not want to see Stalin get the upper hand in the war in the east. Pius XII and President Roosevelt went round and round regarding lend-lease with the Soviets.[94] Pius XI's encyclical *Divini Redemptoris* had forbidden Catholics to cooperate with communism, which seemed exactly what lend-lease amounted to. Against his better judgment, Pope Pius gave in regarding lend-lease, but he hoped that assistance to Soviet Russia would be limited. Cardinal Edward Mooney managed an end run around the encyclical by explaining to U.S. Catholics that helping Russians was not the same thing as helping communism.[95] There was some truth to this, as American foodstuffs virtually kept Russians alive during the rest of the war.

Clearly, Pope Pius's view of World War II differed from that of the Allies. For the Allies, the war would be an uncompromising struggle to the end with Nazi Germany, not with Communist Russia, which became an ally after Germany invaded Soviet Russia. The pope wanted the termination of the war to have the result of moving Soviet Union's boundaries far from Central Europe. As German armies pushed into western Russia, taking huge areas from the Baltic to the Black Sea, the outcome of the struggle looked propitious to Pius XII. Harold Tittmann reported in the summer of 1942 that the pope did not believe the Allies could win the war and that he hoped a stalemate would produce a negotiated peace in Germany's favor. The U.S. state department told Tittmann to let the Vatican know that the Allies intended to fight Nazism to the bitter end.[96] President Roosevelt told the pope that the United States wanted to wage a "moral crusade" against evil (the Nazis), a diplomatic miscalculation on the president's part. Pius suffered from no delusions about Hitler's evil designs for the Church. But for the Vatican, the threat Hitler posed would wane, whereas the threat of communism would grow because ideological movements endure much longer than the human lifespan—Hitler's, in this instance. The pope did not see Hitler's attack on the Soviet Union as a crusade, but he knew that German Communists had been Hitler's sworn enemies during his struggle to seize power. Pius saw Christian Germany, not Hitler's Germany, as a bulwark against the spread of Russian communism into the west.[97] The pope expressed himself to Tittmann unambiguously on this point: the Communist menace was much more insidious than the Nazi menace.[98] Although he did not say this until after the war, there is no doubt that this was how Pius felt during the war. Pius XII answered the Allies' 1942 Casablanca Declaration, which called for an unconditional surrender, with a call for a just peace in his 1943 Christmas address, a peace that would spare Germany a Götterdämmerung.[99]

Looking back, we can understand where Pius XII was coming from when he in effect told Catholic Poles that they were Job. They were suffering because of the Nazi occupation just as all European Catholics were destined to suffer in a postwar Nazified continent. Pope Pius had no illusions about Hitler's brutality and began making arrangements in 1942 for prominent Catholics to flee to Argentina when it became a matter of life or death for them. Yes, Catholics would suffer, but in the process the European Church would be "cleansed" of those who only paid it lip service and thereby strengthened.[100] After Hitler's death, Nazi-style fascism would give way to the "garden variety" of fascism that supported religion, as the fascism of Mussolini, Perón, Franco, and Salazar did. Roosevelt's lend-lease aid to the Soviet Union was a bitter pill for Pope Pius to swallow. He believed that if communism emerged victorious after the war, the Catholic Church itself would be faced with a life-or-death struggle. The pope based his decision not to speak out about the moral outrages Nazis perpetrated against Catholics in Poland in the hope of avoiding moral outrages Communists would perpetrate against the entire Church if they prevailed against Nazi Germany. This was a flawed and mistaken political judgment. In the postwar and Cold War eras, East European Communist regimes did not commit genocide as the Nazis and Ustaša had done in Poland and Yugoslavia.

3
PIUS XII'S 1942
CHRISTMAS MESSAGE
GENOCIDE DECRIED

Although the word genocide would not be coined until 1944, Pius XII denounced what we now commonly understand as genocide in his Christmas message of 1942. The pope's radio address did not shape history; it did not stop the Nazi or Ustaša genocides. Yet it was an important step in the pontificate of Pius XII, one that won approval throughout the western world except in Germany. Those familiar with *The Catholic Church and the Holocaust* will notice that I have modified my views to a considerable extent regarding Pius XII's genocide statement of 1942. But my view has not changed regarding the Vatican's essential passivity in collecting and disseminating genocide information. This chapter attempts to understand what brought the pope to break out of his self-imposed silence and assesses the impact of his words.

To formulate a positive judgment about the December address of 1942 is to join, or rejoin, a conversation that historians and others (Pius XII's apologists and detractors) have carried on for some time. The historical debate about Pius and the Holocaust is nearly as long-standing as Holocaust study itself. The multivolume publication in the 1960s of the Vatican's sources, *Actes et Documents,* jump-started serious historical thought about Pope Pius and the Holocaust.[1] Two seminal articles about the Vatican and the Jews of Rome appeared in the 1960s and 1970s, the first by Leonidas Hill in the *Journal of Modern History* and the other by eminent British historian Owen Chadwick in the *Journal of Ecclesiastical History.*[2] But unlike mainstream Holocaust studies, which have made impressive strides over the last three decades, scholarship about Pius XII and the Holocaust has not keep pace after its promising start. It has been mired down betimes in one or another elementary dispute: the pope's silence saved lives, the pope's silence cost lives; the pope's 1942 message was clear, the pope's 1942 message was not clear. Curiously, historian Walter Laqueur does not mention the pope's address at all in his well-known book, *The Terrible Secret,* perhaps because acknowledging it would mean that the developing Holocaust was not a secret after all.[3] In fact, the Christmas address signaled adaptability rather than uniform rigidity at the Vatican in the middle of the Holocaust years. The Holy See was in search of a new path for papal policy.

Pius XII's committed apologists and detractors are alike in their compulsive desire to come to premature closure. This investigation of a critical point during the Holocaust years aims to provide access to an open-minded inquiry about Pius XII and the Holocaust. The wealth of detail and innumerable surprises that resulted from the opening of the Vatican's interwar archives means that at this point we see the wartime period only through a glass darkly.[4] Historians know that they are in the middle of scholarly exploration, not at its end. The murder of Polish Catholics and Jews moved Pius XII to reshape the Vatican's course. We will not know precisely what other considerations brought him to this decision until the Vatican's archives for World War II are made available, but we may cautiously construct the factors that determined Pius's moves.

Historians, myself included, who have been more critical than indulgent in their studies of Pius XII have been rather too dismissive of the 1942 address.[5] Since Pius never spoke out again, the Christmas address has been seen by the pope's critics as falling far short of the mark, given the enormity of the Holocaust. This judgment is premature. Contemporaries, as we will see, viewed the statement in a different light, precisely because it was the pope's initial words about atrocities. Had the pope spoken out again later, we would of course also view the 1942 address as the beginning of the pope's messages rather than his final declaration. We know that the pope would not take up the matter again, but contemporaries did not know that this would be the case. In fact, to assert that Pope Pius himself intended this to be his one and only statement is incorrect. He informed Bishop Konrad Preysing (Berlin) that given the right circumstances, he intended to make a more pointed pronouncement than that of 1942.[6] It follows that we must pay close attention to then current reaction to the pope's message and then inquire, in the following chapter, what circumstances arose to seal the pope's lips.

Because Pope Pius spoke out meaningfully about genocide in Poland at the end of 1942, we can assume that he took seriously the reports, or at least some of the reports, that had come to the Vatican earlier that year. The extent of the information about atrocities that poured into the Vatican seems overwhelming to such a degree that the Vatican's secretary of state appeared to be dissembling when he questioned news of atrocities or said they could not be verified. The reasons the secretariat sometimes gave for the pope's silence before the Christmas address—speaking out would make matters worse for the victims, it would endanger potential victims, when individual bishops speak out they speak for the pope—appear to be lame. Indeed, it could be argued that the Vatican did dissemble in the months preceding December 1942. But there had to have been a turning point that caused the Holy Father to address genocide in the Christmas address. This does not mean that at the end of 1942 Pius XII knew or was convinced of the fact that the Final Solution was in the process of being carried out.

The Vatican's reaction to the news of genocide from Poland is admittedly curious. Vatican spokespersons said that they believed the accounts of atrocities perpetrated on Catholics but doubted the stories of greater atrocities on Jewish victims, despite the two-decade-long Nazi record of radical antisemitism, about which the Vatican was keenly aware. In 1935, Pius XI assigned two Dutch Jesuits the task of analyzing National Socialism. In a thorough study, they came to the conclusion that there could be no compromise between the Church and the Nazis.[7] The Jesuit study even foresaw and condemned the Nazi Lebensraum program, which, as we have seen, resulted in misery or death for millions of Poles.[8] At the same time, a Vatican bishop, Alfredo Ottaviani, wrote a treatise on canon law in 1935 which condemned the idea that the purpose of the state was to promote the purity of blood.[9] Pacelli, who then headed the Vatican secretariat of state, agreed with the Jesuit analysis; before the war began, he had said that the "message of a new materialism of race" contradicted the "joyous news of Christ's teaching."[10] Clearly, quite early on the Vatican understood the social venom of National Socialism. It is difficult, in fact, to accept as a fact that Pacelli as Pope Pius did not give credence to the news of the murder of the Jews.

More than two decades ago, historian Walter Laqueur wrote that the Vatican got so much information about the Holocaust that "but for the tragic character of the subject, it would have been a subject for comedy."[11] Information about atrocities came to the Vatican from a variety of sources:

—its own diplomatic corps, the nuncios in Eastern European countries

—church hierarchy, the bishops in Germany, the Netherlands, and
  Eastern European countries

—Catholics, priests and laypersons alike
—the Polish Government in Exile
—foreign diplomats assigned to the Holy See
—Jews and Jewish organizations

These would be the actors in Laqueur's "comedy," and it cannot be denied that they testified to atrocity after atrocity. What is impressive about the information that was provided to the Holy See is the spectrum of its provenance. Although historian David Alvarez argues rightly that other governments knew about atrocities before—shortly before—the Vatican did, he does not question the fact that intelligence was collected from a variety of sources about ongoing mass murder.[12] Australian historian Paul O'Shea has counted the references to Jews in volume eight of *Actes et Documents*, finding 107 for the period prior to December 1942. O'Shea found a sharp jump in the number of references to Jews after June 1941, a date that corresponds with the German invasion of Russia and the onset of murder of Jews by the mobile killing squads. However, the disclosures covered not just the activity of the killing squads but every aspect of the Nazis' murdering process.[13] A number of historians have listed or discussed atrocity data received at the Vatican.[14]

For most of 1942, the Vatican stonewalled regarding the Nazis' intent in the face of continuous information about atrocities perpetrated on Yugoslav Jews and Orthodox Serbs and on Polish Catholics and Jews from many different sources. Even if the Vatican held back from admitting genocide, its personnel worked to alleviate the victims' lot. In September 1942, for example, Cardinal Secretary of State Maglione instructed the nuncio in Vichy France, Valerio Valeri, to request that Vichy Prime Minister Pierre Laval mitigate the severity of measures taken against Jews in the unoccupied zone.[15] The nuncio could not persuade Laval or Marshal Petain to stop the persecution of Jews or reduce it. Later, however, Valeri succeeded in getting Laval to arrange that the families of the 12,000 Jewish women and children herded into the Vélodrome d'Hiver in Paris would remain together. Maglione mentioned that the intervention of the Holy See in favor of Jews in Italy, where Nazi pressure to participate in atrocities was not as effective as in France and the inclination of the Italian people against persecution was strong, had met with much greater success. He did not give particulars about the intervention. In spite of these efforts by the Holy See, when diplomats pressed the pope to condemn mass murder, Maglione responded with ineffectual dodges that have provoked the suspicion and impatience of historians operating, of course, with hindsight knowledge of the Holocaust. Papal silence also provoked the suspicion and impatience of Poles when they told the Holy See about German atrocities and how they were being deprived of the sacraments. Undecided about what to do for much of the year, Pius left the job of temporizing to his secretary of state.

That the Holy See was unable to confirm atrocity reports became Cardinal Maglione's rickety crutch. But when a Ukrainian bishop wrote that over 200,000 people had been murdered, what was there to confirm? Were bishops for some reason unreliable on the matter of mass murder? Had the Holy See not heard exactly the same from Polish bishops? Not infrequently, the Holy See received information relating to the same atrocity from more than one source. In the spring of 1942, Pope Pius learned from three of his own diplomats stationed in Hungary, Switzerland, and Slovakia that Slovak Jews were to be deported and murdered. In June, word came to the Vatican from the Polish Government in Exile that these Jews had been killed. If the Vatican had learned in advance that mass murder of a particular population was to take place and then learned a few months later that the murders of those people had been perpetrated, would that not constitute confirmation? In the fall, Roosevelt's envoy Myron Taylor informed Maglione that the Warsaw Jews were being deported and killed in specially constructed killing centers. The cardinal replied that he had heard similar news a few days earlier ("incredible killings take place every day; it appears that by the middle of October they wish to empty out entire ghettos of hundreds of thousand of languishing unfortunates"[16]), but he could not verify the accuracy of the reports. In this instance, an American diplomat (Taylor), an Italian national (Malvezzi), and a Catholic clergyman (Abbot Scavizzi) independently told the Vatican the same news about killings en masse. By any measure, does this not amount to a confirmation? But the cardinal secretary of state played for time, refusing to even use words like "killed" or "massacred." He had heard, he said in words reminiscent of Nazi euphemisms, of "severe measures."[17]

In 1942, when the question of whether Jews were being murdered systematically arose, the Holy See's office of the secretariat of state and the U.S. State Department reacted similarly. Neither displayed much interest in the matter. Late in 1942, a state department official told a U.S. congressman that stories about atrocities could not be confirmed. When Rabbi Stephen Wise proposed a declaration warning that Hitler planned to exterminate all European Jews, the State Department "wanted to have nothing to do" with it.[18] After a 26-nation alliance against the Axis powers called the United Nations issued an official pronouncement about German atrocities in December of that year, R. B. Reams of the State Department said that the problem with the proclamation was that the United States as a consequence would have to do something to "help these people."[19]

Cardinal Maglione's other feeble crutch was his repeated protests that the Vatican was doing everything it could to alleviate the suffering of "non-Aryans," or words to that effect. Indeed, the Holy See often did work to save Jews when specific situations were brought to its attention. But there was an essential passivity regarding the secretariat's conduct of affairs relating to mass murder. Regarding Maglione's oft-repeated rejoinder to the effect that something could not be confirmed, it must be noted that he never took steps to confirm the many reports of atrocities that flowed to his office. Had Pope Pius wished to do so, he could have assembled a comprehensive picture of the genocidal crimes of the Nazis from information that had come to him from Eastern and Western European bishops and nuncios and from secular sources. Cardinal Maglione showed no interest in doing this, nor did Pope Pius show any interest in disseminating a comprehensive overview of the genocide in progress to the national churches. For most of the year 1942, the Holy See temporized and sometimes even dissembled when genocidal information was brought to its attention.

Very late in 1942 Pius XII began to consider a change of course that would eventuate in his Christmas address of that year. Vatican documents and those of other governments allow us to lift the curtain enough to peek at what went on behind the scenes at the Holy See. In the fall, more documentation about Nazi genocide of Jews, notably Gerhart Riegner's famous "final solution" memo of late August 1942 (which was omitted from the *Actes et Documents*) became known. In his work for the World Jewish Congress in Switzerland, Riegner had learned from an anti-Nazi German industrialist of Hitler's intention to settle "the Jewish question in Europe." The Nazis intended to murder all of the Jews of Europe by asphyxiation using "prussic acid." Thus, amazingly, even as the gas chambers of the death camps were just beginning to approach full capacity, accurate information about them became available.[20] Riegner wrote that his source should be considered very reliable, and he asked authorities to confirm or deny his information. Riegner sent a cable to the U.S. State Department and, through Nuncio Filippo Bernardini, to the Holy See. Much to Gerhart Riegner's dismay, nothing happened. The State Department sat on the telegram because of its "fantastic allegation" instead of forwarding it to Rabbi Stephen Wise, as Riegner wanted. The Vatican also gave the telegram a chilly reception. Secretary of State Luigi Maglione said in October 1942 that the Vatican could not corroborate Riegner's memo on the final solution.[21] In fact, however, the Riegner cable had made a greater impression on Pope Pius than Maglione was willing to admit.

During the summer months before the Riegner cable, Pope Pius had

FIGURES 3 AND 4. Berlin-born Gerhart Moritz Riegner (*left*) was a Jewish lawyer
and director of the World Jewish Congress in Geneva, Switzerland, during
World War II. Jan Karski (*right*), Polish underground hero, in 1942.
Karski informed Prime Minister Churchill and President Roosevelt about
the Nazi extermination policy in Poland. The efforts of Riegner and Karski
led to the United Nations' condemnation of genocide late in 1942.
Courtesy of the United States Holocaust Memorial Museum.

begun to come under fire for ignoring the mass murder of civilians in
Eastern Europe. The pope, Harold Tittmann reported, was

> having to withstand a constant stream of criticism from pro-ally sources
> for refusing to speak out against the violations of the moral and natural
> laws perpetrated by the Axis powers. It is pointed out that the Holy Father
> appears to be occupying himself exclusively with spiritual matters, chari-
> table acts, and rhetoric, while adopting an ostrich-like policy toward the
> notorious atrocities.
>
> It is felt that as a consequence of this exasperating attitude, the great
> moral authority enjoyed by the papacy throughout the world under Pius XI
> has today been notably diminished.[22]

More criticism calling Pius XII's moral authority into question
emerged that fall. Shortly after the Vatican received word of alleged
atrocities from the nuncio in Switzerland, predominantly Catholic countries hit Pope Pius with a blunt challenge to his authority. In September,
four Latin American nations—Brazil, Uruguay, Peru, and Cuba—along
with two European countries—Belgium and Poland—sent démarches to
the Holy See, which, though worded slightly differently, warned Pius

about the loss of papal moral authority. "A policy of silence in regard to such offenses [in Poland] against the conscience of the world must necessarily involve a renunciation of moral leadership and a consequent atrophy of the influence and authority of the Vatican."[23] Tittmann notified Secretary of State Hull that the Jesuits supported the resolution of the Catholic nations, adding that Undersecretary of State Montini had remarked that "the time may come when Pius XII will feel obliged to speak out."[24] The charge of a renunciation of moral leadership had to have wounded Pope Pius. Thus, at the same time that Polish bishops were independently warning Pius about loss of faith in him among the Catholics of Poland, a number of other Catholic states brought the same concern to his attention, and not in varnished diplomatspeak. Catholics since the time of the first Vatican Council in 1870 had been obliged to believe in the infallibility of the pope when he spoke ex cathedra on matters of faith and morals. Protestants had traditionally rejected papal authority, but now Catholics were warning Pius XII about a decline in his moral authority because of his silence. Both Great Britain and the United States joined the assault, but it was surely the messages from the Catholic countries that shook Pope Pius.

Pius XII, who considered diplomacy to be his forte, was being put on the defensive by accredited diplomats. The Peruvian ambassador to the Holy See, Diomedes Arias Schreiber, reported in November to his government that the Polish ambassador had informed Pius XII about the atrocities being committed in his country, pressuring the pope to speak out.[25] Harold Tittmann and Francis d'Arcy Osborne, the English minister to the Holy See, likewise pressed Pope Pius to speak out about the atrocities: "Is there not a moral issue at stake which does not admit of neutrality?" Osborne asked.[26] Commenting to himself, Under-Secretary of State Domenico Tardini wrote in his diary, "I could not but agree."[27] We may speculate, on the basis of another Tardini memo to be discussed below, that his agreement reflected a shift in thinking at the Vatican at some point very late in 1942.

From inside the Vatican, Wladimir Ledokowski, superior general of the Society of Jesus, added his voice to those of the diplomats. Before his death in December, Ledokowski, called "the black pope" because of his influence, urged the Holy Father to condemn German atrocities.[28] In December, a memo to the U.S. State Department reported that the pope was disturbed by the "undescribable savagery" of the German occupation in Poland.[29] Worse was to come. Later that month, Pope Pius heard from the Polish ambassador that approximately 1 million Jews had already been exterminated.[30] The massacre was not limited to occupied Poland.

That same month Pius was informed by the bishop of Riga, Latvia, that most Jews there had been exterminated. Thus, in the fall of 1942, especially the months of November and December, Pope Pius was besieged with news about atrocities.

More moral pressure came to the pope when the Allies condemned the genocide of the Jews in December 17, 1942.[31] The efforts of Jan Karski and Gerhart Riegner were the tripwire for the Allied declaration. Karski, a courier for the Polish underground, led an adventuresome and dangerous life smuggling information in and out of his occupied country. Jews secreted him into the Warsaw ghetto and later into the Belzec death camp. The sight of emaciated corpses on the streets of the ghetto and of bodies piled up at Belzec sickened him. In November, Karski, as we have seen, carried a message from Polish Jews to the pope asking him to excommunicate those who perpetrated atrocities. On December 18, President Raczkiewicz of the Polish Government in Exile wrote to Pope Pius asking him to intervene. In an effort to press the Church into action, Karski also saw cardinals Spellman, Mooney, and Stritch and the apostolic delegate to the United States, Amleto Cicognani. Karski also personally carried his message from Polish Jews to world leaders such as Roosevelt and Churchill, urging them to take extraordinary measures to stop the extermination process. His meetings with foreign affairs statesmen Anthony Eden and Lord Selborne and with top state department members Cordell Hull and Henry Stimson contributed materially to the United Nations' declaration of December 17th.[32]

In November, the U.S. State Department at last confirmed the content of Gerhart Riegner's "final solution" cable of August. Rabbi Wise, the leading American spokesperson regarding the Jewish disaster, broke the news to the media that same month. This effort together with that of Karski pushed the issue of a United Nations' declaration forward in spite of some state department opposition. In the end the U.S. naysayers only managed to weaken the declaration somewhat by insisting on the removal of the phrase "no room for doubt" in reference to the certitude of the atrocity information. The final wording referred to the "bestial policy of cold-blooded extermination" and said that "the number of European victims of these bloody cruelties is reckoned in many hundreds of thousands of entirely innocent men, women and children."[33] Thus, even with some deletions, the United Nations declaration amounted to a strong and unequivocal condemnation of genocide.

The December 17th statement must have set the Holy See scurrying to play catch-up. After having been curtly told several times by a number of nations that the Vatican was squandering its moral authority, Pius XII found himself in the embarrassing position of being overshadowed by a

FIGURE 5. Eugenio Cardinal Pacelli at Mt. Vernon in 1936. During his
visit of that year to the United States, the cardinal secretary of state said that
the Soviet Union was the greatest threat to the western world. Later, as
Pope Pius XII, he would consistently hold to this view.
*NCWC/OGS Photographic Collection, American Catholic History
Research Center and University Archives, The Catholic
University of America, Washington, D.C.*

secular institution. The United Nations, not even yet an officially charted
body, held court on genocide before the centuries-old papacy with its
rather recent claim of moral infallibility got around to it. U.S. and British envoys to the Vatican held the pope's feet to the fire. After having
unsuccessfully sought an audience to discuss Riegner's information with
the pope, Tittmann twice asked for an official Vatican response to the
Riegner cable. Subsequently, both Tittmann and Osborne urged the Holy
See to endorse the declaration of the Allies. For too long the Vatican had
temporized about mass murder in Poland, first of Catholics, then of Jews.
With the international declaration, Pius was brought to the realization
that events had passed him by.

Let us pause to look at recent history as Pius XII might have viewed
it. During the 1930s, Pope Pius XI had worked to construct a system
of concordats with European states that would clear the path for the
Church to attend to the religious affairs of Catholics and protect the faith

of believers. The advent of fascism had seemed to hold out the promise to Pius XI that the days of the Protestant reformation, the Enlightenment, liberalism, and socialism were over.[34] Eugenio Pacelli was one of the main architects of the concordats, first as nuncio to Germany, then as the cardinal secretary of state when he concluded the all-important Lateran Treaty with Italy in 1929 that finally ended the decades-long bitter dispute between church and state. By the time of his elevation to the throne of St. Peter, the concordat system was in place with all major Central and Eastern European countries with substantial Catholic populations as well as with the two Iberian nations. Rome viewed the recent concordats with Italy and then Germany as major achievements, even though Nazism had been denounced by many German bishops who, left to their own, would not have sought a concordat with Hitler. Among others, Cardinal Karl Schulte in Cologne had seen the futility of striking a legal contract with a lawless regime.[35] With great expectations, the Vatican had pressed on. Pacelli pushed through the negotiations with Nazis, and he determinedly sustained the concordat in the face of repeated German violations. "The world will see," Pius had said in March 1939, "that we tried everything in order to live in peace with Germany."[36] Soon thereafter, Pius XI's strategy of concordats and Pius XII's concordat strategy with the Nazis foundered on the rocks of World War II. Germany had repeatedly violated the concordat, and now it was the country that was denying Poles access to the sacraments, the exact opposite of the Church's intent in the concordats. For a year and a half, Germany and the Soviet Union, the nations that constituted the Vatican's two worst enemies by its own appraisal—Nazism and Soviet bolshevism—had been allies, a baffling, altogether unanticipated pact. Mussolini had fallen from grace as the "model fascist" when he copied racist Nazi laws after disparaging them earlier. Pope Pius XII, left holding a withered fascist flower, looked back on the wreckage of the Holy See's ten years of work. The new pope was at a loss as to where to turn or what to do other than to attempt to nurse the sick fascist patients back to health. But time and the events of the war were passing Pope Pius by. After the international declaration condemning genocide, Pius XII knew that somehow the Vatican's policies needed to be modified.

As Pius turned his thoughts in December to his annual Christmas address, black clouds hovered above. A French bishop, interviewed shortly after his audience with the pope, painted the following picture of the pope:

> [Pius XII] is terrified of savagery of the present war. He is revolted by the religious persecutions in countries under German domination and the con-

tinual attacks to which the Vatican and [Pius] himself are subjected in Italy are unbearable for him; recently [Italian minister of state Roberto] Farinacci requested the denunciation of the Lateran agreements and the internment and isolation of the entire Vatican administration. Relations with royal family about as bad. [Pius] wants Rome considered as the papal city not an enemy city. Results of investigation in Poland: the attitude of the Russians much more humane than the Germans. The German administration, headed by the bullies of the party, showed an unbelievable lack of order (in administering Poland) compensated by undescribable savagery.[37]

No mention is made here of the savagery of Catholics in Croatia against both Christians and Jews. Nevertheless, Pius would have had reason to see a silver lining on the horizon, since Germany and Soviet Russia were no longer allied after Hitler's double-cross of Stalin in the summer of 1941. But the deplorable conduct of the German occupation forces overshadowed any cause for hopefulness.

The Christmas Message

By the end of 1942, Pope Pius could recall during his adult lifetime two mass murders in Africa and one in the Middle East. Since the word genocide did not yet exist, these mass murders did not convey the same sense to him that they do to us in a post-Auschwitz era. He would not have been aware that the pattern of genocide would come to characterize the twentieth century. But the contemporary brutality and mass murders unleashed by World War II deeply troubled the new pope in the second full year of his pontificate.

Pius XII decided that he could not ignore the issue. The Christmas message he crafted fit the circumstances as he saw them—that is to say, he addressed principles and omitted particulars. The pope spoke out against "arbitrary attacks" and opposed those who violated the "juridical safety of individuals." Pius said that the state had no right to "herd people around as though they were a lifeless thing." He spoke of "anguished cries" of the victims, a clear reference to the atrocities. Pius lamented the fact that some who called themselves Christian were perpetrators. Near the end of the discourse, Pius condemned genocide when he mentioned "the hundreds of thousands of persons who, without any fault on their part, sometimes only because of their nationality or race, have been consigned to death or to a slow decline."[38] Although not as bluntly stated as the United Nations' declaration earlier that month, Pius unmistakably denounced genocide.

The papal address did not mention the perpetrators or the victims by name. Of course, the pope could not mention Polish Catholics without mentioning Jews. To have mentioned both of them would have infuriated the Polish Church because Pope Pius had failed to mention his own Catholics in a timely manner when they had begged him to do so.[39] In July 1942, it will be recalled, the order was given for Polish Jews to be taken from their workplaces to places of extermination. Polish Catholics replaced these Jews. This process could not, however, be accomplished everywhere simultaneously or anywhere overnight. For this reason, the Polish Church still registered bitter complaints late in the year about the pope's abandonment of them. In the meantime, the murder of the Jews was well under way everywhere except in the yet-to-be built killing facilities at Auschwitz-Birkenau. Had the pope publicly decried the atrocities perpetrated against the Catholics earlier, he could then have mentioned both groups in his Christmas message. Because he had failed to do this, he dared not risk alienating the Polish Church by waiting until the genocide of Jews had begun before alluding to the fate of Catholics. The pope's failure to condemn Nazi atrocities against Catholic Poles in a timely manner—a baffling omission—turned out to be a crucial mistake.

But why did not Pius mention the killers by name? The answer lies in the Church's irrevocable opposition to Marxist communism and fear of Russian bolshevism that had become dramatic during the two world wars. Pope Leo XIII first condemned communism as a social and economic system in 1878 in the encyclical *Quod Apostolici Muneris*. Pope Leo repeated the condemnation numerous times, notably in *Rerum Novarum* (1891). Each subsequent pope reaffirmed Leo XIII's condemnation. When communism took on the form of Russian bolshevism, Pope Pius XI railed against it. During the worldwide depression of the 1930s, when the Soviet five-year plan seemed to be a model of economic growth, Pius said in *Quadragesimo Anno* that communism was not the remedy. Again in *Caritate Christi Compulsi* of May 1932, the pope labeled communism the "most perilous of all evils." Communism had one aim: "to wage an atrocious war against all religion and God."[40] Pius XI returned to this theme in 1936 in *Dilectissima Nobis* and the following year in *Divini Redemptoris*. The Vatican could and did negotiate with fascist governments because they were not godless. It felt that of the two systems of government, the greater danger lay in communism and that Christianity was its antidote. This view took concrete form when Pope Pius XI used the exact words of the internal investigation by the Congregation of the Holy Office in condemning communism but significantly cushioned that office's condemnation of National Socialism in the encyclical *Mit brennender Sorge*—obviously a conscious choice.[41]

Because communism was atheistic, there could be no compromise with it (*Divini Redemptoris*). Pius XII inherited this tradition of fierce rejection of communism and reaffirmed it in *La Solennita della Pentecoste,* given June 1, 1941, just a few weeks before the German invasion of Russia. In view of the Vatican's tradition of unalterable opposition to communism, it was natural for Pius XII to view World War II as a showdown between the Christian West and the Bolshevist East. No inch of territory should fall to the Soviets. Germany, which he did not mention as the perpetrator of atrocities in the Christmas address, was to be the vanguard in this decisive encounter. The pope walked a fine line in holding to this view: Germany, not the Nazis, would be decisive in the confrontation between Christianity and communism.

Because we lack documentation about the behind-the-scenes thinking at the Vatican, we cannot be completely certain why Pope Pius failed to identify Germany as the perpetrator of the genocide he was condemning late in the year 1942. Apparently, the murder of thousands of Catholic Poles and hudreds of thousands of Polish and European Jews did not deter Pius XII from the path so clearly laid out in 1937 when the decision was made to "lighten up" on the severe language the Holy Office had used to condemn Nazi racism. By the end of 1942 the world war had raged for one complete year, at which time the military situation seemed bleak to the Allies. Not so for Pope Pius. First, it seemed possible, and from the pope's perspective, hopeful that with the German army deep in Soviet territory the war might finally come to an end with the boudaries of the Soviet Union far removed from Western Europe and, possibly, that Communist leadership would founder as a result thereof. Pius did not, as we have seen, think in 1942 that the Allies would prevail.[42] Pius liked to think in terms of Christian Germany fighting Communist atheism rather than of Hitler as a crusader.[43] Second, we know from both Vatican insiders who were close to the pope and from the dispatched of Harold Tittmann and D'Arcy Osborne that Pius very dearly wished to play the role of a mediator to bring peace to Europe. Thus, wanting the war to end with a status quo as it was in that December of 1942 and hoping to be the broker of the peace, Pius XII protected his neutrality by not naming Germany as the atrocity perpetrator in his Christmas message.

The Vatican's newspaper *L'Osservatore Romano* warped news coverage of the war at the expense of Communist Russia. Even though German atrocities in western Poland against Catholics far outpaced those of the Soviet army in the eastern half of the occupied country, *L'Osservatore* repeatedly relayed information about closed churches and murders perpetrated in the name of communism. When the Germans deported people in the western sector, *L'Osservatore* referred to the action as a "transfer," but when the Soviets did the same, the newspaper said the victims were deported. At a time when Germans were terrorizing Polish priests and depriving Poles of their religion, something the Vatican was well aware of, *L'Osservatore Romano* referred to the "terrorist methods" of the Soviets in assassinating Polish priests.[44] When Bishop Leon Wetmanski died in October 1941, *L'Osservatore* carried the news but did not mention that he had died in Auschwitz.

Uppermost in Pius XII's mind was the religious significance of the war in Europe. During the first year and a half, the period when Germans, including of course German Catholics, were murdering Polish priests and depriving the populace of the sacraments, Pius was reported in March 1941 to be profoundly discouraged and depressed.[45] If there had to be war, he could not have envisioned less fortunate circumstances—two anti-Christian rulers dividing up Catholic Poland. Just a few months later, when Germany invaded Soviet Russia, Pius was encouraged. A year later, when German prospects in western Russia looked promising, the pope linked the war to popular spirituality, dedicating the world to Our Lady of Fatima, who had appeared in Portugal in 1917 (same year as the Bolshevik revolution) and promised that Russia would be converted if the world were to be dedicated to her Immaculate Heart. On the same day in 1917 that Benedict XV had raised Eugenio Pacelli to the episcopacy, the Virgin Mary had appeared for the first time to three peasant children in Portugal.[46] This coincidence made a deep and lasting impression on the young bishop. To celebrate the silver anniversary of the apparitions at Fatima, Pius dedicated Russia to the Immaculate Heart, and in December 1942, he repeated the dedication in a solemn liturgical ceremony in St. Peter's basilica in the presence of the diplomatic corps. For Pope Pius, German atrocities were an immediate concern but Soviet communism was the greater evil.

Reaction to the Christmas Message

In the short term, Pius XII's address was well received, except by the Nazis and their Jewish victims in Poland. The message quieted the diplomatic corps of the western world. In reporting on the address to the State Department, the office of the U.S. envoy at the Vatican specifically referred to the line in the pope's talk that referred to genocide.[47] The Christmas message went a long way toward shoring up the papacy's moral authority, which was, no doubt, one of Pius's objectives. A distinct decline in the number of challenges to the pope's conduct of the Holy

See's affairs followed the Christmas message, at least until the fall of 1943, when the Nazis began seizing Italian Jews.

When Harold Tittmann visited with Pope Pius at the traditional Christmas audience, they parlayed as diplomats customarily do. Tittmann reported to the State Department that he thought Pius was sincere in believing that the meaning of his words that referred to atrocities should satisfy those who had been urging him to speak out. Pius showed surprise when Tittmann said there were some who did not share the pope's opinion. The pope then told Tittmann that his words referred to Poles, Jews, and hostages. The audience ended amicably; Tittmann agreed with Pius when he said that "taken as a whole . . . his message should be welcomed by the American people."[48]

Tittmann had tried to use the audience to keep pressure on the Holy See to speak out about the Holocaust because of the advantage such a statement would give to the Allies. But Tittmann's actual opinion of the papal Christmas message was more positive than the diplomatic stance he took during the audience. Early in January, Tittmann wired the State Department that "taken as a whole, the message may be regarded as an arraignment of totalitarianism. Furthermore, the reference to the persecution of the Jews and mass deportations is unmistakable."[49] There were some, Tittmann reported, who wanted the pope to point a finger and name names. But it is clear that Tittmann thought approvingly of the pope's Christmas message. Curiously, in his memoir Tittmann (or his son, who edited the papers) did not mention that the reference to Jews was obvious. The memoir quoted Tittmann's first dispatch on the New Year's audience to the State Department verbatim but then omitted his subsequent report in which he said that the reference to Jews was unmistakable.[50] The reason for the omission is that Tittmann wanted to incorporate in his memoir a speech he made at St. Louis University in 1961 after he had retired from diplomatic service in which he gave Pope Pius's reasons for keeping silent about the Holocaust. The omission in the memoir of Tittmann's positive assessment of the Christmas address and the ambassador's subsequent talk at the university distort the historical record. Ambassador Tittmann admired Pope Pius and obviously put words in the pope's mouth in his university address with the intention of defending him.[51]

Western newspapers applauded the pope's message or took approving notice of it. The *New York Times* report praised the pope. That Pius had omitted specific reference to Jews was not even alluded to, much less criticized. The report singled out and quoted a few of Pope Pius's phrases, such as "arbitrary attacks," and specifically mentioned the phrase the pope had used to condemn genocide. Two other newspapers, the *Bal-*

timore Sun and the *Chicago Tribune,* pointed out that the pope had
mentioned no nations by name. But both presses quoted the phrase that
referred to genocide, "consigned to death." Interestingly, although both
reports pointedly said that the pope also condemned Marxist socialism,
they noted that he also denounced racial superiority. The *Washington
Evening Star* did not run a news story on the Christmas message but
included a reference to it in the lead editorial that dealt with President
Roosevelt's Christmas radio address. This association of president and
pope naturally cast Pius XII in a favorable light. The London *Times* did
not cover the pope's message, probably only because the paper did not
publish on the 25th, 26th, or 27th. All of the papers that devoted copy to
Pius's address did so positively, although it was not page-one news in any
of them.[52] Pope Pius had not hit the Nazis hard enough to capture headlines. The address was quite abstract and mostly proclaimed principles.
The lay Catholic journal *Commonweal* editorialized that it is "difficult
to realize that certain sections [of the pope's message] are issued in the
very midst of a world cataclysm."[53] In *America,* the other major Catholic
journal, John LaFarge emphasized Pope Pius's antipathy toward communism: the pope, he said, had condemned and still did condemn "the
various forms of Marxist Socialism."[54] John LaFarge wrote that most of
the encyclical had to do with free enterprise and private property and
the rights of labor; he did not mention atrocities, whether by Russians
or Germans.[55] The two U.S. publications, *Commonweal* and *America,*
had done more to report on the Holocaust than any other religious or
secular journal in the United States, but, remarkably, they did not pick up
Pius XII's words condemning genocide. It may be that, unlike the secular
press, the Catholic weeklies thought the pope's words about atrocities
were too few and too indefinite.

Jews also approved, except, of course, Jews in Poland. Gerhart Riegner at the Swiss office of the World Jewish Congress in Bern considered
the message to be "very important," even if, later on, he found it less
impressive. As Riegner later wrote, he had never felt so hopeless as he did
during the months following his "final solution" cable. Having "waited
in despair for some reaction from the allied world to my reports," he
quite naturally felt buoyed by Pope Pius's words.[56] At least in this respect,
the Christmas message had a long-term effect, as it opened the door for
the World Jewish Congress to seek a Vatican intervention for the predicament of European Jews during the rest of the war.

Reaction to the Christmas message from within the Church varied.
Interestingly, Bishop Preysing in Berlin thought the pope's words referred
to Jews but were not specific enough. Poles thought the pope had referred
to them, the suffering Catholics, but that he should have identified the

Germans as perpetrators. Pius wrote to Preysing in April of 1943 saying that his words were well understood, meaning that he had referred to the Jews about whom the Berlin bishop was greatly concerned.[57] Although the Poles wished the Nazis had been singled out, they began to agree early in 1943, now that they had replaced the Jews in the labor force, with what they perceived as the wisdom of Pius XII's tactics during the first years of the war.[58]

The most meaningful, and at the same time most puzzling, reaction to the Christmas message came from the Dutch Church. The racial question arose from the outset of the Dutch Church's confrontation with the German occupational authorities. Dutch historian J. M. Snoek asserts that in comparison to other Netherlands churches, the Catholic Church there behaved very favorably toward the Jews.[59] To a considerable extent the credit for this record goes to the main player in the Netherlands Church, the archbishop of Utrecht, Johannes de Jong. When the Germans occupied Holland, de Jong said that he did not intend to be another Innitzer.[60] He meant that he had no intention of rolling out the red carpet for Hitler as Cardinal Theodore Innitzer had done in Vienna, which had infuriated Pope Pius XI. In fact, de Jong ordered his priests to deny the sacraments to Nazi Dutchmen.

The first "action" against Dutch Jews came in July 1942. Among the Jews the Nazis deported were some who had converted to the Christian religion. The Christian churches protested this outrage and planned to communicate their protest to the Dutch people toward the end of the month. The Nazis, however, promised the mainline Protestant Church that if they refrained from a public announcement, no additional Christian "Jews" of their denomination would be transported. Seeking to save lives, the Church remained silent, but the Catholic Church and some smaller Protestant denominations went ahead with the public pronouncement against the Nazis.[61]

Thereupon, the papal nuncio in Berlin, Orsenigo, notified the Vatican that the protest of the Church had forced the German occupiers to end deportations. In fact, just the opposite occurred. After the protest, the Nazis seized, deported, and murdered Catholics of Jewish heritage. Among the victims was Edith Stein, who had warned Pius XI nearly ten years earlier about Nazi racism, predicting that it would claim "many victims."[62] Twice de Jong had personally pleaded for the seized Jews to the Nazi Kommissar of the Netherlands, Arthur Seyss-Inquart. After the war, Seyss-Inquart admitted that he had deported the Catholic "Jews" in revenge for the public protest by the Church on behalf of all Jews.[63] More than in any other country on the continent of Europe, the Dutch Catholic Church dealt with Nazi racist policy in a timely and bold manner.

What moved the Dutch Church to challenge the Nazis? De Jong saw in Pius XII's 1942 Christmas message a signal for other Catholics to publicly confront Nazi Germany. When the Dutch bishops protested Nazi treatment of Jews in a pastoral letter, they said that they "were following a path indicated by our Holy Father, the Pope," and they quoted from Pius XII's Christmas address: "The Church would be untrue to herself, ceasing to be a mother, if she turned a deaf ear to children's anguished cries."[64] Directly addressing the Reich Kommissar, the bishops accused him of violating the "foundations of Christian life, . . . Justice, Mercy and Liberty." The bishops indicted Seyss-Inquart for his "persecution and execution of Jewish fellow-citizens," for executing hostages, and for imprisoning churchmen in concentration camps under conditions that led to their deaths. In concluding their pastoral letter, the bishops expressed their sympathy for Jews and for converted Jews and forbade the faithful from collaborating with the occupation authorities.

The pastoral letter of the Dutch Church is as amazing as it is puzzling. It is extraordinary in its frankness. Going well beyond anything Pope Pius had said in December, the bishops accused the German occupation authorities of sinning in their exercise of power. Unlike Pius XII, the Dutch Church named names. Also remarkable is their direct reference to Jews, something the pope could not do for reasons mentioned above. The bishops made it very clear that they would not be satisfied if the Germans seized Jewish citizens while leaving converted Jews alone. It is, of course, critical to note that the Dutch Catholic leaders took their cue from the pope's Christmas radio address.

The protest of the Dutch bishops is puzzling because of its singularity.[65] No other national church even came close to duplicating what church leaders did in the Netherlands. Objections to genocide did occur the year after the pope's message—for example, in the fall by Archbishop Stepinać in Croatia and Cardinal Schuster in Milan, Italy.[66] While one could speculate that these two bishops took their cue from the Christmas letter, there is no known link between the pope's Christmas message and their statements. Most puzzling is the case of bishops in Vichy France. In the summer of 1942 they had issued a protest letter that took exception to the treatment of Jews, referring to them explicitly.[67] That same year, when a church group rescued Jewish children and Vichy officials demanded that the group surrender the children, Cardinal Gerlier (Lyons) denied their request, saying that the rescue symbolized a protest of the government's treatment of Jews.[68] Information from a Catholic information service that was passed on to the OSS also indicates Cardinal Gerlier's opposition to the Nazi deportation of Jews. Gerlier urged Catholics to refuse to surrender children they had hidden to the Nazis.[69]

Why, then, did the French not take inspiration from Pius's Christmas address as the Dutch had?[70] Charles Journet, the eminent Swiss Catholic theologian, asked in March 1943, "after finally waking up, why have they gone back to sleep?"[71]

French historian Jacques Duquesne has noted that the French bishops were well aware of the confrontational stance the Dutch Church took. Meeting in December 1942, the French Vichy bishops reasoned, however, that their situation differed from that of the Netherlands because theirs was a legitimate government—that of Marshal Petain— whereas the Dutch were directly under the thumb of the Nazi Seyss-Inquart. French bishops decided that they had to maintain the authority of the state, which meant supporting Petain. In January 1943, Cardinal Suhard had two long discussions with Pope Pius, who agreed with the point of view the bishops had taken. Pius advised them not to demand overly much of Petain and to be reasonable in their expectations.[72] Thus, with the backing of Pius XII, the French Vichy hierarchy discontinued its criticism of Nazi cruelty toward Jews. In the words of Charles Journet, they had become "unfortunately spiritually impotent."[73]

Information originating from Pius XII and transmitted to the OSS by Felix Morlion, a Belgian Dominican code-named "Blackie" by his handlers, indicated the pope's strong displeasure with French Church leaders! During the war, Morlion started a Catholic press agency called Pro Deo and spent several years in the United States, where he became a well-known public figure. After Morlion moved to Rome, Pius told him about a conversation he had had with Cardinal Pierre Gerlier, whose rise in the hierarchy the pope had personally sponsored. "Blackie" related that

> at a certain point the pope asked, have the Germans kept the armistice agreements? Gerlier answered no, they are the conquerors. The pope then rose and said severely: I cannot understand that a prince of the church accepts this. You should oppose this way of action. You should remember the sentence [the Germans] engraved on a monument in Germany to their dead of World War I, "to the conquered dead, the conquered who are going to conquer."[74]

Gerlier's audience with Pius took place in November 1944. The Holy See had not objected to Vichy's antisemitic legislation in 1941 and 1942. The pope had counseled French bishops two years earlier not to press the Petain government about its treatment of Jews. Had Pius XII now reversed himself? Or did his disagreement with Gerlier have nothing to do with Jews? "Blackie" reported that Georges Bidault of the French resistance was highly critical of cardinals Suhard and Gerlier, the latter because after his early refusal to cooperate with roundups of Jews, he had made many concessions to the Petain regime regarding its antisemitism.[75] But in this report, Morlion was not recounting the pope's reprimand to Gerlier. If the pope wanted to criticize French bishops on this score, his reprimand came much too late to do any good. Why would Pius be showing displeasure about treatment of French Jews at such a late date? Actually, it would have been completely out of character for Pius to have been referring to French Jews, because, as we will see, he did not encourage Dutch or German bishops in 1943 to confront the Nazis regarding their treatment of Jews. We must conclude that either Morlion made up his report to the OSS out of whole cloth or the pope was vexed about some other matter that did not pertain to Jews, such as the deportation of French men and women to Germany as forced laborers.[76]

In Germany, Bishop Preysing issued a strongly worded statement (though not nearly as blunt as the pastoral letter of the Dutch bishops) in November 1942 in which he said that it was never permissible to "deprive a person of another race his human rights."[77] Why did Preysing not follow up this assertion with stronger words in 1943? It may be that he and Margarete Sommer drew inspiration from the pope's Christmas message, leading them to try to galvanize church leaders in Germany to confront Hitler with the truth of the Holocaust in August 1943 at the bishops' annual meeting in Fulda, but we have no proof of such a linkage.[78]

It is easier to explain what allowed the Dutch bishops to issue an explicit protest than to suggest why others failed to do so. Holland, a small country, had fewer bishops than most European countries. This made it easier for them, presumably, to speak with one voice. Also of great importance, Archbishop de Jong, the highest-ranking Dutch bishop, took the lead in opposing antisemitism, making it easy for the others to follow suit. Regarding the situation of the Jews, the bishops of every other country, including—most unfortunately—Germany, were divided as to what action, if any, was to be taken. Even the Italian hierarchy in the shadow of Rome itself demonstrated a complete lack of unanimity when it came to assisting Jews or of following up on the pope's Christmas message.[79] Europeans were prejudiced against Jews to a greater or lesser extent, but the Netherlands bishops could count on widespread Dutch support for their protest statement. Although Holland lost a large percentage of its Jews to the Holocaust, antisemitism was not a significant contributing factor to that calamity.[80]

Difficult as it is to understand why other national churches did not take up the cry of protest, the fact that the Dutch Church did so is proof of the efficacy of Pius XII's Christmas message.

In contrast to the Dutch, the Polish Government in Exile in London was dissatisfied with the pope's Christmas message. The month before Christmas, underground courier Karski had carried a message from Polish Jews to the Polish government's office in London asking that it request the pope to excommunicate German Catholics who were engaging in murder. Early in January, right after the Christmas message, Wladislas Raczkiewiez, president of the exiled Polish government, notified the Vatican that what was happening to the Jews in Poland would later happen to the Catholics.[81] The obvious intent of the warning was to trigger a papal protest, but, as we have seen, by January 1943 Pius had already gotten word from Poland of improved conditions for Catholics. The Polish ambassador to the Holy See was also disappointed that the pope did not identify the Germans as the perpetrators.[82] Clearly, Polish Jews and the Government in Exile wanted a more trenchant papal condemnation about the murderous events taking place in Poland.

The German perpetrators of genocide were also displeased with what Pius XII had said. This, of course, was to be expected. Though he did not mention them by name, it is clear that the shoe fit Germany when the pope spoke about herding people around and violating peoples' rights to juridical safety. To show Germany's displeasure, its diplomatic staff boycotted the pope's Christmas eve liturgy. Pope Pius soothed the Nazis' ruffled feathers when Diego von Bergen, the German ambassador to the Vatican, paid his New Year's visit. The pope drew him aside and assured him that he and Germany were at one regarding bolshevism: Stalin, not Hitler was the new Attila the Hun.[83] This amounted to encouragement for Berlin to think that the Christmas message was aimed at Moscow, not them.[84]

It cannot be denied that opinion about Pius XII's 1942 Christmas address in the western world was positive. Although western diplomats had hoped Pope Pius would describe the killing methods the Germans used without necessarily mentioning who the killers were, most people understood that he could not do this while still claiming neutrality. Also, it was generally recognized that the pope stood at the head of a universal Church and therefore could not single out wartime Greater Germany (most of whose citizens were Catholic after the annexation of Austria) for condemnation.

Pius XII's 1942 Christmas address must not be taken as proof or even as an indication that he then knew the scope of the Holocaust. He knew only that mass murder, what we now call genocide, was under way. We cannot expect Pius to have been thinking ahead, to have been anticipating the Holocaust. Rather, the Christmas address should be read with a view to past Vatican statements about communism and Nazism. Weighing the twin evils against each other before war began, the Holy See determined that Soviet bolshevism was a greater danger in the long run than Nazi racism. In the middle of the war, Pius once again weighed one against the other and this time determined that Nazi racism and nationalism had to be denounced. People were being murdered, Pius said, "because of their nationality or race." No doubt the pope still thought in terms of communism being the greater enemy in the long term, but in the short term it was necessary for him to safeguard his moral authority by denouncing genocide.

When Rolf Hochhuth introduced Pius XII in his famous play The Deputy, he instructed the actor to capture the pope's "aristocratic coldness" and the "icy glint" of his eyes. In this way the playwright launched the controversy that has haunted the image of Pope Pius—whether or not he kept silent about the genocide of the Jews. That question can be settled: Pius XII did not keep silent. The 1942 Christmas address assuaged negative opinion about Pius XII in the western hemisphere and directly led the bold Dutch Church to challenge the Nazi Holocaust.

4
1943

PIUS XII REVERSES COURSE

In early May 1943, a letter from a Dutch priest to Pope Pius XII reached the Vatican. At the end of that month, the first of the four new gas chamber-crematoria complexes that would liquidate about one million people began functioning at Auschwitz-Birkenau. The letter pleaded for papal action on behalf of the Jews. After reading the letter, Under-Secretary of State Tardini reflected that "it's not such an easy thing" to help the Jews.[1] Tardini's thoughts signaled a change in the direction of papal policy regarding the Holocaust even though just a few months earlier the pope had spoken about the victims of World War II in his Christmas message. In 1943, Pope Pius decided that he needed to try to control events taking place in Rome rather than those taking place in Poland.

After having assessed, or reassessed, Pius XII's 1942 Christmas address, we may pose the question why it was both his first and his last pronouncement on genocide. If, as seems certain, the pope intended to speak again, why did he fail to do so? World War II and the Holocaust would persist for two and a half more years. At what point did Pope Pius make the decision not to raise his voice for a second time? That determination came in the spring or, at the latest, the summer of 1943, only a few months after the auspicious Christmas message—auspicious from a western point of view, at least. The Vatican's published documents provide glimpses behind the Holy See's closed doors that allow us to make an educated guess regarding the timing of a turnabout. Moreover, the circumstances of the war—the momentous developments of the spring and summer—produced a flurry of documents now available in the U.S. national archives. These also suggest guideposts for interpreting the Vatican's reappraisal of its position regarding the predicament of European Jews.

The pope's denunciation of genocide in his Christmas message was expressed by his dismay that "hundreds of thousands of persons, who, without any fault on their part, sometimes only because of their nationality or race, have been consigned to death or to a slow decline." Six weeks later, in early February 1943, the pope delivered an allocution to the college of cardinals in which he again referred to the suffering of people because of their nationality or race. His words were very similar to those of the Christmas message but with one remarkable change: in this message he referred to people "destined . . . to forced extermination."[2] Extermination! Only a few months prior to this time the Vatican had said it could not confirm Riegner's "final solution" warning. It appears that a significant shift had taken place at the Vatican.

Confirmation of this fact came two months later in May. Cardinal Secretary of State Luigi Maglione wrote the following memo to himself:

> After months and months of transports of thousands and thousands of persons about whom nothing more is known, this can be explained in no other way than death. Special death camps near Lublin and near Brest Litovsk. It is told that they are locked up several hundred at a time in chambers where they are finished off with gas.[3]

We do not know all of the additional information that came to the Holy See that triggered this remarkable admission. Certainly the Vatican continued to receive regular disclosures. In January, President in Exile Raczkiewicz detailed Nazi horrors in Poland. In March, Bishop Preysing wrote of the almost certain death of the Berlin Jews who had just been dispatched to the east (they were in fact immediately murdered at Auschwitz). In any event, what the Holy See had long said (and continued to say until late 1942)—that it could not confirm "rumors" about mass murder—it now no longer doubted. That the Holy See did not know the exact places of the mass executions matters not at all. Pius now knew the essence of the Holocaust.

Just five days after Maglione wrote his memo to himself, the Vatican received the letter from a Dutch priest, Father De Witte, of the Redemptorist Order. What the priest wanted was nothing less than Pius XII's intervention in the matter of the killing of the Jews. Extreme circumstances, he said, call for extreme remedies. The message was certified by Archbishop de Jong, who wrote a cover letter.[4] Clearly, the Dutch Church was proceeding here along the path that had led it to protest the "transportation" of Jewish citizens in February 1943. Based on its interpretation of the 1942 papal Christmas message, the Dutch Church—not unreasonably—expected the Holy See to back up its bold challenge to the German occupiers.

Their expectations were not realized. The Vatican's response to the Dutch priest's plea is found in a memo of Under-Secretary of State Tardini who, thinking to himself, pondered what to do.[5] The Dutch Church was already well informed about what the Holy See "has done for the Jews," Tardini reasoned, thinking no doubt about the Dutch Church's reference to the 1942 Christmas message. Tardini wondered if perhaps the Vatican could work with the Red Cross to help the Dutch Jews emigrate, but he immediately rejected the idea since Nuncio Orsenigo in Berlin would not be able to get permission from the Germans for them to emigrate and Spain and Portugal would only provide temporary transit visas. So, Tardini mused, it would probably be best to respond that the Vatican would continue to do whatever it could. Wanting to take some immediate action, Tardini determined that he would refer the letter from the Netherlands Church to the rector of the Dutch seminary college in Rome. While proposing to reply in this way to the Dutch Church, Tardini thought to himself that helping the Jews "is not such an easy thing."[6]

What is the significance of the Tardini memo? Remarkably, a communication from Holland that came at the height of the Holocaust and carried the weight of approval of that country's most prominent Catholic leader *did not reach the eyes of Pius XII*. Rather than bring the matter to the attention of the pope, Tardini decided, probably after a discussion with Cardinal Maglione, his immediate superior, to refer the matter to the rector of the Dutch college in Rome who "has on many occasions interested himself in the question of the Jews of Holland."[7] A more minimal reply to the Dutch cannot be imagined. It is clear from the Tardini memo that he took the initiative in answering de Witte's letter. He did not consult with the pope.

It might appear from Monsignor Tardini's words—"it's not easy to help the Jews"—that he did not care about what happened to them, that he was callous. This is not the case. Just six months earlier, Tardini had admitted to diplomats Francis D'Arcy Osborne and Myron Taylor that he had to agree with them that the pope needed to speak out against the atrocities being perpetrated on the Jews.[8] His memo to himself indicates, rather, a new resolve at the Vatican based on Holocaust data it no longer doubted. Tardini, very much a Vatican insider and a veteran of the secretariat who reported to Pope Pius every day, knew the score.[9] The Holy See had come to the conclusion that if the Germans were doing the unthinkable and the unimaginable—building death camps and gassing facilities in a foreign land to which the Jews of Europe were to be "transported" and killed—the Vatican was helpless to do anything to stop the process. "Its not easy to help the Jews" might be equated with "we cannot stop the trains."

There is another indication of the Holy See's about-face regarding the Holocaust. In June 1943, Pope Pius gave the encyclical *Mystici Corporis Christi* (The Mystical Body of Christ) in which he argued that the physical church—the *visible* church—constituted the mystical body of Christ.[10] In making his case for the Church, Pius referred to Judaism: "On the cross then the Old Law died, soon to be buried and to be a bearer of death." *And to be a bearer of death!* Could anyone, knowing what was befalling the Jews at that very moment in the first half of 1943, write those words in a merely figurative sense? This seems quite unlikely, but it does not mean that Pius wished for the Jews to be killed off.[11] The encyclical, which went on to belabor the point about the visible church, may be taken as an indication that in the spring of 1943 Pope Pius had resolved to remain silent about what he thought he could do nothing about (the Jews) and to attend to concerns that he might be able to control, matters that had to do with Rome and Vatican City within it, *the visible church*. Presumably aware of the pope's decision, Monsignor Tardini seems to have thought it unnecessary to bring the letter of the Dutch Church to the pope's attention. After finally admitting the fate of the Jews and gaining an accurate insight into the Nazi killing machine, the Holy See came to the conclusion that helping the Jews "is not a very easy matter."

By the summer of 1943, Pope Pius had toned down his rhetoric considerably when referring to the Holocaust. The word "extermination," which he had used in February in his in-house address, does not appear in his subsequent public addresses. Instead, in June the pope talked rather obliquely about Poles "who have been cruelly tried and others like them." "Others like them" meant Jews, but Pius was careful not to use the word. He referred to people "sometimes dying because of nationality or descent." The phrase "sometimes dying" entirely minimized the truth about Jews as Pope Pius certainly knew it by this date. Taking the position, rightly or wrongly, that it was better not to say anything that might make the situation worse for potential victims, Pius said "do not expect from us now that we give you here the details."[12] He *knew* the details! But the main emphasis of the pope's June 3rd address did not involve genocide; Pius XII concerned himself with the killing of hostages, presumably because of the activity of Roman partisans against the Nazis, and about aerial bombardment, which was getting closer and closer to Rome. The language the pope used in the summer of 1943 with reference to the Holocaust may be taken as another clue that in the spring the Vatican had adopted a new course, a policy of control. Pope Pius wanted to control the fate of the *visible* church.

It was the circumstances of the war that generated the pope's thoughts about control—about protecting the visible church. By the spring and summer of 1943 the outcome of World War II looked entirely different to Pius than it had in 1942. Previously he had not thought the Allies could win the war; rather, he believed that it would end in a stalemate.[13] But just before the time the Vatican had become convinced that the Holocaust was indeed under way, the Soviet army had won the battle of Stalingrad, killing or capturing half a million German soldiers. Another major battle ensued that summer at Kursk, which the Germans again lost. In the meantime, an enormous Allied amphibious force had landed on the shores of North Africa. Within one week of the time when Maglione admitted to himself that Jews were being murdered in gas chambers, Erwin Rommel's troops had been driven off the African continent, the Germans suffering in the process losses equal at least to those of Stalingrad. With the Allies now ruling the Mediterranean, there was no doubt about where the next theater of war would be—Italy. The dangers this situation would bring to Rome and to Vatican City could not be overestimated as far as Pius XII was concerned. He was determined to do what he could to control these dangers to the visible church.

Furthermore, events in Italy hugely complicated that theater in general and Rome in particular. The overthrow of Mussolini and the fascist government of Italy in July was followed by the overthrow of the successor regime of Marshal Pieto Badoglio. In September, the Germans reappointed Mussolini, who now ruled as a puppet of the Nazis. German armed forces overran most of Italy even as Allied forces successfully invaded the boot of Italy. Since Rome was not only the capital of the country but also the most important railroad, highway, and airport nexus linking the northern and southern halves of the peninsula, there was every likelihood that it would become the focal point of hostilities. Nothing could be more ominous for Pius XII's visible church.

As if these factors were not enough, the domestic situation in Rome became vexed by two developments. Prior to the time of Mussolini's fall, the number of people who participated in the Italian resistance forces was small. After Mussolini returned as a puppet of Hitler, Italian nationalists of every stripe, from Communists to Catholics, became involved in resistance. What, Pius XII wondered, would come of resistance turmoil? He had witnessed a similar situation in Munich after World War I which gave rise to his great dread, a Communist regime. Thus, the Italian underground constituted yet another factor for Pius to attempt to control. Last in chronological order came the question of Roman Jews. The Holy See knew what was transpiring in faraway Poland; now the Holocaust would also come home to Italy since the Germans were determined to carry out the deportation of Jews there, as they had been doing in other European countries. For the moment—the spring and summer—this was not yet a problem, but when and if it became one, Pope Pius would be forced to decide where his first priorities lay when it came to issues of control.

The Vatican and the Jews of Rome

Holocaust reality came to the Vatican in the fall. Because the Jews of Rome were seized in October, "under his very windows," the question of the pope's silence has become the focus of intense historical debate and analysis. The situation at the time of the pope's 1942 Christmas address differed vastly from the situation the Holy See encountered the following summer and fall. After dissembling or procrastinating for two years, the Vatican at last came around to the reality of the Holocaust late in 1942, although the full extent of it was not yet perceived. Mass murder took place far away in Poland. It did not yet touch Italy or Italians. After the puppet Mussolini government came to power in the fall of 1943 and Germany overran and occupied most of Italy, the reality of the Holocaust squarely confronted the Vatican.

Several months after the 1942 Christmas radio address the Holy See fell back into passivity when critical situations for Jews came to its attention. In the summer and fall of 1943, Jews in Croatia and southeast France were in danger of being captured by the Ustaša or Gestapo. The Vatican was asked to intercede in one instance by the World Jewish Congress and in the other by the Catholic rescuer Father Benedetto (Marie-Benoit Peteul), but it did not respond productively to either request. Presented with appeals to help in very concretely detailed situations, the Holy See replied vaguely and blandly: "The Holy See has already involved itself in favor of the Jews mentioned." In fact, its involvement was minimal at best.[14]

The bearing of the Holy See did not change as Germans began murdering Italian Jews in northern Italy in September. The Nazis in some cases made no attempt to conceal their crimes, openly discarding the corpses of victims in the Lago Maggiore, a resort area. The Vatican would certainly have learned of these crimes and must have drawn the conclusion that Jews in the Eternal City would likely become victims in due time.[15] When under-secretaries of state Montini and Tardini first got wind of possible actions against Roman Jews in mid-September, their reaction set the Vatican on a course that would prevail in the following critical month of October. The under-secretaries decided that the best course of action was to see if Germany's ambassador to the Holy See, Ernst von Weizsäcker, could ward off danger to people "of whatever race."[16] The compatibility of German and Vatican diplomats during the crisis month of October should not surprise us. They shared, as Robert Katz has written, the same goals—to "save the Jews and save the silence" of the pope.[17]

And to save Pope Pius himself, it might be added. When Hitler learned of Mussolini's overthrow, he vowed in a rage to occupy Rome. Asked if this included Vatican City, Hitler vowed to pull every one of the mongrels out of their lair—a reference to the pope and curial cardinals. Hitler's crude remark delighted the madly anti-Catholic apostate Josef Goebbels, who took note of it in a July entry in his diary.[18] The German diplomatic corps in Rome, who were mostly sympathetic to the pope, sought to eliminate the threat. Pius himself took the threat seriously, according to his German housekeeper, Sister Pasqualina Lehnert.[19] Vatican personnel also took Hitler at his word, as did all of the diplomats accredited to the Holy See who notified Cardinal Maglione of their intention to accompany the pope should the Germans remove him. Tittmann wrote that this "gave pleasure to His Holiness at a moment when he was especially beset with anxieties."[20] Thus, Hitler's threat was believed in Rome and in Vatican City.

In fact, however, the threat backfired. Greater Germany was predominantly Catholic. If the Nazis were to manhandle the pope, serious dissent and disruption could not be ruled out at a time when Germany's war fortunes were ebbing. There were also serious propaganda disadvantages to consider. Western newspapers, anticipating the worse, were full of reports of Pius being taken prisoner. Anne O'Hare McCormick wrote in the *New York Times* that the pope was now more a prisoner of Rome than he had ever been (a reference to the pope's status before the 1929 Lateran Treaty).[21] Hastily backpedaling, the Nazi minister for foreign affairs, Joachim von Ribbentrop, assured the pope again and again that the sovereign status of Vatican City would not be violated. In late September, the Nazi newspaper *Völkische Beobachter* assured Rome that the Vatican's territories would be respected by German occupying forces.[22] Berlin sought a public assurance from the Vatican that the occupational forces in Rome had indeed respected the Holy See's sovereignty in order to put the Führer's blunder to rest.[23]

The Vatican's "good conduct" statement was still pending when the events that preceded the October 16th seizure of Rome's Jews and the *razzia* took place. During the first weeks of October, various members of the German military and diplomatic corps in Rome attempted to prevent Berlin's effort to deport Rome's Jews. It would be presumptuous to assert that their efforts came about at the Vatican's request, but it is highly likely that the Holy See was kept abreast of their actions, and at certain points we can be certain of the secretariat's knowledge and participation.

Hitler's angry impropriety and its aftermath had occurred as Nazis murdered Jews in northern Italy and as they occupied the Eternal City. In view of these circumstances, Montini and Tardini in the Vatican secretariat felt it would be best if German diplomats, rather than the Vatican, took the necessary steps to protect Rome's Jews should this prove necessary. As long as the Vatican did not meddle in Nazi antisemitic violence in Rome, there would be no danger of Hitler flying into another rage that would force Minister Ribbentrop to go back on his word that Nazis would not violate the sovereignty of Vatican City. The Vatican knew about a telegram from Berlin instructing the SS in Rome to seize the city's Jews, and it worked out an explicit understanding with German diplomats as to how the crisis was to be handled. This understanding was reached in a timely manner—that is, several weeks before the October 16th *razzia*, perhaps as early as late September. At some point, the secretariat instructed Bishop Hudal, rector of the German National Church near the Piazza Navona, to compile a list of all Vatican properties scattered in and about the city of Rome for the purpose of preventing Germans from searching them. As concern grew that the German occupational forces might set upon the Jews, Hudal's task was taken over by Ambassador Weizsäcker himself.[24] Weizsäcker sent hundreds of "letters of protection" to all Vatican properties in Rome guaranteeing them extraterritorial status. He did this on the widest possible basis and even provided the German occupational forces with a map designating the location of these properties. The commandant of Rome, General Stahel, approved of Weizsäcker's plan.[25] The map would prevent German soldiers from making a mistake. Should Nazis, searching for Jews, show up in one of the marked places, they would be shown a document from the German ambassador indicating they had no business there. It is inconceivable that Weizsäcker would have done this without the knowledge of the Holy See, especially since he took over the task from Bishop Hudal. Weizsäcker and the Holy See's action accomplished a double purpose. First, with no danger that Berlin would blame the Vatican, Jews could escape by hiding in one of the extraterritorial properties. Second, because Weizsäcker's letter prevented Germans from violating Vatican property, he could claim that he was ensuring just what Berlin wanted—a public assurance that the Germans had behaved well in Rome.

The Weizsäcker-Vatican gambit was nothing if not shrewd, but it had a fatal flaw. To succeed, Roman Jews would have to see their peril and take advantage of the Vatican properties. It fell to Albrecht von Kassel, Weizsäcker's assistant, to spread the word among Rome's Jews of their chance to find a safe harbor in one of the Vatican's properties.[26] But leaving house and home is never an easy decision, and the leaders of the Jewish community, Dante Almansi and Ugo Foà, both respected fascist civic functionaries before their release from their civic occupations due to Mussolini's antisemitic laws, saw no cause for alarm. Naturally, Roman Jews took the word of these two men over that of a German, even though the Chief Rabbi of Rome, Israel Zolli, prophesied a Nazi slaughter.[27]

If the Holy Father himself had warned the Jewish community, would they have believed him and saved themselves? That cannot be taken for granted. Before Italian unification, Rome's Jews lived under the rule of the pope and were often subjected to economic and social discrimination and very unpleasant religious humiliation.[28] Just how much residual resentment toward papal rule lingered during the seven decades before October 1943 is unclear. But Pope Pius gave them no warning. Historian David Wyman believes that Roosevelt, Churchill, and Pius were at fault for not repeatedly driving home the message that deportation meant definite death. Certainly all three could have done so. Auschwitz escapee Rudolph Vrba asked rhetorically after the Holocaust, "Would anybody [have been able to] get me on a train alive to Auschwitz if I had this information?"[29] Pope Pius made Vatican properties available to those who wished to hide but left it to the well-intentioned Germans to spread the alarm. Had Pius done so himself he would have had to do it clandestinely or go through Foà and Almansi.[30] A public alert would most likely have led the Nazis to violate the extraterritorial status of Vatican properties when the moment came to seize the Jews. Thus, the purpose of Weizsäcker's strategy would have been thwarted. Unlike Churchill and Roosevelt, Pope Pius found himself in the immediate proximity of Holocaust action when the Nazis set upon Rome's Jews. Any warning from the pope might have been more effective had it taken place much earlier and then been renewed in early October as the Nazis prepared to capture their victims.

In the end—that is, in the days before October 16—very few Jews availed themselves of opportunities to hide. Historian Susan Zuccotti found no evidence that the populations of convents and monasteries surged before the fateful day. Very likely that held true for Vatican properties as well. Zuccotti found that not only would the Vatican not help Father Benedetti, known as the Jewish priest because of his indefatigable efforts on their behalf, but it discouraged his work.[31] Why would the Holy See engage in an effort to provide shelter for Jews while deterring Benedetti? The difference in the two situations lay in the fact that the members of the Holy See prevailed upon the Germans to write the letters of extraterritoriality and warn the Jews while they themselves stood aside. At the very least, the Vatican-Weizsäcker arrangement shows that the Holy See took steps to help Roman Jews.[32]

The police attaché to the German embassy in Rome, SS Lieutenant Colonel Herbert Kappler, somehow became aware of the Vatican-Weizsäcker design and reported to Berlin that the Holy See was helping Jewish refugees. Kappler wanted Berlin to know that Pope Pius would be opposed to the idea of deporting Jews.[33] Kappler is notorious for holding the Jews of Rome for ransom, demanding 50 kilograms of gold from them in return for his assurance that they would not be molested. For this reason, Kappler has usually been viewed as an insidiously evil person since he did not keep his word. But he may actually have meant well. The fact that the gold was duly shipped off to Berlin suggests that Kappler aimed more to bribe Berlin than to shake down the Jews. In his cover letter to Reichssicherheitshauptamt chief Ernst Kaltenbrunner, Kappler mentioned several credible reasons for not deporting the Jews and said it would be a mistake to do so.[34] Little did he know that 50 kilograms of gold (about $56,000 in 1943 dollars) would not begin to tempt Berlin, given its voracious wartime appetite for the precious metal.[35] Whatever his true intentions were, Kappler was found guilty of extortion by an Italian court after the war.[36] The OSS reported on October 6th that in addition to Kappler, General Reiner Stahel, commandant of Rome, and Field Marshall General Albert Kesselring opposed the deportation of Jews.[37]

Kappler's demand for the gold of Rome's Jews brought about the direct involvement of Pius XII in the events culminating in the October 16th catastrophe. The Jewish community of Rome fell into a panic as word spread of Kappler's threat. He was known to be ruthless, and the Jews knew he was not bluffing when he threatened their lives if they did not come up with the gold. In consternation, they turned to the pope, who offered, as requested, to help them raise the needed amount. The Vatican's promised gold, tendered as a loan payable whenever and with no interest, appeared generous. In fact, it was not (for reasons explained in the following chapter). In the end, the loan proved unnecessary, as Roman Jews managed to collect what was demanded of them by September 28. So ended the first chapter of the drama of October. With no word of thanks for the extorted gold, Berlin cabled back crisply on October 11th, telling Kappler to seize the Jews without delay.[38]

By the first week of the fateful month of October, the circle of would-be German protectors of Rome's Jews had widened to include both Weizsäcker and von Kessel at the Vatican post and Eitel Friedrich Möllhausen, acting ambassador to Italy.[39] On the 6th, Kappler told von Ribbentrop at the foreign ministry in Berlin that officials "in Rome were going to Field Marshal Kesselring to suggest that the Jews could be better used as laborers in Italy," and Möllhausen cabled him that General Stahel opposed the idea of deporting Jews to "liquidate" them.[40] He added boldly that he thought it would be "better business" to use the manpower productively in Rome and said that he and Kappler would propose this to Field Marshal Kesselring. Möllhausen signed off with "Please advise." Without waiting for a reply, Möllhausen sent a second telegram to Berlin the next day saying that the field marshal had asked Kappler to postpone the roundup of Jews. Through Weizsäcker the Vatican was kept informed of these developments.[41] Pius XII knew of the plan to murder Roman Jews.

Möllhausen's brashness cost him his job. On the 9th, von Ribbentrop answered the diplomat's telegram, telling him to mind his own business. Furious that Möllhausen had used the word "liquidate" in his telegram, von Ribbentrop launched an investigation, only to learn that the diplomat had used the word purposefully because he was upset at the idea of killing the Jews.[42] By then it had become clear to officials in Berlin that everyone in Rome, both the military, the SS, and diplomats, opposed their plan to kill the Jews. Knowing they could not be trusted to carry out their dirty work, Himmler put matters in the capable hands of Adolf Eichmann, who in turn sent Theodore Dannecker, the SS captain who had neatly carried out the liquidation of Parisian Jews, to Rome. During the contest of wills between Berlin and the Germans in Rome that played itself out in early October, the Vatican stood in the background. That would change.

Lacking enough men under his command to carry out the roundup of about 8,000 Roman Jews, Dannecker pressed Kappler to provide him with additional manpower and a list of the addresses of his quarry. Kappler caved in.[43] Dannecker got the list and the additional troopers from Commandant Stahel, who, like Kappler, gave way under pressure.[44] "Disaster struck," historian Zuccotti wrote, "early in the morning of the Sabbath, October 16, 1943 . . . in the cold rain of a dreary dawn."[45] The Germans surrounded the ghetto and, aided with the addresses of their victims, went from door to door awakening sleeping Jews. The terrified Jews were given twenty minutes to put their possessions into a bag or suitcase and assemble outside in the rain. The Germans nabbed over 1,000 Jews, almost 900 of whom were women and children. Later that morning they were taken to the Military College, a building several blocks away from the Basilica of St. Peter. There they awaited an unknown fate.

It was at this point in the catastrophe that the Holy See became directly involved in events. Cardinal Maglione requested Ambassador Weizsäcker to come to the secretariat to discuss the actions the Germans had taken, and a letter threatening a papal protest was drafted and telegraphed to Berlin. Both events took place on the 16th, the day of the roundup.

The letter in question is known as the Hudal letter. Bishop Alois Hudal was the rector of the German National Church of Rome and of the Santa Maria dell' Anima seminary. Hudal, as we will see, did not compose the letter, but it went out to Ribbentrop, the Nazi foreign minister, under his name. It read:

> I must speak to you of a matter of great urgency. An authoritative Vatican dignitary, who is close to the Holy Father, has just told me that this morning a series of arrests of Jews of Italian nationality has been initiated. In the interests of the good relations that have existed until now between the Vatican and the High Command of the German Armed Forces . . . I earnestly request that you order the immediate suspension of these arrests both in Rome and its environs. Otherwise I fear that the Pope will take a position in public as being against this action, one which would undoubtedly be used by the anti-German propagandists as a weapon against us Germans.[46]

The author or authors of the message clearly intended to make von Ribbentrop think that his urgent request for a Vatican statement of good conduct by the Germans was in the balance. Hence the line "in the interests of good relations" and the warning about "anti-German propagandists."

The Vatican claimed the initiative for Hudal's letter. It was in its interest to do so as the letter puts Pius XII on record as opposing the German assault on the Jews of the Eternal City, his Episcopal See. According to *Actes et Documents,* the pope's nephew, Carlo Pacelli, had Hudal send the letter to General Rainer Stahel, commandant of Rome, for him to forward to Berlin.[47] Although this may literally be true, it does not demonstrate that the initiative came from the Vatican. It is more than a little strange that a nephew of the pope, a prince who had no official curial office, should be the one to deliver the directive to the bishop. There was an obvious intent here to avoid the usual channel, the Holy

See's secretariat. After the war, Albrecht von Kessel declared that the Hudal letter did not originate with the bishop.[48] And the letter was not written by Hudal but was merely signed by him. Weizsäcker, von Kessel, Gerhart Gumpel (a junior diplomat posted to Rome), and, perhaps, General Stahel himself, to whom the letter was sent en route to Berlin, wrote it.[49] Thus, the letter was a joint undertaking by the Holy See and the German diplomatic corps.

If the same routine of the very recent past was followed on October 16th, Montini and Tardini summoned Weizsäcker and the three of them put their heads together to work out an appropriate strategy. This would mean finding a suitable person—Bishop Hudal—to act as a spokesperson for a message of an unnamed person who was "close to the Holy Father," meaning Prince Carlo Pacelli. Once the Vatican and German diplomats agreed in principle on the letter's content, they settled on Hudal as its "author." That Pope Pius himself was involved is not out of the question by any means.

The choice of Bishop Hudal as the purported letter-writer points again to Vatican involvement in the design to rescue the Jews without risking a papal statement of denunciation.[50] Hudal was a Vatican outsider whom the Nazis thought was an insider. During the previous decade, Hudal had tried to convince Pius XI that racism was not the heart and soul of Nazism, and he had succeeded for a while. But the Austrian bishop's book, *The Foundations of National Socialism*, which Hitler himself had read and thrust in the face of the German hierarchy, had infuriated Pius XI. After the book's publication in 1936, Hudal no longer had the pope's ear, but his demotion was not public knowledge.[51] A schemer, Hudal stayed on in Rome as rector of the German National Church and looked for the day when he could once again be an important curial player. In the meantime he became known in Rome as the most outspoken pro-Nazi clergyman, one who hobnobbed with top German occupational authorities like Commandant General Stahel. Hudal, who must have been overjoyed that the Vatican was once again turning to him with the matter of the letter, was merely being used by the secretariat because of his reputation in Nazi inner circles.

Ambassador Weizsäcker backed up Hudal's letter with his own telegram to Berlin only a few hours later. This again suggests the connivance of the secretariat and Weizsäcker's fingerprints on the Hudal letter. Weizsäcker assured von Ribbentrop that Hudal knew whereof he spoke and he sent the same signal—it would be bad propaganda to deport the Jews of Rome—to furrow the brow of the foreign minister. But the matter would blow over, Weizsäcker suggested, if the detained Jews were released to do labor service in Italy.[52] The cunning ambassador worded his message most intriguingly by suggesting that it was the curia who was upset by the *razzia,* in effect telling Berlin to be careful lest Pius XII be pushed over the edge into a denunciation. Weizsäcker did this by comparing the pope to some French bishops who the previous year had clearly spoken out about "similar incidents" and by comparing him to his predecessor, Pius XI, "a man of more spontaneous temperament." Years later one of the early defenders of Pius XII, Robert Graham, S.J., who assisted in editing *Actes et Documents,* excoriated Ambassador Weizsäcker for originating the picture of a pusillanimous pope with his telegram.[53] In his zeal to prop up Pope Pius, Graham completely overlooked the historical context and Weizsäcker's objective. The Jews were still at that moment in detention in Rome. Releasing them, the ambassador said, would "muffle" the Vatican's negative reaction. Left unsaid, but implied, was the statement that deporting them might very well push Pius XII over the edge into denunciation of Nazi actions in Rome.[54]

The Hudal letter and the Weizsäcker telegram of October 16th reveal that in the crisis of the day, the Vatican and German diplomats worked together to try to protect Rome's Jews.

As the Jews were rounded up and confined near the Vatican in temporary detention, Secretary of State Maglione summoned Weizsäcker to discuss the situation.[55] This meeting ranks as one of the most dramatic scenes of Holocaust historiography. Because of the drama and because distinguished British historian Owen Chadwick focused on it, the diplomatic aspect of the seizure of the Jews "under his very windows" has taken center stage in accounts of the *razzia* in Rome. I contend that its centrality has resulted from Holocaust scholarship that has directed attention to the issue of papal silence about the *razzia* to the detriment of examination other concerns of the day.[56] The importance of the *razzia* historically and in historical literature is not to be denied, but we will see that issues other than the pope's silence weighed equally heavily—indeed, perhaps more heavily—on his mind.

Historians are in unanimous or near-unanimous agreement that Cardinal Maglione did not protest the seizure of the Roman Jews when he met with the German ambassador.[57] A papal protest, such as the Christmas address of 1942, does not come into question; Pius XII did not himself address the October 16th roundup. *L'Osservatore Romano,* the Vatican newspaper, did address the issue a week later on the 25th, at which time most of the "transported" Jews had met their end or were about to do so in the Birkenau gas chambers. The article said that the Holy Father's charity was universal, extending to all races. The piece was so belated and vague that an American diarist living in occupied Rome, a nun writing under the name of Jane Scrivener who picked up on all news that concerned occupied Rome, the Vatican, and the Jews, failed to mention it at all.[58] Romans themselves, however, assumed that the article was a swipe at the hated occupying Germans.[59] They were angry that the Germans had seized and deported women and children.[60] But what appeared in the Vatican's newspaper in no way compares with a papal statement from the throne of St. Peter. Newly released documents of the U.S. national archives also fail to establish that the pope protested. The police attaché to the German embassy in Rome, SS officer Herbert Kappler, notified Berlin prior to the roundup on October 16th that Pope Pius would be opposed to the idea of deporting Jews, saying that the Vatican had been helping Jewish refugees. He did not report that the pope protested the deportations afterward.[61] Likewise, Ambassador Weizsäcker asserted the same absence of a protest in a letter to his mother on October 22nd: "Fortunately so far no one has taken a public position."[62]

Historians—as opposed to writers whose sole objective is to defend Pius XII—are not in agreement with the editors of *Actes et Documents,* who maintained that Maglione succeeded in registering a papal protest of the roundup of the Jews.[63] Putting aside the issue of whether or not Maglione protested, I argue that protest was not what he wanted to accomplish when he summoned the German ambassador on the morning (probably) of the 16th. The record of the meeting, as set down by the cardinal, reads as follows:

> I asked him [Weizsäcker] to intervene in favor of those poor people. I spoke to him as best as I could in the name of humanity and Christian charity.
>
> The Ambassador, who already knew about the arrests . . . replied to me in all sincerity, saying with some emotion: "I am always waiting for you to ask me: Why do you remain in this position of yours?"
>
> I exclaimed: No, Mr. Ambassador, I would never presume to ask you such a question. I simply wish to say to you, Excellency, you who have a good and tender heart, try to save these many innocent people. It is painful for the Holy Father, painful beyond words, that right here in Rome, under the eyes of the Common Father, so many people are to suffer only because of their particular descent—
>
> The Ambassador, after some moments of reflection, asked me: "What would the Holy See do if these things were to continue?"
>
> I replied: The Holy See would not want to be faced with the need to express its disapproval.
>
> The Ambassador observed: For more than four years I have followed and admired the attitude of the Holy See. It has succeeded in steering the boat amid all shapes and sizes of rocks without running aground and, even though it has greater faith in the Allies, it has maintained a perfect equi-

librium. Now, just as the boat is about to reach port, is it worth it, I ask myself, to put it all at risk. I am thinking of the consequences that such a step by the Holy See would provoke—

These measures come from the highest level: "Will your Eminence leave me free not to report this official conversation?"

I observed that I had asked him to intervene appealing to his sentiments of humanity. I was leaving it to his judgment whether or not to mention our conversation, which had been so friendly.[64]

If we disregard the spin of the editors of *Actes et Documents*—to wit, that Maglione was registering a protest—it can be seen that the objective was to induce Weizsäcker to take action to get the Jews released. The cardinal was well aware, of course, that German diplomats had been working with his office to register places where Jews could hide. Trusting in the experience of the past few weeks, Maglione urged the Germans to continue to handle the situation. As Robert Katz observed, a detached reading of the cardinal's minute shows it to be "a desperate plea to save the Jews," not a protest against the Nazi roundup.[65] When Ambassador Weizsäcker interjected that "these matters come from the highest level," he was intimating that Hitler would retaliate, as earlier he had indeed threatened to do, if the pope publicly protested. "Is it worth it . . . to put all at risk?" What those words conveyed to Pope Pius, I discuss immediately below. Further, the cardinal never even alluded to the possibility of a papal protest until the ambassador prompted him to do so. The cardinal ended the meeting by returning to his original intent—an appeal on the basis of Weizsäcker's "sentiments of humanity" to intervene. It was not in Weizsäcker's power to do so. The Vatican underestimated Hitler's determination to seize Rome's Jews even if it meant a papal protest. When German diplomats attempted to thwart the *razzia*, Himmler dressed down Ribbentrop, telling him in effect to mind his own business. The editors of *Actes et Documents*, writing after the publication of Hochhuth's famous (or infamous) play *The Deputy*, spun the Maglione minute to imply that the Vatican had protested. There was no protest.

After the Holy See became convinced in the spring of 1943 that what we now call the Holocaust was indeed under way, Pope Pius shifted to a policy of control, thinking he was not able to hinder the Nazi genocide. The October 16th *razzia* intensely tested the pope's new policy, but he stuck to it. What exactly did Pius XII want to control? The issues that most concerned him were as follows:

1) Protection of Rome, the Eternal City, from destruction by aerial bombardment. Even before his 1942 Christmas address Pope Pius was

FIGURE 6. Myron C. Taylor, the personal representative of the U.S. president
to Pope Pius XII, was often absent from Rome. On those occasions, his assistant,
Harold H. Tittmann, Jr., conducted U.S. affairs with the Vatican.
Courtesy of the Truman Presidential Museum and Library.

worried about possible bombing in Italy. For this reason, the Peruvian
ambassador to the Holy See thought the pontiff would not mention the
atrocities at that time.[66] Obviously, the ambassador was thinking in terms
of German retaliation, but as the war progressed, it was the Allies, not
the Germans, who worried Pius. Judging from the Vatican's diplomatic
correspondence, no issue weighed on Pius XII's mind as much during
the war as aerial bombardment. The U.S. national archives hold page
after page of entreaties and warnings from the Holy See on this issue.[67]
No issue occupied Tittmann's attention more than the Vatican's com-
munications about the bombing of Rome. Pius warned Taylor in the fall
of 1941 that if the British bombed Rome he would not remain silent; he
repeated the warning in writing.[68] As early as December 1942, Tittmann
cautioned the State Department that the Vatican might be gearing up for
a "solemn protest" should Rome be bombed.[69] Then, as the danger of
aerial bombardment grew, Tittmann warned again that the pope would
be "constrained to protest" if it should become a reality.[70] No such threat
of protest was ever made regarding the fate of Jews.

FIGURE 7. Pius XII and Myron C. Taylor, the president's personal envoy to
Pope Pius XII. The pope is reading a message the president sent to him. March 15, 1940.
Courtesy of the United States Holocaust Memorial Museum.

In June 1943, the Vatican's warnings through Tittmann about bombing of Italian targets continued steadily, especially as the bombs neared Rome. On June 24, James Dunn of the U.S. State Department replied to Tittmann, informing him that the War Department would not dignify the "fantastic charges" about the bombings with a reply.[71] On June 26, the Vatican told the apostolic delegate to the United States, Amleto Cicognani, to let the president know in no uncertain terms that Rome must not be bombed. Secretary of State Hull drafted a response to Cicognani for President Roosevelt to review. On the 28th, FDR told Hull that he would have to let the Holy See know that "war is war," meaning that since the Germans were using Rome for their military operations, the city could not be spared.[72] The next day, Hull relayed the president's message to Cicognani, telling him that for twenty years Italian fascists had been killing Greeks, Ethiopians, and Albanians, implying that if Italians died because of aerial attacks nothing could be done about it.[73]

On July 20, Allied bombs devastated the area around the Basilica of St. Lawrence, causing extensive damage to the church structure. Pius wrote President Roosevelt to entreat him to stop the bombardment.[74] "Every district," Pius wrote Roosevelt, "in some districts every street, has its irreplaceable monuments of faith and art and Christian culture, [which] cannot be attacked without inflicting an incomparable loss on the patrimony of Religion and Civilization."[75] As soon as the Allied Fifth Army occupied Rome in June 1944, the Holy See grew concerned about German bombing. On June 10th, Maglione wrote to the army command to ask that the military make its headquarters outside the central city or outside the city altogether.[76] What might affect the *visible* church registered intensely in the pope's thinking.

2) Guarding Rome from becoming a second Stalingrad, an issue that was obviously closely related to bombing. Pope Pius sought to win open-city status for Rome from the belligerents, both to avoid bombing and so the Holy City would not become the site of a major artillery battle between the Allies and the Germans. The pope feared that Rome would be destroyed by ground fighting, as had happened in the largest city to the south, Naples.[77] Also, the fact that the Pacelli family was Roman did not escape Tittmann's attention. Writing to Washington about the pope's desire for a declaration that Rome was an open city, Tittmann made the most unflattering comment about the Vatican of his entire years of service there: "As the war closes in on Italy, one is impressed, although hardly surprised, by the increasing vividness with which the underlying Italianate character of the Holy See is being revealed."[78] Ambassador Weizsäcker, quoting a Catholic colleague in the diplomatic corps, wrote similarly: "The curia is the most Italian of all institutions and the most Italian characteristic is fear."[79] In April 1943, the Peruvian ambassador to the Vatican said that Pope Pius was not so much thinking of peace negotiations in his Christmas address "as to the position of the cities of Italy, particularly Rome, in view of the constant air attacks and the announcement of their ceaseless repetition, made continuously from London." Consequently, he said, the Holy See was continually pursuing open-city status for Rome.[80] The problem was that the Germans were using Rome and its transportation facilities for their war effort. In June 1943, President Roosevelt explained that Rome could not be declared an open city until the Germans left.[81] Once the Mussolini government was in disgrace, the Romans looked to Pope Pius to save them "as if," Ambassador Weizsäcker wrote, "the Germans, the Italians, and the Allies will all obey him."[82] After the Allies occupied Rome, Pope Pius asked General Alexander to declare Rome an open city and remove Allied forces. The "general gave the final quietus to the Open City obsession by telling the pope that it was a matter that he could not discuss."[83]

3) Avoiding a Communist uprising in Rome. Even if Pius had succeeded in having Rome accepted as an open city, he would still have been
apprehensive about communism. The pope believed that in the interlude
between the German evacuation and the Allied occupation, Bolshevik
insurgents had a perfect window of opportunity to seize power. This
problem—to some extent imaginary—occupied Pius XII's mind just before and after the *razzia*. Communist bands near Rome might attack the
city, Pius worried, if they were not controlled after the Germans evacu-
ated.[84] Pius contacted Osborne to ask if the Germans and the Allies might
not be willing to cooperate to shut out the feared Communists.[85] The
pope still had this on his mind three days after the *razzia,* so he asked
the Germans to increase their military presence in Rome to thwart the
Italian partisans he suspected of being Communists (and some were).[86]
In the event of a Nazi seizure of Vatican City, Pope Pius did not intend
to defend himself, but he very much intended to do so if it came to blows
with the Communists. To this end, between September and December
1943, the Vatican increased the Holy See's guard from 400 to 1400 men[87]
and put in an order to the Swiss firm that manufactured machine guns
for the German army for twenty automatic rifles and 60,000 cartridges.[88]
Pope Pius wanted a greater German police presence in Rome because he
feared the partisans could open the door to a general uprising that the
Communists would exploit. Pius found himself obliged "to identify the
security of the [German] occupiers with that of the Holy See."[89] Pius
wanted order—German order—in Rome for as long as the Germans occupied the city. In March 1944, 320 Italian hostages were murdered by
German authorities, Kappler and others, at the Ardeatine Caves outside
the city. The editor of *L'Osservatore Romano* wrote a "vibrant protest"
against the massacre, but Pope Pius revised the piece in such a way as
to make the partisans the guilty party instead of the Germans.[90] During
these months, Pope Pius undoubtedly thought back to his days as Nuncio
Pacelli in Munich when he stared down a gun-toting revolutionary during the Kurt Eisner Communist uprising at the end of World War I. But
the situation in Italy differed from that of postwar Germany in 1919.
Communist Party secretary Palmiro Togliatti promised in April 1944 to
support a government of national unity comprised of all major parties.
Togliatti kept his word, but Pius distrusted him from the beginning. As
soon as the Allies occupied Rome, Pius asked them, as he had asked the
Germans, to provide ample security for Rome. In the critical days of
October 1943, Pope Pius thought and worried a great deal about Communists, perhaps much more so than about Jews.

4) Preventing the Germans from seizing Vatican City and the pope.
If the pope had sharply protested the seizure and deportation of Ro-

man Jews on October 16th or immediately thereafter, it is quite possible that an enraged Hitler would have given orders to invade Vatican City and abduct Pius XII. That is exactly what Weizsäcker meant by "Is it worth it . . . to put all at risk?" In the absence of a papal protest, Berlin anxiously awaited the word of approval from the Vatican regarding the proper conduct of German soldiers in Rome. On October 18th, Ambassador Weizsäcker went to Cardinal Maglione's office and, finding that the secretary of state was still fretting about the *razzia*, wondered whether the moment was opportune to press for the statement of good German conduct.[91] Weizsäcker got what Berlin wanted; the assurance of good conduct came on October 19th as 1,000 Roman Jews were en route to Auschwitz.[92] Thereafter the Vatican continued to deal warily with the unpredictable German dictator. But by the end of the fateful month of October, Pius felt optimistic that the Germans would leave Rome without taking him prisoner.[93]

5) Protecting the remaining Jews in hiding in Rome. Ambassador Weizsäcker had warned the Vatican that a strong protest about the *razzia* could provoke a second roundup of the thousands of Jews still in hiding in Rome. A large number of the remaining Jews, perhaps more than 6,000, found shelter, many in religious properties such as monasteries and convents. But some, a much smaller number, took refuge in properties that belonged to the Vatican although they were not located within Vatican City. Given the number of letters of protection that Weizsäcker issued, it is clear that many of the letters went to religious institutions that were not owned by the Holy See. After the *razzia*, General Stahel and Weizsäcker continued to pass out the letters and placards for display in windows.[94] Thus, many Jews who went into hiding after the 16th would have found safety in a property that did not belong to the Vatican but had a letter of protection asserting that it did. These properties were not to be violated (searched) because such an action would endanger the pending good conduct pronouncement that Berlin sought from the Holy See. Of course, Weizsäcker's action also worked to protect any Jews who had found refuge in Vatican properties. It goes without saying that Pope Pius and secretariat personnel would have been informed of Weizsäcker's effort. A few months before the end of the war, Tardini told a member of the U.S. delegation to the Vatican that clergy in Rome had given asylum to approximately 6,000 Jews during the Nazi occupation, from early September 1943 to June 5, 1945. Approximately 180 Catholic religious homes and institutions, including the Lateran and Gregorian universities, offered asylum to Jews, who were thereby rescued and saved from fascists and Nazis.[95] If the Vatican protested the October 16th *razzia*, the Jews yet in hiding might be jeopardized, Weizsäcker warned, and

the Vatican policy of control would be jeopardized—indeed, probably quashed irretrievably.

Thus, a papal protest on or after October 16th might have resulted in double jeopardy: both the Jews *and* the Vatican might have been put at risk. In this case, the Vatican's speculation ran toward Germany, not the Allies. Hitler's rage toward the Holy See was still a fresh memory inside Vatican City. Given his volatility, a protest regarding Jews could have set him off, leading to a ruthless attack both on the pope and the remaining Roman Jews, or so the Holy See might have reasonably supposed. Weizsäcker, after all, warned that a second roundup was not unlikely in the event of a protest. Actually, seizing the remaining Jews would not have been practical for the Germans. After October 16th, the Jews had acquired new identities and new addresses. About 6,700 survivors of the *razzia* had intermingled with 200,000 anti-fascist gentiles hiding out in Rome. Ferreting out the Jews posed a virtually impossible task; the SS no longer had a list of Jewish places of residence.[96]

Those who see a protest in Cardinal Maglione's minute of October 16th and conclude that it stopped the Germans from seizing more Jews are mistaken on two counts.[97] First, circumstances made a mass roundup virtually impossible after October 16th, and second, German and Italian fascists continued to seize Jews individually when opportunity arose. At the end of 1943, for example, fascists raided several Vatican properties, including the Oriental Institute, where they seized Jews and gentiles of various political stripes.[98] This was not an isolated incident.[99] Minister Osborne made this quite clear to the pope. In a remarkable interview with Pius XII two weeks after the *razzia*, Osborne mentioned several of the points of concern that I have singled out:

> On Nov. 1, 1943 the British minister had an audience with Pope XII. The pope was concerned about food. Wanted the Allies to bring in provisions because the Germans would probably take all the food with them. The result would be famine and disorder in the city, the pope believed. Pope Pius XII was concerned about the period after the Germans left and before the Allies came in.
> The minister said that the Germans were not obeying the "open city" status of Rome. . . . [They were] arresting Italians and "applying their usual merciless methods of persecution of the Jews." I said it was the opinion of a number of people that the [pope] underestimated his own moral authority and the high respect in which it was held by the Nazis because of the Catholic population of Germany; I added that I was inclined to share this opinion and I urged him to bear it in mind if push came to shove during the transition period. Conversation then turned to Russia and I mentioned that Stalin was now allowing the orthodox religion. He then reiterated the usual anxieties in respect of Communism to which I replied that Commu-

nism was derived from economic conditions that were the responsibility of the governments of individual countries and was not a political infection disseminated from Moscow.[100]

During the audience, Minister Osborne clearly stated that the Germans continued to molest individual Jews as opportunity arose.

Except for the last concern about the Jews on my list, all of the pope's issues of control related to the physical continuation of the city of Rome and safety of the Holy See. Had the pope protested the October 16th *razzia,* Pius might have lost control over all the five issues he was concerned about, at least in his mind. So he did not protest. But which of the five issues was paramount in his thinking? The answer to that question is unequivocal: saving the city of Rome, not the Jews.

The preservation of a city seems trivial and petty in the face of the Holocaust. But in the mind of Pius XII, Rome, the Eternal City, anchored the faith of Catholics around the world. Pius believed that Rome, in his mind the birthplace of Christianity, symbolized the visible church for Catholics worldwide. If the heart of Christendom were to be destroyed (or seized by Communists) the faith of Catholics would also fall. Pius never said this to any diplomat, nor did anyone in the secretariat do so. But he confided it in a letter to Bishop Preysing, who wanted the pope to speak out against the Holocaust.[101] Thus, when Pius XII addressed the issue directly about why he kept silent after the *razzia,* he pointed to concerns about the safety of the city, not the safety of the remaining Jews. An American who had an audience with the pope three days after the *razzia* reported that Pius worried about the possible destruction of Rome because of the war and about a possible Communist insurrection. He did not mention Jews.[102] On October 11th, Maglione had mentioned the same priorities to Osborne.[103] Gerhart Riegner saw in the letter to Bishop Preysing the true reason for Pius XII's failure to speak out after the 1942 Christmas address. His perception was squarely on the mark.[104]

When the Germans seized Rome's Jews on October 16th, all of the issues of control crowded together simultaneously in Pius XII's thoughts. It is a mistake to isolate any one of the issues, such as the famous Weizsäcker-Maglione meeting or the Hudal letter, from the others. Certainly, the circumstances surrounding the entire *razzia,* including its prelude and aftermath, are devilishly complex and challenging for historians. The facts, however, point to an interpretation that is consistent with Pius's policy of control. The pope moved immediately after October 16th to solidify his control of events that affected, or potentially affected, the city of Rome. On October 19th, the Vatican publicly acknowledged the good behavior of German troops in Rome (as requested by Berlin), asked for more German police to control Communists in Rome, and pressured the United States to give assurances that Allied troops would not attack the city. An additional week and a half passed before *L'Osservatore Romano* printed the Vatican's reaction, such as it was, to the *razzia*.

Unraveling the several interweaving threads that Pius XII held in his hands at the critical moment of October 16, 1943, is a complex process. Still, it is clear that an out-and-out protest would have meant loss of control of the issues that were important to the pope. Ambassador Weizsäcker reported that a few days before the seizure of the Jews, Pius's foremost concern pertained to the safety of Rome.[105] What was uppermost in Pius XII's mind immediately after the *razzia* was concern for Rome, not concern for the remaining Roman Jews. In this regard, no document compares in importance with the letter Pope Pius wrote to Bishop Preysing in March 1944. Preysing's letter of the previous March had precisely addressed the issue of the Jewish plight versus physical destruction by aerial bombardment. Terrible as the air raids were, Preysing wrote, what was happening to Berlin's Jews was worse. Five months later Pius, XII faced exactly that situation. Speaking out to protest the October 16th roundup would likely or, at least possibly, have led to a Roman Stalingrad. Pius XII would not allow the Eternal City to be destroyed if he could prevent it. No document in the eleven volumes of *Actes et Documents* addresses the Holocaust issue as directly as the March 1944 letter to Preysing; in no other document does Pope Pius himself address the issue so directly, and in no other document does the mind of Pius XII reveal itself so clearly and unambiguously.

When Pius got around to answering Preysing's letter of March 1943, he began by saying that Preysing's "eight letters of 1943 and five letters of 1944" were at hand. Preysing had presumably been urging (perhaps even pressing) the pope about the murder of the Jews. (My indefiniteness here derives from the fact that the editors of *Actes et Documents* omitted nearly all of Preysing's letters. Of course, it is possible that the Vatican purged the letters prior to the editors' work.) Pius told Preysing that he had two reasons for not allowing Rome to be endangered, a reference to what he felt would happen if he protested the roundup of Jews. First, "in consideration of Catholics worldwide [it is] a matter of conscience for Us" to protect the city because of the "uniqueness of the Holy City in the history of mankind." Rome had been the center of "Christendom since the beginning of the church of Jesus Christ," and it was that "distinction and purpose which gave the city its special character." Second, Pius said that he had to keep Rome out of the war to preserve his impartiality among Catholics on both sides of the conflict. In this letter, Pope Pius made clear that preventing bombardment of Rome was more important to him than protecting the city's Jews.[106]

The Killing of the Jews of Hungary

If, as I have argued, the threat of German retaliation was the critical factor governing Pope Pius during the fall crisis involving the Roman Jews, then he must have felt greatly relieved when the Allies became Rome's occupational force in June of 1944. Most important, the turnabout in occupying forces had been accomplished with almost no destruction within the Eternal City. Myron Taylor found that Pius, once free of Nazis, was now "eager to co-operate in the endeavor to save Jewish lives." Pius said that "neither history nor his conscience would forgive him if he made no effort to save at this psychological juncture further threatened lives."[107] It is impossible to say what Pius meant by "this psychological juncture," but the threat of the murder of over half a million Hungarian Jews in 1944 would become a test of the pope's new resolve.

The onset of genocide in Hungary came upon the Jews with terrible swiftness. The Germans occupied the country in mid-March and by July nearly 300,000 Jews had been transported to Auschwitz and gassed and cremated there. Several reasons accounted for the swiftness of the genocide. I have described these along with the conflicting advice from bishops within Hungary—some favoring supporting the Jews, others favoring doing nothing to hinder the Germans—in *The Catholic Church and the Holocaust*.[108] Here I concentrate on Pius XII and his resolve "to . . . save threatened lives." To be successful, Pius needed to overcome the resistance to act of the primate of Hungary, Justinian Serédi—a resistance rooted in obstinacy or indifference or indecision.

From March to July, Serédi heard from Endre Hamvas, the bishop of Csanad, who told the primate that

> it was painful to see the Jews herded here from Zenta, Magyarkanizsa and Zombor. About two thousands of them had to leave their homes hastily with little packs on their backs. The local authorities did not know where to accommodate them on short notice, thus they have been put up for the time being in the synagogue, the Jewish school and the pigpens of the salami factory (the latter have been standing empty for several months). Sometimes up to 80 persons are crammed into a school room, men women, children and aged people together.[109]

Then, in June, Bishop Hamvas publicly protested the deportation of hundreds and hundreds of thousands of people, among whom were "innocent children, defenseless women, helpless old and pitifully sick persons."[110] But in May, a higher-ranking bishop, Archbishop Gyula Czapic of the diocese of Eger, had counseled Serédi "that what is happening to the Jews at the present time is nothing but appropriate punishment for their misdeeds in the past."[111] Clearly, opinion about what the Hungarian Church should do about the predicament of the country's Jews was sharply divided. Which direction would the primate take? One thing is certain: unlike Archbishop Johannes de Jong, who on his own authority had challenged the occupying German administrators about Dutch Jews in 1943, Serédi did not act independently and decisively.

Voices outside Hungary also advised Cardinal Serédi. In March, the War Refugee Board, which Franklin D. Roosevelt had created very belatedly in January 1944 to coordinate efforts to rescue Jews, urged Pius XII to become involved in saving Hungarian Jews. The War Refugee Board quickly learned that the Vatican had already told the representatives of the Holy See in Hungary to "do everything possible for the relief of the Jews."[112] The principal representative of the Vatican in Hungary was Nuncio Angelo Rotta, who strongly sided with the Hungarian bishops who were urging the primate to speak out on behalf of the Jews. In June, Rotta told Cardinal Serédi in the name of the pope that what was happening to the Jews was "abominable and dishonorable."[113] On the first day of the deportation of Jews, the nuncio contacted members of Regent Miklós Horthy's government, telling them that "the whole world knows what deportation means in practice." Rotta told them that he protested in his official position as the apostolic nuncio.[114] On June 8, Rotta challenged Cardinal Serédi as intensely as he had the government, asking the primate why the Hungarian bishops were not confronting the government. At this, the cardinal became incensed. What is the "utility of the Apostolic Nuntiature in Budapest" which "does nothing and nobody knows if it ever did anything?" he asked.[115]

Although Pius had resolved to do what he could to save the Jews, he required a good bit of prodding before he finally intervened toward the end of June. One source of pressure came from the Auschwitz Protocol. In April, two Czechs, Rudolph Vrba and Alfred Wetzler, escaped from Auschwitz and made their way to Slovakia, where they divulged in great detail the operations of the death camp. Vrba and Wetzler's information was corroborated by other escapees. When authorities in Slovakia became convinced of the truth of what the escapees told them, they drew up what became known as the Auschwitz Protocol, translated it into German and Hungarian, and circulated it in Europe. Authorities in Switzerland gave it wider circulation and credence because of a cover letter by prominent Protestant churchmen, including Karl Barth and W. A. Visser t'Hooft.[116] When a copy of the Auschwitz Protocol reached the Vatican, the pope sent a messenger to Bratislava to verify its authenticity, even though he had known for well over a year that Jews were being gassed en masse. The Auschwitz Protocol subjected Pope Pius to the same kind of pressure he had felt late in 1942 when the United Nations decried the murder of the Jews. Undoubtedly, the pope did not want to find himself trailing behind the denunciations of other voices and institutions about the events in Hungary. The king of Sweden had, in fact, already urged Regent Horthy to stop the persecution.[117]

In addition, a number of people appealed directly to Pius. The chief rabbis of Palestine, Isaac Herzog and Ben-Zion Meir Uziel; the War Refugee Board; the Archbishop of Westminster at the behest of the British World Jewish Council; and Archbishop Edward Mooney at the behest of Leon Kubowitzki of the United States as well as others prodded Pius to do something. He finally sent Regent Horthy an open (public) telegram on June 25, urging him to "do everything in his power to save as many unfortunate people [as possible] from further pain and sorrow."[118] The appeal to Horthy, historian Randolph Braham has written, was weak—a "discreet diplomatic appeal" that did not mention the Jews by name.[119] Furthermore, it was not pain and sorrow but death that faced the Jews. And the pope's message was sent "three weeks after the liberation of Rome by the Allies, when any threat of German attack on the Vatican was gone."[120] Even though the pope's letter was not as strong as it could have been, Horthy was flooded with letters from around the world, including a very threatening one from President Roosevelt. These outbursts directly led to a cessation of deportations.

The pope's telegram moved Cardinal Serédi to do something at last. In July, when all of the Jews of Hungary were dead except those living in Budapest, Serédi issued a pastoral letter opposing deportations. It is significant that Pius intervened directly with Horthy instead of with the Hungarian bishops through the primate. When Serédi blew up at Nuncio Rotta, he concluded his rant by saying that "it is deceitful for the Apostolic See to carry on diplomatic relations with that German government which carries out the atrocities."[121] This statement backed Pope Pius into the corner. It implied that if Rome pushed too hard, Serédi would respond, possibly publicly, by asking why the Vatican still recognized the legitimacy of Nazi Germany. Judging from how the pope dealt with the cardinal after June, it appears that the primate's outburst made Pius resolve to mollify him rather than press him.

The cessation of deportations to Auschwitz proved to be no more than a summer respite. The fall—October—was again fateful, as it had been in Rome the year before. It was then that Frenenc Szalasi, the leader of the fascist Arrow Cross Party, became prime minister and the new government immediately began to persecute the Jews again. Not surprisingly, after the murders in the first half of 1944, the United States and the World Jewish Congress turned again to the Vatican to forestall the killing of the remaining three to four hundred thousand Jews. On October 10, Taylor learned from the state department of "another step in the process of mass extermination" in Hungary. State wanted Taylor to get word to the Holy See because "it would seem that the most impressive means of achieving the purpose of our government to bring this message to the attention of the Hungarian authorities would be through the intercession of the Vatican."[122] Taylor heard the same dire news about extermination of the remaining Hungarian Jews from the London office of the World Jewish Congress, which also appealed direct to Pope Pius to intervene. The U.S. State Department and the British Foreign Office directed Taylor and Osborne to "encourage such a course."[123] Pius knew that the news from the west was accurate because Nuncio Rotta had cabled Rome with news of "great cruelty." On October 16, the U.S. State Department again asked that the Holy See communicate through Rotta the Allied warning to Hungarian authorities to stop cooperating with the German deportations.[124] Two days later, the U.S. asked the Holy See to communicate to the German ambassador the intention of the Allies to hold those responsible for the atrocities in Hungary accountable.[125] There is nothing in Weizsäcker's papers to indicate that the pope conveyed the message. After his audience with Pius on the following day, Taylor cabled Roosevelt that the "pope [would] make a special appeal for the salvation of the Jews in Hungary."[126]

The Vatican and Rotta kept in steady contact. The nuncio was told of the appeals from all sides for the pope's intervention and instructed to avail himself "of the collaboration of the episcopate" to energize Catholics to practice charity toward the persecuted.[127] But here exactly was the rub. The Hungarian episcopate was badly divided. There were those like bishops Morton, Apor, and Hamvas who spoke out distinctly against persecution, but they did not have the ear of the cardinal.[128] Pressure from Rome did succeed, however, in nudging Cardinal Serédi to designate Sunday, October 29th, as a national day of prayer on which a collection would be taken up for refugees. Of course, the pope's plea to the episcopate had no effect on Szalasi's fascist regime. But Nuncio Rotta insisted "in the name of the Holy See on an improvement of conditions" for Jews and extracted a statement from Szalasi that the Jews would neither "be deported nor annihilated."[129]

The intensity of appeals to the Holy See in October may be taken as an accurate barometer of the danger to the 300,000 to 400,000 Jews remaining in Hungary. Late in the month the Vatican received still another plea from London and Washington, this time for a radio broadcast by the Holy Father to Hungary. Prompted by the War Refugee Board, the State Department told Taylor "urgently to approach the pope with the suggestion that he deliver a broadcast to the people and clergy appealing to them to temporarily conceal Jews and oppose the deportation and extermination of these people to the full extent of their powers."[130] Instead of a radio broadcast, Pius responded, very weakly, by sending a congratulatory word to Serédi for his plan to make October 29th a day of prayer and monetary support for Jews. This was very far indeed from what was asked of the Holy See—a direct appeal by Pope Pius to the Hungarian Catholic people. In early November, Gowen, an assistant to Myron Taylor, sent word that "it was fear of communism that in the fall of that year dissuaded Pope Pius from making a radio broadcast," at the behest of the U.S. War Refugee Board and the U.S. State Department, to save 65,000 Jews about to be deported from Hungary and murdered at Auschwitz-Birkenau.[131] Osborne provided London with a not altogether different but fuller explanation for why the pope turned down the request to give a radio broadcast. Osborne said that if he made such an announcement about Jews in Hungary he would have to make a similar statement regarding "Russian treatment of Poles and Baltic populations."[132] This was surely a hollow excuse. Pius knew very well that the Soviets were not engaged in a Nazi-style genocide or anything like it, and he knew that the Soviet's treatment of Poles could not begin to compare with the bestiality of the Nazis from 1940 to 1943 in occupied Poland.

There is no doubt that Pius XII did more to save the Jews in Hungary than in any other country. In no other instance did he intervene directly with a foreign government. Even though by that time it was clear that Germany would lose the war and that Rome was out of Hitler's reach, credit must be given for his intervention. In the end, although about 450,000 Hungarian Jews perished, some of the credit for saving the remaining 30 percent of the Jewish population belongs to Pius XII. (Of course, this leaves unattended the question of his silence *before* the deportation of the 450,000.) The fact remains, however, that he could have done more. As before, the Vatican remained passively active regarding Jewish concerns. His failure to appeal directly by radio to Hungarian Catholics left some of them uninhibited in their rapaciousness—forcing starving Jews to pay usurious prices for bread or taking clothes for bread for in the winter months when the Arrow Cross Party had begun again with persecution.

The Vatican received detailed information from a Hungarian priest about the pitiable condition of the Jews—children and the elderly whipped and dragging "themselves along starving, frozen, limping" twenty or thirty kilometers a day without food or a place to sleep at night. (This letter was omitted from *Actes et Documents*.)[133] During the last months of their torture, Nuncio Rotta worked heroically to save them and alleviate their suffering (for which he was later named Righteous Gentile among the Nations by Yad Vashem). Once the Vatican supported his work with a donation of an unspecified amount, but the initiative for helping the Jews was Rotta's alone; he received no instructions from the Vatican for his relief work.[134] American Jews continued to appeal to the Vatican for more intervention by the Holy See late in December 1944. The Vatican replied that it was no longer possible for the pope to be in contact with Nuncio Rotta. Instead, Monsignor Tardini instructed the nuncio to Germany to recommend that the Nazis follow principles of "humanity and justice" regarding the Hungarian Jews. Clearly it was disingenuous for Pope Pius to have such a message sent to Nazis in Berlin knowing, as he had for some time, that their murderous agenda left no inch of room for humanity and justice.[135] His success in Hungary notwithstanding, Pius XII missed a wide-open opportunity to join with Nuncio Rotta in a determined effort to end the misery of the Jews.

In this and the previous chapter we have looked closely at the perennial theme of Pius XII and the Holocaust. Several threads run through the war years that distracted the pope from attending first and foremost to genocide. Separately the threads appear as single twisted snarls that kept the pope from attending to what we generally today, more than a half century later, believe should have been his principal preoccupation. But together the threads weave a pattern that was the pope's actual principal preoccupation—preserving the Church. That preserving a Church that had not had its finest hour in the service of humanity would leave it indelibly stained was not a thought that came to him.

Preserving the Church meant protecting it from communism, meant preserving concordats, meant saving its architectural and artistic treasures in the Eternal City. The pope's mind dwelled on these concerns. When the Nazis reigned over most of Europe, Pius, as we will see, considered how Catholics could survive by emigrating to South America. Then, when Germany's war fortunes flagged, he thought about how Nazis could emigrate to Argentina and be useful against communism. While genocide was under way, he gave audiences to various people, some of whom were Nazi collaborators, to work on these strategies—correspondence about which we do not read a word in *Actes et Documents*.

When the war came to Italy, Pius XII was very proactive in his efforts to save the structures of the Eternal City while remaining passively active with regard to that city's Jews. The result was near-total success for the buildings but only very partial success for the Jewish people. There can be only one reason for the whimpering, absurd plea in the final months of the Holocaust for the Nazis to treat Jews "justly and humanely": Pope Pius did not want to place the concordat at risk with the end of the Nazi regime so close at hand. Only when his moral authority was called into question in 1942 did the pope speak out in his Christmas address. Whether staving off genocide or staving off challenges to his authority was his first objective we do not yet know. In short, we must come to the realization that Pius XII had a number of concerns on his mind other than the destiny of the Jews. Certainly one of them was communism in Italy, which not only threatened the country's Christian way of life but also the financial foundation of the Vatican.

5

PAPAL CAPITALISM
DURING
WORLD WAR II

What did money mean to Pius XII? Shortly after Harold Tittmann began work at the Vatican in 1940 as second in command in President Roosevelt's mission, he was invited to an audience with Pope Pius. Tittmann was led to a hidden elevator that ascended to the pope's private quarters. The room was furnished traditionally in heavy upholstery. Tittmann was asked to take a seat on the divan. After a few moments, Pius XII entered the room and sat at the other end of the couch. Following some casual chitchat, Pius told the American that he had a New York bank account about which the city's cardinal, Francis Spellman, knew nothing. The pope asked Tittmann to tell Myron Taylor to tell Spellman to have this account listed with the Treasury Department like other Vatican accounts so that it would not be blocked. The FBI reported in 1941 that the account had a balance of $61,999 (about $848,500 in 2006 dollars).[1] Pius then told the diplomat to keep their meeting a complete secret, even the fact that it had taken place in his private quarters.[2] Tittmann continued on at the Vatican for eight years but would never again set foot in the pope's private quarters. For Pope Pius, money mattered.

The commencement of the pontificate of Eugenio Pacelli coincided with the year, 1939, that marked the beginning of World War II. The new pope complained, without overly exaggerating, that he faced a more critical political situation in Europe than any modern pope (one of his namesakes, Pius VI, had died a prisoner of Napoleon Bonaparte). One thing Pope Pius did not have fret about was the wealth of Vatican City, which without exaggeration easily surpassed that of his modern predecessors.

The nineteenth century saw huge economic transitions in western society. For most of the century, popes and cardinals came from Italian aristocratic stock, and, like other European nobility in the early industrial era, they fell on hard economic times. One avenue of escape from financial hardship, marrying into the moneyed bourgeoisie, was blocked for celibate clerics. (After the Counter-Reformation in the sixteenth century, popes no longer took mistresses, although some aristocratic cardinals and bishops continued the practice for the next two centuries.) Popes had recourse to European bankers to bail them out of economic straits, although they disdained bourgeois new money and Jews who were associated with it. Pope Gregory XVI, who treated the Jews of the Roman ghetto so atrociously that the most conservative head of state in Europe, Austria's Chancellor Metternich, begged him to lighten up, borrowed money in 1831 from the Jewish Rothschild bank to pay to put down an uprising of the liberal middle class.[3] Pope Gregory's successor, the equally antisemitic Pius IX, also sought a loan from the Rothschild bank, which he obtained only after promising to improve the living conditions in the Roman ghetto, a pledge on which he subsequently reneged.[4] Clearly, the transition from an agricultural to an industrial economy strained the Vatican, one of the last aristocratic landlords of Europe.

Two other momentous changes occurred in Vatican finances before Pius XII ascended the throne of St. Peter. The papal estates, which stretched across the breadth of Italy from sea to sea, blocked national unification. Yet step by step, northern and southern Italy had fused into one nation by 1861 under the leadership of unlikely partners, the liberal Count Cavour and the radical Giuseppe Garibaldi, a merger which robbed the Holy See of its age-old patrimony. Afterward, Pope Pius IX found himself isolated in Rome, protected by French troops from being completely swallowed up by the nationalist movement. Napoleon III wanted to drum up Catholic support by supporting the pope, but the friendly occupation of papal Rome by French forces ended in 1870 when the French were called home to fight in the Franco-Prussian War. The ancient capital of Italy assumed that role once again. Pope Pius, chagrined, retreated behind the walled area that became known as Vatican City.[5] The Roman Question—the relation of the popes to the Italian government—remained unsolved from 1870 to 1929, when the Lateran Treaty was signed. It infuriated Pius IX that the city the popes had ruled for centuries was now ruled by a hostile liberal government. Refusing to leave the area allotted to him by the government, the pope became a "prisoner of the Vatican." Time after time over the next fifty years, the popes tried to recover the Patrimony of St. Peter.[6]

If the popes found themselves diplomatically disempowered by nationalism, the loss of the papal states helped them adjust to the economic liquidity of the industrial world. Deprived of the feudal dues of the vast papal states, the Vatican became dependent on voluntary contributions from throngs of the faithful, who made pilgrimages year after year to Rome to support their besieged leader.[7] A second major source of funds came from Peter's Pence, a medieval tax that was revived in the late nineteenth century. In its modern form, Peter's Pence drew from contributions from middle-class Catholics and, especially, from the masses—that is, from rural Catholics and blue-collar workers, still at that time largely free of socialist infiltration. In the last quarter of the century, American Catholics began to weigh in heavily with their contributions to the pope's purse. Using trusted intermediaries to cloak its financial dealings, the Vatican invested intensively in the construction boom in the city of Rome. "So, irony of ironies," historian John Pollard wrote, "the millions given by the faithful in support of the 'prisoner of the Vatican' was going to support the development and embellishment of the capital city of the pope's 'jailer,' the usurper of his temporal power."[8] But, shamelessly, Pope Pius X also used some of the "offerings of the faithful poor" to bail out bankrupt members of the Roman Catholic aristocracy, including members of his own family.[9] He was not the only pope to do so.

The final great turning point in papal financial affairs prior to Pius XII's pontificate was the Lateran Treaty between Italy and the Vatican State in 1929. The agreement regularized relations between the two states. To compensate the Holy See for the loss of its patrimony, Italy gave the pope 750 million lire and 1,000 million in government bonds (amounting to about $90 million, or a little over $1 billion in 2006 dollars).[10] Pius XI wanted nearly double that amount, and Mussolini initially agreed before reconsidering.[11] The Lateran Treaty dramatically improved the Vatican's finances. Previously, the Vatican could only make marginal investments, since most of the cash contributions flowing into it had to be used for current expenses and extensive charity. After 1929, the Vatican invested around the world in the capitalist marketplace.

Pius XI's predecessors had become accustomed to using laymen as financial advisors and investors. The Roman Pacelli family was prominent. Ernesto Pacelli distinguished himself as Pope Leo XIII's advisor and banker, and Francesco Pacelli, the brother of future Pius XII Eugenio Pacelli, negotiated the financial aspects of the Lateran Treaty's indemnity.[12] Pope Pius XI, the pope who rebuilt Vatican City, making it into an "imperial papacy," chose another layman, the highly intelligent and extremely capable Bernardino Nogara, as his in-house financial manager and investor.[13]

Nogara's credentials were indeed outstanding. Pollard characterizes his career as spectacular.[14] The Milan native excelled in both engineering and finance. He directed engineering operations in England, Bulgaria, and the Ottoman Empire. His financial abilities led the Italian government to appoint him to its delegation for economic negotiations at Versailles after World War I and later to appoint him to manage the industry section of the Inter-Allied Commission that executed the Dawes Plan in Berlin.[15] Subsequently, he sat on the board of the Banca Commerciale Italiana in Milan, Italy's largest bank, and eventually became its vice president. After the signing of the Lateran Treaty, Pius XI created a new office, the Special Administration of the Holy See, to be caretaker of the funds the Holy See realized by the treaty.[16] Pope Pius named Nogara the director of the new office, in which capacity he answered directly to the pope rather than to the two other Vatican financial offices, the Vatican bank and the office that handled previously acquired liquid and nonliquid assets purchased through Peter's Pence.[17] In fact, his influence may well have extended over all Vatican fiscal offices. Tittmann, a friend of Nogara, described him as being in effect the Vatican secretary of the treasury.[18]

Achille Ratti, Pope Pius XI, favored those who, like the Nogara family, came from his native Lombardy, and he appointed more than a few of them to his administration. A remarkable number of Bernardino's siblings served the Church in a variety of capacities. The pope's favoritism toward residents of Milan and the religious loyalty of the Nogara clan led naturally to the appointment of Bernardino.[19] Those factors and, of course, the proven ability of the young engineer from the distinguished Milan institute, the Politecnico, made Nogara a natural choice. He worked for Pius XI from 1929, when the Special Administration was created, and he was appointed its head until the pope's death in 1939. He continued under Pope Pius XII until 1954. An ability to move fluidly in the highest circles of industry and politics as well as the Church marked Nogara's career. He remained a consultant to Pius XII until his death in 1954.

As the effects of the 1929 stock-market crash hit Europe, Nogara restructured the Vatican's portfolio in two ways. First, he transferred funds into the Holy See's gold reserve, at that time worth 100 million lire (about $12 million).[20] Second, he put the Vatican into the real estate business, not, as before, as an investor, but as an entrepreneur. Nogara was anything but timid. He contemplated buying the office headquarters of Europe's two largest travel agencies, Wagons Lit in Paris and Thomas Cook in London. When these prospects did not materialize, Nogara settled on residential properties in Paris, London, Coventry, and Lausanne, some of which were housing for the working and middle classes. In these operations, Nogara launched companies and appointed chief executive officers to manage the properties that still exist today.[21] Nogara then established a holding company, Grolux, into which the profits of these investments would flow on behalf of his papal Special Administration office. Grolux, which had tidy profits from 1932 to 1935, was housed in Luxembourg, where, by law, companies were not open to the public.[22]

While Nogara broadened papal investments internationally, he also intensified holdings in Italy. These ventures included "financial institutions, manufacturing and utility companies."[23] Nogara became a board member of a mind-boggling number of major Italian companies, including Assicurazioni Generali, Italy's biggest insurance company and one of the largest in the world. The Vatican acquired a controlling interest in the Società Generale Immobiliare, the largest construction company in Italy, destined to become one of the largest in the world after extending operations in the western hemisphere. Considering the investments already in the Vatican portfolio, "it is clear that the Vatican had consolidated its hold over the economy of the Italian capital city."[24] By placing businessmen with close ties to the Vatican on the boards of these companies, Nogara could keep track of his investments, making sure that they benefited Vatican capital. After the economic depression after 1929, the Italian government passed legislation to bail out and reorganize the country's banks. Nogara, who was a party to the negotiations the reorganization entailed, knew exactly which industries and companies would stand to do well, and, equipped with this insider information, purchased large portions of shares in these companies. By any reckoning Nogara wisely and profitably invested the considerable funds that came to the Holy See as part of the Lateran settlement. All in all, the Vatican in the person of Bernardino Nogara took its place with the captains of industry in Italy: the Banca Commerciale Italiana, Assicurazioni, Pirelli, and FIAT.[25]

If Pope Pius XII inherited a fat portfolio, he also inherited a money-minded curial bureaucracy. The transition after 1870 from a feudal landed economy to an industrial capital-based economy ushered in a money culture to which Vatican officials had had ample time to acclimate themselves by the middle of the twentieth century. Top Vatican officials from the pope on down regularly involved themselves in one way or another in the Holy See's finances.[26] An American bishop, Joseph Patrick Hurley, a Vatican diplomat who was stationed in Rome from 1934 to 1940 and sporadically thereafter, had a ringside seat for observing the curia's money culture. What the bishop saw he did not like. When passing out papal honors, Hurley noted, the curia would charge Italians 500 lire but it would charge Americans $500, explaining, enigmatically, that the fee was calculated in the currency of the recipient's country. (At that time one dollar bought over seven lire.) A disgusted Hurley wrote in a diary entry, "Corruption of petty officials in the Papal Court. Panhandling at audiences. Hawking of biglietti [tickets] by guides. . . . A disgrace felt keenly by most foreign Catholics who are approached or who see others, non-Cath[olics] approached."[27] The money culture extended to Mass stipends.[28] Consequently, Americans who, like Hurley, held positions at the Vatican or at one or the other American seminary of the many religious orders resolved among themselves not to present their visiting fellow Americans to Italian ecclesiastics, "even the most high placed, for fear of the resultant bad impressions made."[29]

But the curial bureaucracy devised a system for milking the American cash cow. They would find a cooperative American priest stationed in Rome to put them in touch with Americans with deep pockets when they visited the Eternal City. This even worked with Protestants, according to an observation made by the Italian ambassador to the United States. "Because they have no aristocracy, the Americans are particularly susceptible to this form of flattery. The rich Protestant Mellon of Philadelphia has just been made a Papal Marquis."[30] The clerical "spotter," who fingered wealthy prospects, would suggest donations to this or that curial office or charity. In return, "all doors were open to the prosperous Americans who saw Rome under the tutelage of this young Amer[ican] priest. The knock-down man [would become] a monsignor himself, and later, when he had perhaps reached the limit of his usefulness because his toadyism had aroused a good deal of talk, he was conveniently shipped back to America—as a bishop."[31]

Although Hurley did not accuse Rome of simony, the selling of church offices, he came close. The Holy Father's apostolic delegate to the United States nominated candidates for bishoprics "in the only way he knows anything about—by intrigue, by balancing fortune against fortune, by personal favoritism. Result is that we get mediocre men. Neutral gray is the color of the U.S. Purple." (The ecclesiastical and liturgical attire of bishops is purple.) Consequently, Hurley explained, the office of apostolic delegate to the United States was the post ambitious Vatican Italians sought the most. Although the apostolic delegate was not paid very much, he had "unlimited possibilities for making money and the red hat [of the cardinalate] at the end of it." Over time, Hurley predicted, the cash-based system for choosing prelates would undermine the American Church:

> No matter how sanctimonious the exterior, how disarming the impression, you may be sure that the majority of the American Bishops are what they are by servility, flattery, sucking [up] or worse. The climbers among the priests, who are looked upon with disgust by most of their brethren, will be the Bishops of tomorrow. Both in Mental[ity] and morale, the priests

are far above the average of the Bishops. But that high standard cannot last long when it is sapped by the cynicism which comes from the spectacle of bad example in high places.[32]

As Hurly saw it, Rome rewarded those who rewarded it with cash. In the twentieth century this meant, above all, the American Church, whose bishops were caught in a race to see who could outdo the other in Peter's Pence donations to the Holy Father. "Money transferred from other funds [to Peter's Pence] in order to hold their own with another bishop," wrote Hurley. In 1924, Pius XI chose to raise one of his biggest benefactors to the cardinalate—George Mundelein of Chicago, who rewarded the pope with a gift of $1 million at the time of the World Eucharistic Congress held in the Windy City in 1928.[33] For the first time in the entire history of the American Church, there were two U.S. cardinals. U.S. bishops continued for the remainder of the century to fill the Holy See's coffers. This paid off handsomely in terms of ecclesiastical promotions. Today the U.S. Church of 67 million Catholics counts thirteen cardinals, eleven of whom can vote in papal conclaves. The less-well-to-do churches of Brazil, Mexico, and the Philippines, which have a combined Catholic population of 340 million, have altogether only fifteen cardinals, only nine of whom are electors.[34] John Pollard has argued persuasively that the dollar power of the American Church paid off for career-minded prelates.

Clearly, at the time of Bishop Hurley's tenure in Rome, on the eve of the elevation of Pius XII to the papacy, a money culture had struck deep roots in the day-to-day affairs of the Vatican and many of the national churches affiliated with it. This had occurred everywhere in modern society; it was inevitable that it would befall the Vatican. Modern popes, including the curia veteran, Eugenio Pacelli, were unavoidably part of that culture. Pius XII's closeted meeting with Harold Tittmann regarding his hidden New York bank account signals that the new pope was not at all unmindful of his money. During the war, Nogara met with Pius XII, keeping him apprised his investments, just as he had done under Pope Pius XI. There were no intermediaries between the pope and Nogara, who, for whatever reason, did not take notes of his conferences with the new pope as he had under Pius XI.[35] No record exists in *Actes et Documents*. Historians must make do with information gleaned from documents in the U.S. national archives, because Pius XII chose to do much of his banking through New York banks. The information at hand is scanty in comparison to the record Nogara compiled for the period 1931–1939, but nevertheless it is substantial.

Since Vatican City was a neutral state, as far as the war was concerned, Nogara had to be circumspect about investments lest Vatican funds in Allied or Axis countries become blocked. Although his experiences as a negotiator at Versailles after World War I made him chary of investing in Germany, his ties to Italian companies pulled him into the Nazi orbit during World War II.[36] It was not necessary or even economically feasible for the Vatican to divest itself of assets held in England, the United States, Italy, or elsewhere. Having said this, the question nevertheless remains as to whether indiscriminate investing was ethical given the racial nature of Germany's aggression. Was the Holy See prepared to make a profit during the war regardless of where a profit was to be made?

Pius XII Secures Vatican Gold and Opens an Account with Chase Manhattan Bank

On May 17, 1940, Myron Taylor sent a telegram from Rome to President Roosevelt marked "strictly confidential for the president."

> The Vatican secretary of state has asked of you the following favor:
> The Vatican state has a sizable amount of gold bars on deposit in a bank in a belligerent country now possible to ship to NY. Would like to deposit for safekeeping in trust with NY bankers and does not wish to sell. Desires permission of our govt through you to assure as in case of other states with deposits in America that the gold will be intact and in all ways free under our laws. Vatican very anxious to avoid publicity.[37]

Italy, presumably, was the "belligerent country." What, however, did Taylor mean by "a sizable amount of gold bars"? Since Nogara had taken care after the stock market crash to convert a certain amount of Vatican assets to gold, we must assume that the transfer entailed considerably more than 100 million lire. At the same time as this transfer of gold, the Vatican transferred $7,665,000 worth of gold from England to the United States.[38] Although Vatican gold lay outside the sphere of Nogara's Special Administration, it is unthinkable that Pius would take this action without his advice. The transfers of gold took place without public knowledge, just as Pope Pius wished. By withdrawing Vatican gold from the continent, the pope saved it, in all likelihood, from the fate of the wealth of other countries, whose reserves were stolen by Germany in the course of the war. It was, obviously, the circumstance of the war that moved the Holy See to take this action. Noteworthy is the timing of the transfer from England—during the Battle of Britain.

After Germany's blitzkrieg invasion of Poland in September 1939 and its subsequent occupation of the western portion of the country, Hitler turned the attention of his generals westward. By the end of the following year, more blitzkrieg had delivered Denmark, Norway, Luxemburg, the Low Countries, and northern France to German control, while southern France, Vichy, remained nominally and temporarily free. (The Vatican, Switzerland, Sweden, Spain, and Portugal remained neutral.) In 1941, the same fate befell the Balkan countries, where Nazi puppet governments took power. The Vatican had representatives or missions of one sort or another in all of these countries, and they needed to be maintained. Since this would be impossible or highly problematic to do through Germany's Reichsbank, the Holy See turned to the United States for help.[39] In the summer of 1941, Harold Tittmann notified the U.S. Department of State that the Vatican's situation had become critical. Having converted its liquid assets to dollars, the Holy See found that it could not carry on normal diplomatic and Church business in those countries now occupied by Germany because they were "blocked" by the Allies or because they were allied with Germany. Pleading for the Vatican, Tittmann wrote that these assets were "strictly necessary to the very life of the Holy See."[40]

U.S. secretary of the treasury Henry Morgenthau had his personnel look into the Holy See's request and in April 1942 gave permission for the United States to make an exception so the Vatican could meet its obligations in the blocked countries that required it to spend money in Axis-dominated countries. In fact, the United States went out of its way to cooperate with the Holy See. It told the Vatican that if the Swiss denied the request of the Vatican's U.S. bank, Chase Manhattan of New York, to make dollar-franc exchanges, the Treasury Department would simply buy francs on the open market and make them available to the Vatican.[41] The arrangement allowed the Vatican to maintain liquidity throughout Europe, where the Swiss franc was honored everywhere. The Treasury Department was willing to make the exception for the Holy See both because the amount of money in question was too small to be of any appreciable use to Germany and because the Vatican said it needed the money for its mission of charitable works, including assistance to prisoners of war. The agreement of the Treasury Department seems generous but surprising in one aspect. One of the purposes the Vatican stipulated in its request for funds for the Low Countries was for proselytizing—a clear violation of the American principle of separation of church and state. I suspect, however, that the between-the-lines meaning was "converting Jews," a practice that many believed could save them.

The amount of money converted through the U.S. treasury during the war varied from year to year—never less than \$1 million or more than \$3 million. This amount, the Vatican told treasury officials, would cover its operating expenses in Vatican City and on the rest of the continent. The budget broke down along the following lines:

Nunciatures	\$117,000
Religious and charitable works; missionary works	\$307,000
Vatican City and congregations (offices)	\$476,000
Swiss Guards	\$50,000
Money orders, etc.	\$50,000
Transactions involving protection of principal, reinvestments, and transfers of principal[42]	\$300,000

Swiss francs were needed for expenditures of about \$40,000 in each of the blocked countries—those under Nazi occupation—as well as for Italy, which demanded that the Holy See pay for its services and utilities in a currency backed by gold. But not all of the dollars were to be converted to Swiss francs. In the above budget, the first the Vatican proposed, \$55,000 was requested in Spanish pesetas and \$214,000 in Portuguese escudos. Of these amounts \$155,000 was earmarked for food for the Vatican; in other words, for food shipments from the Iberian Peninsula to Vatican City. This allocation was peculiar, as we will see, but, again, the dollar amount was small, and the Treasury Department let it slip by.[43]

In its application to the Treasury Department, the Vatican assured the United States that "the sums in question are intended for payments exclusively in countries whose assets have been frozen, or in territories occupied by enemy nations. This designation, however, does not include Germany and Japan nor the territories occupied by this latter." In other words, no money would be expended in the two countries that were at war with the United States. The Vatican could not include Italy, which was also at war with the Allies, because most of its employees were naturally Italians. Still, the wording of the Vatican's request is curious, to say the least. Neither Spain nor Portugal were occupied countries, and their assets were not frozen. Indeed, Germany carried on essential wartime financial transactions with the Iberian nations. Also, one might reasonably ask, what exactly would the \$300,000 "transactions" allocation entail?

All in all, the Vatican's request raises as many questions as it answers. The Holy See enjoyed considerable liquidity in Europe independent of the currency transfers through the Chase bank. The Vatican bank and Nogara's Special Administration held many bank accounts in Europe and worldwide.[44] Historian Ron Chernow lists five (one each in New

York, London, Paris, Holland, Stockholm, and Switzerland), but there were actually many more.[45] It was not as if the Chase Manhattan Bank in New York was a lone player. Historian Gerald Feldman has demonstrated how eager Germans were to expand business operations into western Europe, which meant that regular financial transactions would take place as they had in the past.[46] Thus, Nogara's cloaked real estate companies continued to operate during the war as before. Of course, Germany blocked funds that would flow to Allied countries, but that obviously excluded the Vatican, which had, and used, its account in the Reichsbank.[47] The Vatican could move funds with ease around Europe through Swiss banks. In 1946, a Swiss banker estimated Vatican holdings in Switzerland to be about a $250,000 in Swiss francs.[48] Toward the very end of the war, the Vatican transferred 300,000 francs from Swiss banks to an Italian bank.[49] Doubtless many other transactions occurred that U.S. intelligence did not know about.

The FBI tracked Vatican investments as well as it could until the Vatican's agreement with the Treasury Department began in 1942.[50] In May 1942, Hoover informed the State Department that Italian utility companies had paid the J. P. Morgan Bank $56,335, which the bank had forwarded to the apostolic delegate in Washington, D.C.[51] In 1941, FBI director J. Edgar Hoover had informed the State Department that Nogara's Special Administration's account had been credited $2,000 from a Vatican equity in Argentina.[52] Given Nogara's extraordinary investments during the 1930s, these sums would only be a fraction of the interest and dividends that were owed the Vatican annually. In addition, the Vatican could still count on large Peter's Pence contributions by U.S. Catholics, whose offerings far outpaced those of other countries around the world. Only in certain European countries were Vatican funds blocked. Germany's contribution, which was second only to that of the United States, was cut off. What this means very simply is that while the Vatican could continue during the war to pursue bank transactions worldwide, it needed a safe harbor for its gold in a place where it could obtain plentiful Swiss francs. The U.S. treasury obliged.

Within a year of the Vatican's agreement with the United States, the Holy See broke its word. Himmler's SS reported in the spring of 1943 that the Vatican had sent $45,000 to Japan to assist in the care of its wounded.[53] When word of this reached the Treasury Department, officials were understandably infuriated. It certainly appeared that the Vatican had played a treacherous double game. After having reached a financial agreement with the United States, Germany—and even worse, the SS—disclosed that its ally, Japan, would get Vatican money via Switzerland. Promptly and angrily, the United States swore that it would cut off the funds going from Chase to Switzerland for conversion to francs.[54] Caught red-handed, the Holy See beat a hasty retreat. Tittmann quickly notified the United States that

> the Vatican states that the recent notice appearing in Axis press to the effect that the pope has given $45,000 to the Japanese government to be used for Japanese wounded soldiers and sailors was untrue. The money was in fact sent to the apost[olic] delegate in Japan for the relief of war sufferers and more particularly for the relief of prisoners of war in Japanese hands.[55]

This limp attempt to explain the deception did little to improve the Vatican's situation. It had sent money to Japan—a direct violation of the Holy See's written word. Even if what Tittmann reported was true—and this seems doubtful because the amount in question is exactly the same as the Vatican had specified for blocked countries in Europe—it broke faith as far as the Treasury Department was concerned. The United States would never have obliged the Vatican's request had it known that any money would go to Japan, regardless of its source or purpose. Tittmann's explanation also makes it clear that the Vatican did not, after all, depend entirely on the United States for its liquidity, as originally claimed.

In 1964, Harold Tittmann, by then Ambassador Tittmann and retired from the State Department, received permission to revisit the documents in the national archives pertaining to the Japan-Vatican controversy. Tittmann wanted to set the record straight in his memoirs, and he indicated in a 1964 letter to the archives that Pius XII had sent "his very close friend Engineer [Enrico] Galeazzi," the top administrator of Vatican City, to Washington to iron things out. Upon reaching the United States in July 1943, Galeazzi learned that Rome had just been bombed for the first time, for which reason he immediately returned to Italy without making any contact with the Treasury Department. Tittmann was unable to discover any extenuating circumstances in the U.S. archives that would exonerate the Holy See and consequently makes no mention of the controversy in his memoirs.[56]

After refusing to accommodate the Vatican any longer by purchasing francs from the Swiss, the Treasury Department let the matter drop. It did not block Vatican accounts in the United States, so the Holy See could acquire Swiss francs from friendly governments in South America that could then be sent to the Vatican's Chase Manhattan account. Although the Vatican's conduct clearly broke faith with the Treasury Department, the affair did not strain relations between President Roosevelt and Pius XII.

The Holy See Buys a Bank

World War II brought the Vatican new opportunities for making money and new risks for losing it. The Vatican's extensive real estate holdings stood in danger of being destroyed, and some of them were. Interest on bonds and dividends on equities could be blocked, and some of them were. National Peter's Pence contributions to the Vatican could be blocked, and some were. On the other hand, Nogara capitalized on new possibilities. One of these was a bank, the Banque Française et Italienne, which, because its operating location was in South America, went by its American name, Banco Sudameris. Actually not a single bank but a chain of banks, Sudameris included eight banks in five countries with sixteen sub-branches. The bank had served the public for the first half of the twentieth century, and it thus had name recognition and the backing of two of Europe's best-known banks.

Although Sudameris was an established reliable enterprise when the Vatican bought controlling interest in it in November 1941, it was having difficulty because of the war. Both the United States and Great Britain had put the bank and its South American directors on their blacklists. One reason for this was that just before France fell to Germany, the Banque de Paris et des Pays Bas sold the controlling interest of Sudameris to its Italian partner, Banca Commerciale Italiana of Milan, an action which the British, stretching a point, called treasonous. But since Britain had put any business or corporation that was in an enemy country or controlled by an enemy country on its blacklist, Sudameris could not escape this fate.[57]

There was a second reason for blacklisting Sudameris. In order to make it appear that it was an independent South American corporation, Sudameris shifted its management to Buenos Aires under an Italian national, Giovanni F. Malagodi, and his assistant, a French (Vichy) national, André Cavin. But the Allies were not convinced. When one of the Sudameris banks in Chile became overdrawn, Malagodi asked Milan to send funds to shore up the bank. So it was not independent. Other intelligence intercepts made it clear that Malagodi still got his orders from Milan.[58]

In addition, the Allies did not like Malagodi or Cavin. They were nothing other than fascists, the British complained, who acted in a manner "inimical to British interests." The distrust was merited. In June 1940, Malagodi instructed all of the Sudameris branch banks to "retain British assets in their possession and to disregard any instructions to transfer to the Bank of London South American bills for collection or securities held for the account of other British banks."[59] Malagodi did not do this as an act of retaliation, since Sudameris funds in England were not frozen until after Italy declared war on the Allies on June 11. Malagodi and Cavin "stood out," the British charged, "as bitter and traitorous enem[ies], even before Italy entered the war." In the eyes of the Allies, Sudameris was simply an Axis bank. In February 1942, the American embassy in Chile notified Secretary of State Cordell Hull that there was "conclusive evidence" showing that Sudameris "was acting in collusion with the German banks there, in attempting to bribe certain Chilean officials by means of overdrafts" (meaning that they were allowed overdrafts).[60]

When the Holy See bought controlling interest in Sudameris in late November 1941, it held 70,000 shares. Its Milanese and Parisian partners held 40,000 each.[61] The Allies had information, however, that the Vatican would not make any decisions that would not be in the best interests of the other shareholders. It appeared to the Americans and British that the Vatican's purchase was a contrived operation and that Milan continued to run Sudameris through Malagodi and Cavin.[62] And, of course, since Bernardino Nogara sat on the board of Milan's Banca Commerciale Italiana, it seemed likely to the Allies that a secret understanding existed regarding the Vatican's purchase. The fact that the Vatican's shares in Sudameris were nested in a Swiss holding company, Profima, added to the Allies' suspicion that Nogara cloaked the true nature of the Vatican's purchase.[63] This was not the case. For purely financial reasons, Nogara had "transformed Profima from being purely a property company into a holding company able to participate in all forms of commercial, industrial, property and financial enterprises" as far back as 1938.[64] In 1945, the managing director of the Banca Commerciale Italiana, Raffaele Mattioli, testified that the reason the Vatican made the purchase anonymously through Profima was so that Profima could be the entity that told the Germans that shares were no longer available for them to buy. Only if the Germans pressed the bank would they learn that the Vatican had actually bought the bank.[65] There is solid evidence showing that, indeed, the shares were offered to the Vatican for purchase only after the Germans had approached the Milan bank asking to buy in.[66] Nogara, of course, knew that Sudameris was blacklisted when he bought the additional shares.

Why would Nogara buy a pig in a poke—a blacklisted bank? For a number of reasons, but mostly to turn a profit for the Vatican's portfolio. Other considerations for the purchase seem somewhat plausible if less compelling: the hope that the Sudameris bank could come off the black-list because its new owner was the Vatican; the hope that the Vatican could keep the bank out of German hands; and, perhaps more important than anyone can say, because Nogara was instrumental in founding the bank prior to World War I and wanted to see it succeed. But his hope that Sudameris would be delisted because the Vatican owned it proved to be wishful thinking. Throughout the war and even afterward, the Allies persisted in thinking that Nogara's action could only be seen as cloaking.[67]

One other consideration must not be overlooked—the timing of the Vatican's purchase, November 1941. Germany, formerly an ally of the Soviet Union, had sent its armies eastward into Russia in the summer of that year. One year later, Harold Tittmann reported to the State Department that the Holy See did not think the Allies could win the war. The Vatican hoped that whichever side held the upper hand after the winter campaign of 1942–1943 would sue for peace, one that would that would turn out to be advantageous for Germany.[68] It would also be financially advantageous for the Vatican. With its fascist clientele, Sudameris would be likely to pay handsome dividends in the years to come as German and Italian business, already established in South America, spread. Special Administration director Nogara would not see this as unusual, having grown accustomed to doing business for more than a decade in fascist Italy. Inside the Vatican, curial opinion was split; some clerics favored fascist government and some favored democratic government.

Bypassing Nogara, Harold Tittmann took the unusual step of cautioning Cardinal Secretary of State Maglione against buying into the blacklisted Sudameris.[69] It is quite exceptional that the United States would consider the purchase to be so important that it would ask Tittmann to carry their objections over the head of Nogara to Maglione, warning him that Sudameris gave preference to the Axis powers. The United States did this, obviously, to suggest that morally the democratic nations were in the right in the struggle against the aggressive fascists. In the mid-1930s, when the Vatican commissioned Dutch Jesuits to produce an analysis of Nazism, they warned that Hitler's Lebensraum foreign policy amounted to racial aggression. Now, in the second half of 1941, that aggression was taking its toll on Polish Catholics and Polish and Russian Jews. But the Vatican went ahead with the purchase of Sudameris. In November of 1941, in spite of the racial nature of German aggression, it evidently did not occur to the Vatican that indiscriminate investing had ethical implications.

Blacklisting caused Sudameris considerable financial loss. A run on its banks in Argentina in February 1942 created a crisis. The branches held deposits of 41,289,400 pesos, or about $12 million in 1942 dollars. Malagodi could not cover the run by withdrawing Sudameris funds or those of its Parisian and Milanese founders from the Chase Manhattan bank or other U.S. banks because these had been blocked since early 1941.[70] In order to avoid a collapse of Sudameris branches, Banco de la Nacion, the Argentine national bank, arranged a cash deposit of 3 million pesos. Sudameris had to repay the loan and 3.25 percent interest on the bailout.[71] In neighboring Brazil, Sudameris banks were actually liquidated by the government in August 1942.[72]

From the moment of its purchase of Sudameris, the Vatican tried ceaselessly to have it removed from the proclaimed list.[73] Why? The answer may simply be that Nogara wished to protect his investment. The Vatican, after all, owned shares in dozens of corporations that were blacklisted either by the Allied or Axis countries. But the Holy See left no stone unturned in its efforts to get one company, Sudameris, delisted. Because the Vatican was a neutral nation, it thought that legally the Allies should not be blacklisting its corporation, which was operating in neutral countries. The Holy See pressed its case to such an extent that it reached the top of the State Department, and a standoff between the Vatican secretary of state and the U.S. secretary of state ensued. Cardinal Maglione instructed his nuncios in Brazil and Argentina to work at their end to have the ban lifted and pressed Tittmann and Taylor again and again to request that the United States review its case. In June 1944, Hull wrote Myron Taylor saying that Sudameris could not be removed from the blacklist for the usual reasons, namely, that the Americans had reliable information that the bank was still really run by Milan or Paris and that its directors had not stopped operating in favor of the fascists.[74] The Allies saw fascist economic activity in South America as insidious. Early in 1943, the U.S. Board of Economic Warfare wrote that

> Germany has no need of spies. They get all the information they need through insurance and re-insurance companies, and they predominate in this field over all others. 45% of all receipts internationally are German companies. Aside from this they have the advantage of influencing the social and economic life of South American countries.[75]

In fact, Malagodi was making serious efforts to comply with the Allies' "Rules for Economic Warfare" to get Sudameris delisted. Malagodi notified Nogara that he had assured the Allies in his September 27, 1943, letter that he would "liquidate all facilities and creditor accounts pertaining to our other customers" (meaning those the Allies were suspicious of).[76]

No matter what steps Nogara took to placate the Americans, they responded negatively. Only a few months after Hull's last communication to Taylor, Nogara renewed his request. The Americans were occupying Rome by this time, and Nogara offered to have two Rome-based appointees take over directorship of Sudameris, promising that they would do so in way that would respect Allied interests to the fullest.[77] Throughout the blacklisting ordeal, Nogara consistently said that he had purchased the additional shares of Sudameris simply to turn a profit for the Vatican. The investment, Nogara said,

> was in the nature of a speculation as the price was very low. Since the assets are in South and North American securities and since the shares were paid for in French francs, the Profima, as result of the devaluation of the French franc, has realized a considerable book profit on the deal.[78]

As if to prove the legitimacy of the transaction with the Banca Commerciale Italiana that brought Sudameris to Profima, Nogara offered to sell half the Vatican's shares to any American investor. This, he surely thought, would speed up the delisting.

But no American investor came forward, and the State Department stuck stubbornly to its position. In September, Hull wrote to Taylor again, giving information about very specific issues the Americans wanted clarified:

—the nature of the agreement between the Paris and Milan banks
—the nature of the agreement between those banks and Profima
—how and in what currency Profima had paid for the stock
—who the actual owner of Profima might be[79]

Even though the State Department's own investigation, the Marino Report, recognized Nogara's claim that profit was the motive for his purchase of Sudameris, the Americans distrusted the pedigree of Sudameris and Profima.[80] Clearly, Pius XII put a high priority on freeing Sudameris. But nothing Nogara or Maglione, both of whom reported directly to the pope, could do would cut through the stalemate. The standoff boiled down to two views of fascism. For the Vatican, which had done business with fascists in balmier prewar days, Sudameris was business as usual. For the Allies, fascism represented aggression and suppression of rights. With a continental war under way that the United States would soon join, that was the message Tittmann wanted to impart in November 1941 when he warned Maglione about Sudameris, a message the cardinal did not take to heart. Nogara cannot be faulted for his honest efforts to free Sudameris. The Allies simply did not believe that a change in ownership from the Banca Commerciale Italiana to Profima would rout out the ingrained fascist culture in all of the Sudameris banks and sub-branches of the bank in South America. Sudameris would remain on the blacklist until August 1945, well after the end of the war.

The Holy See Buys Stock in an Insurance Corporation

Not for everyone were the interwar fascist years in Italy balmy. In 1938, Mussolini's government enacted laws that mirrored the Nuremberg laws that severely restricted Jews economically and socially. Suddenly Jewish schoolchildren could no longer attend public schools. Civil service employees lost their jobs. Jewish employees of businesses in the private sector also found themselves among the unemployed. This purge included Jewish employees of the highly developed Italian insurance industry, which accounted for about one-quarter of the country's gross national product.[81] Although Italy's Blackshirts did not brew up the horrible antisemitic violence of the November pogrom in Germany or ghettoize Jews, they strictly enforced Mussolini's anti-Jewish laws. In a word, the legislation constituted a disaster for the Jews of Italy.[82]

In 1938, when the antisemitic laws were passed in Italy, the Vatican found itself at the tail end of a nearly 2,000-year tradition of antisemitism that it sponsored under a rubric it preferred—anti-Judaism. Early in the fifth century, St. Augustine wrote *The City of God,* a book that profoundly influenced western civilization. For Jews, it meant rescue from the viciousness of earlier church fathers, because Augustine singled them out as the erstwhile chosen people whom Christians were not to kill. Eighteenth-century philosopher Moses Mendelssohn believed that this Augustinian precept saved European Jews from extinction. This was only partly true; Jews during the Middle Ages were at times eliminated by murder or expulsion. Also, in medieval times social custom began to override Church teaching regarding Jews. The folklore superstition of blood libel that accused Jews of sacrificing Christians, especially children, for ritual purposes struck deep roots. Official Church condemnation of blood libel in the twelfth and thirteenth centuries failed to suppress it. Thus, while Jews benefited from Augustine's legacy, his precept did not rescue them from discrimination at the hands of Christians. As James Carroll has pointed out in *Constantine's Sword,* Jews were only tolerated after Constantine's Edict of Milan in 313, which, in effect, made Christianity a state religion. Augustine left the policy of minimal toleration in place a century later when he wrote *The City of God,* but his guideline of promoting conversion of the Jews prevented Christians from murdering them. This tradition of not killing Jews that the Augustinian precept established held the Church (and Jew as well) in its grasp for centuries. Hitler and the Nazis sought to end it, and temporarily succeeded in doing so.

Modern popes, seldom demurring, fell in step with tradition and even with the blood libel folklore that a few of their predecessors had censured. When British cardinals asked the Vatican to officially denounce the blood libel about ritual murder at the turn of the twentieth century, the Vatican refused, saying it could not comply just "to satisfy a few dupes" in England.[83] In both the nineteenth and twentieth centuries, the Vatican newspapers *L'Osservatore Romano* and *Civilta Catholica* and Vatican radio continued to endorse stories of blood libel, the latter newspaper even at the time of the Holocaust.[84] The popes could have stopped the Vatican papers at any time from printing copy on ritual murder. When Pope Benedict XV was elected in 1914, he prevented the Vatican's newspaper from carrying material on blood libel. Other popes, including Pius XII (in the case of *Civilta Catholica*) failed to follow Benedict's example.[85] Jews under Vatican rule in the papal states prior to 1870 were subject to public humiliation at the hands of the Church, ghettoization in inhumane conditions, and economic restrictions. Down through the centuries, even to 1998 when the Vatican published its official "apology" for the Holocaust in the document *We Remember*, the Holy See never understood that its distinction between anti-Judaism and antisemitism was paper thin.[86] Time and again, what the Church called anti-Judaism led to the physical elimination of Jews. As it played out on the street, neither the Jewish victim nor the gentile protagonist could tell the difference between anti-Judaism and antisemitism.

To his credit, Pius XI saw in the fascist antisemitism of his day the arrogance of the totalitarian state. Alarmed by the new culture of blood-racial purity, he assigned American Jesuit John LaFarge the task of writing a draft of a papal encyclical condemning racism. By September 1938, the draft was completed with the assistance of two Jesuits, Gustav Gundlach and Gustave Desbousquois. Too often their draft has been belittled as bland, even counterproductive.[87] In fact, the draft criticized fascist denial of the natural rights of Jews and the practice of withholding justice and love on account of racism. The Church, the Jesuits wrote, saw these abuses with sorrow. It recommended that the pope renew the Vatican's 1928 condemnation of antisemitism. Pius XI's assignment and the resulting submission of the Jesuit draft came at an extremely timely moment. The following month, Italy promulgated its antisemitic laws, even though only four years before, Mussolini had called Hitler's antisemitism "complete craziness." Italy's racial laws contradicted the Lateran agreement between the Italian state and the Vatican, and Pope Pius XI had no intention of letting the disagreement fall between the cracks.[88] The standoff between dictator and pope escalated until Pius XI's death. After that, Pius XII let the matter drop.[89]

Such was the situation of the near and distant past when Nogara bought shares in an Italian insurance company called La Fondiaria on behalf of the Vatican in 1940. The venture's innocuous appearance belied its significance. Historian and survivor Rudolf Vrba once described the Holocaust as "murder and grand larceny."[90] Ever so insidiously, the Vatican's purchase of Fondiaria linked it to the murder and larceny of the Holocaust. Coming closer to home and the realities of 1940 Italy, the purchase aligned the Vatican with fascist antisemitism.

The Vatican's venture into the insurance industry may seem like a dismal undertaking at best, but the ramifications of the purchase deserve exploration. Fondiaria, like Sudameris, looked like a sound investment prospect to Nogara. An English insurance company, Norwich Union, founded in 1797 and authorized to do business in Italy in 1910, was sequestered in October of 1940 by the Italian government as alien property. After the company was liquidated, its entire portfolio of transport, fire, and accident policies was handed over to Fondiaria.[91] Acting no doubt on a tip, very likely either from internationally known insurance players Arnoldo Frigessi or Edgardo Morpurgo, Nogara bought 585 shares of Fondiaria Vita (life insurance) and 200 shares of Fondiaria Infortuni (accident insurance) shortly before the assets of Norwich Union were given to it.[92] Fondiaria sold life, transport, fire, and accident policies and ranked as Italy's fourth largest insurance company.[93] After the Allies occupied Italy, the military government arrested Emanuale Trigona, president of Fondiaria.

What is the significance of this seemingly insignificant small financial venture? Less than two years after Fondiaria fired its Jewish employees, the Vatican had no qualms about investing in the company. At the time of the April 1933 boycott of Jewish stores in Germany, the Holy See advised the Catholic Church in that country that it should do what it could to "alleviate the suffering of German Jews."[94] Much more suffering had befallen European Jews between the April boycott and 1940, when the Vatican bought shares of Fondiaria. Wave after wave of antisemitic legislation and social prejudice washed over Germany and Eastern European countries. In 1935, the Nuremberg Laws fundamentally abrogated what shred of legitimacy the Augustinian precept still retained. From then on, a Jew was a Jew whether he had converted to Christianity or not. How would the Church respond? In the spring of 1938, when Hungary passed antisemitic legislation, Cardinal Pacelli, speaking at the international Eucharistic congress in Budapest, still thought in terms of St. Augustine: Jews even today curse Jesus and reject Him in their hearts.[95] In other words, Jews were getting their just deserts. But later that year, Pope Pius XI began to move beyond the Augustinian precept. In September, when Italy began its persecution of Jews, Pius XI made his famous "Spiritually, we are all Semites" address, in which he roundly condemned antisemitism as "a hateful movement." Pacelli, soon to be Pius XII, did not see his predecessor's point. One might expect that just seven years after advising German Catholics to alleviate the Jews' suffering, the Vatican would refuse on principle to buy into a company that had fired its Jews in order to protest against the suffering of Italian Jews. This is not the choice the Vatican made.

Did Nogara and Pope Pius XII discuss the purchase of Fondiaria? Did they talk about its significance at all? There is no record of the meetings between Nogara and Pius, at least none that have been published by the Vatican. We can only assume that Pope Pius still thought in 1940 in terms of his Budapest address in 1938. In other words, Jews were deserving of social and economic penalties because they had rejected their savior. It may be objected that we do not even know if Pope Pius discussed Fondiaria with Nogara. In the absence of documentation from the Vatican, we cannot say that he did, but only wonder what an investor might talk about with his financial adviser if not about new acquisitions.

Before turning to the broader, more serious ramifications of owning shares in an insurance company during the Holocaust, a second ethical aspect of the purchase of Fondiaria, though minor, deserves mention. Putting Norwich Union's business under Italian trusteeship did not violate wartime convention. Although Italy and England were at war, the Vatican was not. While a neutral country would not be expected to give up its prior investments in belligerent countries, investing during the war in Fondiaria would signify doing business with the enemy as far as the Allies were concerned. Had they known about the Vatican's investment in Fondiaria, they would have blocked all of the Holy See's banking accounts in New York and all of its business interests in the United States and Great Britain. It goes without saying that the U.S. treasury would not have tolerated the currency exchange with the Vatican that facilitated the Holy See's continental missions. In plain language, the Vatican's purchase of Fondiaria shares amounted to a betrayal of trust. Nogara and Pius XII had to know this.

Deeper waters lay ahead. During the war, Italian insurance companies cooperated with their German counterparts in ruthlessly expanding business in Eastern Europe. Outright expropriation of some insurance companies—probably owned by Jews—became common in occupied Poland where the immense Munich-Re and Assicurazioni Generali companies controlled about 50 percent of all insurance business.[96] Other gentile-owned insurance companies lost clients because of price-fixing by the big German and Italian insurers but were allowed to continue doing business in fields that the foreigners had no interest in.[97] Expropriation caused the volume of business to accelerate quickly, necessitating cooperation between large German and Italian insurance companies.[98] Working together helped private insurance interests in their efforts to keep state insurance (meaning National Socialist efforts to nationalize the industry) from horning in on their territory.[99] In February 1941, Italian and German insurance companies made a formal agreement about paying insurance claims because they were doing a "greatly increased amount of business in the occupied territories."[100] The agreement included just about all types of insurance: liability, auto, rail transport, theft, group accident, construction (including construction of concentration camp facilities), fire, private businesses taken from Jews, and properties seized from the Catholic Church.[101] Recalling Vrba's definition of the Holocaust, "murder and grand larceny," we see how closely and directly insurance companies became mired in genocide. Industries in which ghettoized Jews worked to save their lives during the Holocaust had to be insured. IG Farben's immense Monowitz factory and countless smaller ones in which Jews were worked to death had to be insured.[102] Gold seized by Nazis or taken from corpses of the gas chamber victims had to be transported to the Reichsbank; the transport trains had to be insured. Rail transportation insurance obviously included trains heading for Auschwitz and the other death camps in occupied Poland.[103]

Whereas the big German insurance company Allianz and its subsidiary, Munich-Re, called the shots in the Protectorate of Bohemia and Moravia and the General Government, Italian reinsurance companies dominated in southeastern Europe, including Greece.[104] Reinsurance companies had played a vital role in the growth of international insurance. Only through reinsurance could individual companies survive great catastrophes such as the 1906 San Francisco earthquake or the 1921 burning of the Printemps department store in Paris.[105] The volume of business that grew out of Axis expansion into areas where Italian insurance played a large role led to the pooling of resources in the form of overarching reinsurance companies such as Unione Italiana di Riassicurazione, Assicurazioni d'Italia, and Compagnia di Roma.[106] The latter company owed its existence to Italy's nationalization of Lloyd's portfolios but grew to play its share in the new insurance opportunities in Eastern Europe.[107] The Italian reinsurance pools were actually consortiums of voluntary investments on the part of individual insurance firms. Fondiaria, for example, owned 12,000 shares of Roma and shares in Unione Italiana. These companies also did business in Germany. Fondiaria did business in Germany both directly and indirectly by apportioning risks to the big reinsurance pools. Fondiaria Incendio shared risks directly with the giant German reinsurance company, Munich Re, and Fondiaria Infortuni did so to an even greater extent.

Like water finding a downhill path, Vatican money found its way to the grisly side of the Holocaust. It was only a trickle in a river of business connections that interlaced Italian insurance companies through large consortiums and their business relations in turn with the big German insurance companies. When Fondiaria did business directly with Munich Re or some other German company implicated in the Holocaust, the path of Vatican money to the site of the Holocaust was more direct but not more substantial. But no matter how small the amount, Vatican money found its way into Eastern Europe during World War II and the Holocaust.

Did Pius XII know that his investment in Fondiaria funded larceny and murder? Did Nogara? History is not so dramatic or simple. When Nogara bought shares of Fondiaria in 1940, the mobile killing squads had not yet begun their murderous march east. Nor had death camps been erected in German-occupied Poland. Let us search out the proper context of the Vatican's entry into the insurance market.

Insurance was an international enterprise by nature. Italians Frigessi and Morpurgo were giants in this line of business activity. They knew very well what had befallen their co-religionists in neighboring Germany after the Nuremberg Laws were passed in 1935 (implemented in 1936) and Kristallnacht took place in November 1938. They knew that Jews had lost their radios, autos, homes, business properties, and bank accounts. They knew that the Nazi regime had thwarted Jews who tried to avoid the emigration assessment called the flight tax by taking out insurance policies in foreign countries.[108] By the time the war began, they knew that their insurance counterparts in the Reich had, in the words of historian Gerald Feldman, undermined the "elementary principles of legal and business ethics."[109] And yet, knowing all this, in October 1940, Frigessi told Kurt Schmitt, head of Allianz that

> at the present time [it is] the task of the German and Italian insurance companies to create an institution that can as far as possible take over the position of the English Lloyd's. . . . The initiative for this should come from the Italian and German companies.[110]

That was the same month, October, that the Italian government shut down Lloyds, Norwich Union, and other alien insurance companies in Italy. There is no doubt that Nogara knew which way the wind was blowing when he bought Fondiaria shares for the Vatican just before the sequestering of English insurance in Italy. After all, by the mid-1930s, the Vatican held a substantial interest in Assicurazioni Generali, Italy's biggest insurance company, and men with Vatican connections sat on its board.[111] Nogara, operating with insider information, would have known that the fascist countries were about to remake the European insurance industry. And, like Frigessi, he would have known that this would come at the expense of Jews—and not just insurance executives, insurance salesmen, and lower-level employees. Every Jew in Europe with a connection to the European insurance industry would suffer a financial loss.

So did Nogara let Pius XII know about all this? No. Nogara was not in the habit of educating his papal employers about the implications of his acquisitions on their behalf. Beginning with Pope Leo XIII's foundational encyclical, *Rerum Novarum*, some four decades before Nogara came on the papal scene, the Church had expressed serious reservations about industrial capitalism. Although the Church consistently upheld the right of private property, the Holy See inveighed against the exploitation of the working class in an unbridled capitalist industrial society.[112] Pius XI, who had appointed Nogara, weighed in heavily against capitalism in knee-jerk fashion after the consequences of the stock-market crash in 1929 spread around the world. He roundly condemned "monopoly capitalism" and "internationalism of finance." But, canon law be damned, Nogara excelled at just this brand of investment capitalism on behalf of the Vatican. History, often enough, does not make sense; theory and practice under Pope Pius XI were entirely disconnected.[113] To say that Nogara did not educate Pius XI about his investments is to altogether understate the situation within the Vatican.

Nogara's lack of concern under Pius XI about the impact of Vatican investment on the working class in Italy slipped easily into lack of concern about the impact of Vatican investments on Jews across Europe. Popes Pius XI and XII certainly knew by 1939 that Jews, rich and poor, were being despoiled of their property in Hitler's Germany. Frigessi knew this and so, presumably, did Nogara, who was on Assicurazione Generali's board. By 1939, the Holy See ought to have had ethical concerns about holding extensive stocks in Assicurazioni because of the company's willingness to block loans on policies held by Germans (meaning of course German Jews). Thus, by 1940, when Nogara bought shares in Fondiaria, he had good reason to know that his investment could lead to further shady business. Nogara was not in the habit of considering the ethical ramifications of his investments, and Pius XI and Pius XII never checked him on that score.

In late 1939, Pius learned of the mass despoilment of Polish Catholics and Jews. By the summer of 1941, he knew that the property of French Jews had been taken from them. The Church had always preached the right to private property to counter Marxist communism. Now, as fascists stole the property of Jews, it said nothing.[114] On the contrary, Nogara's retention of stock in Assicurazioni Generali and his investment in Fondiaria participated with the process by which Italians and Germans stole the assets of Jews. Lack of concern became accommodation, and accommodation became participation—unwitting but nevertheless unpardonable participation on Pius XII's part. The Vatican failed to enforce on itself its own teaching regarding modern capitalism. Perhaps this should not surprise us. Pius XII would need two more years before he spoke out about genocide.

Assuming that Nogara told the pope about buying into Fondiaria, we wonder what Pope Pius thought and said about it. Did he think back about the Jews who had recently lost their jobs at Fondiaria? Did he ask why it was timely to buy insurance stock? Did he wonder why Fondiaria's assets grew shortly after Nogara bought into it? Did he suggest that some of the profit from Fondiaria's good fortune be used to support unemployed Jews? These are questions that beg for answers, but it is quite possible that none of them occurred to Pius XII, whose attitude was that Jews had crucified their Messiah and continued to reject him.

The Vatican Bank and Imperiled Jews

During the years when the Holy See was trying again and again to have Sudameris removed from the Allies' blacklist, Pius XII learned repeatedly with greater and greater urgency about the plight of Jews. Eventually, as we have seen, he was moved to speak out about genocide in his Christmas 1942 address. After that, the critical hour for the Jews of Italy in general and those of Rome in particular came unavoidably to his attention. Two opportunities arose for the Holy See to use the resources of its Vatican City bank to help the imperiled Jews. Let us briefly review how Pope Pius dealt with these opportunities.

First came the run-up to the crisis of October 16, 1943, the day the SS seized the Jews of Rome. Before this fateful event, SS Lieutenant Colonel Herbert Kappler, chief of German security police in Rome, offered the

Jewish community a chance to buy their deliverance by providing him with 50 kilograms of gold. Whether Kappler's proposition amounted to cruel and deceitful extortion or was an attempt to stall Berlin's order to seize the Jews by showing that they could be useful for Germany's war effort is not certain.[115] Either way, his demand caused panic in the Jewish community of Rome. Jewish leaders Dante Almansi and Ugo Foà scrambled to meet Kappler's demand for over 100 pounds of gold. The SS officer had made it clear that failure to come up with the ransom would cost Jews their lives.[116]

For centuries, Jews had lived in Rome under pontifical rule—often, as we have seen, very unpleasant rule. Since 1938, they had endured even more unpleasant fascist authority, and the Holy See was financially and politically aligned with this authority. Pius XII made no social or economic objections to Mussolini's antisemitic policies. But in late September 1943, a new authority, the SS, threatened Jews with deportation, which the Vatican well knew usually meant death. The ancient Augustinian precept that guided Pope Pius taught that Jewish life was to be preserved. How would the pope react to the German threat?

Pius XII promised to loan the Jews whatever amount they needed to meet the demand for gold. This act might at first seem generous, but several factors must be considered. First, the offer was probably made in response to a request rather than a spontaneous gesture. Second, although the conditions of the loan were liberal (there was no interest and no deadline for repayment), it was a loan, not a gift. Third, the loan was conditional; it would become real only if the Jews could not raise the full sum themselves. The offer did not relieve Rome's Jews of the tremendous pressure they felt in their financial crisis.

Just how generous was Pope Pius's offer? Consider that the Vatican had taken care a few years earlier to deposit many millions of dollars' worth of gold in the United States, something in the range of $20 million. The Jews of Rome needed only a tiny fraction of that amount—about $61,600. Consider that the Vatican was an international corporation with multiple millions invested in stocks and bonds. Consider that the Vatican through its own bank and through its banking arrangements in New York and a number of other great cities could readily access its funds, something Jews could not do. Consider finally that in 1940 the American Jewish community had *given* Pope Pius $125,000—double the amount demanded by Kappler—for the relief of Catholic war refugees.[117] Two and a half years later, with the lives of Jews in Rome on the line, Pope Pius offered a *loan* for only that amount of gold that the Jewish community could not muster. The Jews had acted generously; Pius XII did not.

A few months after Kappler reneged on his word and double-crossed Rome's Jews, the Holy See had another opportunity to allow its bank in Vatican City (not Sudameris) to assist Italian Jews, and again it failed to do so. This would have cost the Vatican nothing; the money in question came from the American Joint Distribution Committee (AJDC). In the spring of 1944, the AJDC wanted to send $20,000 to assist Delasem, the Italian Jewish rescue operation that was trying to provide for thousands of hidden Jews.[118] In this instance, it needed funds to hide and feed Jewish children. Settimio Sorani, director of the Rome branch of Delasem, conveyed the situation: "The orphanage is still occupied by nuns; it will provide complete assistance (lodging, school and food) for 50 children [but] more than 440 children, sons of deported parents, under 10 years of age are in desperate need."[119] Sorani begged for help.

The question came down to getting the money in the hands of the right people in Rome—Jews, and not other Italians, who were still at war with the Allies and for whom there was little sympathy in England. The British suggested that the Americans funnel their money to the Vatican bank, from whence it could be delivered quietly and secretly into the hands of the Delasem organization.[120] There is no doubt but that such a transfer through the Vatican bank would have gone smoothly because the Delasem operation was well known inside Vatican City. Both Osborne, the English minister at the Vatican, and Tittmann, the American envoy, had done what they could over the previous months to lend a helping hand to Settimio Sorani. Furthermore, Sorani's right-hand man, Padre Benedetto, known affectionately as "the Jewish priest" because of his ongoing care and protection of the surviving Jewish population, had connections inside Vatican City. On at least one occasion, he had personally met with Pius XII to enlist his support for Jews fleeing the Gestapo. These connections between Delasem's leaders and various Vatican individuals assured that the $20,000 would end up safely and quietly in the hands of Settimio Sorani and Padre Benedetto. The scheme never became reality, however, because the Vatican refused to allow its bank to be used for this purpose.

Just a few months later, events demonstrated that funds could easily flow through the Vatican bank. In August 1944, Harold Tittmann received $5,000 that was transferred to him from the J. P. Morgan Bank in New York through Nogara's Special Administration office at the Vatican. Subsequently, an additional $5,000 dollars came to Tittmann, this time through the Vatican bank itself.[121] Tittmann was to use these funds for the benefit of American prisoners of war in Italy. Why was the Holy See willing to use its bank to help the POWs but not the Jewish orphans and other survivors whom Delasem was assisting? We must rule out that mere chance led to the different outcomes of the several occurrences. Cardinal Maglione "categorically refused" to consider using the Vatican bank to help Delasem, saying that he did not even want to make suggestions on the subject.[122] Thus, the decision not to allow the use of the Vatican bank to funnel money to Delasem was a very conscious one.

Harold Tittmann's research for his memoir throws a sharp light on some of these events. Writing to his friend Abba Schwartz in 1961, Tittmann explained that he had reached the point in his research that "concerns the treatment of the Jews in Rome after September 10 1943 [*sic*] when the Germans moved in and took over the city of Rome."[123] Tittmann wrote

> Something very bad happened on October 16 1943 for the Jews in Rome. And for the Jews in the north of Italy, then under the Salo Government, came the "Statuto di Verona" in February 1944. But I do not really know the details of these two events, but would like to.[124]

Tittmann added that he had a copy of a memo written by "Settimo Serani" (Settimio Sorani), but he noted that "while the Germans were still occupying Rome, he [Sorani] could not say too much." Tittmann was under the impression that the Vatican had done much to help the Jews during the time span he was researching. He mentioned in a subsequent communication the "fine job" the Vatican had done in getting Latin American countries to recognize passports of Polish Jews interned at a detention camp in Vittel, France.[125]

After a fruitless search of the records of the AJDC and an equally fruitless search of Delasem's records in Italy, Tittmann got in touch with Settimio Sorani himself, who, according to the Rome headquarters of the AJDC, was "the person in possession of voluminous documentation."[126] Sorani wrote a long letter to Tittmann on January 22, 1962, saying that he would provide the information about Delasem's work "when Rome was cut off from the rest of Italy after Sept. 8, 1943." It turns out, however, that Sorani did not possess "voluminous documentation" and had to rely on memory. Recalling his meetings with Tittmann during this time, Sorani wrote that

> I came to see you for the first time in November 1943, asking you to transmit to the Joint in New York a desperate appeal for assistance for thousand Jews who needed help. I turned to you again at the end of March 1944 to claim the first remittance of $20.000 in a form of a letter of credit. The second remittance of $100.000 came at the right time before June 4th.[127]

Thus, we learn that the needed funds for the Jews hidden throughout the city of Rome did indeed reach Sorani but through the International Red

Cross, not through the Vatican.[128] Sorani told Tittmann that he would recall for him the events of the period in question, including specifically the *razzia*, although "the memories are painful, and I try to forget." In fact, the memories must have proved too painful, for Sorani did not even mention the October 16 *razzia* that Tittmann had specifically mentioned in his original request for help and which Sorani said he would address as he began his account.

Sorani started the essential, central part of his communication with a tribute to Padre Benedetto, "one of the noblest characters I have ever met. He was my most valued fellow-worker," through whom I "maintained my contacts with the Vatican and Italian authorities." What Sorani wished to communicate to Tittmann was that while Benedetto lived according to the precept of love of neighbor found in Leviticus and the "Christian teachings," others, both Protestants and Catholics, did not. In this context, Sorani turned his thoughts to the Vatican and continued in a somewhat garbled passage,

> Since what was expected, and not only by us Jews, was a move by the Vatican, other than giving orders to help us financially (?) publicly the persecutors. What was expected—An outspoken and loud outcry of condemnation of what was well known to the Vatican, a condemnation in such a way that it would have put a restraint on the part of the Christian world on the unheard of crimes, which were taking place unpunished. That is the reason we were disillusioned. (The question mark is Sorani's.)[129]

Tittmann's expectations that the AJDC and ultimately Sorani would be able to provide details of Vatican assistance to the Jews of Rome were not fulfilled. Only in one respect did Sorani allude to help from the Holy See. In accounting for various kinds of assistance Delasem received, Sorani mentioned provisions from the International Red Cross and clothing from Monsignor Antonio Riberi, head of the Pontifical Commission of Assistance, which "was a real support." Financial support came, of course, from the AJDC. By 1962, time may have eroded the accuracy of Sorani's recollections. In his report at the time, May 1944, it was clear that neither clothing nor money came from the Vatican, nor, for the most part, did food.[130]

Sorani's disillusionment with the Vatican in 1943 became Tittmann's disillusionment in 1962. The former envoy to the Vatican had clearly begun his quest thinking that he would be able to throw a shining light on Pius XII just after he had come under eclipse after Rolf Hochhuth published his sensational play, *The Deputy*, in 1960. In his letter to Tittmann, Sorani said that he remembered the American diplomat "perfectly well, always courteous, always willing to help." It was clear that the same accolades could not be tendered to Pope Pius. Generously, Tittmann, passing up a perfectly legitimate opportunity to present himself in a favorable light, decided not to mention anything at all about Pius XII and the Jews of Rome. Not even the famous roundup of October 16, 1943, can be found in Tittmann's memoir.

In addition to Settimio Sorani, there is one other eyewitness to the predicament of Roman Jews during the German occupation who has not yet been discussed in historical literature. Reuben Resnik worked for the AJDC in Italy during the war and became its director in that country after the war. Resnik, an American Jew, could function for the AJDC in Rome while the city was still under German rule because he was actually an OSS agent who worked with anti-Nazi partisans. In November, a few months after the war ended, Resnik, accompanied by Dr. A. Leon Kubowitzki, secretary-general of the World Jewish Congress, went to the Vatican to pay their respects to the leader of the Catholic Church. This is what Resnik said on that occasion:

> I thanked him in the name of the American Joint Distribution Committee for the splendid work that had been done by the Catholic clergy in Italy and the great mass of the Catholic people during the period of enemy occupation for the Jewish people in need.[131]

In a statement made years later, in 1988, Resnik was profuse in his praise of Italian Catholics, many of whom he mentioned by name for their efforts to save Jews during the Nazi occupation: cardinals Roncalli and Boetto (Genoa), Boetto's secretary Padre Repetto, Padre Salvi, Monsignor Basalen, and, of course, Padre Benedetto. But Resnik had no words of gratitude for Pius XII:

> While I was received in private audience and otherwise honored by the Vatican, I must be frank to tell you that I was not a great admirer of top Vatican policy with respect to the Holocaust. During its height there was constant apologizing by the Vatican for its inability to do anything about it when as a matter of fact no effort was made to do anything about it.[132]

Resnik went on to say that he believed his audience with Pope Pius was just for publicity purposes. Afterward, he said, "a big story was published in the Vatican paper, the Osservatore Romano," that was picked up worldwide. It is difficult to say to what extent Resnik was influenced by adverse publicity and opinion about Pius XII over nearly three decades, but his criticism of the pope squares with the wording of the message of gratitude he made in the 1945 audience.

We may conclude that Sorani's and Resnik's statements made during the war and immediately after it and their statements made years later accurately reflect the absence of concentrated concern by Pope Pius for Roman Jews during the German occupation of that city. This attitude would explain the offer of only a loan just before the October *razzia* and the Vatican's refusal to allow the bank of Vatican City to facilitate an exchange of funds to benefit Delasem.

Fool's Gold

That's what the gold-digger's nuggets were called that looked like gold but weren't—fool's gold. During the war, the Vatican probably profited from trade in gold, but it was tainted gold, tainted by wolfram ore—fool's gold. I conclude this chapter on Vatican capitalism by exploring the mining industry in the Iberian Peninsula and Nogara's apparent investment in it. "Apparent" is the operative word in what follows because there is only strong evidence. In the absence of the Vatican's own records, there is no absolute proof that the Vatican exploited the peninsular mining bonanza.

Until the onset of World War II, tungsten, derived from wolfram, had largely been used only for light bulb filaments. So vital was wolfram or tungsten for World War II military hardware that no country could wage war without it. But this metal element, whose hardness approached that of diamonds, could be found in abundance on the European continent only in the Iberian Peninsula. When steel was reinforced with tungsten carbide, it could turn out artillery shells capable of crippling a tank, to name just one of its myriad military uses. Germany's Gerlich anti-tank gun could penetrate the steel of a Russian T-34 tank. Germany consumed 160 tons of pure tungsten every month during the war.[133] Until Operation Barbarossa, Germany was able to import tungsten via the Transiberian Railroad. Had Hitler subsequently been unable to procure tungsten from the Iberian Peninsula, the war would have ended in months if not weeks.

The two Iberian countries, Spain and Portugal, were neutral. They found themselves in a position to realize unheard-of profits as their exports soared, and they capitalized on their good fortune. Antonio de Oliveira Salazar, the industrious dictator of Portugal, agreed to sell tungsten on the open market but on a fifty-fifty basis, half to Allied countries and half to Axis countries.[134] Spain also sold to both Germany and the Allies. This arrangement ignited a bidding war between Germany on the one side and the United States and England on the other; neither the United States or Britain needed Iberian tungsten because they could obtain it elsewhere. Their strategy was to starve Germany of the ore if at all possible. This competition set off a mad scramble for tungsten by Spanish and Portuguese citizens. Mining it often amounted to just picking it up where it lay exposed on the ground. Salazar had to double the wages of olive pickers to keep them harvesting food instead of tungsten, and Franco in Spain had to use force to keep civil bureaucrats at their desks. Wildcat miners became so numerous in Galicia that a problem arose when the Allies ran low on pesetas, the currency that the fossickers demanded for their metallic treasure.

Driven by the war and the market, the price of tungsten rose to a high of $22,000 a ton. Spain added a high export tax that amounted to $13.5 million a year.[135] The United States could pay the ever-escalating price for its share of the tungsten, but Great Britain could not and ended by running up an IOU to Portugal alone for $322 million.[136] Germany would have been in similar straits had it not stolen the gold of the countries it occupied or those that had Nazi puppet rulers. Germany took $53 million from Austria, $33 million from Czechoslovakia, $16 million from Poland (and Danzig), $154 million from Holland, $223 million from Belgium, $25 million from Yugoslavia, $5 million from Luxembourg, $63 million from Italy, and $32 million from Hungary, for a total of just over $600 million.[137] At the end of the war, Germany had paid out $741 million of its mostly ill-begotten gold. Much of this treasure poured into the Iberian countries. Spain got $123 million from Germany alone.[138] Portugal started the war with $64 million of gold in its vaults and ended up in 1945 with $356 million.[139]

Let us revisit the Vatican's disbursement schedule at the time it asked the U.S. Treasury Department if it could use the country's facilities to exchange dollars for Swiss francs. In addition to the francs, the Vatican's budget specified $55,000 in Spanish pesetas and $214,000 in Portuguese escudos. An additional $300,000 fell loosely under the rubric of transactions.[140] Nogara shifted funds from other countries to Spain and Portugal as well, but we do not know to what extent he did so. He certainly had the capability to do this, but because the Vatican's books remain closed we have no way of knowing how much more he funneled to the Iberian Peninsula. Why was the budget for Spain and Portugal so much higher than for other European countries?

The Vatican told the U.S. Treasury Department that about half of the money in pesetas and escudos, $155,000, would be allocated to buying foodstuffs to import to Vatican City. This seems highly unlikely. Severe food shortages plagued Spain. The government could not even guarantee the bread supply in many districts. "People actually died of starvation," notes one scholar.[141] Governments have been known to let their people starve while exporting grains but this did not seem to be the case with Spain, nor would it speak well of the Vatican if it knowingly took bread out of the mouths of the poor. Portugal, which was better off than Spain, nevertheless was importing basic foodstuffs during the war as before.[142] The Allies allowed Salazar to export certain foodstuffs that the country imported from its colonies, but these were to go to Spain.[143] The Allies kept watch over the Iberian coast to make sure that additional foods could not get to Germany via the peninsula. It is possible that Portugal exported sardines to the Vatican, that being one of its major export commodities, but this seems unlikely. When Argentina tried to send a shipload of food to the Vatican in October 1943, it was held up for months because the British did not want to issue the navicert without which no seaborne vessel was safe.[144] I have found no records of exports to the Vatican either by land or sea from the Iberian Peninsula. Furthermore, food was as scarce in Vatican City as it was elsewhere in Italy. Pope Pius rationed food at the same rate as the Italian government, and during the war years Italians suffered increasingly as their diet moved from restricted to severely restricted.[145] All of these factors lead one to conclude that the $155,000 food item in the Vatican budget actually had a different purpose. Even if it did pay for imports, that still leaves another approximately $150,000 unaccounted for along with whatever other funds Nogara might have shifted to the two Iberian countries.

Of course the next question is, if the money was not for food, what was it for, and the obvious answer is to cash in on the mining bonanza. Nogara's skills were exactly right for venturing capital into mining. Earlier in his career, Nogara, a degreed engineer, had had experience in mining in England, on the continent, and in the Near East. As the potential for tungsten began to be developed in the fine-tool industry during the interwar years, Nogara would have immediately grasped the magnitude of the discovery. When World War II broke out, Nogara would have understood why tungsten carbide would be the high-tech metal of the conflict. This is the context that induces us to ask whether the timing of the Holy See's application to the United States for Swiss francs, Spanish pesetas, and Portuguese escudos in the summer of 1941 was happenstance. That marked exactly the moment of the war when Hitler double-crossed Stalin and invaded the Soviet Union, thus ending shipments of tungsten to Germany through Russia. Was it happenstance that the Holy See transferred $10,000 from the National City Bank of New York to the Banco Espirito Santo e Comercial de Lisbon in November 1941?[146] How many other such transfers from how many other banks were there?

Let us recall Nogara's credentials in international finance. While still involved with mining, Nogara was appointed a representative of the major Italian bank, the Banca Commerciale, in Istanbul. "Such was the reputation he had developed," writes John Pollard, "that Nogara was appointed to the Italian delegation to the Economic Committee at the Versailles Peace Conference of 1919."[147] As a consequence of these various appointments, Nogara had established firm personal contacts with leading financial persons in Italy and abroad. After Pius XI appointed him to head the Special Administration, Nogara diversified Vatican funds, making banking deposits worldwide. In addition, Nogara made substantial investments in gold and currencies, especially sterling silver.[148]

We can readily grasp the possibilities that the Iberian Peninsula represented in 1941 to a person with Nogara's mining and financial expertise. Did he guess right? Did Vatican funds do well in the Iberian Peninsula during the war? The investment in Portugal, at least, turned out to be extremely lucrative. We have already seen how much of the gold in Europe found its way to Salazar's bank as a result of the competition between Germany and the Allies for tungsten. What happened to that gold? A fraction of it took the following route:

Germany sent its gold, or gold it had stolen, to Swiss banks

Germany debited gold and Swiss francs to Portugal for tungsten

Portugal sold Swiss francs to the U.S. Treasury Department

Chase Manhattan Bank debited the Vatican to pay the U.S. Treasury Department for Swiss francs

The Vatican invested Swiss francs in Portugal

To satisfy the Vatican appetite for Swiss francs, the U.S. treasury bought 1 million dollars' worth of them from Sweden and 900,000 dollars' worth from Portugal in 1943.[149] The apostolic delegate in the United States was the person who controlled the Vatican's account at Chase. In May of 1942, the United States assured the Vatican that it would continue to try to provide the Swiss francs the Holy See requested. In 1943, the Treasury Department found ways to simplify this arrangement. A treasury official wrote:

> Since it appears that this government is committed to make Swiss francs available to the Vatican and because the Vatican authorities have permitted this government and certain Latin American governments to remit funds to their representatives at the Vatican by the deposit of dollars to the account of the Vatican authorities at J.P. Morgan Company in New York, thus obviating the necessity of remitting through Switzerland, FF would recommend the request be approved.[150]

This international movement of funds worked nicely until the Vatican upset the applecart by sending $45,000 to Japan in late summer 1943. After that, Nogara had to find francs and escudos elsewhere.

Of course the amount of German gold involved in the chain outlined above constituted only a tiny fraction of the amount that ended up in Portuguese banks. What did Portugal do with the gold? The collapse of the U.S. stock market in 1929 and the subsequent international economic depression caused most countries to abandon the gold standard. This circumstance no doubt dictated Salazar's policy of buying foreign currencies with some of his accumulated stash of gold while keeping the remainder. In this way Portugal would be protected should the world return to the gold standard in the not-distant future, as many thought likely. If, on the other hand, currencies floated freely, the value of the escudo against other currencies should appreciate considerably, as would at least some of the other currencies that Salazar acquired. Thus, we find that in October 1944, Portugal bought 259 million British pounds, $89 million U.S. dollars, 32 million Swiss francs, and the currencies of eleven other countries. The following month, Portugal bought 132 million British pounds, $47 million U.S. dollars, and smaller sums in the currencies of thirteen other countries.[151] In spite of these extraordinary expenditures, Salazar still had a great deal of gold in his vaults toward the end of the war. The Tripartite Commission for the Restitution of Monetary Gold estimated that about $124 million in gold stolen by Germany reached Portugal. The Bretton Woods conference determined that looted gold had to be returned to its rightful owners. Switzerland, Sweden, and Spain complied with the ruling, but Portugal refused.[152] Salazar had taken care to have Germany pass its gold through Swiss banks rather than having it sent directly from German banks to Portugal. Since it was not known at the time that the Swiss were Hitler's bankers, funneling German payments through Switzerland for the Portuguese exports of tungsten gave the transactions a semblance of regularity. So, at any rate, argued Salazar. The Allies found the Portuguese dictator a stubborn negotiator. When Salazar refused to return the 44 tons of gold the Allies initially demanded, they reduced their demand to 38, then to 21, then to 7, and finally to only 4 tons.[153] Thus, in the end, Portugal pocketed most of the stolen German gold.

How then did Nogara exploit Portugal's windfall? As there are no records, we can only guess. One possibility is that the Vatican bought Portuguese bonds. The vast infusion of money from Axis and Allied nations flooded Portugal with cash. The country's industrial base could not begin to absorb the cash in the form of investments.[154] To control the situation as best he could, Salazar floated a bond in the spring of 1943 in order to "take funds out of circulation."[155] Nogara may have purchased the bond, which promised 2.75 percent annual interest. There may have been other bonds as well. A second possibility is that the government allowed the Vatican to buy stock directly in its mining enterprise. Given the warm relations between Salazar and the Holy See, it does not seem out of the question that Salazar would allow the Holy See to share in a very minor way in the tungsten miracle. A third likelihood is that Nogara bought escudos in the expectation that their value would soar. As early as 1943 the escudo was worth six times more to the dollar than it had been before the war. No doubt more complex possibilities for exploiting Portugal's bonanza existed. Nogara's skill in this regard certainly outpaced this historian's speculations about how he would manipulate the situation.

It was a known fact in 1944 that Germany had stolen the gold reserves of a number of European countries and that much of that gold had ended up in Portugal. A person of Nogara's financial experience and savvy would have known this much earlier. After all, as a result of his work at the Versailles peace conference, Nogara was well acquainted with Germany's economic situation at a time when the world was still operating on the gold standard. The conclusion is unavoidable: Nogara indirectly trafficked in the arms race and did so knowing that any resulting profit derived from stolen property. (On the other hand, Nogara would not have known that a minuscule portion of the gold sent to Portugal had been extracted from the mouths of corpses—Holocaust victims.) If Portugal exemplifies how the greedy drive for profit removed compunctions about "consorting with the Nazi regime and receiving its looted treasures," the same judgment applies to the Holy See.[156] Pius XII paid as little attention to the ethical implications of Nogara's venture capital in Iberian mining as Pius XI had to the involvement of the Vatican's financial holdings in industries profiting from the Italo-Ethiopian war in 1935.[157]

A second aspect of funneling money to the Iberian peninsular countries jangles an ethical nerve center. The Vatican indicated that the funds sent to Spain and Portugal were for food exports. As far as I have been able to determine, that was not the truth. Furthermore, under no circumstances would the U.S. treasury have facilitated the dollar-franc exchange had it known that the francs would be used to make a profit at the expense of the United States in a bidding war for tungsten. If, as it seems, that was the purpose of the currency exchange, then clearly the Vatican betrayed the trust of the United States. If these verdicts rest too greatly on surmise, let the Vatican open its books for clarity's sake.

"Modern Capitalism Is Absolutely Irreligious"

Appropriating this observation of John Maynard Keynes, R. H. Tawney wrote in his famous book *Religion and the Rise of Capitalism* that the "Christian virtues that allowed capitalism to come into being and become dominant" had become extinct.[158] Capitalism, Tawney believed, had become nothing but "a mad grab for money" that had nothing to do with Christian morality. In their teachings since Leo XIII, the popes had insisted that capitalism be tempered by moral considerations. Why did the popes not follow their own teaching? Perhaps the deep scar left by the loss of the papal states explains why Nogara's hands were left unfettered. Having lost their landed patrimony, Pius XI and XII would have been eager to preserve their liquid patrimony. Still, this seems a weak leg on which to stand when it comes to neglecting one's own moral directives. In fact, John Pollard gives credence to the opinion that Nogara accepted the appointment to the Special Administration only on the condition that he not "be restricted by religious or doctrinal considerations."[159] Whether or not any such agreement was actually struck does not really matter so much if, as seems certain, Nogara was prepared to make a profit during the war regardless of where or how a profit was to be made.

The forays of this chapter into Vatican wartime capitalism present an unflattering picture. The manner in which its financial dealings touched on the Holocaust only deepens concern about the Holy See's financial activity. Let us review the ledger:

The Vatican appears to have been less than honest in applying to the United States for banking privileges.

The Vatican's purchase of Sudameris indicates its ambivalence, not impartiality, about the war's outcome.

The Vatican's purchase of Fondiaria stock indicates Pius XII's lack of concern for Italian Jews.

The Vatican's failure to assist Delasem indicates the same.

The Vatican's retention of Assicurazione Generali stock shows a lack of prudent papal oversight.

The Vatican *apparently* sought profit by exploiting the high-tech tungsten armaments race.

The Vatican broke its word with the United States by investing in Fondiaria and (apparently) in the tungsten trade.

The Vatican also broke its word to the United States when it sent $45,000 to Japan.

Much, of course, could be forgiven the Vatican if it had lavishly provided for the victims of the war, whether they were refugees or POWs.

The Vatican had traditionally been liberal with its funds for charitable purposes. When such charity benefited Italy, it was a way to both assist the poor and silence anticlerical voices. But the Vatican spent much as well outside Italy. Benedict XV had spent millions for the poor, for refugees, and for POWs during World War I. In 1920, he "raised 50 million lire for famine relief in Russia."[160] Pius XI had carried on the relief work of his predecessor. Given the strong papal tradition of humanitarian work, it seems entirely likely that Pius XII gave as liberally as Benedict XV and Pius XI before him. Pius XII sent a donation of an unspecified amount to the nuncio of Hungary, Angelo Rotta, who distinguished himself for his remarkable efforts to save Jews.[161] Earlier, in 1940, the Vatican on two occasions contributed small amounts of money—3,000 and 10,000 lire—for Jews.[162] There is not much evidence to suggest that Pope Pius XII characteristically dipped into papal finances to assist Jews, but should this turn out to be the case, then some of the Holy See's ethical breaches itemized above will seem picayune. We do not yet know the extent of the largess of Pius XII during World War II.[163] What we know is that when the *razzia* occurred, Pope Pius offered the desperate Roman Jews only a loan and that he failed to assist Delasem's rescue work when Jews at his doorstep were in dire need.

6

THE FIRST COLD WAR
WARRIOR

At the end of the war, thirteen years remained of Pius XII's papacy, years that included the onset of the Cold War in the summer of 1947. But for the pope, the Cold War did not begin in 1947. It began, rather, in 1945, and had been presaged by the defeat of the German army at Stalingrad in 1943. Pope Pius was the world's first Cold War warrior.

During the years after World War II, Pius XII believed that a military showdown between the Soviet Union and the west would occur. If that were to happen, it would have his blessing. On several occasions Pope Pius actually urged war. Only in 1948 did he sound a warning about atomic warfare, and even then, he hedged somewhat. The following year, in an address in which the pope banned any political accommodation with communism, he referred to his mostly male audience as "soldiers prepared for battle." The pope's entire "tone and bearing was that of a militant leader who was prepared to engage the enemy at whatever cost."[1]

Adolf Hitler committed suicide on April 30, 1945. Admiral Karl Dönitz assumed control of the German government and the army surrendered. On May 8th, Truman and Churchill announced V-E day, the end of the war in Europe. Much of the western world rejoiced ecstatically. Pope Pius did not. The war had ended exactly as Pius XII hoped it would not—that is, with the Soviet Union looming over western Germany and Western Europe and with a hostile Communist Yugoslavia backed up on Italy. In spite of the just-concluded Holocaust, the pope believed that "Russian Communists were even more nationalistic and more brutal than the Germans."[2]

The view from Vatican City was almost totally dismal. Jesuit Father Schiltz, paraphrasing Pius XII, said that "neither during the war, nor now that it is finished, have Americans been able to comprehend the fatal damage which they have inflicted on this continent, casting it into the depths of misery by aerial bombardment." Pius spoke with good reason about the depths of misery that wracked Europe. Bombed out and devastated, Europe, Pius believed, was now ripe for plucking by Communists. The Americans had blundered fatefully by rejecting Admiral Dönitz's offer after Hitler's suicide: "Sirs, if you wish, here we are brought to our knees, but permit us to join you against communism."[3]

Europeans turned angry eyes toward Germany after the war, not so much because of what Hitler had done to the Jews but because of what he had done to them. But Pope Pius, choosing not to add to Germany's burden of guilt, blamed the Anglo-Americans for Europe's devastation.[4] While it is true that their carpet bombing had taken an enormous toll that included many children and the aged, Pius should not have singled out the Allies. But his larger point concerned, of course, the Soviet threat, and here he glimpsed the future squarely, as the Anglo-Americans were to learn.

The immediate Communist threat menaced Pope Pius in two ways. The Communist party in Italy would soon become the largest in Western Europe, and it was capably led by Palmiro Togliatti, whom Pius believed was a Russian agent.[5] Also near to home lay the second Communist threat, Marshal Josip Tito in Yugoslavia. Even before the end of the war Tito had begun to settle the score with the Ustaša, which meant with the Catholic Church as well because of the close relations between the two. While Togliatti's Communists menaced Pius domestically, in the pope's mind anyway, Tito menaced him as a nearby armed aggressor. What can be detected in the pope's alarm is an extension of his twofold wartime anxiety when he worried about Rome's destruction from without and from within, by Communists at home. A Togliatti government with Communist Tito next door would go far to make that nightmare a reality. Pope Pius exaggerated his peril, but the Church in Italy was undeniably facing a challenge, perhaps even a severe test. The Berlin Airlift and eventual building of the Berlin Wall, where one American president after another posed for a photo opportunity, has diverted historical memory away from Italy, where the contest between communism and the free world was first met—in Trieste.

Farther afield Pope Pius saw an equally dangerous situation. The predominantly Catholic countries of Eastern Europe would inevitably fall in the shadow of Soviet Russia and atheistic communism. For the first time, a Roman pontiff would have to deal with that situation and on a truly massive scale. In late 1944 and early 1945, Stalin ordered a dozen priest-professors in Lublin murdered and deported 400 additional priests to "the frozen tundra of interior Russia."[6] In Pius's mind, Western Europe would be next. "*Paupertas meretrix,* poverty is the greatest seducer, and Europe's total impoverishment," Pius thought in 1946, "is driving her straight into the Communist embrace."[7] Of course, if this were to be the fate of Western Europe in the north, the same destiny would befall cisalpine Europe. Pius did not think the Americans were capable of fighting off the Red menace, because, as he said, they "are too unfamiliar with Europe and its problems."[8] Here he was entirely mistaken, but it would take two years from the end of the war for the Americans to prove themselves—"a steep learning curve," in the words of historian Tony Judt.[9]

Half of Pius's beloved Germany already found itself in the grasp of the Soviets at the war's end. Consequently, what concerned the pope was not that country's recent horrendous past but its future. Westerners, having seen the pictures from Buchenwald, Dachau, and other concentration camps, looked aghast at the Germans. When German citizens were marched past the corpses of starved Jews, they diverted their eyes from them. Like the Germans, Pope Pius refused to look at the pictures that Tittmann and Osborne had prepared for him that demonstrated the complicity of ordinary Germans in the Holocaust. After the war Pius showed more interest in using ideologically committed fascists to fight communism than he did in bringing those of them who had perpetrated crimes against Jews to justice. This is why, as we will see in subsequent chapters, he protected Ustaša criminals in Rome. Pope Pius defended the Germans themselves, at least German Catholics, whom, he incorrectly opined, had resisted Hitler with all their hearts.[10] During the war, Pius had wanted German Christians to be the bulwark against Russian communism; he did not afterward want to see them guilt-ridden because of what they had done to the Jews, nor did he want to see them fall victim to Soviet communism.

In only one respect had the war ended well for Pius XII. He emerged as the savior of Rome. In his efforts to save the Eternal City, Pope Pius acted proactively. This contrasts with his passively active response to the Holocaust. When approached by the World Jewish Congress or the bishop of Berlin or the Dutch Church or any one of a number of diplomats about the murder of the Jews, the Vatican had a stock reply: the Holy See will continue to do all that it can to alleviate those suffering on account of the war. At times the Vatican actually did take remedial action. But this was always *in response* to a request. When it came to saving Rome, on the other hand, Pope Pius was proactive. Again and again he contacted Washington, as we have seen, imploring the Allies not to bomb Rome. When he could not extract a promise not to bomb, he threatened them with a public protest. Noting the contrast between Pope Pius's passivity when it came to the Jews and his proaction when it came to bombing, British minister Osborne had told Secretary of State Maglione in December 1942 that "instead of thinking of nothing but the bombing of Rome, the [Holy See] should consider [its] duties in respect to the unprecedented crime against humanity of Hitler's campaign of extermination of the Jews."[11]

Pope Pius paid the chiding no heed. Rome had to be saved, and in saving the city the pope won the favor and admiration of Romans. Ambassador Weizsäcker noted that with Mussolini either sacked or in discredit, Pius stood to gain enormous prestige if he could protect the Eternal City from bombs.[12] Early in the war, before Italy became a combatant, fascist youth had surrounded Pope Pius's car, screaming at him "death to the pope." The protest may have been staged as a warning to Pius XII to stop urging Mussolini to stay out of the war, but the incident inhibited the pope, who did not venture out of Vatican City again.[13] Not, that is, until three years later when the Basilica of St. John Lateran was bombed along with the surrounding neighborhood. Instinctively, Pius realized it was his moment, and he hastened to the badly damaged church. Historian Paul O'Shea described the scene: as fires burned, sirens sounded, and ambulances screeched, Pius, his white robes stained with dirt and blood, heard confessions and anointed the dying. The "effect was electric."[14] Pope Pius had reconquered Rome. From then on, the eyes of Romans were on the pope, not on the disgraced dictator or the king. With civil government humiliated and enfeebled, Pius XII stood tall as the protector of the Eternal City. Tittmann reported that he "was now enjoying unprecedented popularity both in the capital and elsewhere in Italy."[15] Weizsäcker disclosed that both sides had respected the pope's wishes, even if they were unwilling to grant Rome the status of an open city. Pius had created a "nimbus" over Rome, Weizsäcker wrote, and "both of the wars' combatants fell under the spell of this nimbus."[16] The OSS, paraphrasing the local media, filed this report:

> On March 12, 1944, all the bells of Rome rang out to summon the people to the piazza of St. Peter's. The pope wanted to speak to the people of Rome. The crowd gathered and the Holy Father spoke urging them to feed and clothe the needy, etc. When he finished he exclaimed "Hands off Rome! Those responsible, be prudent!" The crowd left with new hope. And it happened as he ordered. On June 5th [the day after the Allied occupation of Rome] the people returned to St. Peter's to applaud their savior—the

Roman pope saved Rome. After that Romans said to each other that we
must listen to his advice to rebuild our Italy. And so Rome, capital of Italy,
but first of all, moral capital of the world, was spiritually re-given to the
pope.[17]

The refusal of the Anglo-Americans to grant Rome open-city status greatly annoyed Pius and probably accounts for his one-sided finger-pointing
after the war regarding aerial bombardments. But in one single respect,
preserving the sanctuary of the Eternal City, Pius could be pleased with
himself and with the outcome of World War II. The pope's highly favorable stature among the Italians was a matter of great importance as the
country turned its attention to domestic politics in 1945.[18]

What most of the world feared in that year was a Nazi-style German revival; what Pius feared was communism. As Pope Pius read the
past, he stood at the end of a long history of enmity between the Vatican
and communism. Decades before World War II, atheistic communism
had horrified the Holy See. As we saw in chapter 3, Pope Leo XIII first
condemned communism as a social and economic system in 1878 in his
encyclical *Quod Apostolici Muneris* and then repeated the condemnation numerous times, notably in *Rerum Novarum* (1891). By this time,
European socialism had become Marxist, or at least pseudo-Marxist.
The German Socialist Party, the continent's largest and most successful,
talked the talk of revolution and atheism under its fiery leader, August
Bebel. The socialist agenda called for the disestablishment of (state-supported) churches and seizure of private property, including the Church's,
by the proletariat (actually, the state).

Such an agenda threatened the Vatican at its roots. Having lost
most of its landed patrimony, which had stretched from the west to the
east coasts of Italy, to the liberal movement of nationalism, the Vatican
viewed communism as the next catastrophe. From 1870 to the end of
World War I, regaining the Vatican's lost territories constituted the single
greatest concern of successive popes, every one of whom repeated Pope
Leo's condemnation of Marxist socialism.[19] During the last quarter of
the nineteenth century, concern over its lost patrimony often seemed to
occupy the Vatican more than spiritual matters.

The Church's irrevocable opposition to Marxist communism and
subsequent fear of Russian bolshevism became dramatic during the two
world wars. When in 1917 communism took on the form of bolshevism
and the revolutionary socialist agenda became a reality in Russia, the
popes ratcheted up their anti-communist rhetoric. The danger that Bolshevist communism would spread to Western Europe became obvious
after World War I. Amid general chaos, a number of German cities wit-

nessed revolutionary movements in which Marxists participated. Nuncio
Pacelli had a ringside seat on Kurt Eisner's temporarily successful putsch
in Munich. Pacelli famously stared down a Communist revolutionary
who had barged into his residence near the fashionable Karolinenplatz
and held the future pope at gunpoint. That many of the Communists
were Jews—Leon Trotsky, Karl Liebknecht, "Red Rosy" Luxemburg,
and Eisner, to name only a few (and Marx himself, of course)—registered
at the Holy See. As these events took place in Germany, Achille Ratti, the
papal nuncio in Poland, witnessed the Soviet army's abuses of Catholics,
mistreatments which left the future Pope Pius XI deeply distrustful of
communism.[20]

The worldwide depression of the 1930s greatly boosted the Vatican's
fear of the Communist menace. To many western onlookers, the Soviet
five-year plan appeared to be a model of economic growth. Pope Pius
XI feared that "the determined atheists of Moscow and the Comintern
would attempt to use the social distress to further their own political
ends."[21] As the depression worsened, Pope Pius launched an anti-Bol-
shevist campaign with a "solemn expiatory Mass for Russia and its persecuted Catholics in St. Peter's on 19 March, 1930."[22] In his encyclical
Quadragesimo Anno, Pius wrote that communism was not the remedy
for the west's ailing economies. Again in *Caritate Christi Compulsi* of
May 1932 the pope lambasted bolshevism, saying that it aimed to ex-
plode "every bond of law, human or divine; they engage openly and in
secret in a relentless struggle against religion and against God Himself."
Communism, Pius said, was the "most perilous of all evils." Pius XI
would return to this theme relentlessly.[23]

During the interwar era, the Vatican favored Europe's fascist governments because they were not godless. There could be no compromise
with atheistic communism (as Pius XI noted in the 1937 encyclical *Divini
Redemptoris*). Cardinal Pacelli fully agreed with this assessment. During his visit to the United States in 1936, Pacelli told Myron Taylor that
the Soviet Union was the greatest threat looming over the future of the
west.[24] The fascist governments of Western Europe seemed an antidote
to communism in papal eyes. Largely for this reason Pius XI welcomed
Hitler and signed the concordat with Germany early in 1933. The pope
wanted Italy's fascist leader Benito Mussolini to work with other western
Christian countries against Bolshevist Russia.[25] By the mid-1930s, however, the racism of Nazi Germany had become apparent to Pius XI, and
the Vatican began nervously to hedge its bets, unable to decide whether
its new foe, Nazism, or its traditional enemy, communism, spelled the
greater danger.[26]

Pius XII repeated past denunciations and added his own. In 1941, he emphasized the right to private property and importance of ownership in *La Solennita della Pentecoste* (which commemorated *Rerum Novarum*). While admitting a need for wider distribution of property, Pope Pius asserted that Christians cannot have a social order that denies possession of private property.[27] Wasting no time, Pius attacked communism in his first postwar Christmas address, saying that it placed the interest of the state over that of the individual.[28] In a directive to a French labor leader, Pius pointed out the advantage of corporate units over nationalization of industry.[29] The 1947 encyclical *Mediator Dei* emphasized the need for religious observance to counteract the threat that atheist communism "presents to [religion's] very existence."[30] In the following year, Pius XII actually excommunicated Catholics if they joined a communist party or supported communism. In his 1949 letter to the German bishops on the occasion of their annual *Katholikentag,* Pius stressed the binding force of his decrees against communism.[31] He wrote to the workers of Spain in 1951 promoting the right to property and condemning class warfare.[32] In 1952, Pius reiterated his condemnation of communism and consecrated Russia once again to the Immaculate Heart of Mary.[33] Similar messages supporting private property and condemning communism continued for the remaining years of Pius XII's papacy.

How, in turn, did Moscow view Pope Pius? Reporting on a *Pravda* article, American diplomat George Kennan summed it up succinctly:

> Pope never censure[d] Hitler or Mussolini. Pope asks for lenient treatment of Nazi prisoner[s] and war criminals. During the war Vatican hatched plan for a peace at Russia's expense. Vatican is closely connected with monopoly capital through banks and concerns of many countries.[34]

The Kremlin's perceptions of Rome, it must be said, were every bit as accurate as Rome's perceptions of Moscow. Be that as it may, the two antagonists headed on a collision course. Without doubt, Pius believed at the end of World War II that the showdown between the two belief systems would boil over in devastated postwar Europe during his papacy. The chance that the eruption would first come in Italy seemed only too real.

Italy, 1945–1948

With the end of the war in sight, U.S. secretary of state Cordell Hull wrote to Tittmann suggesting that he attempt to quiet the pope's fear of communism. What caused a nation to fall to communism, Hull said, was "the internal financial weakness of a country."[35] Such theorizing made no impact on the pope, who continued to make known his concern about Soviet Communist advances into the west in his 1944 Christmas address.[36] Closer to home, Pius worried that it might already be too late to save Italy from communism. In a 45-minute audience with an American, he noted the Communist infiltration of Italian farmers, and he reacted angrily to Don Luigi Sturzo, founder of the Italian Popular Party, who had pointed to the need for cooperation during the war between Catholics and Communists in an article in the *New York Times*.[37]

As the war drew inexorably toward its conclusion, Europeans searched for some political design or framework to fill the gap left by the demise of fascism. The freewheeling laissez-faire liberalism of the nineteenth century was out of the question; rather, some kind of an economy controlled or directed by a nonfascist state found favor. Some Italian Catholics wanted to experiment with a Catholic-Communist parliamentary democracy that would embrace some of Marx's social teachings while eschewing materialism. In Pius's eyes, however, this amounted to letting a communist foot in the door, Togliatti's to be sure, whom Pius distrusted. Thus, in July 1944, Pius XII denounced the Catholic-Communist movement that was just aborning.[38] Early in 1945 the Holy See returned to the issue of "Christian Leftists." The movement, the Vatican said, was not in line with Catholic teaching and could only turn out to be a halfway house for communism. An OSS operative reported that "the Vatican seems to prefer that part of the group still small becomes outspoken Communist now, rather than [later] have a full grown left party instrument of Communists."[39] *L'Osservatore Romano* carried an article on January 4 criticizing the movement. Intelligence reports noted that Pius XII himself handled this question and claimed that his close advisor, Montini, would have dealt with the activity differently—a debatable opinion.[40] *L'Osservatore Romano* returned to the question of the Christian Leftists in May, repeating the Vatican's condemnation and asserting that "the leaders of the party have no right to parade themselves as spokespersons of the church."[41]

Immediately after the war, Palmiro Togliatti committed the Communist Party of Italy to parliamentary democracy, not to revolution or Moscow-led militarism.[42] Pius XII refused to give the party a chance to demonstrate its sincerity. Myron Taylor reported to the State Department that the pope's concern about the activity and potential of the Communist Party in Italy was resolute and ongoing. "The pope has consistently repeated these possibilities since my first interview after the liberation of

Rome in June last."[43] Pius seemed to feed on his suspicions. In conversation with presidential envoy Taylor in 1945, before the end of the war, the pope reported that the head of the Communist Party in Italy had given instructions to the party in Sicily to beef up Communist membership in the Italian army so that it could join with the Russian army in overtaking all of Europe. The pope's statement absolutely dumbfounded Taylor.[44] Recovering from his astonishment, Taylor pointed out that the Italian army was too small and too dependent on U.S. supplies to function against the United States and that the Russian army was too far from its base to attempt any such military action. The exchange spotlights Pius XII's frenzied distrust of communism in general and of the Italian Communists in particular.

The hypertense atmosphere inside Vatican City did not let up. In 1946, Pius thought in terms of the necessity or inevitability of war. In January, speaking to a group of U.S. senators, the pope said (in English): "If only peace could be had for crying PEACE, PEACE: but it can't."[45] In July, Pius said in reference to a possible peace conference: "Objective justice of the peace (which is humanly impossible to attain) should be set aside for the fundamental necessity of fighting and overcoming the Communist menace which threatens all peoples."[46] Cardinal Tisserant believed a Soviet invasion of Europe was imminent. He told U.S. envoy Franklin Gowen that the Soviets were in a "favorable position to overrun western Europe," which would allow them to seize leftover German weapons from the war.[47] Late in 1946, Pius dwelled on the likelihood of a Soviet invasion of Italy, the possible purpose of which would be to take him hostage to Russia so that the Americans would not drop an atomic bomb on them! Pius resolved to stay put within Vatican City if the Russians came. Under-Secretary of State Tardini, perhaps trying to assuage his anxiety, suggested that it would be better to relocate somewhere outside of Italy, where he could continue to shepherd his flock. Three planeloads would suffice to transport the Vatican archives, and the diplomatic corps would be sure to follow! Tardini believed that ultimately the pope would follow his advice.[48]

Nerves in the Vatican remained taut in 1947. Montini and the pope worried in the fall about a Russian invasion of northern Italy. Montini wanted to know if any of the American diplomats had heard the rumor that Russia had moved a half million Yugoslavian troops to the Italian border.[49] No one had. The French ambassador to the Vatican, Jacques Maritain, expressed his wonder about the Holy See's sophomoric conduct of its external affairs. The ambassador told Graham Parsons of the U.S. mission that it "was extraordinary, the course of the church in world affairs was literally ruled by three men: the pope, Tardini and Montini."[50] Parsons's assessment of the diplomatic scene inside Vatican City soon after his arrival in Rome was that reality did not live up to the reputation the Vatican had as a fruitful listening post. To Parsons, the personnel in the secretariat seemed underinformed about affairs. In the guessing game that went on inside the secretariat (which included the pope, of course) concern about local Communist insurrections alternated with worries about an invasion. Just as during the war the pope had wanted both the German and Allied occupying forces to be a strong presence in Rome so as to put down the Communist uprisings that the he felt were likely, so in late 1947 Pius believed the withdrawal of Allied occupational forces was premature.[51]

Pius XII remained a hawkish warrior in 1948. Late in the year Tardini and envoy Paxton T. Dunn of the U.S. mission had a "very confidential" discussion. Tardini wanted to assure the United States that the Italian people could be safely relied on to go with the west in the event of a military showdown with the Soviet Union. Ideologically, economically, and culturally—the monsignor specified art, literature, and Latin background—Italians belonged to western traditions. The people had no interest in class struggles or in Communist ideology. Having laid the groundwork, Tardini then made his pitch (Dunn paraphrased Tardini):

> Italy is presently disarmed and therefore can only be neutral if war breaks out. But if armed Italy will go with West. *It would seem logical therefore [to] consider rearming Italy now in spite [of the] peace treaty rather than postponing her rearmament until after [the] outbreak of war.* (emphasis added)

Tardini cautioned Dunn that no word of the pope's push for Italy's rearmament should leak out. The Communists, he said, continually harped on the fact that Pius sided with imperialist western powers, and the Holy See wanted to avoid "giving any impression [that the] Vatican is encouraging Italy's rearmament."[52]

Atomic warfare finally led Pope Pius to modify his hawkishness. In a February 1948 allocution on nuclear research and warfare, the pope deplored the terrible destructiveness of the atom bomb and urged that war be avoided in the future because of it. But in the words of Parsons, he "stepped lightly" around the issue by not condemning the discoverers of the atomic bomb or those who used it, and he did not attempt to exclude continued possession of it.[53] Pius XII's warning, such as it was, came tardily. American bombers stationed in Great Britain at the time of the Berlin Airlift in 1948 were already equipped to carry atomic bombs, of which the United States had fifty-six ready for use.[54] The pope praised American Jesuit Edmund Walsh, who believed the United States should not hesitate to use the atom bomb in a first strike.[55] Furthermore, the pope's concerns about avoiding war did not preclude his attempts to induce the United States to arm the Italian army.

Pope Pius's extremely pessimistic frame of mind prior to the 1948 national elections and the Marshall Plan caused him to fret about how Italians would conduct themselves at the polls. Prior to the elections in 1946, Pius's close collaborator in the secretariat, Tardini, felt confidant that the party favored by the Vatican, the Christian Democrats under Alcide de Gasperi, would win a majority of the votes. But Pius thought otherwise, as Tittmann cabled the secretary of state:

> The pope felt that proposed unanimity of action on part of Communists and left wing socialists in election campaign together with application of terrorist technique by these parties at voting time could bring about majority for this group which would mean leftist dictatorship in Italy. It was all very well, the pope said, for people to say Communists were losing in popularity, but it should not be forgotten that they still remain the best organized and most active party with indefatigable will to power and seemingly limitless funds.[56]

Pius pulled out all the stops to cajole Italians to vote against communism, asking them whether they would "continue to build on the solid rock of Christianity, on the recognition of a personal God, on belief in spiritual dignity and eternal destiny, or whether they will prefer to entrust their future fates to the impassive omnipotence of a materialistic state without unworldly ideals, without religion and without God."[57] The Christian Democrats won, and de Gasperi formed a coalition government with the Communist and Socialist parties.

Paradoxically, Vatican policy regarding Soviet Russia moderated momentarily in 1947, just as the real Cold War unfolded. Several unrelated factors worked together to bring about the redirection. Togliatti demonstrated his commitment to government by democratic give and take by allowing the Lateran Treaty to become part of Italy's new constitution. In this way, a reopening of the wound between church and state that had plagued the Holy See and Italian politics from 1870 to 1929 was avoided. Togliatti's move had to have echoed profoundly inside the walls of Vatican City. In an unrelated matter, the Vatican was disappointed in the lack of support the United States showed for Archbishop Stepinać during his trial in Yugoslavia. In historian Peter Kent's view, a third factor was the "incipient division of Europe" into eastern and western blocs, which Montini thought could be avoided by a more conciliatory attitude toward Communist leaders. Newly released documents suggest that this interpretation may be correct. Graham Parsons notified the U.S. State Department in July that French ambassador Jacques Maritain had given a speech in which he had said that the "church had to strive for peace and therefore could not endorse a holy war against Russia."[58] Earlier, in 1946, Maritain had been upset by the Vatican's hostile attitude toward the Soviets. Montini, who was a close friend of Maritain, asked the ambassador's permission to quote the speech in *L'Osservatore Romano*. The article and previous editorials in the Vatican paper by its editor, Count della Torre, pointed to a new direction in papal diplomacy but at the same time caused eyebrows to raise because of the implied compromise with communism. Parsons reported to the U.S. Department of State that della Torre's editorials were obscure and confusing. "His recent misrepresentation of the Vatican's position was very embarrassing to the Vatican," Parsons wrote, indicating some vacillating or indecision within the Vatican.[59] Pope Pius cleared the air as far as the United States was concerned when he referred to the Marshall Plan. He spoke

> with deep feeling and gratitude of U.S. assistance to world, making clear that without this assistance situation would indeed be desperate. In every way pope emphasized Communist menace which he characterized as much more insidious than Nazi menace. . . . He seemed especially preoccupied by Yugoslav situation which he considered worst of all Moscow dominated countries.[60]

The Holy See was certainly not being conciliatory regarding Yugoslavia, for it was precisely in June and July, as we will see in chapter 11, that Pope Pius pressured the United States and Great Britain not to return war criminals to Tito who were wanted for trial in that country. At any rate, the effect of the Marshall Plan, announced at the same time as the developments just described, left the Vatican with little choice regarding its position on European affairs, because the Soviets refused to allow Eastern European countries to accept economic aid from the United States. East and West drifted inevitably apart. By the end of the year, Montini reported that Pope Pius was "quasi americano."[61]

The 1948 parliamentary elections brought out the warrior in Pope Pius once again. In an attempt to unseat the Christian Democrats, the Communists and Socialists decided to unify their slate so as not to split the vote on the left. After a 35-minute audience with Pius, American Anne O'Hare McCormick said that the pope had told her forcefully that he would remain within Vatican City if the Communists won the election. The pope, she said, was very pessimistic about the poll's outcome, more so than Montini.[62] Evidently, Pius XII was thinking in terms of returning to the "prisoner of the Vatican" status that had kept popes locked up in Vatican City after 1870.

The Holy See stood to lose much if a leftist government came to power—including money. After the war the Italian economy had not undergone any kind of a basic restructuring. This meant that the major industrial giants, who were interlocked financially, continued to function as they had in fascist times. After the war, de Gasperi wedded Christian Democracy to the existing economy by setting up a "clientalistic system of patronage."[63] The Vatican, as we have seen, had deeply invested in most of Italy's major industries, and Bernardino Nogara had worked with men on the boards of these corporations with solid Vatican sympathies and connections. The nationalization of some or all of Italy's industrial powers would bring about financial losses to the Holy See on a drastic scale. Interestingly, Communist Togliatti was less enthusiastic about nationalization than the socialist party was.[64]

Although Togliatti's inclusion of the Lateran Treaty in the new constitution assured the continuance of a state-supported Church in Italy and his party refrained from antagonizing the Church, Pope Pius feared that a leftist government victory in 1948 would inevitably lead to the ruin of Christianity and Christian life in Italy. Once again the pope pulled out all stops to rally Italian Catholics in the spring of 1948 to safeguard the Christian Democratic government. Catholic propaganda before the election was apocalyptic: "God or Satan, Christ or antichrist, civilization or barbarism, liberty or slavery."[65] Because churchmen were not supposed to meddle in politics, the Vatican's support for de Gasperi's party took the form of denunciations of communist philosophy. American statesman George Marshall complimented Pope Pius for an address he gave in February, saying that his strictures against communism would have a "profound effect on liberty loving people everywhere."[66] Other high churchmen inside and outside Vatican City spoke pointedly about the political conduct of Catholics. Cardinal Tisserant, a French citizen who was titular bishop of Italy, said that "Catholics favoring or propagating the principles of Marxist socialist-communism" would be exposing themselves to a "loss of faith" and a "conflict of conscience" and that they would be cooperating in the "diffusion of false doctrines."[67] Cardinal Shuster of Milan went even further in asserting that it constituted a "serious offense for the faithful to give their vote to a candidate or list of candidates that are manifestly contrary to the Church or to the application of religious principles and Christian morality in public life."[68] Other Italian cardinals and bishops spoke in a similar vein.

To counter Communist activists on the hustings and in the streets, the Vatican mobilized the Catholic Action movement, for which it found a vigorous leader in Luigi Gedda. An observer working for U.S. Catholic bishops reported that Gedda was an organizing genius in dealing with the working class and added that he met frequently with Pius XII.[69] A special cadre of Catholic Action called the Catholic Vanguard Movement was formed to activate healthy men of "excellent physical condition" between the ages of 18 and 35. They were to act as the militant branch of Catholic Action. The pope told them they could use "all legal means that right puts in your hands" to counter hostile antichurch mobs or demonstrations.[70] It was beginning to sound like the elections would be an occasion for vigilante street-brawling. The Irish ambassador to the Holy See, Joseph Walshe, believed the Vanguard Movement to be "very effective in overcoming political apathy of non-Communist Italians." Catholic Action was not the only group that was put to work in the interest of the Church in the spring election. War criminals, who were hiding out in ecclesiastical institutions, copied and distributed handbills, posters, and pro–Christian Democratic literature.[71] The U.S. Central Intelligence Agency funded Premiere Alcide de Gasperi's party with millions, some of which was funneled to it through the Vatican. Monsignor Montini "actually ran a campaign 'slush fund' based on the sale of U.S. army surplus, through the Vatican bank."[72] U.S. CIA agents also smeared Communist candidates and hired goons to intimidate voters.[73] These efforts made a mockery of the Lateran Treaty, which had called for the Church to stay out of politics. For Pope Pius, the fight against communism in the 1948 election was a no-holds-barred contest.

The combined efforts of Pius XII, the Italian hierarchy and clergy, laymen, and non-Italian operatives of one sort or another produced a major victory for the Christian Democrats in 1948, who fared even better than in the previous year's elections. De Gasperri's party won 48 percent of the vote and half of the seats in the new parliament. The Communist-Socialist slate was limited to just under 31 percent of the vote. After the elections, diplomats noticed that the pope seemed more relaxed and assured.

Yugoslavia

To some unknown extent, the anxiety Pius XII experienced over postwar domestic affairs prior to the 1948 elections was stoked by Italy's next-door neighbor, Yugoslavia, and its hostile dictator, Marshal Tito. Western military personnel believed in 1945 that if Stalin provoked World War III it would breakout in Trieste, the city on the Adriatic Sea contested by Yugoslavia and Italy.[74] The murderous excesses of the puppet Ustaša regime under Ante Pavelić had destroyed the fragile fabric of the Yugoslavia of Versailles and opened the door to Communist partisans under Marshal Tito during the last two years of the war. As Hitler's war fortunes collapsed, so did Pavelić's. Tito emerged from the war as the de facto dictator of a restored Yugoslavia and as the strongest Communist leader of any Eastern European nation. Without help from the Soviets, Tito had purged his country of the fascist Ustaša regime. His support among the populace, though contested, was greater than that of any other Eastern European Communist leader. After the war, Tito took steps to expand Yugoslavia both in the east and west, which, in the latter case, had to come at Italy's expense. War seemed a possibility, because no one knew that Josef Stalin had no agenda for starting World War III.[75]

Because Catholic Church members, both lay and ordained, had been directly and indirectly involved in the genocide the Ustaša had perpetrated, Tito's partisans retaliated against the Church even before the end of the war. After visiting Croatia in February 1945, English Catholic novelist Evelyn Waugh reported that partisans had killed fourteen priests. Waugh explained that "the task of the partisans was made easier in that the clergy as a whole had undoubtedly compromised the church by tolerating the pro-axis Ustashis, if not actively collaborating with them."[76] Waugh met with Tardini and with Britain's minister Osborne (because the British shared postwar oversight of Yugoslavia with the Soviet Union), and, separately, with Pope Pius, whose "greatest concern" was Tito, not the compromised Church. By March 1945, there were reports that the partisans had murdered 160 Catholic priests.[77] April brought more of the same news. Partisans had massacred an undetermined number of Franciscans, who had been singled out because of their complicity in the murders of Serbs and Jews under Pavelić. They had destroyed fifteen Franciscan monasteries. They were attacking archbishops Stepinać and Sarić on the radio and were accusing Sarić of being a war criminal.[78] By the end of the year, the number of priests who had been killed had reached 270. For the Holy See, the situation had become intolerable.

Pope Pius looked for a way to rescue the Church and settled on sending an American bishop, Joseph Patrick Hurley, as an envoy to the Tito government.[79] Perhaps Pius thought that an American would carry more weight with Tito, since anyone with a connection to fascism would be out of the question. Also, Tito was receiving millions of dollars of aid from the United Nations Relief and Rehabilitation Administration,

FIGURE 8. Ustaša dictator Ante Pavelić with Benedictine Abbot Guiseppe Ramiro Marcone, Pius XII's apostolic visitor to Croatia, in 1941. The close ties of many bishops and priests with the murderous Ustaša led to the persecution of the Church in Yugoslavia after the war under Communist dictator Marshal Tito. *Courtesy of the United States Holocaust Memorial Museum.*

about three-fourths of which came from U.S. dollars, a spigot which he presumably would not want shut off.[80] Hurley went to Yugoslavia early in 1946, carrying the title of regent, one that did not grant official Vatican recognition of Yugoslavia. Hurley's mission was to mend fences with Tito and to try to arrive at a relationship with the Holy See that was less constrained. Montini told U.S. envoy Franklin Gowen that Hurley's mission "was very difficult and important."[81] Apparently what Pope Pius had in mind was a carrot-and-stick approach to Tito. Hurley was the carrot. The stick would be U.S. military muscle. For example, in January, the same month that Hurley took up his post, the apostolic delegate to the United States, Amleto Cicognani, told Secretary of State Edward Stettinius that only armed force could rectify the situation in Yugoslavia.[82] In March, in conversation with Harold Tittmann, Pope Pius urged that something be done about Yugoslavia. "When I asked what, he said 'perhaps a show of force.'"[83]

Hurley arrived on the scene in Belgrade too late to change the course of events. In the immediate postwar period, Tito had sought to come to an understanding with Yugoslav Church leaders—on his terms. These were totally unacceptable. The murder and disappearance of priests, closing of schools and seminaries, elimination of Church social work programs and publications, and other severe constraints demonstrated to the hierarchy that Tito's intent was "the spread of materialism and atheism throughout Yugoslavia."[84] Archbishop Stepinać wrote an open letter to Tito late in 1945 indicating that his policies had created an unbridgeable gap. The leaders of the Communist regime, the bishops were convinced, had already decided "that there was to be no real role for the Catholic Church in postwar Yugoslavia."[85]

After Hurley arrived, Tito asked him to see if the Vatican would recall Archbishop Stepinać to Rome. The prelate had come to stand for opposition to communism and to the regime, and he was immensely popular with Croats. British diplomats reported to the Foreign Office that the archbishop was "now almost the only man of whom the authorities are afraid."[86] The Holy See decided to let Stepinać choose his destiny; he chose to remain with his flock. During the summer of 1946, Tito toured Yugoslavia trying to fan the flames of patriotism over the question of Trieste. The pope, Tito asserted, opposed Yugoslavia's claim. Attempting to use the issue to deflate Stepinać's popularity, Tito asked the Yugoslav people why the clergy obeyed a foreign enemy instead of siding with the Yugoslav claim. In September the hierarchy responded, denying Tito's claims and detailing a list of government abuses of the Church.[87]

Unable to make Church leaders bend, Tito decided to break them. In August, Bishop Rozman of Ljubljana was put on trial in absentia for war crimes. It was a warm-up for proceedings against Stepinać. British occupational authorities had recommended a year earlier that "bishop Gregoric Roxman [sic] . . . should be arrested and interned as a Ustaša collaborator."[88] The Ustaša priest, Krunoslav Draganović, the principal player who was organizing resistance to Tito among Ustaša refugees and fugitives in Rome, asked permission to travel to Austria to bring Rozman to Italy and safety. After Rozman was found guilty, Stepinać was arrested in September on three charges: supporting the Ustaša government, urging forced conversions of Orthodox Serbs to Roman Catholicism, and encouraging Ustaša resistance to Yugoslavia.[89] The archbishop was found guilty and sentenced to sixteen years in prison.

The nature of the charges against Stepinać point conclusively to the fact that his was to be a show trial. Recognizing this, Stepinać refused to defend himself during court proceedings. He might easily have done so, making use of the materials he had sent to Monsignor Juretić in Switzerland. The issue of his defiance in the courtroom deserves further exploration. Unlike Bishop Rozman, Stepinać was not accused of being a war criminal. As we have seen in the first chapter, that charge could easily be refuted with the result that Tito's communist regime would be viewed in the west as repressive and unjust. Stepinać could also have refuted a charge that he was forcing conversions, which probably was made to gain Serb sympathy for the regime, although the archbishop failed to do so except with curt denials. The charge that he supported the Ustaša regime was, of course, true, as everyone knew. But Stepinać's record clearly showed that he had not supported the regime's murderous rampage against Serbs and Jews; defending himself regarding the Ustaša's criminal excesses would have demonstrated the archbishop's opposition to genocide. But to the final charge that he had encouraged the Ustaša or the Croatian Peasant Party to overthrow the Tito government, Stepinać had no defense. Furthermore, to have defended the charge would have led to awkward questions and negative propaganda about the Holy See.

Archbishop Stepinać could not defend himself against the charge of seeking to overthrow the government because he had allowed the state papers of the self-exiled Ustaša regime to be stashed in his episcopal residence, evidently when Pavelić's fascists fled the country.[90] The fact that these papers would serve the Ustaša should it regain control of the country, as was its intention, would itself be incriminating. Why else would they be saved rather than turned over to authorities? More to the point, the papers undoubtedly contained incriminating information about individuals who had functioned in the genocidal Ustaša government. And where were many of these individuals at the time? In Rome, hiding out in ecclesiastical properties awaiting a local or a Europe-wide conflict so that they could return to Yugoslavia to overthrow Tito. In a secret memo to the American ambassador to Yugoslavia, Stepinać had referred to this crusade movement, the Krizari. Other former Ustaši whose names would turn up in the papers hidden in Stepinać's residence were in detention camps awaiting possible extradition by British authorities.[91] At this point the United States and Great Britain took quite seriously their agreement to the 1943 Moscow Declaration to return possible war criminals to the state of their crimes for persecution. The Vatican, as we will see in chapter 11, was actively seeking to weaken the resolve of the occupational authorities regarding the declaration. Thus, had Stepinać defended himself against the charge of promoting a return of the Ustaša, it would necessarily put the Vatican in a very embarrassing position because it harbored the exiles and sought to exempt them from the declaration.

Truth be known, Archbishop Stepinać would not have wanted to see a resurrection of the Pavelić government. Rather, a regime under Vlatko Maćek's Peasant Party would have been Stepinać's choice because it was both moral and democratic but was still Croatian nationalistically.[92] And there was a possibility that refugee Croats and some Ustaši would support a new government under Maćek.[93] But this, of course, was nothing more than a possibility piggybacking on the chance of domestic turmoil in Yugoslavia or the outbreak of World War III. Stepinać felt that if in the end Pavelić outmaneuvered Maćek, then so be it; he would continue his nationalistic support but with moral objections to his criminal behavior. The popularity of the archbishop made him the automatic rallying point of any non-Communist effort. For this reason he was in danger of being shot by Communist thugs even before the trial.[94] But as far as Stepinać's trial was concerned, it made no difference which party he favored, since he was guilty of plotting against the legitimate state which had the support of Great Britain as a result of the postwar assignment of territorial oversight among the Allies.

As historian Charles Gallagher points out, Stepinać's conviction brought about bad feelings at the Vatican toward the United States for not supporting the archbishop during his trial. This the United States could hardly do, as it had information from as far back as 1945 that indicated that Stepinać had directed the Krizari resistance movement.[95] Although the Vatican publicly and firmly supported Stepinać's innocence, it could do this only if the archbishop remained silent.[96] If Stepinać had responded to the charges against him, his defense would have inevitably unraveled, exposing the Vatican's support of the genocidal Pavelić. The diplomatic nicety of the fact that the Holy See sent an apostolic visitor instead of a nuncio to the Ustaša regime did not conceal the fact that Pius XII wanted a strong Catholic state in the Balkans. At no time had the Holy See denounced the Ustaša's murders. Quite the contrary, it had carefully tiptoed around the question.[97] Bad blood between the Holy See and the United States over Yugoslavia continued two years after the archbishop's trial, when Tito was expelled from Stalin's East-bloc Cominform and the United States extended a $25 million loan to the renegade Communist dictator without demanding freedom of religious practice as a condition. Stalin's dismissal of Tito did nothing to improve Pius XII's opinion of the Yugoslav Communist, whom he considered a "cruel, ambitious dictator of the worst type [who is] utterly unreliable and dangerous."[98]

Stepinac's silence in the courtroom served several purposes. It preserved the show-trial character of the proceeding. It avoided a public airing of the Krizari movement, Stepinac's link to it, and its ties to war criminals living in Rome under Vatican protection. Finally, it kept the book closed on the issue of Vatican's wartime support of Pavelić. After the archbishop's trial, the Yugoslav situation remained an open sore as far as Pius XII was concerned. Late in 1947, in conversation with the new British minister to the Vatican, Sir Victor Perowne, Pius kept bringing their conversation back to Yugoslavia, where, he said, in comparison to other Eastern European countries, "the suppression of the church is relatively far advanced and the threat to Italy much greater."[99]

Eastern Zonal Germany

During the last year of World War II, Pius XII grew anxious about the postwar reconstruction of Europe. With each great advance of the Red Army toward Western Europe, the pope's distress grew. The war had begun when Germany attacked Poland; it was now ending with Poland more than likely controlled by the Kremlin. To everyone in the west, but especially to Catholics in Great Britain and the United States, Poland's fate seemed unfair. To reassure his Catholic voters and win them over to his policy of friendship with the Soviet Union, President Roosevelt sent a Polish-American priest, Stanislas Orlemanski, on a mission to Russia to discuss the religious rights of Poles with Stalin. In April 1944, Orlemanski met with Stalin, who "confirmed both orally and in a signed document that the Soviet government would never carry out a policy of coercion and persecution of the Catholic Church and that he was willing to join Pius XII in the struggle against religious persecution."[100] President Roosevelt believed Stalin was sincere. Pope Pius did not. The Vatican rejected the Orlemanski mission out of hand. Subsequent missions sent by the American president with similar intent met with the same response.[101]

Having chosen a hard line by rejecting Stalin's concession, Pius XII had to formulate his own ideas for the postwar settlement. Although these were less likely to be realized than Stalin's promises would have been, Pius forged ahead with his own plans for the continent's reconfiguration, which necessarily included Germany. What the pope had in mind was the formation of a multinational Catholic state in Central Europe that would replace the old and defunct Austro-Hungarian Empire. The large and multinational but Catholic state would act as a check on the Soviet Union. In November and again in December 1944, the pope met with Prince Ruprecht of the Wittelsbach house of Bavaria to discuss the possibility of fusing the south German state with another German state, Saxony, and with Austria.[102] The new entity could either be a kingdom under the Hapsburgs or a Christian social republic.[103] At some point the Vatican hoped to include Hungary in the new Catholic bloc. An intelligence report noted that "the Vatican thinks that it is still possible to work for an agreement with the Soviets, in order to save Hungary from another Soviet experiment."[104] At the end of the war Pius continued to push for a negotiated peace, one that would be "just and equitable," but one that would severely limit Soviet influence in Eastern Europe.[105] Any joining of a German state such as Bavaria with a Central European state would, of course, have eliminated it from its share in Germany's responsibility for the war and crimes committed during it, and Austrian Nazis and army personnel had gravely implicated themselves in war crimes. Pope Pius simply did not think in the same terms as the Allies. The pope was still pressing for a Central European Catholic state when he met after the war in September with generals Dwight Eisenhower and Mark Clark.[106]

Neither of the generals had a hand in planning the reconfiguration of postwar Europe, so it is not surprising that Pius XII's vision of a Catholic state remained just that, a vision. What became a reality instead was zonal Germany. For four years after the war, the Allied armies occupied Germany, each controlling a zone and each controlling a sector of Berlin. The experience of the Catholic Church in the east, the Russian zone, diverged radically from that of the Church in the other three zones in the west. In addition, neither the eastern or western zonal situations bore any resemblance to the experience that the Vatican had in postwar Italy. Catholics in the Soviet zone constituted only a small minority of the population, whereas in most other Eastern European countries controlled by the Soviet Union they were a dominant majority. The situation in zonal Germany presented a black-and-white contrast: in the eastern zone, the Vatican exercised zero influence, but in the western zones, the Holy See managed considerable leverage.

Although in eastern Germany the institutional Church and the Communist government eventually found a way to get along with each other, there was no indication that this would be the case during the years of zonal Germany.[107] In fact, control of the Church by German Communists turned the Vatican's nightmare of religion under communism into reality. Even worse, the Communist government bureaucrats were often ex-Nazis.[108] Thus, Communist officials such as Walter Ulbricht, who equated the institutional Church with institutional superstition, could rely on former Nazis, who only yesterday in Hitler's time had oppressed and harassed the Church, to administer more bad medicine to it.

In Communist ideology, religion, like liberalism, was a dying phenomenon. Accordingly, the state resolved to prevent institutional churches from having any voice in public affairs, understood in the broadest sense. But whether Communists liked them or not, the churches existed. What were Communist officials to do with "dying church institutions" that had massive memberships? Because the churches and Communists had both opposed fascism, there appeared to be some chance of cooperation between the two in the immediate postwar years. Socialist-minded Protestant ministers experimented with forming an alliance of sorts between communism and religion. But "religious socialism" died quickly, a victim of the Cold War. Communist leader Walter Ulbricht, who emerged to take control of institutional religion in the Russian zone, viewed it as a "foreign body" in socialist society.[109] In the new spin, the German Catholic Church and the Vatican were viewed as fascist partners in Hitler's seizure of power.[110]

In Bishop Konrad Preysing of Berlin, Pius XII had the ideal person to deal with the Communist regime in the east zone—ideal for the pope, at least. The bishop and the pope had not seen eye to eye regarding Nazism; Preysing's stubborn opposition to the Nazi regime found no counterpart in Pope Pius. But when it came to communism, the two were on the same page. Bishop Preysing was the perfect complement for the pope's stubborn fixed attitude toward communism. In 1946, at the first postwar expansion of the college of cardinals, Pius named Preysing to the consistory. With that, Cardinal Preysing became the highest-ranking Catholic authority in the eastern and Communist sector of zonal Germany.

Like Josef Stalin, Wilhelm Pieck, the first Communist leader of the Russian zone, thought that the 1933 concordat between Germany and the Vatican had Nazi fingerprints on it.[111] There was no question of a reinstatement of the concordat under the Communists. Rather, the Catholic Church found itself cut off from the state, facing what must have appeared to Preysing as terminal conditions. There were no seminaries to educate new priests, no Catholic schools, no religious instruction in schools, no financial support to compensate for seized church property, and very little religious literature.[112] Still, the Holy See might have reflected that what the Communists did to the Church in zonal Germany could not compare with the persecution the Nazis had subjected the Church to in occupied Poland during the war. Cutting the Church off financially and educationally from society did nothing to reduce the number of Catholics, who numbered close to 3 million, in that sector.

The situation was tailor-made for the schmoozing skills of another Catholic bishop, Heinrich Wienken. For ten years, Wienken, acting as the executive secretary of Catholic bishops in Nazi Germany, had bargained and wheedled with mid-level Nazi bureaucrats to make the best of the bad situation the Church found itself in. Wienken and Preysing were opposites. While Preysing had urged a sharp break with the Nazis, Wienken willingly worked with the hand the Church had been dealt. As soon as the Nazi regime was replaced with a Communist one in the eastern zone, Wienken set about building bridges with any Communist bureaucrat who would give him a hearing. This must have occasioned a few strange scenarios: one day Wienken would be talking with a Nazi, the next day with a Communist—who would be the same person. In 1943, after his residence in Berlin was destroyed by Allied bombs, Preysing moved to what later became the western sector of Berlin, and he remained there after the war. Wienken, however, who lived and worked in the Communist sector, made useful contacts with Communists who saw that, like it or not, a sizable minority of their citizens were Catholics. In time, other bishops in the Soviet sector began to see the advantages of Bishop Wienken's approach.

The Holy Office decree of excommunication of July 1, 1949, brought matters to a head in Eastern Europe and in the eastern zone of Germany. Any Catholic who belonged to the Communist Party or who believed in or supported communism was excommunicated. "In Soviet eyes Churchill was the leading European anti-Bolshevik statesman of the post-revolutionary era. Pius XII was his ecclesiastical equivalent."[113] To Stalin, Churchill's Iron Curtain pronouncement was the first announcement of the Cold War, followed by Pope Pius's decree of excommunication, which was a declaration of holy war against communism. And so it was. In fact, the decree had disastrous consequences for the Catholic Church's capacity to survive the advent of Communist regimes in eastern Europe.[114] Communist leaders and Catholic bishops in zonal Germany wrestled with the decree, attempting to "interpret" it for local conditions. Ulbricht thought that Catholic members of the Communist Party should just switch their membership to the Freier deutscher Gewerkschaftbund, a workers' organization. Wienken and others wanted to differentiate between philosophical communism and its socialist or political aspects, in this way providing a way out for lay Catholics.[115] When the German bishops met at their annual meeting in Fulda in 1950, they dodged the decree of excommunication, saying that they did not wish to be party to the political and economic conflicts between Communist and anti-Communist powers.

Wienken and other like-minded bishops continued to work toward a modus vivendi with the Communist regime. Bishop Spülbeck recalled in 1968 that the bishops had wanted the Church to work toward rebuilding the country, to be engaged, and to participate politically. But Cardinal Preysing continued to take a hard line.[116] The Communists were willing to bend somewhat in dealing with the Catholic population because the later got cash support from West German co-religionists. The economically faltering East German regime was badly in need of West German Marks. In late 1949, he informed the Vatican that in his opinion no working arrangement should come about with Communists until the rights of the Church were both recognized and implemented.[117] Pope Pius, who was not in close touch with the situation in the Communist sector, was critical of Wienken: "[He] yields too early; not firm enough; was that way with the Nazis."[118] In a unilateral attempt to resolve the episcopal rift, Preysing sought to have Wienken dismissed as the executive secretary of German bishops (both in the east and west) so that he would lose his ex officio position as the spokesperson for German bishops with the German Democratic Republic.[119] This was not successful. In December 1950, Cardinal Konrad Preysing died. His great misfortune was that Pius XII had not supported his effort to persuade the bishops at Fulda in 1943 to speak out about the Holocaust, only to support his position during the rift with other East German bishops after the war when, in fact, a more conciliatory tactic would have been better for Catholics and their Church.[120] With Preysing's death, the road was open for the bishops to adopt Wienken's approach to dealing with Communists.

Western Zonal Germany

In the western sectors of zonal Germany, Pius XII could play a much more active and direct role than in the east. When the occupational authorities allowed political activity to revive—first locally, then regionally, then nationally—the Social Democratic Party and the Christian Democratic Party and its counterpart in Bavaria dominated elections. Communism was not a problem in the western sectors, as it was in France, Italy, and, of course, eastern zonal Germany. Furthermore, Germans appeared to be cured, at least for the time being, of their infatuation with the politics of the radical right. This situation allowed Pope Pius to concentrate on establishing, or reestablishing, the concordat between Germany and the Vatican. As in Italy with the Lateran Treaty, so in Germany the concordat was the indispensable foundation for church-state relations, in the pope's eyes. Never mind that had it been left up to Germany's bishops there would never have been a concordat in 1933 or a revival of it in the postwar era. Instead of breaking off diplomatic relations with the genocidal

Hitler regime, as Bishop Preysing had wanted, Pius had preferred to press Nazis to live up to the agreement, even though this was clearly a hopeless proposition. The war ended with the concordat between Germany and the Vatican intact.

But, of course, Germany was not intact. When at some future point Germany recovered its sovereignty, what obligation, if any, would it have to reinstate the concordat? For the pope, the idea of reinstatement constituted a misconception; the concordat had not been severed by either the state or the Church and therefore continued to exist. But neither the occupational authorities nor the German bishops thought in these terms. For this reason, Pius XII made the issue of the concordat his greatest concern regarding zonal Germany. The pope still hoped that the eastern sector would be obliged to accept the agreement long after there was any realistic possibility that the Communist regime would do so.

Pius XII made his insistence that the concordat be renewed very clear to his apostolic visitor to zonal Germany, Aloisius Muench.[121] In July 1946, when Muench met with Pope Pius for the first time, the concordat was uppermost on the pontiff's mind.[122] The following year when Muench traveled to Rome, he told the pope that the word "concordat" was objectionable to Americans and the English. Pius responded, "[You] must not consider objections; hold firm against opposition."[123] Pius was pleased when the 1948 draft of the new Bonn constitution (for West Germany) incorporated the concordat. The pope wanted the exact same concordat as the one he had fashioned fifteen years earlier—no changes. Pius complained that the military governor of the U.S. zone, Lucius Clay, was overly rigid in his duties. Muench, by this time less in awe of the pope than he had been in earlier meetings and more familiar with current German affairs than the pontiff, thought it was the pope who was too rigid. "Pius interprets most everything according to this or that phrase of the concordat," he wrote in his diary.[124] It was not unusual for Pius to talk about nothing but the concordat when Muench met with him each year, and these meetings could last more than an hour, sometimes several. In 1949, when the German parliament was debating the concordat and considering changes, Pius refused to bend: it had to be adopted to "the last detail." Pius told Muench that he had to "talk up to the Germans, stand firm."[125] The pope's charge must have reminded Muench of what Cardinal Bernardini had told him three years earlier at the time of Muench's first audience with the pope: "Pius thinks that he's still the nuncio in Germany."[126]

The inflexibility of Pius XII regarding the concordat can be understood in terms of both his past and current affairs in Europe. The 1933

German concordat had been Cardinal Secretary of State Pacelli's task—that is, he had made it his task, refusing to let his successor do the negotiating with the Nazis. In April, Cardinal Pacelli had burned the midnight oil working and reworking drafts. It was natural for him to look back on it as the foundational piece in relations with the German state. Had it been another's work, the concordat would not have given him a sense of personal accomplishment and he might have questioned his policy of letting Hitler walk all over it without breaking off diplomatic relations; the United States had made the opposite choice in 1938. As things stood, he could not distance himself from his handiwork. The pope's micromanagement governing style also contributed to his desire to preserve the concordat. Pope Pius believed he could manage state-church affairs in Germany with his concordat. From the point of view of current affairs in Rome, it seemed that everything was coming undone and becoming unstable in the postwar era. Keeping up with events in countries in the Eastern European Communist bloc was a daily juggling act. Domestically, in the west, democratic governments faced leftist challenges that, as we have seen, worried the pope deeply. In the midst of all of this unevenness and flux, the concordat offered a rock-solid basis on which church and state could, at least in those countries where a concordat was in force, carry on their affairs amicably and profitably for the Church.

As a corollary to his policy about concordats, Pius looked to build good will among Germans by supporting them morally and materially. The pope believed that the top Nazis deserved to be tried at Nuremberg, and he cooperated to a certain extent in providing evidence of Nazi persecution of the Church. But for Pope Pius, the mass of German people bore no responsibility for Nazi crimes against the Jews. In 1946, when the Vatican objected to the massive denazification process in Germany, it asserted that teachers, who were forced to become Nazi party members or lose their jobs, routinely sabotaged the Nazi regime in the classroom. Occupational authorities found no evidence to corroborate the Holy See's statement. Although the pope believed and said that Catholics generally had opposed Hitler, this was not the case. They had remained loyal to their Catholic Center Party at the polls during Hitler's political surge in 1931 and 1932, but very few could be said to have opposed him once in power. In fact, Austrian Catholics enthusiastically welcomed the Nazis and joined the party in disproportionate numbers compared to Germans.

Germans naturally welcomed Pius XII's moral support after the war. As Cardinal Bernardini told Bishop Muench, he was their "sole friend" during that period.[127] When Bishop Muench spoke publicly in Germany, he always told the Germans of Pius XII's love for them. In the first expansion of the college of cardinals after the war in 1946, Preysing, who had been the most anti-Nazi bishop, and Clemens August Graf von Galen, the most outspoken bishop to oppose Nazi euthanasia programs, were made cardinals.[128] By raising Preysing and von Galen to the cardinalate, Pius furnished Catholics and the Church with a solidly anti-Nazi profile which, in fact, neither Catholics nor the Church had. The pope's words and actions drew the loyalty of Germans toward Rome and allowed them to wrap themselves in a blanket of innocence.[129]

Pius also drew the Germans' admiration because of his material support immediately after the war during several extremely hard years. In a letter to Cardinal Michael Faulhaber written in November 1946, Pope Pius encouraged the Germans not to despair, saying that he would try to ease their situation by contacting the United States and Great Britain.[130] The Vatican sent care packages to German POWs, many of whom were not released for months, sometimes more than a year, after the war. The packages contained articles of clothing, which were much needed because of the scarcity of coal for heating, that were distributed indiscriminately to Protestant and Catholic servicemen. Pius XII also sent enormous amounts of food by train to Germans, who during the first postwar years were reduced to less than the bare minimum in calorie consumption. Former president Herbert Hoover praised Pope Pius, saying that he had sent 5 to 7 million dollars' worth of foodstuffs for the Germans.[131] German nun and longtime secretary to Pope Pius, Sister Pasqualina, organized food shipments to Germany and told Bishop Muench how much Pope Pius appreciated Muench's show of good will toward all Germans. Occupational authorities, who generally believed the Germans deserved to suffer, did not appreciate the pope's efforts. Naturally, in a time when the Allies were trying and finding guilty countless Germans at Nuremberg and in army trials in the four zones and forcing other Germans to go through denazification trials, the largess and moral support of Pius XII made a deep impression on the German public. Their appreciation showed politically when Germans supported the pope's goal of incorporating the concordat into the constitution (Basic Law) of the Federal Republic of Germany.

German War Criminals and the Cold War

Since most of the war criminals of World War II were German nationals, Pius XII's pleas for clemency for them appears, like the concordat, to have been a papal policy addressing only Germany. This was not the case. Clemency for fascists, wherever they were, appeared to the pope to be insurance against communism. Thus, in 1946, the Holy See wrote to the Italian government, "calling attention to the large number of persons currently being sentenced to death by the Italian courts" and pleading for these "unfortunate persons."[132] By late 1945, 320 Italian fascists had been given the death sentence, forty-three of which had been carried out. The Holy See intervened for those not yet executed and in doing so pointed out that just as it had intervened with the Nazi occupational authorities on behalf of condemned Italians during the war, so now it intervened on behalf of the fascists. In fact, the implication that the circumstances were alike did not obtain. Those duly tried in Italian courts had been found guilty of specific crimes, whereas those the Nazis had murdered were innocent hostages who paid with their lives in Nazi revenge for partisan sabotage.

However, most convictions for war crimes occurred in zonal Germany. In the American zone alone, more than 1,400 were convicted. The question of the fate of convicted war criminals had arisen in 1946 and 1947, "cold war" years for Pius XII, and would play itself out in western zonal Germany in the context of the actual Cold War. By 1948, the focus of tension between east and west had shifted from Italy to Germany, whose onetime capital city, Berlin, had become the hot point. General Lucius Clay sensed the turn. Early in March, he famously telegrammed President Truman that for many months he had felt that "war was unlikely." Now he said he had the "feeling that it may come with dramatic suddenness." In July, the Soviets blocked off all surface access to Berlin. Clay answered with the Berlin Airlift. The fusion of the three western zones into one zone—which created bizonal Germany—presaged the Berlin crisis and foreshadowed the East-West standoff, a permanent fixture of the Cold War. The forces at play during the early years of the impasse determined the lot of convicted German war criminals.

What were these forces? On the European side, the Vatican, the churches, and the state in what would become the Federal Republic of Germany and the overwhelming majority of the German people urged blanket pardons for convicted war criminals. Occupational authorities, all of whom feared a revival of Nazism, opposed this idea. On the other side of the Atlantic Ocean, some U.S. congressmen, a not-insignificant number of jurists, and Catholic bishops whose greatest concern was communism found reason to question the trials and their sentences when they heard negative reports from Bishop Muench about these proceedings. American public opinion, however, continued to see punishment of war criminals as a matter of justice. The fact that some American jurists questioned the legality of the war crimes trials while some politicians in high office wanted the German question settled so as to get on with the real enemy, the Soviets, gave Pius XII and German bishops plenty of room to plead for imprisoned war criminals.[133]

Similar to his intervention in Italy, in 1948, Pope Pius urged blanket clemency for convicted criminals in the Landsberg Prison in southern Germany. (Earlier he had sought clemency for murderers Arthur Greiser and Hans Frank, among others.) The war criminals at Landsberg wore the red jackets issued to the worst offenders, those sentenced to death. Included in their number were Oswald Pohl, who had overseen the organization of the death camps, and Otto Ohlendorf, who had commanded a mobile killing squad, as well as more "small-time" murderers such as Dr. Hans Eisele, whose victims probably numbered around 1,000. After ten of the red-jacketed convicts (none of the above) were hung in October 1948, Pius XII wrote to President Harry Truman asking for mercy for the remaining war criminals, petitioning him to support the appeal of German bishops that "further sentences of capital punishments in Germany [be] reduced to less severe punishments."[134] Working through the apostolic delegate to the United States, Monsignor Amleto Cicognani, who in turn enlisted the help of the anti-Communist hawk, Jesuit Edmund Walsh, the Vatican sent a memorandum to Secretary of the Army Kenneth Royall emphasizing "the desire of the Holy See to present to the Allied authorities a plea of mercy in behalf of the German nationals condemned to death."[135] Pius also intervened directly on their behalf with the military governor of the American zone, General Lucius Clay. Clay replied that he could not grant blanket clemency because the criminals had been convicted of specific heinous crimes.[136]

In its appeals after the October executions, the Holy See asserted that it sought justice tempered with mercy. In a carefully worded statement addressed to all four zonal authorities, the Vatican said that "without any violation of justice, it is hoped that [occupational authorities will] commute the existing death sentences into other penalties at least in those cases where there is even a slight doubt of guilt or where mitigating circumstances may be found."[137] The Holy See wanted the United States to know that the executions had "shocked" the German people.[138] Most Germans believed that attestations of good character sufficed to anchor "a slight doubt of guilt." Thus, Oswald Pohl, a "just and steadfast man, helpful and good," could not be guilty of overseeing the murder of millions.[139] Hitler's doctor, who headed Nazi euthanasia murders, was described by Catholic nuns as "gentle in his behavior" and a "high-minded person" who would not likely be guilty of war crimes.[140] Bishop Wienken pleaded for the "euthanasia killer" Victor Brack on the grounds that he did not have a "criminal cast of mind."[141] The Holy See shared the view of most Germans that the Nuremberg Trial and subsequent zonal trails constituted victors' justice, for one thing because Soviet authorities had been guilty of crimes as horrendous as those of which the accused had been convicted. Only in a very general sense was this the case. Stalin had allowed millions of kulak farmers to languish and die for economic reasons rooted in Marxist theory and had executed other Russians because of his paranoia. These murders took place in the Soviet Union, and the victims were Russian nationals. In contrast, Germany had established death camps in a foreign land and then murdered millions of Jews from all over Europe. In any case, it is difficult to believe the Holy See's claim that death sentences of convicted Nazis would constitute a violation of justice, since six months earlier in the summer of 1947 it had pressured the United States and Great Britain to release Ustaša war criminals in custody in Italy without undergoing any juridical process at all.[142]

No doubt the statement that justice would not be violated was the work of Bishop Muench, who collaborated in the wording of the Vatican's appeal to zonal authorities. Muench, who acted as the Catholic liaison to U.S. occupational authorities, regularly dealt with Military Governor General Clay and his successors regarding convicted war criminals. In the process Muench became acquainted with the facts of many of the cases, which he characterized as "shocking" in a letter to his sister.[143] He knew that the convictions and death sentences of these criminals had served justice. For this reason, Muench lost patience with hot-headed nationalists such as the auxiliary bishop of Munich, Johannes Neuhäusler, whom he lectured: "Whatever the many voices might be saying, one voice must be heard. That is the voice of justice, so that the people's sense of justice is not dragged into the grave with the executed [men] of Landsberg" Prison.[144] Muench wanted to "give justice its proper due," as he wrote the U.S. political advisor for Germany, Robert Murphy, in 1948.

Besides appeals for blanket pardons or wholesale commutations of sentences, the Vatican not infrequently appealed particular cases. But unlike Muench, the Holy See did not investigate the evidence that led to a conviction. A case in point is that of the commander of the German Army Medical Corps from 1941 to 1945, Dr. Siegfried Handloser. His defenders told the Vatican that Handloser was unaware of the experiments being carried out on the internees of concentration camps and that the doctors concerned were not directly under his command. "In any event," the appeal said, "doctor Handloser would have been unable to

prevent such experiments since his position dit [*sic*] not give him any real
power of command over his subordinates."[145] The plea seems preposter-
ous, as did a supposedly extenuating circumstance: consideration should
be given to Dr. Handloser because he had saved the Benedictine monastery of Maria Laach from Nazi oppression. The Holy See submitted the
Handloser petition to the United States, making it clear that the Vatican
itself was not the petitioner. But the Vatican had not investigated the
merits of the case for Handloser, and in forwarding the appeal it brought
pressure to bear on Allied authorities. Handloser had been found guilty
at Nuremberg and given life. In 1951, U.S. High Commissioner McCloy,
who meticulously reviewed each case, reduced the sentence to twenty
years.[146] Handloser was indeed guilty.

Rome launched the attack on the war crimes trials in 1946, and
German Church leaders readily took up the cue. In that year, Cardinal
von Galen published an outrageous assault on the occupational authorities, *The Sense of Justice and Questionable Justice.*[147] Von Galen, an
ardent German nationalist who had established his name in his homeland because of his bold objection to the Nazi euthanasia programs,
now proclaimed that the Nuremberg trials were not about justice but
about the defamation of the German people. In Cologne, Cardinal Josef
Frings took up von Galen's argument in his 1946 New Year's Eve ser-
mon. Frings couched his objections to Nuremberg in legal jargon that
hid his true intent to dismantle Allied trials and verdicts: "The Allies
had followed a 'pagan and naive' optimism for taking it upon themselves to make judgments on guilt or innocence."[148] Other Catholic and
Protestant Church leaders joined in the refrain; the most strident voice
was that of the auxiliary bishop of Munich, Johannes Neuhäusler. With
unquestionable credentials as a former Dachau prisoner, Neuhäusler in
1949 contacted U.S. senator Joseph McCarthy, who, Muench assured
him, was "a good Catholic and an outspoken opponent regarding what
happened in the course of the Landsberg trials."[149] McCarthy had indeed
brought about serious "damage to the war crimes program" through his
rantings in the Senate.[150] The coordinated and combined interventions of
several parties on both sides of the Atlantic took a toll on General Clay
and his successors, who periodically stayed and commuted sentences of
convicted war criminals.

In 1949, the drive for clemency by American politicians and jurists,
German politicians, the German churches, and Pius XII reached a cli-
max when the Cold War grew hot. Both the United States and Great
Britain were willing to commit standing forces on the continent to offset
a massive Soviet military presence in the east. But the Anglo-Americans

believed that if western Germany was to be protected from the Soviet Bear, the Germans should contribute to the military effort. Talk of rearming Germany immediately led Germans to insist that any war criminals still in detention be set free: German politicians, including Chancellor Adenauer, and German generals held that executing any additional criminals or even detaining them sullied the "honor" of the German military, derailing any possible contribution it could make to the defense of the west.[151] The German parliament aggressively entered the act once the Federal Republic became a reality in the fall. All three major parties, Adenauer's, the German Socialist Party, and the Free Democrats with their heavily ex-Nazi membership, joined hands to denounce continued Allied detention of Germans whom they believed, one and all, to be innocent of any crimes.[152]

At one with Pius XII, the German elite wanted to bury Germany's past along with its infamy. The pope continued to press the Americans to release the war criminals, so much so that his own envoy to Germany, now Nuncio Muench, had to deter him. Muench knew that Clay and his successors had acted responsibly and conscientiously in reviewing cases for clemency. As the time for Otto Ohlendorf's execution drew near, an organization of former Nazis urged sympathetic Germans of high and good standing to prompt the Holy See to intervene on behalf of the perpetrator. Muench was contacted by the same group, leading him to warn the Holy See to desist lest the good name of Pope Pius become associated with German Nazis.[153] It is especially noteworthy and revealing that the pope's own envoy to the Federal Republic of Germany had to forestall Pius XII regarding clemency for convicted war criminals. U.S. High Commissioner McCloy refused to grant clemency to Ohlendorf and the five others who were executed in the summer of 1951, causing outrage in Germany.[154] But for all intents and purposes, that marked the end the controversy over war criminals. The German parliament succeeded in blackmailing occupational authorities into dismantling the war crimes program.[155] The ever-increasing concern with Soviet military intentions led to ever-decreasing concern that the Nazis would rise again like the phoenix. Amnesty for war criminals was the price that had to be paid for German contribution to the defense of the west.[156]

Europe and Beyond

George Kennan's now-famous "long telegram" of February 1946 pointed American foreign policy toward containment of the Soviet Union in

Europe. The following year the Marshall Plan for European recovery, which was initially an anodyne for Pius XII, became a bittersweet pill because it resulted in an East-West division of Europe. The west's economic course of free trade that was energized by U.S. capital was followed by the Schuman Plan to integrate Europe's economy, sparking a period of economic growth the continent had not seen since the heyday of the industrial revolution. Meanwhile, autarchy in the East doomed nations within the Soviet bloc to gradual but continual economic stagnation. Pope Pius opposed the partitioning of Europe into halves that left heavily Catholic countries to deal with the atheistic Soviets. The chaotic situation in the East in the immediate aftermath of the war nettled the micromanaging pope, who felt out of touch with events. Under-Secretary of State Tardini reported that Pius was "depressed, nervous, and irresolute" about them.[157] Kennan's containment policy held no promise of improving things. The first Cold War warrior wanted to roll back communism, not contain it.

Still, there could be no doubt about which party the Vatican favored in the developing East-West standoff. In February 1948, Secretary of State George Marshall told the American envoy to the Vatican that "you should at first opportunity inform pope in person [that] this government has welcomed his recent statements in opposition to Communist philosophy."[158] In dealing with the emerging East bloc of nations, Pius chose a one-size-fits-all strategy—a hard anti-Communist line. Historian Peter Kent has thoroughly reviewed papal policy during the early Cold War in Eastern Europe, documenting the difficulties the Vatican faced, not a few of which were of its own doing. Pope Pius's inflexibility, on the one hand, and indecisiveness, on the other, placed Eastern European Church leaders in the awkward position of either blindly following Rome or doing what was best for conditions of the Church in their separate countries.[159]

Nowhere was this more evident than in Poland. Peacetime relations of the Holy See with Poland got off to a poor start. Polish Catholics' hard feelings about how the pope had abandoned them—as they saw it—during the first three years of the war had subsided but not dissolved. Washington learned that the "Polish people are as Catholic as in the past, but anti-Vatican due to the failure of [the] present pope to support [the] Polish people at time of the German invasion."[160] Poles wanted the Holy Father to speak out against the new potential menace of Soviet oppression, but Pius failed to mention the restoration of a greater Poland in an early postwar address and avoided coming to terms with the issue when approached by the Polish ambassador to the Vatican, Kazimierz Papée.[161] Poles were still nettled by the pope's appointment of a German bishop to a Polish bishopric and of another German as apostolic administrator within Poland during the war. *L'Osservatore Romano* asserted that these appointments had been necessary measures because the Germans had removed Poles in the Greater Reich portion of occupied Poland and replaced them with ethnic Germans and the Vatican claimed that it was only a temporary step. Nevertheless, there was no denying that the appointments had violated the concordat between Poland and the Vatican. *L'Osservatore Romano* maintained that Communists in Poland, not the Polish people, had resurrected the thorny issue.[162] But, in fact, it was the Poles who were angry with the pope.[163]

Poles were also riled by the Vatican's failure to recognize the postwar boundaries of their country. After the war, Stalin increased the buffer zone between Germany and the Soviet Union by annexing 69,000 square miles of territory in eastern Poland and compensating the Poles by annexing 40,000 square miles of German territory—minus many of its Germans—to Poland in the west.[164] The acquired western land benefited Poland considerably, of course, but the loss of this predominantly agricultural territory devastated Germany. Each year before the war, the area in question had produced 194,000 tons of butter, enough to provide for all of Germany, and sufficient grain, 8 million metric tons, to feed well over half of the population.[165] Poles realized that this arrangement was the best they could hope for under postwar conditions. But Pope Pius refused to recognize the new Oder-Neisse boundary of Poland.[166] Here again, the pope seemed to Poles to prefer German interests over their quite legitimate interests. Why, they wondered, should not Germany be punished for the aggression against Poland that had incited World War II and for its crimes in occupied Poland during the war? The partitioning of the western part of Poland had been a European pastime for nearly two centuries—"she weeps but she takes," Prussia's Frederic the Great had cynically said of Austria's Maria Theresa—without any consideration of what Poles themselves wanted. When the most recent realignment benefited Poland, it rankled Polish national feeling that Pius XII refused to recognize it.

Likewise, Pius refused to recognize Poland's Communist-dominated postwar government in spite of the fact that it was treating the Church tolerably well. Polish bishops were quite prepared to deal with the postwar regime because of its indulgent attitude in religious matters, which contrasted sharply with what they had experienced under the Germans a few years before. But when Pius continued to recognize the Polish Government in Exile, the home regime retaliated by abrogating the concordat of 1925 between Poland and the Vatican. The Polish hierarchy, like its

German counterpart, did not object to this state of affairs because it left its members with "considerable independence in their dealings with the government."[167] Bishop Sapieha, who was more respected than Cardinal Hlond (who had fled the country at the time of the German occupation), and another popular bishop, Adamski of Katowice, did not believe that Pope Pius had dealt fairly with Poland in his wartime appointments. Controversy swirled around Bishop Splett, whom Pius appointed during the war, who banned liturgy in Polish and refused to allow Polish priests to return to their parishes after the war, when they were released from concentration camps.[168] The pope found himself in the awkward position—largely of his own doing—of being out of favor with the Polish Church, both shepherds and flock, and out of favor with the Communist government at the same time.

It was in the context of this stressful situation that the Kielce massacre took place in July 1946. A boy who had run away from home blamed Jews for his disappearance when he returned after a few days' absence.[169] The boy's tale, reminiscent of the age-old myth of blood libel, set off a massacre which cost more than forty Jewish lives in Kielce and many more across Poland. Pope Pius, pressed by Rabbi Philip Bernstein in a private audience in September to hold religious antisemitism in Poland accountable for the crime, put the blame for Kielce on the Communist regime instead of on antisemitism.[170] Church leaders in Poland also refused to blame the traditional antisemitism of the Catholic populace for the calamity. Cardinal Hlond blamed the Communist regime instead, asserting that Jews were much too prominent in it. Thus, in a tragic way, the Kielce massacre sutured the ruptured relationship between Polish bishops and the pope.

The realigned relationship was short lived. In 1947, the Holy See began talks with the Communist regime after forbidding the Polish hierarchy to do so. Church leaders were not consulted in the bilateral discussion, which the Vatican successfully used to pressure the government to put a good face on Pius XII's lack of help for Poland during the war.[171] The rift between Rome and the bishops widened when the Holy See failed to create new dioceses in the western territories that were taken from Germany and annexed to Poland after the war. The failure demonstrated again that Pius preferred German over Polish interests. As historian Peter Kent relates, the Polish hierarchy issued a pastoral letter in September that was purposefully so offensive to the government that it derailed relations between it and the Vatican. Pius XII's dealings with the Polish Church during and after the war constituted an ongoing fiasco. Polish best interests continuously took a back seat to Pope Pius's political designs or expectations for Europe.[172]

Beyond Europe, the worrisome pope looked toward South America. Before becoming the pope, Pius XII had traveled more extensively than any other pontiff. His journeys had provided him with an awareness of the universality of the Church that very likely was more concrete than it had been for his predecessors. Like many others, including a number of heads of state, Pius believed that Josef Stalin was planning an aggressive expansion of communism. Pope Pius told Taylor in the spring of 1945 that Moscow radio threatened "that the Twentieth Century is a century of bolshevism and that its mission will be carried to the end of the world by the Red Army."[173] If this were to happen, the universal Church would be faced with a universal challenge. Beyond Europe, Pius XII worried with good reason, especially about the spread of communism in the economically awakening countries of Catholic South America.

The Holy See's reluctance to discharge German nationals residing in Vatican properties in Rome and the pope's appeals on behalf of convicted war criminals should correctly be seen as part of a larger design to combat international communism. The U.S. State Department considered the Vatican to be one of the most recalcitrant counties in the matter of postwar harboring of Germans, and officials fretted about how to induce the pope to surrender them. The State Department considered embarrassing the Vatican with publicity or even expelling the pope's envoy, Muench, from zonal Germany.[174] From the pope's perspective, the Nazis and their European collaborators were fascists who had opposed communism prior to the war and fought against it during the war. The Vatican wanted to save these fighters for another day in the struggle between religion and atheism. It sought clemency for war criminals just as it sought to have released fugitive criminals who were in custody but not yet tried and just as it abetted the escape of fugitives to safe harbors in South America, where they could be enlisted in the anti-Communist campaign the pope anticipated.[175] Under the guise of traditional Christian clemency, the Vatican systematically pursued a political cause. Pope Pius, a Polish official pointed out, would ask for clemency for the likes of Arthur Greiser, a Nazi who had murdered thousands of Polish Jews and gentiles, but would not ask Franco to intervene on behalf of Spanish Republicans.[176]

In the end, to what extent did Pope Pius XII shape the coming of the Cold War? The question could be answered in a straightforward manner if only historians agreed as to why the Cold War developed. But agreement has eluded them. After the collapse of communism in Eastern Europe, some American analysts pointed to the importance of "moral ambiguities" in bringing about the Cold War and the importance of advocacy of human rights in ending it. "The greatest danger that can befall us in coping with this problem of Soviet Communism," George Kennan had written in the conclusion to the long telegram, "is that we shall allow ourselves to become like those with whom we are coping."[177] That, unfortunately, is what happened, in the view of some historians. Moral ambiguities—atomic warfare, Truman's interference (supposedly on behalf of freedom) in Greece and Turkey, gross intrusions by the CIA in Italian domestic politics, Eisenhower's talk of a Sino-Soviet bloc, and Kennedy's exaggerations about a "missile gap"—were pretexts that spurred on the East-West estrangement. At the very outset, economic considerations motivated American statesmen, who "were driven less by a desire to help others than by an ideological conviction that their own political economy of freedom would be jeopardized if a totalitarian foe [the Soviet Union] became too powerful in Western Europe."[178] If the moral ambiguities argument prevails, Pope Pius's pleas for leniency for convicted perpetrators of atrocities and his assistance to fugitives from justice after the Holocaust must certainly be added to the top of the list of moral ambiguities that brought about the Cold War. Because the United States and, eventually, Great Britain became complicit in this undercover activity, Pius XII's ethical trespasses must be seen as a fundamental moral ambiguity underpinning the Cold War.[179]

In his vast study of postwar Europe, historian Tony Judt disregards moral ambiguity or any other western provocation in accounting for the coming of the Cold War. In Judt's view, it came to pass inevitably, rooted in history. Although Pius XII does not figure largely in Judt's analysis—indeed, he is not mentioned with regard to the origin of the Cold War—he must be counted as the first Cold War warrior because he more accurately foresaw the future than his contemporaries. For the American proconsuls in zonal Germany, Nazism was a distraction from the fundamental incompatibility of communism and capitalism. Among U.S. Secretary of State Acheson and proconsuls McCloy, Clay, and Harriman, "there was a consensus that concessions would have to be made to democratic leaders like Konrad Adenauer, so as to keep Germany out of the hands of rabid nationalists," meaning Nazis.[180] German nationalism was not a distraction for Pope Pius.

For Judt, "the Cold War began not after the Second World War but following the end of the First."[181] Neither the Truman Doctrine nor the Marshall Plan nor any other western act triggered the Cold War, Judt argues. It was, rather, a product of history and the result of the relative positions of the Red Army and British and American forces at the end of World War II.[182] A divided Germany became the solution to the Cold

War. Bringing about a democratic and prosperous western Germany on the heels of Nazi Germany—veritably on top of it—was an "odious" but necessary step as a bulwark against communism.[183] For Pope Pius, it was not odious. Communism had to be forestalled, not to preserve economic freedom in the west but to save Christianity. Pius, Judt would argue, bore no responsibility for the coming of the Cold War just because he accurately foresaw it. Pius may certainly be faulted for missteps in dealing with the various regimes of Communist countries, but he cannot be faulted for creating them, any more than any other Westerner.

It was how the Cold War ended that led historians to point to "moral ambiguities" as its incubator. The Conference on Security and Cooperation in Europe, which was held at Helsinki in 1975 with thirty-four nations attending, established for the first time "a basis in international law upon which states could protest human rights violations inside other states."[184] Not since the presidency of Harry Truman had there been an opportunity "to make containment work by standing for, rather than by compromising, American ideals."[185] Although historians have not adverted to Pius XII as a key player in begetting the Cold War, they have not been shy about crediting successive popes in its unraveling. The groundwork that led to Helsinki's human rights agreement began with Pius XII's immediate successor, Pope John XXIII.

In the spring of 1945, Nuncio Angelo Roncalli met with the other ambassadors accredited to the French government of General de Gaulle. As the diplomats assembled, one stood apart, isolated by the rest—the Soviet ambassador. When Roncalli entered the room, he "went directly to him immediately and greeted him warmly which delighted the Russian."[186] The Soviets did not forget. When Roncalli became Pope John XXIII, he addressed himself at once to "all men of good will." The day for excommunicating Communist sympathizers thereby ended. In November 1961, Soviet chairman Nikita Khrushchev sent Pope John birthday greetings. To the consternation of the curial establishment, the pope telegrammed his thanks. Christmas greetings came the following year, and in 1963 the Soviet chairman sent his son-in-law to Rome to meet with John XXIII. Soon after that Pope John issued the encyclical *Pacem in Terris* calling for international peaceful coexistence.[187] The Cold War iceberg had begun to melt. As Pope Paul VI, Giovanni Montini, Pius's longtime collaborator in the papal secretariat, followed the path of John XXIII. In his speech at the United Nations in the fall of 1965, Pope Paul's words "jamais plus la guerre, jamais plus la guerre!" rang out resoundingly.

Although they disagree sharply about just about every aspect of the

Cold War, Judt and John Lewis Gaddis agree on the role of Pius XII's successors in ending it. Karol Wojtyla, John Paul II, completed the "work of Popes John XXIII and Paul VI," leading the "Church into a new era."[188] Soon after John Paul visited his native Poland in the summer of 1979, the workers' rights movement of Solidarnošč began, "a stirring prologue to the narrative of Communism's collapse."[189] Pius XII foresaw the Cold War, but unlike John XXIII, he was unable to foresee how it might end.

7
THE ORIGIN OF THE VATICAN RATLINES

During World War II, Pope Pius sought an end to the conflict at the expense of Communist Soviet Russia. Such an outcome presupposed a negotiated resolution to hostilities, which the pope very much wanted to believe to be a possibility. Pius, a realist, knew that the Allies would not accept a negotiated peace that did not spell an end to Hitler and his Nazis. How could this come about? During the war, the Vatican contemplated a muddled scheme that provided a way for refugees, including Nazis, to emigrate from Europe. One route led from Germany to Spain and thence to Argentina, the other from Germany to Rome to Genoa to South America. The two ratlines developed independently of each other, but, in time, the operators of the two routes collaborated.

The Vatican's ratline has always been thought of as a postwar episode that facilitated the escape of fascists, including war criminals. And so it was. But its origin lies earlier, during the war, before alarm about war criminals arose. To grasp this we must view the early war situation as part of on ongoing mindset at the Vatican that stretched from the 1930s to the Cold War. Seen from this perspective, it becomes clear that the Vatican's ratline did not come about initially to benefit war criminals, although it is undeniable that that is what it ended up doing.

The link between the 1930s and the ratline that developed after the war was Bishop Alois Hudal, a little and little-known Austrian with a big head. Hudal was in favor at the Vatican for a few years during the interwar period, but when he fell out of favor, he hung around and emerged as a prime player in the ratline scheme of the immediate postwar era. A coterie of Argentine diplomats that included Juan Carlos Goyeneche linked the Vatican and the Spanish ratline. Hudal and the Argentines independently concocted schemes whereby Nazis would help the Church fight communism. This plan hooked Pope Pius, who was ever fearful of Communists marching relentlessly onward. We turn first to Hudal.

During the 1930s, the Holy See had dithered, unable to decide whether its traditional foe, communism, or its new enemy, Nazism, posed the greater threat. Seizing the opportunity to promote himself, Bishop Hudal hatched a pro-Nazi plan of action. The Austrian bishop, an antisemitic pan-German nationalist, was first and foremost a self-serving schemer. According to historian Peter Godman, Hudal aimed to reconcile Nazism with Catholicism and emerge as the mediator who brilliantly conjoined the two. While proclaiming loudly that racism did not constitute the core of Nazism, Hudal secretly denounced Hitler's regime to the Holy See. Hudal pursued this foolish strategy, condemning the "bad" in Nazism so that it could be injected with the "good" of Catholicism. The Austrian bishop, who had been appointed rector of the German National Church in Rome in 1933, got Pius XI's ear by claiming that Nazism injected with Christianity would become the vanguard against bolshevism.[1]

Eugenio Pacelli should have known better. As nuncio to Germany, he had once written the Holy See that compromise with Nazis was impossible. As Vatican secretary of state during the 1930s, he could have shot down Hudal's wacky plan. Alarming evidence against the Nazis had accumulated daily. The ink on the concordat had not yet dried when the Nazis began ignoring it, most notably in 1934 when a racist sterilization law was passed that obviously contradicted Pius XI's recent encyclical, *Casti Conubii*. On June 30th, the famous Night of Long Knives when the top echelon of the Sturm Abteilung (SA) was eliminated, the Nazis also murdered Erich Klausener, the most prominent lay Catholic in Germany.[2] Neither the Vatican nor German bishops responded to this crime. Instead of denouncing national socialism, Pius XI assigned two Dutch Jesuits to investigate Nazi racism. The call for an investigation amounted to a nondecision on the part of Pacelli and Pius XI, neither of whom wanted to see the concordat with Germany broken.

The 1936 report of the Dutch priests on the Hitler regime found that racism was the heart and soul of Nazi philosophy. No compromise, they said, was possible with Catholicism. Hudal continued to say just the opposite. Hitler was a moderate, he said. German expansion into Eastern Europe, the Nazi program of Lebensraum, would drive Bolshevist Russia back. In their indecisiveness, Pacelli and Pius XI gave the study of the Dutch Jesuits to one in-house committee at the Vatican after another, which accomplished nothing except to kill time which, in Rome, seemed to stand still. In the meantime, Hitler unveiled the Nuremberg Laws in 1935. As the laws were being put into effect in 1936, the Vatican finally concluded that the Holy See should uphold the "law of justice and love toward all races," by no means excluding the Semitic race. "Here, for the first time among the documents of the Holy Office, the problem of anti-Semitism is mentioned explicitly."[3]

Thus, Hudal's loopy ideas of Nazi Christians lost ground inside the Vatican, but the Austrian prelate fought back, publishing first an article and then a book in which he argued that Nazi antisemitism constituted a "special case" which was justified by Jewish purveyance of "soulless materialism."[4] Hitler loved the book; Pius XI hated it. The pope wanted to put the book on the Index of Forbidden Books, but Pacelli persuaded him to have the Vatican's newspaper denounce it instead. Hudal, once considered for a cardinal's red hat, had done himself in. Pacelli, meanwhile, contented himself with doing battle on an ad hoc basis with Nazi violations of the concordat, avoiding an all-out confrontation. In the end, it was not the schemer Hudal who forestalled a blunt rejection of Nazi racism by the Holy See but the Spanish civil war.

From 1936 to 1939, Spain was the site of intramural ideological warfare in Europe. During the bloody civil war, Communists were responsible for murdering scores of priests and nuns among the over 30,000 total fatalities in the conflict. Insurgents under General Francisco Franco could not have prevailed had he not been assisted by thousands of soldiers and military hardware from Germany and Italy. In this way, the idea of Pius XI in the early 1930s for a coalition of Christian nations against communism became a reality in the latter years of that decade.[5] Authoritarian regimes had demonstrated that they could effectively combat bolshevism.

In a three-hour meeting in Hitler's Obersalzburg redoubt in the Bavarian Alps, the Führer taunted Cardinal Faulhaber with Hudal's idea that the Church and Nazis could work in tandem to destroy communism. Spain was the proof, and the Führer waved the little bishop's book in the cardinal's face. Hitler lectured Faulhaber about the danger that communism would spread from Spain to France and insisted that only Germany could stop the Bolshevist menace.[6] Pius XI and Pacelli needed little convincing about the significance of the war in Spain, which led them to a fateful decision. In 1937, the pope issued two encyclicals. In *Divini Redemptoris*, he harshly condemned communism once again, while in *Mit brennender Sorge* he criticized racism in carefully measured words. As Peter Godman has pointed out, this was a political decision that ignored the immorality of Nazi racism as it had been discerned by in-house committees at the Vatican.[7] Although the Holy See had abandoned Hudal's ideas, the Spanish civil war confirmed that fascism could indeed be used to fight bolshevism. This was a lesson in practical politics that neither Hudal nor Pacelli would forget, which explains why after World War II, they would engage in ratline activity.

Equivocating about their conviction regarding the evil of antisemitism, Pacelli and Pius XI, working with several German prelates, produced *Mit brennender Sorge* in 1937. Smuggled into Germany and read simultaneously from Catholic pulpits in March, it infuriated the Nazis because it decried racism. But in fact, the encyclical stepped lightly around the issue of racism so as to keep the concordat intact. Cardinal Pacelli's fingerprints are on *Mit brennender Sorge,* for, as Gerhart Besier has reasoned, the cardinal secretary's chances of succeeding Pius XI would have been greatly diminished had Hitler done away with the concordat, the cardinal's handiwork.[8]

Time passed, and the tentacles of Nazi antisemitism penetrated ever more deeply into the German social fabric, ripping Jews apart from it. Though the oppression in Italy was not as extreme as it was in Germany, Italian Jews also found themselves increasingly the targets of state-sponsored prejudice. Probably aware that he had not dealt acutely enough with fascist antisemitism, Pius XI commissioned yet another study of racism in 1938. Three Jesuits, this time a German, an American, and a Frenchman, were asked to draft an encyclical. Because of in-house Vatican subterfuge, the encyclical, *Humani Generis Unitas* (The Unity of Humankind), never came to light.[9] Had it been given, *Humani Generis* would have clearly delineated the immorality of racism. "All the rhetoric of 'racial impurity . . . ends by being uniquely the struggle against the Jews.'" The papal edict would have deplored the situation of the Jews who were denied "legal protection against violence and robbery, exposed to every form of insult and public degradation, innocent persons [who] are treated as criminals . . . traitors . . . outlaws."[10] A moment of truth slipped by.

Clearly, the notion that western European fascism would do battle with communism grew to be commonplace in the 1930s. Only Hudal carried the idea to the extreme, believing that top Nazis, whose antisemitism he justified, would be infused with Christianity and then do battle with bolshevism. Pius XI eventually scoffed at Hudal's naiveté, but the irksome bishop held fast, waiting for another day to breathe life into his theory. That day would come at the end of World War II. During that conflict, the Vatican consistently thought of Soviet bolshevism as its primary enemy. Starting from this outlook, Pope Pius XII entertained various schemes that in one way or another worked against the spread of communism. But because the war concluded with the Soviet Union threatening Western Europe, what evolved from these schemes was the Vatican's postwar effort to use Nazi fascists to combat communism. The idea that Hudal had unsuccessfully floated in the 1930s came full circle. The Vatican sparked new life into Hudal's plan when Pius XII's close advisor Father Leiber wrote to the Austrian bishop at the time of Germany's invasion of the Soviet Union, telling him that in some sense he could look at the mission as a crusade.[11] Here, the Vatican was simply leading Hudal on, for the pope himself did not subscribe to the crusade notion.[12] What Pius XI had eschewed Pius XII took up under quite different circumstances, and Hudal's dream of the 1930s became the Holy See's postwar ratline in the 1940s. To see how this linkage came into place we must briefly review diplomatic intrigue at the Vatican during the war.

The Spanish Ratline

Early in the war a coterie of German army officers, hoping to avoid a two-front war, plotted to overthrow Hitler and come to terms with Germany's western enemies. The officers saw Pope Pius as the best intermediary and enlisted a Munich lawyer, Josef Müller, to engage the Vatican.[13] The prospect of eliminating Hitler while preserving a strong anti-Soviet Germany was too good to be passed up. Pius XII, breaking all rules of neutrality, accepted the role of intermediary. The pope's willingness to go along with the plot can be reckoned, historian Klemens von Klemperer, quoting Harold C. Deutsch, pointed out, as "among the most astounding events in the modern history of the papacy."[14] Although the negotiations had realistic possibilities, they eventually fell through. Pius XII made a dangerous gamble. When German intelligence uncovered the plot including the pope's role, only Hitler's irresponsible rejection of sound German intelligence saved Pope Pius from dire consequences.[15] History can be fickle; had Hitler had the good sense to rely on competent German intelligence, Pius XII would now stand out in the record of World War II as a hero.

As the war progressed, the Vatican remained flexible but steadfast in opposition to bolshevism. From Rome's perspective, matters took a turn for the better in the summer of 1941 when Germany attacked its ally, the Soviet Union. At least now Europe's two main enemies of Christianity were not aligned. In the view of a high-ranking Vatican diplomat, Archbishop Filippo Bernardini, a Nazified Europe would lead to only a temporary persecution of the Church, which, like metal in fire, would purify Catholicism.[16] Pius XII and President Roosevelt went round and round in the fall of 1941 regarding the wisdom of the United States arming Stalin's army through the lend-lease program.[17] Both sides exaggerated, the president postulating freedom of religion under Stalin and the Holy See emphasizing Soviet abuses in eastern occupied Poland when it certainly knew that German atrocities in western occupied Poland far exceeded those in the east.[18] Monsignor Tardini suggested giving the Soviets enough help to keep Hitler's army busy far away in Eastern Europe but not enough to allow Stalin's army into the heartland of Europe.[19] Clearly, the Vatican had no love of Hitler's Germany, but its fear of Bolshevist Russia offset its contempt for Nazism.

By the summer of 1942, a powerful Germany held sway over a Nazified Europe. In the judgment of Pope Pius, Germany's grasp on the continent could not be successfully challenged, at least not in the foreseeable future. Harold Tittmann sent word to the State Department that Pius did not think the Allies would prevail in the war. The pope, Tittmann reported, expected that whichever side emerged victorious from the coming struggle for Moscow, Stalingrad, and Leningrad would sue for an advantageous peace.[20] This would present Pope Pius with the opportunity to play the peacemaker, a role he would certainly relish.[21] The Vatican newspaper promoted the aptness of the pope for peace negotiations.

Such was the war's status when Argentina came forward with a harebrained design for peace with Pius XII playing a central role. Spain, Portugal, Argentina, and the Vatican together with Germany would be the nucleus of an Iberio-American bloc that would sponsor a worldwide political realignment. Archival records from Argentina that have been exploited by Uki Goñi disclose that in the spring of 1942, Juan Carlos Goyeneche, accompanied by Spain's ambassador to Germany, Adrián Escobar, was sent by the Argentine government to engage top Nazis, Foreign Minister Ribbentrop and Reichsminister Himmler, in peace talks based on the continuance of the status quo—that is, a Nazified Europe. After concluding talks with the Germans, Goyeneche traveled to Rome to meet with Vatican officials. Goyeneche had sound family and official credentials. The foreign minister of Argentina, Enrique Ruiz Guiñazú, and his close advisor, Mario Amadeo—both of whom had formerly served as ambassadors to the Holy See where they had been close to Under-Secretary of State Montini—authorized Goyeneche's mission.[22] The Argentine envoy had a private audience with Pius XII and the Argentine ambassador met with Secretary of State Maglione to discuss the peace plan. Afterward, Goyeneche returned to Germany for a follow-up conference with Ribbentrop.

The 1940 peace plan—the plot to overthrow Hitler—and the 1942 peace plan had one thing in common: both victimized the Soviet Union. But besides being scatterbrained, the 1942 peace plan differed from the 1940 plot to overthrow Hitler in that the top Nazis would not be eliminated. A nazified Europe would remain intact, a situation which promised persecution of the Christian churches. Most likely for this reason in June 1941, Pius XII proposed open borders for would-be emigrants.[23] The Vatican succeeded in getting the Argentinians to agree that after the war, European Catholics who felt themselves in mortal danger from the Nazis could emigrate to their country. The Argentine foreign minister cabled his ambassador to the Vatican suggesting that the two neutral states, Argentina and the Vatican, mediate a peace. On October 6, 1942, Ambassador Llobet replied to the foreign minister that he had met with Monsignor Maglione, who "suggested to me that the pontiff would be interested in knowing the willingness of the government of the Argentine Republic to apply its immigration laws generously, in order to encourage at the opportune moment European Catholic immigrants to seek the necessary land and capital in our country."[24] Subsequently, a German priest stationed in Rome, Father Anton Weber, who headed the Rome branch of the St. Raphael Society, an organization that gave assistance to Catholic emigrants, traveled to Portugal with plans to continue on to Argentina, presumably to lay the groundwork for immigration of Catholics.[25] This was the innocent origin of what would become the Vatican ratline.

Germany, which by this time was at war with the United States, gained a bridge to the western hemisphere through the proposed peace plan. Argentina would be allowed to seize the Falkland Islands and the Vatican would be named the governor of the city of Jerusalem. A worldwide political realignment indeed!

Argentina continued its talks with Germany and the Vatican in 1943. Juan Perón, who had done military training under Mussolini in 1942, came to power in Argentina in the spring of 1943, assisted by Fifth Column activity organized by Walter Schellenberg, head of German foreign intelligence.[26] When the Soviet Union inaugurated diplomatic relations with Uruguay and Colombia (and with Chile in 1945), the Argentines feared a "Bolshevist penetration of our Continent."[27] Perón wanted to build a South American fascist coalition to oppose communism. The Vatican, naturally, backed him completely. For the same reason—to thwart communism—Pius XII urged Bolivia not to break diplomatic relations with Germany.[28] The issue that had hitherto snagged Iberio-Vatican-Argentine talks with Germany was Christianity. The Nazis had been inflexible in 1942, at which time they persistently deflected discussions about

Christianity, but they were not so sure of themselves in 1943. In a meeting with Himmler, Goyeneche stressed the indestructible roots of Catholicism in Argentina and asserted that if Europe fell to communism, South America would follow. In other words, if the two countries were to team up against bolshevism, religion had to be part of the bargain. Himmler, the man who had been responsible for the death of tens of thousands of Catholic Poles, told Goyeneche to let Pope Pius know that he was "very approachable" on religious matters.[29] After discussions with Himmler, Goyeneche orchestrated understandings with Vichy France, Hungary, Rumania, Slovenia, Italy, Spain, and Portugal, the purpose of which was to organize the Christian order of postwar Europe.

The absurdity of these proceedings need not be belabored. What is of significance in trying to search out the ratline's beginnings is the shift in emphasis from 1942 to 1943. When the Nazis were winning the war in 1942, Christians were at risk. When that superiority came into doubt after Soviet victories at Stalingrad and Kursk in 1943, the fascists understood the potential peril of their future. Although by then many fascists had innocent blood on their hands, they were no longer in a position to scorn religion. So it was that by the fifth year of the war, Hudal's notion that Christian Nazis would do battle with communism came full circle. But in 1944 it was not yet time for Hudal's regrettable reappearance in the pages of history.

The postwar interrogation of German foreign intelligence chief Walter Schellenberg by the Allies makes clear the central role the Vatican was playing in the Iberio-Vatican-Argentine scheme. As Germany's fortunes took a turn for the worse in 1943, Schellenberg intended to use the close contacts that Ambassador Escobar, Goyeneche, and Amadeo had with the Vatican to put out peace feelers. The Argentines made it clear, Schellenberg testified, that the Nazis would have to accept the Catholic element if cooperation was to go forward. Although the Argentines and Spaniards took the diplomatic lead, Schellenberg believed that the Vatican's involvement was essential. Once again the Vatican was hoping that some sort of accord between Nazism and the Church could work against bolshevism.[30]

In the last two years of the war, Spain, not Rome, became the first center of ratline activity that facilitated the escape of Nazi fascists. The Vatican, nevertheless, took part in planning the exodus of fascists from Europe. From the outset, the governments of Iberian nations and the Vatican agreed essentially that Europe was involved in two wars—one an intramural war, the other a war against bolshevism.[31] When the former war ended, the war against communism would continue—if not conducted by Germany, then by the United States and Great Britain. By 1944, it appeared more certain that it would be the United States and Great Britain, not Germany, that would lead the battle against communism. For the previous two years, Spain, Argentina, and the Vatican had been discussing peace and emigration strategies with Germany. In addition, at the Vatican secretariat of state, Monsignor Montini had participated closely as early as 1943 with a Madrid group whose purpose was to "save Europe from bolshevism, prevent communism in Germany and . . . keep in touch with the German military circles and after the collapse of Germany and the fall of the Nazis, *help the military right wing together with a capitalist government seize power*" (italics added).[32] Thus, from the outset the Vatican worked to provide Nazi fugitives with a base of operations.

For a number of reasons Spain offered the best base for such operations for Nazis, both for anti-Communist plots and for hideaways. Though Spain was supposedly neutral, Franco sent the Spanish Blue Division to Germany to fight bolshevism during World War II. Falangists, who were predominant in Spain after the civil war, identified with Nazi ideology, though not with its antireligious policies. Spain's foreign minister, Serrano Suñer, had allowed German military personnel to direct Falangists in anti-Communist "Nazi-fascist activities in those South American countries who have broken off from the Axis."[33] Furthermore, economic cooperation between Germany and Spain had increased during the war, with, as we have seen, much-needed tungsten going to Germany and wheat and gold going back the other way. A number of large German companies had established branches in Spain, where they succeeded in cloaking their operations and identities under an umbrella organization called Sofindus.

Franco, who saw the benefit for Spain's economy, welcomed the Germans and neglected to report them to the Allies, just as during the war he had frustrated the SS by allowing thousands of Jews to find sanctuary in his country. Safehaven, the name the American intelligence community gave to its efforts to deny a safe haven for any stolen Nazi funds, could not successfully track much of the flow of German capital to Spain.[34] Toward the end of the war the transfer of funds out of Germany became substantial; Safehaven was aware that the Iberian Peninsula served as an "underground route for transfers to Latin America."[35] In Schellenberg's opinion, the Church played a central role in Spanish-German-Argentine economic planning that would facilitate emigration to South America. U.S. intelligence corroborated this view: "In 1945 the apostolic nuncio to Argentina reported to the Holy See that financial experts from Argentina and from Spain had conferred in Buenos Aires to plan financial collaboration between the two countries and other Spanish-American countries. The nuncio stated that German financial specialists were also present at the conference."[36] A Señor Chaves, who had been involved with emigration from Europe to Argentina as early as 1943, participated in the transfer of capital. In 1945, Chaves visited the Vatican, possibly to arrange money-laundering through the Vatican-owned South American banking chain, Sudameris.[37] In 1945 and 1946, Safehaven personnel repeatedly complained about Franco's protection of Sofindus companies and funds. The Falange-Nazi link and the liquidity of German capital in Spain and Argentina made Spain the ideal country for ratline activity.

Charles Lesca, a French citizen, and Pierre Daye, a Belgian, organized the first Spanish ratline. In December 1944, Walter Schellenberg flooded Lesca with cash and worked with Spanish intelligence to coordinate the emigration of German fascists. Daye, working out of Madrid, used his government contacts to get German displaced persons and prisoners of war out of detention and find them employment in German firms. By the summer of 1944, the Allies had caught on to the ratline activity. The American embassy notified all consulate personnel to be alert to the whereabouts of war criminals as defined by the Hague conventions in 1907.[38] Both Lesca and Daye were rabid antisemites. Both wrote occasionally for the viciously antisemitic journal *Je Suis Partout*. Lesca was a member of Action Française, an organization that Pius XI had condemned in 1926. Pius XII had lifted the ban in 1939; he liked the anticommunism of Action Française more than he disliked its antisemitism. In January 1943, Pius XII gave Daye his papal blessing during a private audience. The benediction did not help Daye; he was condemned to death by a Belgian court in 1946 for collaboration with the Nazis. Daye escaped to Argentina, where Lesca and Amadeo, Monsignor Montini's confidant, received him.[39] Uki Goñi discovered that it was "through the personal intercession in Rome of French cardinal Eugène Tisserant and the newly consecrated Argentine cardinal Antonio Caggiano that [Lesca and Daye] were first able to flee Europe."[40] Many more war criminals would make use of the ratline that Daye and Lesca, working with Caggiano, had opened. For Cardinal Caggiano, who in 1960 denounced Israel's capture of Adolf Eichmann, no perpetrator of Holocaust atrocities was so heinous as to be undeserving of forgiveness.[41]

By 1946, American intelligence had acquired a clear idea of just whom they were dealing with regarding the influx of Germans into Spain. U.S. agents compiled a list of Nazis in the Miranda POW camp that showed that a great number of war criminals had successfully fled

Germany at the war's end. The partial alphabetical list—partial because it breaks off at the letter "E"—showed that the refugees had helped run a number of notorious concentration camps, including Mauthausen, Ravensbrück, Flossenberg, Dachau, Buchenwald, Natzweiler, Stutthof, and Auschwitz. Several of the men had been officers in the camps.[42] Using the list as a rule of thumb, one may conclude that there were hundreds of war criminals in Spain in 1946. In addition, we can reckon on the presence of thousands of diehard Nazi fascists there.

Although these Germans were obviously on the run, the Vatican was prepared to offer asylum to any and all refugees. As a neutral state, the Vatican had "played no favorites" when Germany occupied Italy, and it continued this policy after the war. But in August of 1943 the Allies had requested that neutral countries not give asylum to war criminals, and the Vatican, among other neutrals, had been notified of this request.[43] After the war the Allies asked that all Axis aliens residing outside of their country of origin be turned over to occupational authorities, who would then ascertain whether such persons would have to stand trial for war crimes. The policy was obviously based on the reaction to the horrors of the Holocaust, which had come to light in news and film media around the world. However, there was no hard-and-fast definition of war crimes. Some formerly neutral countries, Sweden and Switzerland, for example, announced that they would "refuse admission to those aliens whose acts had offended the civilized world."[44] U.S. Secretary of State James Byrnes told Robert Murphy, President Truman's political advisor for occupied (zonal) Germany, that Vatican cooperation in turning over aliens was "negligible."[45] Nevertheless, offering asylum was the Church's policy. While "playing no favorites" during the war made sense for the Vatican, a neutral state, the reality of the Holocaust made such a policy by a church-run state a moral farce in the postwar era.

In fact, the Vatican not only offered asylum to refugees, including fugitives, but it also helped them escape to South America. What had in previous years been only potential "peace and emigration" schemes, and rather loony ones at that, now became definite programs, and the Vatican took the lead. Early in the summer of 1946, Monsignor Montini of the Vatican secretariat told the Argentine ambassador that the Holy Father was interested in helping Catholics of whatever nationality emigrate who for whatever reason found that they were not able to find a livelihood in Europe.[46] The ambassador replied that Argentina would be a good solution to the problem of where to relocate such individuals and learned that the Vatican wanted to set up the technical apparatus to inaugurate and carry out a program of emigration. The specification that the emigrant be Catholic would not turn out to be a sine qua non, as we will see; what mattered had to do with the emigrant's politics, and the bigger the Nazi the greater the anti-Communist became the rule.

War Criminals among the War's Refugees

The Vatican's assistance to emigrating fascists was not a stand-alone operation. It was folded into help for emigrants in general through its Emigration Bureau. Contemporaries estimated that there were about 400,000 mostly Eastern European Catholic displaced persons in zonal Germany, Austria, and Italy after the war. This was just an educated guess. In reality there were well over 1 million, many of whom the United Nations Relief and Rehabilitation Administration was able to repatriate before its charter expired in 1948.[47] That still left nearly 1 million displaced persons seeking to emigrate from Europe to avoid the harsh treatment they would certainly encounter if they were repatriated to their homelands. The Vatican wished to help the Catholic displaced persons, both to avoid cruel treatment of them if they were repatriated and to make use of them in South America to offset Communist propaganda and activity there. If among these hundreds of thousands of displaced persons a relatively small number of fascist war criminals should also find their way across the ocean, the Vatican had no objection. In fact, the Holy See helped them escape. The ratline was the shady side of a larger and, by any reckoning, quite legitimate and constructive program under the auspices of the Vatican Emigration Bureau.

To finance the emigration of hundreds of thousands of people, the Holy See turned to the U.S. Catholic Church. The bishops responded by setting up an agency called War Relief Services under the organizational roof of the National Catholic Welfare Committee (NCWC). In taking this step, the bishops understood that

> its basic function was to assist the bishops in Latin American countries in carrying out the instructions included in the letter of Monsignor Montini, addressed to the nuncios of these countries on September 27, 1946. This letter was the clear expression of the mind of the Holy Father in regard to the responsibility of the church throughout the world to assist in finding new homes for the very large number of people forced to leave Europe.[48]

Thus, the U.S. bishops thought that they were part of a worldwide movement operating under the guidance of the Holy See in a great work of international charity. And so they were. "Any success that the mission had in its work," Monsignor John O'Grady, who was the bishops' point man in South America, reported, "had been due, more than anything else, to the fact that it carried out a program that had been formulated by the Holy See and in which the Holy See had a definite and vital interest."[49]

Pius XII wanted the North American Church to provide his South American emigration enterprise with money, but he also wanted organizational and political savvy. The purpose of Monsignor O'Grady's trip to Latin America was to marshal a system for receiving refugees from abroad into the churches of those countries. At home in the United States, American bishops could use the NCWC as a powerful lobby that reached the president and the highest branches of government. Increasingly after 1946, the bishops found a ready audience in Washington when they voiced their fears about the spread of communism. But without money, especially for maritime transport of displaced persons, Rome's emigration program could not function. The Vatican, which had no intention of using its own money for the project, turned to U.S. Catholics, whose response appears to have been more than adequate. My research of the NCWC archives shows that the U.S. Church expended at least $5 million (nearly $72 million in 2006 dollars) between 1946 and 1950.[50] Some of these dollars supported refugees stuck in displaced persons camps or indigent Germans, but most of it was funneled to Rome. Pope Pius expressed his gratitude to U.S. Catholic leaders in 1948, saying that the bishops were a "shining example of charity" whose efforts made it possible to repair "the ruined fortunes of displaced persons in Europe."[51] The Vatican's Emigration Bureau worked hand in glove with the U.S. bishops' War Relief Services office.

The O'Grady mission produced uneven results. He reported that for the most part the Latin American churches lacked an organizational structure at the diocesan level that would allow them to address the difficulties large-scale immigration would pose. The country that was the exception to the rule was, not surprisingly, Argentina, whose diplomats had interacted with the Vatican on immigration schemes, as we have seen, since the middle years of the war. O'Grady was received by the nuncio, by top Argentine cardinals (including Cardinal Caggiano who, as we have seen, had already been a key organizer in the original Spanish ratline), and by President Perón himself. "The best indication of the results of these negotiations with Argentina," O'Grady reported to the NCWC, "is the fact that more than 5,000 visas have been issued to people in camps in Italy and who are actually waiting for transportation." Neither O'Grady nor the U.S. bishops, who were footing the bill, had control, however, over who those visas were issued to. In setting down policy with the NCWC, the Holy See had let it be known that "in Italy, it is understood that the national committee[s] for emigration [are] in charge of emigration with the Pontifia Commissione d'Assistenza [Pontifical Commission of Assistance] responsible for the resettlement of non-Italians."[52] (The Pontifical Commission of Assistance was what U.S. bishops called the Vatican's Emigration Bureau.) Clearly, U.S. bishops had no control over which displaced persons would be sent on their way to South America.

It would be interesting, but idle, to speculate about what would have occurred had the bishops known that Nazi and Ustaša fascist war criminals would be on the receiving end of U.S. Catholic largess. The bishops had no idea that the Vatican had been working a Latin American ratline since late in the war. In December 1947, the NCWC set up a National Catholic Resettlement Council, which organized immigration into the United States. When the resettlement council met to organize itself, it summoned representatives of various American Catholic ethnic groups, one of which was Croatian. One of its delegates was Adolf (aka Ante) Doshen. After three months and three meetings, the bishops found out who Doshen was—a convicted felon. As secretary-general of the Croatian Homeguard, a pro-fascist organization in the United States, Doshen had collected funds for Ante Pavelić, the Ustaša puppet ruler of Croatia, which was at war with the Allies. The federal district court of the western district of Pennsylvania fined Doshen and sent him to jail on the charges of illegal entry and perjury.[53] As soon as Doshen's identity became known, he was removed from the council. Little did the bishops realize that at that very time of their discovery of Doshen's past and his ties to Pavelić, the Vatican was sheltering Ante Pavelić in Rome. As we will see, Pavelić eventually made his way to Argentina with one of the visas Perón handed out.[54]

At the same time that the Vatican was engaging the U.S. Church, Monsignor Montini was carrying out the discussions with the Argentine ambassador to the Vatican so that emigration of displaced persons could begin. The undertaking sounded legitimate, but it left unsaid the fact that the program was also a cover for "anti-Communist agents who intend to combat the activities of the Communists in South America."[55] Even though Montini had said that the Vatican was interested only in Catholic refugees, American intelligence reported that "the Holy See is specifically in agreement with the Argentine government regarding this emigration project as a cover to allow for counteractive operations against both Communist infiltration and [their] operative objectives in South America."[56] The apprehension of Péron and Pius about communism taking root in South America was not just fantasy. Intelligence reports noted in 1944 that the Soviets were trying to step up their presence and to "culti-

FIGURE 9. Much of dictator Juan Perón's popularity derived from the fashionable Eva, here leaving from a private audience with Pius XII. Perón and the Vatican cooperated on the Nazi ratlines. Perón was excommunicated in 1955 for unrelated reasons. *Courtesy of Bettmann Archive.*

vate the idea of USSR being the leader in progressive development."[57] As far as Pius XII was concerned, the first order of business was to put down communism; that is why he preferred to see fascist war criminals on board ships sailing to the New World rather than rotting in POW camps in zonal Germany. The North American bishops, completely unaware of the ratline aspect of the Vatican's emigration work, agreed wholeheartedly that communism in Latin American was "spreading everywhere" and had to be curbed.

U.S. Catholic Church leaders did not suspect that the Vatican's emigration work which they funded helped war criminals along with the thousands of innocent displaced persons.[58] O'Grady assured the bishops that all of the displaced persons in European camps were "a fine type of people . . . the best people of the countries of their origin." Proof thereof, O'Grady said, was that they are the ones who stood "up and offer[ed] the stiffest resistance to Communistic forces in their respective countries."[59]

The bishops needed little convincing. They were appalled that the British occupational forces had recently forced 15,000 Croats to return to Yugoslavia, where they would face Tito's cruelty. This was in addition to 12,000 who had been repatriated in 1945, all of whom the bishops believed to have been executed. U.S. bishops, who feared for displaced persons if they were returned to Communist countries, worked with a sense of urgency. They had no idea that fascists with shady backgrounds were working for the Holy See's Emigration Bureau, but U.S. intelligence did. Agent Henry Nigrelli provided a detailed account of the Vatican's activity in June 1946:

> The Holy See is involved in a plan to organize emigration to South America.
>
> Don Aurelio Torrazza, secretary to Archbishop Siri of Genoa, is in charge.
>
> Torrazza will lead a pontifical mission to South America.
>
> Baron Robert Fauçon de Tourenne will assist Torrazza.
>
> The cost of emigration will be determined.
>
> The project will be "nursed by the Holy See."
>
> The project will be administered by the pontifical mission [Emigration Bureau].
>
> The actual purpose of the project is to fight communism in South America.[60]

U.S. bishops did not know about Tourenne, who had been a Petain collaborator with the very suspect position of secretary to the minister of refugees and prisoners—in other words, Jews. "Despite the shady political past of Tourenne," Nigrelli reported, "the Holy See is persistent about employing him."[61] That he did not have a passport and could not get one without returning to France to face an uncertain fate because of his handling of Jewish refugees did not bother the Holy See. He would travel as a citizen of Vatican state.

Such is the bizarre history of the origin of the Vatican's ratline, from its emergence in a helter-skelter manner from Bishop Hudal's fanciful convictions in the 1930s to the nebulous schemes of 1942 and 1943 to the Nazi escape routes of 1945 and thereafter. The Vatican's emigration setup was centered in Italy and controlled by the Holy See. A second emigration scheme operated out of Spain. Although fostered by the Vatican, it appears to have been run more independently of Rome than the Italian operation of the Vatican Emigration Bureau. There was, nevertheless, as we will see, a link between the Spanish and Italian setups.

The First Ratline

When Nazis on the lam crossed over the Pyrenees into Spain, they were taken into custody by Spanish authorities, who then passed them on to a network of nonmilitary German nationals who had funds at their disposal to care for the fugitives. The funds came from German accounts that the Allies wanted but were unable to block. In 1946, Father Mohr, a German priest who was unsympathetic toward Hitler's regime visited a German POW camp in Spain and came away disgusted: he "found camps being administered in the old true Nazi spirit. [He] thinks they get money from blocked German accounts in Spain. Spanish authorities treat Nazi prisoners well and non-Nazi prisoners badly. Nazis get very good food, the others very bad food. Mohr returned indignant from his tour of inspection."[62] The fugitive Nazis were outfitted with new clothes and given a weekly allowance.[63] Since the Allies had not occupied neutral Spain during the war, they could do little more than sit by and watch the refugee operation.

In the jargon of the day there were three kinds of refugees, whites, blacks, and grays. Whites were Jews heading mostly for Palestine, blacks were atrocity perpetrators—war criminals heading for South America, and grays were the rest, most but not all of whom were guiltless. When word from U.S. intelligence about escaping blacks reached the State Department, it touched off concern. State sent operative Vincent La Vista to Rome to investigate because there were so many whites, grays, and, reputedly, blacks flowing to and through Italy. La Vista soon reported that he had been able to visit all "the welfare offices in Rome that participate knowingly or unknowingly in illegal emigration. The only person I was unable to contact was the notorious Dr. [Willy] Nix."[64] He reported that there were two principal emigration agencies in Rome, the American Joint Distribution Committee (AJDC) and the Vatican. The AJDC handled whites. The Vatican served blacks and grays without distinguishing between the two. The La Vista report stunned the State Department. It told J. Graham Parsons, its intelligence agent assigned to the Taylor mission at the Vatican, to verify La Vista's work. Relying on information obtained inside the Vatican, Parsons confirmed everything La Vista had written.[65]

When discussing the work of Krunoslav Draganović, one of the Vatican's principal ratline agents in Italy, we will return to the La Vista report.[66] Its importance here lies in the fact that La Vista identified Genoa as the port of embarkation for blacks. German blacks traveling to Spain used the Genoa-Barcelona ship line.

In the same month that La Vista filed his report, May 1947, American intelligence in Spain identified Jose La Boos, a German Catholic priest, as the leader of the Spanish ratline. In April, Boos met with the cardinal primate of Toledo; the papal nuncio to Spain; Franco's foreign minister, Serrano Suñer; and another Catholic priest, Karl Sauer.[67] The meeting took place in Madrid in Suñer's office. Boos's work consisted of shipping relief goods from Spain to impoverished postwar Germany and shipping German blacks to South America. Boos had liaised with the Swiss and German Caritas organizations, the Church's continental charity organization, or so he said. To legitimize his work, Boos claimed to be an authorized agent of the German bishops. Given the high rank of the individuals who attended the April meeting, American intelligence believed that they were engaged in carrying out the anti-Communist emigration plan that the Monsignor Montini had previously set up with Argentina. The embassy official who filed the report on Boos concluded that "right now we can only watch and wait."[68]

Boos had in fact already established the organization in Spain to help fascists, meaning blacks, emigrate. American intelligence had become aware of Boos's group in January 1946, more than a year before the meeting he had requested in Madrid. Since the end of the war, Boos had tended to German refugees who had fled to Spain across the Pyrenees. At some point in 1946 Boos extended his operation in order to help Nazi blacks who had fled to Italy emigrate from there. Boos had been traveling to Rome to coordinate the escape of these Germans. In all likelihood he met there with Bishop Hudal, or Hudal's assistant, Reinhard Kops, who had set up an organization like Boos's in Rome to shelter runaway Nazis on their way to South America.[69] But in January 1947, Boos had arranged to go directly to Genoa, where he met with Father Weber, who, it will be recalled, was working during the war for the St. Raphael Society (to assist German emigrants) at the time of the 1942 Iberio-Vatican-Argentine emigration scheme. In Genoa, Weber and Boos worked together "in order to give the last touches to the magnificently working organization in that place providing German escapees with money and false documents."[70] These German blacks embarked from Genoa en route to Barcelona, there to be received by Boos's Spanish-based operation. In April, the high-ranking churchmen met in Madrid with Foreign Minister Suñer to coordinate the flow of Germans coming from Italy. Suñer agreed to the plan but insisted that the "refugees" be called Central Europeans rather than Germans.[71]

Boos's relief work gained a great deal of publicity in major Spanish newspapers and on national radio (which was run by a Falangist) but not, naturally, his ratline activity. Financing for Boos's operation came from the major pools of German money in Spain—AEG (the Allgemeine Electrizitäts Gesellschaft, the German equivalent of General Electric) and Sofindus. Both Herbert Hellmann, head of AEG-Madrid, and Johannes Bernhardt, overseer of Sofindus, took part in the emigration work in addition to providing money. 200,000 pesetas had been made available for the POW work, of which 65,000 had already been spent for new clothing. Hellmann promised to try to get additional monies from AEG, Siemens, and Telefunken, even though those funds were supposedly blocked.[72] This ample support and the Spanish government's connivance allowed Boos to travel extensively in Europe, bring black Germans by ship from Italy to Spain, hire a staff of about ten people, and open centers of operation at several locations in the country.

The Germans who poured over the Pyrenees into Spain included blacks and grays. Those whom Boos brought from Genoa were only blacks. It fell to Boos's staff, which was headed by the very industrious Clarita Stauffer, to separate the grays from the blacks. The grays—those who had never been Nazis or whose enthusiasm had evaporated with Hitler's suicide—were to be sent back to Germany; the blacks—diehard Nazis—were destined for a South American port. For the moment, however, there was no need to hurry them out of the country. Boos and his group thought that war between the Allies and the Soviet Union would erupt any day. In this case, both grays and blacks would serve against the Bolsheviks in the great continental showdown between Christian fascism and communism. If that day did not come, the blacks would head out to Argentina far from their homeland and prosecution as war criminals, there to enlist once again in the struggle against bolshevism. One way or another, Bishop Hudal's fantasy would come alive. When the continental showdown with communism failed to materialize, Spain, which had been the Jews' highway of exodus from Europe until 1943, became the route of escape for the Jews' tormentors after the war.

Clarita Stauffer's work illustrates how Boos's organization sifted through the grays and the blacks. In February 1947, she visited the Miranda POW camp, from whence she escorted prisoners to Salamanca, a more comfortable facility but still under Spanish custody. Some grays had double identity papers; they would be placed in jobs here and there across the country and "disappear forever." Blacks and those lacking such papers numbered 180. Of that number, 150 qualified as grays in Stauffer's eyes and would return to Germany. "The rest," said an American intelligence report, "has its reasons for not returning."[73]

The Spanish government under dictator Francisco Franco had no objections to having industrious Germans remain in its country. This made it possible for Stauffer to arrange with local authorities for a Spanish person to act as a "guarantor"—one who provided food and lodging—for individual German POWs, who would then be released. This scenario played out at the Salamanca, Barcelona, and Valladolid detention camps. In fact, most of the "guarantors" were fictitious or were Spaniards acting as fronts whose money came from Bernhardt of Sofindus. SS members were among those released. A German woman, Mariane Witte, a former secretary in the Gestapo, looked after the released POWs.[74]

All of this was made possible because Franco liked having fascists who had the German work ethic in his country. The government did nothing to extradite some 500 "priority Germans." Nor did the government act on the seventy POWs, probably all blacks, who were on a most-wanted list, even though the Spaniards had agreed to arrest and extradite them.[75] The Allies complained that the government would not suppress transplanted German industry and would not cooperate in repatriating blacks. But their dissatisfaction did not stop there. The American embassy complained that

> above all the schools have been allowed to continue to operate and relay raw Nazi propaganda to pupils. Nazi culture is practiced in these schools, i.e. holidays, celebrations, military stuff, doctrine, pagan religion. The United Nations regard German schools as the very fountainhead of the evil influence which resulted in the present war, the destruction of Europe and the horrors exemplified by the German concentration camps.[76]

In June 1947, Father Karl Sauer (who had accompanied Boos to the Madrid meeting with the nuncio and Foreign Minister Suñer) paid a courtesy visit to the American embassy. It seemed that Sauer disliked being associated with Boos and wished to make this clear. Hudson Smith of the embassy mentioned that Sauer's name appeared on the letterhead of the Boos organization's stationery. That, Sauer asserted, had happened without his knowledge and he regretted it. Smith then told Sauer that the Allies disapproved of Boos's exaggerations, for example, that 50 percent of German children were starving to death. Sauer asserted that he also disapproved and said that he would stop them. After his visit such statements did indeed cease. Smith concluded that Sauer was a bona fide representative of Swiss Caritas and that Boos only claimed such affiliation. Sauer had produced a letter from Monsignor Montini which said that the pope praised his work, meaning the work of sending relief goods to indigent Germans.[77] Smith concluded from the meeting that Sauer was legitimate and did not accuse or associate him with Boos's work with black German fugitives from justice.

It came as a surprise, therefore, when the American embassy in Buenos Aires notified the embassy in Madrid that Boos and Sauer were working together to ship the fugitives to South America. Early in 1948 the Buenos Aires embassy requested an investigation of two Spanish ratline organizations. One was that of the Caritas association, "of which father Saurer [*sic*] and Rektor Boos appear to be the leaders."[78] The Jesuit provincials of Seville in Spain and of Buenos Aires in Argentina operated the second ratline on both sides of the ocean with the cooperation of Falangists. All of emigrants were black Nazis with falsified identification papers.[79] At the receiving end in Argentina, cells were established to organize the immigrant fascists into anti-Communist groups. By 1948, five such groups of an unknown number had been formed. "A Miss Goyeneche leads [one] group. She is the head of the Accion Catolica and member of the Juan Carlos Goyeneche family, prominent in Argentine diplomatic circles."[80] Miss Goyeneche was in fact the wife of Juan Carlos Goyeneche, the negotiator with top Nazis and the Holy See in the Iberio-Vatican-Argentine scheme of 1942–1943.

The Madrid embassy must have wondered why Sauer had attended the Madrid meeting with Boos and the top church and state officials if he was not working in the Boos enterprise. An investigation began. Almost a year after Sauer's visit with Smith at the American embassy, the Allies discovered the truth—Sauer's Caritas work was a cover to hide his efforts to aid black Germans. Sauer, who turned out to be a Spanish Jesuit, was associated closely with the "Nazi fanatic Clarita Stauffer organization which aids Nazi youth in Spain to escape to the western hemisphere."[81] Sauer, American intelligence discovered, had around half a million pesetas at his disposal, money which he had collected by appealing for funds for the destitute in Germany.

That Father Sauer managed for a while to pull the wool over the eyes of the United States is of little importance. More compelling is the letter of the Buenos Aires embassy testifying to the fact that the scheme that Juan Carlos Goyeneche hatched in 1942 and in modified form in 1943 had become a reality at the end of the war. From the beginning, the Vatican had involved itself closely in this project. There is no doubt that it embraced the policy of using Nazi fascists, including blacks, during the postwar years. As we will see in subsequent chapters, the Spanish ratline was only one of several operating under the aegis of the Vatican. One month after the June 1947 meeting in Madrid of Boos, Sauer, the papal nuncio, the cardinal primate of Toledo, and the foreign minister of Spain, an American diplomat who had been working in the Buenos Aires embassy before being transferred to the embassy in Yugoslavia wrote to the State Department deploring the fact that "the Vatican and Argentina [are conniving] to get guilty people to haven in latter country."[82] A second U.S. diplomat, Hiram Bingham, IV, had earlier notified state of the Vatican-Argentina ratline. Disobeying his American state department superior during the war, Bingham had helped thousands of Jews escape, for which reason he was demoted and posted to Argentina. As early as 1946, Bingham notified Washington of illegal Nazi immigration into that country, "but the state department quashed his efforts to investigate."[83]

A tangle of ideas, human emotions, and changing circumstances generates history. Who would ever imagine that the ratline had evolved from the Vatican's hope for an escape route for Catholics from a nazified Europe? Who would ever expect that different circumstances after the war would lead the Vatican to adopt Bishop Hudal's ludicrous prewar idea of Christianized Nazis battling Communists? What Pius XII dreaded, the war ending with Communist Russia in the center of Europe, had become reality. Giving in to his fear of communism, Pope Pius chose to ignore the distinction between refugees and fugitives, between grays and blacks. Aggressively anti-Communist American Church leaders, ignorant of the ratline, backed the pope with U.S. dollars. Pope Pius may have believed that with Hitler removed from the scene, Nazis would see the light and return to church. Some did. But in the end all that mattered to the pope was that they were anti-Communist fascists. The fear of Pius XII rescued Bishop Hudal from the dustbin of history, truly his rightful place.

8
BISHOP HUDAL'S
RATLINE

By the time of the war, both Pope Pius and Adolf Hitler disliked Bishop Alois Hudal, a unique accomplishment on the part of the feisty Austrian prelate. Soon enough Hudal would acquire new friends—Nazi Holocaust perpetrators whom he rescued from Allied authorities and revenge-hungry Jews. In his postwar memoir, Hudal bragged that he devoted all his charitable work after the war to helping fascists and "so-called war criminals."[1]

Hudal believed that in helping Nazi criminals escape, he was in some small measure accomplishing what had eluded him during the 1930s, the marriage of Nazism and Catholicism. We have already seen the disastrous consequences of this ill-conceived dream, but the eccentric Austrian would not relinquish his fantasy. On his deathbed, one of Hudal's clients, SS officer Wächter, gave verbal expression to the bishop's dream when he told the prelate that he regretted that Hitler and the Church had not come together: "That would have broken bolshevism."[2] Sending Nazis to South America would prepare for the day, Hudal believed, when fascism and bolshevism would again do battle.

What one rather quirky bishop did after the war would not much matter were it not for the degraded moral state of his clientele, the blackest of the black. Hudal was responsible for funneling top-ranking Holocaust perpetrators like Adolf Eichmann to Argentina. In carrying out this rescue work, the bishop engaged in the same effort the Vatican had taken up in Spain and Argentina—using fascists to combat Communists. For this reason we need to ask what Pope Pius knew about Hudal's work and whether Hudal received Vatican support.

When the war began, Hudal's prospects appeared exceedingly dim. The pope was shunning him. In 1939, Pius XII gruffly withdrew papal patronage for Hudal's German National Church. "It's not a Roman custom," the Vatican told the bishop. Later that year, when Hudal sent Christmas greetings to the pope, a reply came from Maglione's office addressed to "the Aryan College" instead of to the College of the Santa Maria dell'Anima, the German national Catholic Church in Rome.[3] When Hudal attempted to lead a group of German and Austrian pilgrims to St. Peter's Basilica and places in the Vatican complex that were normally off limits to visitors except when accompanied by a prelate, the Swiss guard unceremoniously blocked them and turned them away.

Out of favor with Vatican higher-ups who had once sought him out, Hudal had to find ways to operate on his own. This would not be easy, for Hudal soon found out that he was also out of favor with the American army occupying Rome. Romans knew Hudal was a notorious Nazi advocate. His wartime sermons were openly pro-Axis and his previous literary efforts had left a paper trail a mile long. Not until the last Sunday before the American occupation of Rome did Hudal voice anti-Nazi sentiments.[4] Always an unconscionable opportunist of the worst stripe, Hudal feigned the transition from avid Nazi to anti-Nazi overnight.

Such was the notoriety of Hudal's Nazi sentiments that Allied security personnel wasted no time in cramping the bishop's action. Soon after the occupation of Rome early in June 1944, security agents paid an unannounced visit to the bishop's seminary and searched the premises. The pompous prelate was infuriated. The Allies understood exactly what kind of a person they were dealing with. According to an early though undated OSS report, Hudal was "a renegade in the full sense of the word, he belongs to the worst category of priests who dabble in politics, being unscrupulous [and] without character."[5] This probe produced no evidence of Hudal's ratline.

The reason, clearly, is that it did not yet exist. Since the war would not end for nearly another year, Nazis had not yet become fugitives. Had Allied security personnel paid their visit a year later, they might have snared a big Nazi fish. But the visit and subsequent visits put Hudal on his guard.

How and when, then, did the Hudal ratline come into existence? Before the Allies liberated the city of Rome, an informal group of Austrians, including Hudal, looked after Austrian refugees regardless of their political persuasions. It is possible, but uncertain, that a small number of Jews were also assisted. At any rate, the group did not come into conflict with German occupational authorities, with whom Bishop Hudal hobnobbed on every possible occasion. The number of Austrians in the informal group was small and overrepresented by members of the nobility, who presumably had means at their disposal. It is important to note that the

Austrians had begun to assist refugees before the Americans arrived, for this would give them some semblance of credibility.

When the Allied army rolled into Rome, the Austrians raised the Austrian flag over the former Austrian embassy to show, Hudal would later claim in an interview, their appreciation for the liberation. The Austrians wanted to gain official status in the eyes of the Americans and British. They promoted the denazification of Austria and the re-creation of Austria as an independent country. By no means were the Allies fooled by Hudal regarding denazification, but they had no cause to suspect other members of the Austrian circle. To cast their net as widely as possible, the organizers of the Austrian clique founded a nonpolitical association and sought to nominate people of various political sympathies as candidates for office. Hudal's past made him unacceptable as an officer, but documents establish that he was the principal force in establishing the Austrian contingent. At the initial meeting in July 1944, 163 Austrians, or "Greater Germans," showed up. Hudal began the meeting by expressing "the sincere gratitude of those present towards the Allied troops for having victoriously freed the city after years of oppression and persecutions." A moment of silence followed in memory of those killed by Nazis.[6] Allied security concluded its first report on the Austrians by affirming that on the whole the group seemed well intentioned but that "the bishop is more complicated and requires a more prolonged study."[7]

Wanting official status, the Austrians decided to call themselves the Austrian Legation to the Italian Government and to set up shop in the former Austrian embassy. This, however, did not pan out. They were evicted from the embassy by the Swiss, who were in charge of former German property in occupied areas, and the United States refused to give them official recognition. The group moved to a room in the Majestic Hotel and decided to call themselves the Austrian Committee, but after further problems regarding their claim to authority, they settled on being simply the Austrian Office. In spite of these demotions in status, the Austrian circle grew. It hooked new members and support by issuing identity cards to refugees who were ostensibly Austrian but who in fact could be from Greater Germany, or, in other words, German. After Hitler's suicide, German and Nazi refugees would become the rule rather than the exception for this organization. To obtain the card, the applicant submitted to a cursory investigation and was asked to sign a statement acknowledging his or her endorsement of the nonpolitical Austrian Liberation Committee, which was in fact the staff of the Austrian Office. In this way, membership soon grew to 267. Most people signed the endorsement without bothering to read it.[8]

The official signature on the identity cards was that of Alois Hudal.[9] Because the Austrian Office provided a service that the Allied occupation authorities needed and because no other group provided such services, the occupational army recognized it officially. Hudal had played his cards well. In organizing the clique that would become the Austrian Office, he emphasized that they must demonstrate to the Allied occupiers that they intended to help them. The Austrians went out of their way to do just this. According to an OSS report, "as a group they are almost pathetically anxious to do everything to please the Allies. . . . They eagerly clutch at any hint of Allied interest in them however lowly the quarter from which it comes." Thus, very soon after the Allied occupation of Rome, the bishop had secured for himself the niche that he needed to carry on his "charitable" work, fighting communism by merging national socialist fascism with religion in the person of a refugee. If that person happened to be a fugitive SS officer, so much the better for the cause, in Hudal's warped way of thinking. An early but undated OSS report on Hudal described the bishop and the other founders of the Austrian Committee as "a small group of idiots" but accurately predicted that they could become dangerous if they came into contact with the German military.[10] Of course, only a few of the refugees pouring into Rome were fugitive SS officers.

The occupational authorities naturally wanted to know where the Austrian Office got its operating funds. They had two autos at their disposal; the cars, decked out with red-and-white flags, were hard to miss as they moved in and around Rome. Besides the cars and the scarce and costly gasoline they ran on, the Austrian Office rented a hotel room until the Allies took over the Majestic for their own offices. After their eviction, the Austrians presumably paid rent elsewhere. Then there were the expenses generated by the issuance of the identity cards. Registration papers and the cards had to be printed at a time when paper was scarce and at a premium. The busy Austrians also had signs printed up notifying refugees of their whereabouts and purpose. Those who registered for the identity cards were charged only 100 lira—just pennies. Even though several hundred or more individuals forked over the lira, their contributions could not begin to cover the expenses of the Austrian Office.

The OSS had no trouble tracing some of Hudal's support to the Vatican's Pontifical Commission of Assistance. According to Vincent La Vista's investigation, some sixteen national refugee organizations operated under pontifical auspices. Hudal's Austrian Office was just one of many such agencies. Since there was nothing clandestine about the Vatican's support of the many national groups working under it, Allied security personnel had no difficulty linking Hudal with the Vatican. Early reports on the Austrian Office noted that Vatican assistance was obvious. Other reports noted that the Vatican helped out with printing materials. There was nothing objectionable about this work, of course. Indeed, Italian and occupational authorities needed the help of the Red Cross and the various national and Jewish agencies to sort out the flood of refugees in Rome.

After a few months of nosing about, however, the OSS turned up another source of support for Hudal's group—expatriated Germans or Austrians in Argentina. Specifically, OSS agents linked the Austrian Office to Prince Ernst Rüdiger Starhemberg, the vice-chancellor of Austria in the Dollfuss administration and a noted antisemite and hard-nosed fascist. At this time, September 1944, American security agents were probably not yet aware of Vatican links to the Argentine military strongman, soon to be president, Juan Domingo Perón. Thus, the triangle of the Vatican, the Austrian Office, and Perón would not have been apparent. But the connection of the Hudal group to Starhemberg was troubling in itself. The OSS knew that for all of the Austrian Office's protestations of anti-Nazism, most of the founding members were fascists. Bishop Hudal, pretending to be a turncoat anti-Nazi, lied through his teeth to Allied security agents, but other Austrians such as Bishop Graf Carlo Trautmannsdorf-Weinsberg set them straight regarding the rector of the German National Church.[11]

How did the links between Hudal and the Vatican and between Hudal and Argentine fascists come about? Hudal wrote in his memoir that Montini himself came to the German seminary and asked the bishop to take over Jewish refugee work as an agent of the American Joint Distribution Committee. Hudal declined the offer on the grounds that sequestering Jews along with German fascists would endanger his operation. In other words, sooner or later a Jewish survivor would recognize one of the Germans as an atrocity perpetrator.[12] Hudal wrote that this meeting took place in 1939, which, of course, is unthinkable. At that early date there were few if any Jewish refugees and no fascist refugees whatever. The date worked well in Hudal's story; 1939 was the year the Vatican began rebuffing him. On the other hand, it is believable that Montini would try to get Hudal to take on work for the AJDC. That would mean that the Jewish refugees would be funneled to South America rather than to Palestine. According to La Vista, next to the Vatican the AJDC ran the most ambitious emigration service in Rome. (The AJDC's emigration program actually had LST-type landing craft to ferry people across the Mediterranean from Italy to Palestine.) It was run by Padre Maria Benedetto, the

French Capuchin priest who, working for Delasem, had rescued so many Jews during the German occupation of Italy.[13] Since Pius XII opposed the establishment of a Jewish state in Palestine, it makes sense that Montini would have approached Hudal about South America.

Montini, one of Pius XII's closest advisors, knew that Hudal ran the Austrian refugee program, knew that fascists of every stripe would flow through it, and knew that Bishop Hudal, known in Rome for his over-the-top pro-Nazi views, could and would facilitate the escape of war criminals. A likely scenario is that the pesky bishop organized the little band of Austrian "idiots" and from this base built a much larger program, within which he could take over the critical work of producing identification papers for black refugees. In other words, whether the Vatican liked it or not, Hudal was running the Austrian refugee program. But what did it matter to the Vatican if Holocaust perpetrators were benefiting from the Austrian refugee program under the Holy See's umbrella when, at the same time as Hudal was running his ratline from the German Santa Maria dell'Anima seminary, the Vatican itself was colluding in harboring Ustaša Croatian war criminals across town in the San Girolamo degli Illirici, the Croatian seminary of St. Jerome, and underwriting the vast Spanish ratline? The bottom line is that the Vatican made no effort to remove Bishop Hudal from the Austrian refugee program under the Pontifical Commission of Assistance until 1952, at which time all, or almost all, of the perpetrators of World War II atrocities who had not been apprehended had made good their escape.

Argentine writer Uki Goñi has documented a case that illustrates that the Vatican not only allowed Hudal to run the Austrian emigration program but also made use of it. Montini headed the Pontifical Commission of Assistance as part of his work in the papal secretariat. Pope Pius himself would have appointed Montini to head the commission. A German priest, Bruno Wüstenberg, who worked in the secretary of state office, was approached by the fugitive Nazi Bernhard Heilig for help. The convicted war criminal asked for money for a visa and transportation to South America. Wüstenberg refused to help but directed Heilig to Hudal's emigration program. There the Nazi fugitive got the assistance he needed; in 1951, he was employed in the same firm as Adolf Eichmann in Argentina.[14]

German writer Ernst Klee, who benefited from a rare chance to examine Hudal's papers in the archives of the Santa Maria dell'Anima seminary, found that Montini on one occasion sent Hudal 30,000 lira, presumably for the operation of the seminary. In fact, Hudal could use the money however he pleased. Thirty thousand lira was not a lot of money; ship passage to Argentina in those days could cost three times that amount. The Vatican's donation nevertheless confirms what Father Karl Bayer told writer Gitta Sereny, namely that "the pope did provide money [for Hudal's work]; "in driblets at times, but it did come."[15] Some of the money U.S. bishops raised for Pius XII's emigration bureau ended up in Hudal's pocket. We know this as result of the Argentine CEANA commission's research of Hudal's papers.[16] But as we will see, the bishop had other sources of support. Thus, he was able to pay for ship passage for at least some Nazi fugitives. But he did not have the funds to pay for passage for all of the war criminals that needed to get out of Europe to avoid prosecution. He would have done so, of course, had he been able to, but he was also responsible for providing food, shelter, false identification, and, when necessary, concealment. Reinhard Kops, for example, had to come up with 100,000 lira on his own to book passage to Argentina.

Kops, a former Nazi intelligence officer, is of special interest because of his association with Bishop Hudal. Writing under his Argentine name of Juan Maler, Kops provides us with an account of how the bishop's ratline functioned.[17] After arriving in Rome, evidently sometime in 1947, Kops ate at the papal mess hall which was open to any and all of the refugees in Rome. There he met other German-speaking refugees, some of whom, like Kops, were subject to extradition to Germany and court trial. From these birds of a feather, who, Kops assures us, were well educated and from "the best homes," he learned the ropes, and he found his way to Hudal and the Santa Maria dell'Anima through the intermediary, "Aunt Paula." Direct approach to the seminary was chancy because a certain Father Heinemann had to be avoided for some reason, although he, too, was engaged in service for war criminals. Once he was in touch with Bishop Hudal, the "great and good friend" who sheltered the SS, Kops found safety and a new destiny far from Germany and Allied tribunals of justice.[18]

Because the seminary had been raided by U.S. intelligence officers, it was not a possible hiding place for refugees. Hudal placed Kops in a residence of an unidentified religious order whose house was but a short distance from the Vatican on the via Conciliazione leading to St. Peter's Basilica. A good number of refugees fleeing the law lived at this house. They slept on mats in a large hall. At Christmas 1947, some 200 hundred fugitives assembled in the house on the via Conciliazione, some from other hiding places, for a festive meal. After Bishop Hudal welcomed them, the superior of the religious house assured the "pilgrims" that the police would never find them there.[19]

Kops ran the library of the religious order, but he soon learned to run Hudal's ratline, or at least one of them. Hudal recognized that the gregarious north German would function well in his clandestine illegal emigration service. Kops could mix easily in the legitimate world and could bamboozle and beguile. Although a Protestant, he was friendly with the Swiss guards, got himself invited to their mess hall, played cards with them, and avoided Italian and Allied security by using the papal mail service. Soon Kops played the same role at the religious house on the Conciliazione as "Aunt Paula" did for the Santa Maria dell'Anima. He screened new arrivals who were supposed to come to the building in the early evening. Kops checked each one out: what sort of German accent did they have, did it correspond to their story, why did they need a secure shelter?

Franz Rufinengo, an experienced ratline operative, taught Kops how to run Hudal's line.[20] Nazi fugitives could obtain an identity card from Hudal and then apply to the office of the International Red Cross to obtain a passport. If, however, the fugitive Nazi had functioned in some capacity in the murder of the Jews, then an intermediary would have to be sent to the Red Cross office to obtain the needed documents, because there were dozens of Jews at that office every day who also sought the papers that would allow them to emigrate. The danger was acute that a Jewish survivor could recognize a former concentration camp official like Franz Stangl or doctor like Josef Mengele or a lower-ranking guard. Red Cross personnel dealt with thousands and thousands of refugees and could not possibly check out the bona fides of each and every one.

Once the fugitives had identification they could safely venture out of the house to one of the soup kitchens run by the Vatican, the Red Cross, or the United Nations Rehabilitation and Relief Association. Kops said that those lacking a birth or baptismal certificate could get by with two witnesses. In other words, the process could be abused by anyone who needed to do so. Inside the residence on the via Conciliazione, the German fascists plotted against Italian Communists. During the spring 1948 national elections—a most fearful day for Pope Pius, as we have seen, because of the strength of the Communist Party—the fugitives from justice ran a distribution center for the Christian Democratic Party, archenemy of the reds. Flyers and campaign literature was stockpiled in the house of the religious order, from whence it was distributed by the German-speaking illegals to the country's cities and countryside. Hudal's dream of the 1930s had come true.[21]

This is how Kops and other fugitives came into contact with the setup in Genoa, from where ocean liners departed for Argentina and other Latin American countries. Carrying campaign literature of the Christian Democratic Party gave the refugees some cover for their trip to Genoa. Of course, Hudal had long known how to dodge the perils that wanted fugitives faced at the port city. At one point, Hudal struck an arrangement with the Italian police whereby they were to return refugees, whether they were suspected criminals or not, to the place of residence shown on their identity cards. German or Austrian refugees and Croats were supposed to be turned over to the Allies by the Italian police for screening and possible extradition. But many in the Italian police force were former fascists of some sort or other and none of them were Communists. They sympathized with Hudal's work. After functioning well for some (indefinite) period of time, the Hudal arrangement abruptly ended when over 100 Germans mocked the Italian police as their ship cast off from land in Genoa.[22]

Once a fugitive made his way to Genoa with the necessary documents in hand, he sought out the office of the Pontifical Commission of Assistance or the diocesan office for emigrants of Archbishop Giuseppe Siri, both of which had facilities in the Genoa railroad station. Kops worked with these agencies and with a third, the Delegation of Argentine Immigration in Europe that Perón had established to promote emigration to his country. In 1948, Bishop Hudal wrote to President Perón asking for 5,000 Argentine visas.[23] It was at this same time that the American Monsignor O'Grady, thinking his Latin American mission had finally met some success, reported to U.S. bishops that Perón had issued 5,000 visas. How was it possible for Hudal's letter to win notice in Argentina? Pierre Daye, the Nazi collaborator who had helped run the Spanish ratline, escaped from Spain early on to go to Argentina, where he made close contacts with the highest echelon of Perón's circle. He also visited many fugitive fascists, including Ante Pavelić. Among his acquaintances was Prince Ernst Rüdiger Starhemberg, the onetime leader of the Austrian fascist party. Starhemberg, U.S. intelligence suspected, funded Hudal's ratline operation, and he was the bishop's connection to Perón.[24] Many of those who used the visas that Hudal had obtained were undoubtedly war criminals such as Eduard Roschmann and Adolf Eichmann, both of whom had been clients of Hudal's ratline, and Josef Mengele.[25] 1948 marked the year of peak emigration of refugees to Argentina. When they reached Buenos Aires, the Nazi fugitive applicants for residence were processed by former immigrants, who were often themselves war criminals.[26] Kops himself emigrated in 1948. We see then that Monsignor O'Grady's work may have been superfluous.

The identity of some of those the Hudal ratline aided is known. Most

Figures 10 and 11. Franz Stangl (*left*), commandant of the death camps at
Sobibor and Treblinka, where about 1 million Jews were murdered in gas chambers.
Adolf Eichmann (*right*) was put in charge of implementing the murder of European
Jewry. He orchestrated deportations to the death camps in occupied Poland after
the January 1942 meeting at the Berlin suburb of Wannsee to organize killings
at death camps. Eichmann and Stangl along with other genocidal killers such
as Josef Mengele, Eduard Roschmann, and Walter Rauff escaped
justice by emigrating through Bishop Hudal's ratline.
Both photographs courtesy of the United States Holocaust Memorial Museum.

prominent among them would be Adolf Eichmann, the top expert in the
branch of Reinhard Heydrich's intelligence service that dealt with Jewish
affairs—the person who orchestrated deportations to the death camps in
occupied Poland. After the January 1942 meeting at the Berlin suburb
of Wannsee to plan the construction of the death camps, Eichmann was
put in charge of implementing the murder of European Jews. Ten years
after Eichmann emigrated to Argentina, Israeli agents kidnapped him. He
was put on trial in 1961, found guilty, condemned to death, and hung
in 1962.

Josef Mengele was a second highly prominent beneficiary of Hudal's
ratline. Known as the Angel of Death at Auschwitz, Mengele selected
tens if not hundreds of thousands of Jews, sending them to their deaths
in the modernized gas chambers of Auschwitz-Birkenau. With Hudal's
help, the mass murderer immigrated to Argentina. He eventually died in
South America in 1978 and never had to answer for his horrendous role
in the Holocaust.

FIGURES 12 AND 13. Nazi doctor Josef Mengele conducted gruesome "racial" medical operations at Auschwitz and sent many thousands to death at the modern gas-crematorium complexes at Birkenau. Mengele obtained this falsified passport through the services of Bishop Hudal's ratline in Rome.
Mengele's photograph courtesy of the United States Holocaust Memorial Museum.
Photograph of Mengele's passport courtesy of Bettmann Archive.

Yet another blackest of the black fugitives, Franz Stangl, commandant of the death camps at Sobibor and Treblinka, found refuge and escape through the Hudal ratline. Gitta Sereny, who interviewed Stangl in prison, learned that Hudal gave him a place to stay in Rome, a Red Cross passport, pocket money, ship money to Damascus, and a job in Damascus.[27] Eventually tracked down by Simon Wiesenthal, Stangl was extradited from Brazil after sixteen years of freedom and put on trial in the Federal Republic of Germany, where the death penalty had been abolished. A German court sentenced Stangl, who was directly responsible for the murder of approximately 950,000 Jews, to life imprisonment.

Eduard Roschmann, the Butcher of Riga; Walter Rauff, gas van murderer—the list goes on. We will never know just how many of the more or less 60,000 Nazis who emigrated to Argentina did so through the Hudal ratline. The number would doubtless be in the hundreds. Nor will we ever know how many of the 1,000 SS officers who found their way to that country had Hudal to thank for their new lives. Black fugitives found their way to Hudal because he had a "long-time relationship with Himmler's SD [intelligence] espionage service" and kept up contact with many Nazis during the war.[28] The American intelligence officer, who dubbed the early pre-ratline Hudal circle "a little band of idiots," thought that the group would be dangerous if it made contact with German military personnel. Of course, that contact already existed. But in the final analysis, Hudal was more infamous than dangerous.

The Vatican appointed Hudal, the most notorious pro-Nazi bishop in the entire Catholic Church, to head the Austrian branch of the Pontifical Commission of Assistance. No doubt, Pius and Montini held their noses as they picked Hudal for the Austrian division of the commission, but they did not do it *contre-coeur*. They knew exactly what they were getting; Hudal's dalliance with Hitler during the 1930s was a fresh memory in the Vatican. The pope's close advisor, Jesuit Robert Leiber, had written to Hudal at the time of German invasion of the Soviet Union, as noted above, telling him that in some sense he could look upon it as a crusade, in this way reviving the Austrian bishop's illusions.[29] As a history professor at the Jesuit Gregorian University, Leiber had no authority to write such a message to Hudal. Leiber's role as one of Pius XII's closest confidantes allowed the German Jesuit to act as the pope's intermediary and messenger. Vatican officials knew that they could rely on Hudal to do what they themselves were doing, providing fascists, whether gray or black, with passage to South America, where, supposedly, they would be needed to combat Communists. Hudal succeeded to such an extent that he became a magnet for the blackest Nazis. Once these notorious criminals crossed the Alps, they knew they had to locate Bishop Hudal in order to slink out of Europe via his ratline.

After a time, Bishop Hudal became a little too public and a little too obnoxious with his "charitable" aid for Nazi fugitives. In 1949, Hudal wrote an article, "Ein Grüß übers Meer" (An Oversees Greeting) for *Der Weg*, an Argentine magazine edited by Hudal's old crony Reinhard Kops. The journal circulated widely in Argentina and in Germany among unreconstructed Nazis. The article offered readers the usual Hudal pabulum—love of Germanness and the Church—but the Vatican, disliking this kind of publicity, reprimanded Hudal for his effort. After 1949, the flood of refugees had subsided in Italy and the ratlines had begun to dry up. But Hudal persisted, keeping up a running correspondence with Kops and sending him money from time to time for immigrant transactions. Kops and Hudal even discussed plans to expand their operation for Nazi immigration into Colombia.[30]

As the number of Nazi fugitives dwindled steadily, Hudal's zeal for the ratline's cause remained high. Pius XII's patience wore thin. In 1952, he fired Hudal, forcing him to resign from his post as head of the Santa Maria dell'Anima. Hudal allowed his bitterness to bleed through the brief memoir he wrote in 1976.[31] According to German writer Hansjakob Stehle, Hudal took his revenge by providing playwright Rolf Hochhuth, author of *The Deputy*, with the image of a cold and heartless Pope Pius.[32] So ended a nearly 30-year relationship between the Austrian bishop and the Vatican. The degree of influence Hudal managed to exert over top Vatican officials during the 1930s and Pope Pius's use of him in the immediate postwar era is a comment on the ineptness of pontifical governance and its flawed judgment.

9
LOOTED GOLD AND
THE VATICAN

During World War II, vast amounts of gold changed hands in Europe, most of it seized by Germany, from whence it traveled on to neutral countries to pay for vital war matériel. One example is the relatively small amount of looted and state gold (worth hundreds of thousands of dollars, however, in today's money) that Ustaša fascists took to Rome, where the gold was kept in Vatican extraterritorial property or in the Vatican Bank. In either case, top Vatican personnel would have known the whereabouts of the gold.

Before the collapse of the Yugoslav government and the onset of the quisling Ustaša regime in 1941, Yugoslavia's gold was divided up for safekeeping and stashed in various locations. Some of it was hidden in a cave near Mostar, fifty cases were taken to another city, forty-four cases were taken to Herzegovina, and ninety cases remained in Niksic, the site of the original vault. During the war, the Italian government stole 184 cases of this state gold, only to have the Germans seize it.[1] The Italians, however, had not been able to steal the gold that was in Croatia, the rump, fascist puppet state that remained after the collapse of Yugoslavia. This was the gold, or some portion of it, that made its way to Rome after the war.

When they are victims of grand larceny, individuals and states act very much alike; they want their money back. Tito's Yugoslavia appealed to an international committee after the war, asking that Germany return its treasury—its gold. Survivors of the Ustaša terror or their next of kin now living in California have brought a class-action lawsuit in federal court against the Vatican, charging that it profited by the gold the cronies of dictator Pavelić took from them or their families and asking for restitution.[2] Specifically, *Alperin v. Vatican Bank* charges that the Vatican bank laundered and converted "the Ustaša treasury, making deposits in Europe and North and South America, [and] distributing the funds to exiled Ustaša leaders including Pavelić."[3]

In 1997, Swiss banks, after having claimed that they no longer had records of deposits made by European Jews during World War II, were caught red-handed trying to destroy the evidence. In response, President Bill Clinton issued an executive order directing all branches of the U.S. government to open their wartime records for scrutiny and pressured other countries to follow the U.S. example. Fourteen European countries and Canada and Argentina complied, appointing committees to investigate possible Holocaust assets in their homelands. One state refused to comply—the Vatican. The U.S. State Department asked the Holy See to open its bank books, but to no avail.[4] Why would the Holy See, a church-state with ideals commensurate with that standing, need to hide its financial transactions in the face of the willingness of secular states to open theirs to answer legitimate Holocaust-related questions about their finances? The answer may be that the Vatican acted during the war and the Holocaust more like a state than a church. The brief in *Alperin v. Vatican Bank* asks for accountability on the part of the Holy See. Unless the Vatican settles the case and makes restitution, it may be forced, at last, to reveal its wartime bank books. In Catholic moral theology, wrongful possession of another's goods has always required restitution. Lawsuit or no lawsuit, the Vatican, according to its own teaching, should make restitution if it received stolen property during the war or profited from loot that others had stolen.

The principal document state department historians used in 1998 that linked the Vatican to looted gold was the Bigelow dispatch. On October 16, 1946, Emerson Bigelow, writing from Rome, wrote the following report to Harold Glasser, director of monetary research at the U.S. Treasury Department:

> The Ustascha [*sic*] organization (a Croatian fascist organization, headed by Ante Pavelic) removed funds from Jugoslavia estimated to total 350 million Swiss francs. The funds were largely in the form of gold coins.
>
> Of the funds brought from the former Independent Croat State where Jews and Serbs were plundered to support the Ustascha [*sic*] organization in exile, an estimated 150 million Swiss francs were impounded by British authorities at the Austro-Swiss frontier; the balance of approximately 200 million Swiss francs was originally held in the Vatican for safe-keeping. According to rumor a considerable portion of this latter amount has been sent to Spain and Argentina through the Vatican's "pipeline," but it is quite possible this is merely a smokescreen to cover the fact that the treasure remains in its original repository.[5]

Bigelow stated matter-of-factly that the Ustaša removed the gold from Croatia (formerly Yugoslavia) to Rome and the Vatican, where the treasure was used to support the organization in exile. Then Bigelow reported that there was a rumor that the gold had made its way on to Spain and Argentina through the Vatican ratline.

Forty-six million 1946 dollars' worth of gold is an enormous quantity, $474 million in 2006 dollars. How reliable was the Bigelow dispatch? What was the source of his information? Bigelow was not an intelligence agent; his area of competence centered entirely on monetary issues. Because he specialized in just this one area, his report deserves our consideration. Bigelow sent many reports to the Treasury Department during the postwar years on monetary developments worldwide, including one in the summer of 1946 that dealt with a large amount of gold that a Ustaša official had taken to Switzerland. But unfortunately, Bigelow was not in the habit of mentioning the source of his information. And although he seemed confident about what he told Glasser, except for the whereabouts of the gold, his report was filed fourteen months after the time the Ustaša left the Balkans in May 1945.

Bigelow's dispatch gains some credibility from independent concurring testimony. A onetime OSS agent, William Gowen, whom we will have occasion to discuss extensively in the next chapter, has given a deposition as an expert witness in the *Alperin vs. the Vatican Bank* case, asserting that while in Rome in 1947 he learned that in 1946, a Colonel Ivan Babić had transported ten truckloads of gold from Switzerland to the College of San Girolamo Degli Illirici (the Croatian seminary) in Rome near the Vatican. Ten truckloads! The time of the reported transportation coincides with the date of Bigelow's report—October 1946.

For the Ustaša to have taken such a huge shipment from Switzerland presupposes prior gold exchanges between Pavelić's Croatia and Swiss banks. That this happened is entirely credible. An independent commission of experts, the Bergier Commission, linked Swiss banks with Croatian gold transactions during the war.[6] Furthermore, Agent Gowen testified that the Croatian priest Krunoslav Draganović, who is mentioned repeatedly in documents bearing on the Ustaša treasury, bragged to him about the delivery of gold from Switzerland. How credible is Gowen's testimony? He was, after all, recalling an incident that occurred a full half-century earlier to which he was not an eyewitness. On the other hand, a ten-truck convoy headed to Saint Jerome's seminary would certainly have been an unusual sight in 1946. Gowen was on the scene less than a year after the presumed transfer of the gold, and it was his responsibility as an intelligence agent to gather any and all information he could pertaining to the exiled Ustaši living in the college of St. Jerome's, where the gold had supposedly been delivered.

The state department historians who drafted the Eizenstat monograph and pressed the Vatican for its bank data knew that their archival research was incomplete.[7] To encourage other governments to open their books, state department historians quickly sifted through millions of pages of newly released federal documents that had bee made available by government offices as a result of President Clinton's executive order. The U.S. records, it was thought, might indicate the whereabouts of transferred gold that was stolen during the war. When the researchers came across the Bigelow report, which identified the Vatican as a state that possessed stolen gold, they included it in the Eizenstat report. This and other information in the monograph was intended to induce all World War II neutral nations, including explicitly the Vatican, to "take up a moral and political task" that would allow them to "come to terms with [their] own history and responsibility." It took another eight years for a team of historians to work their way through and catalogue the millions of pages of documents. As a result of their work, we have other sources besides the Bigelow report to rely on.

Early on in his storied career as a U.S. spy, Strategic Services Unit agent James Angelton filed a report considerably earlier than that of Bigelow regarding the theft of gold in Croatia. Writing in January 1946, Angelton reported that a large number of Ustaši had fled their country, traveling northward through Klagenfurt, Austria. Angelton does not say when they fled, but we know from other sources that it was in May 1945. Thus, the Angelton report is much closer to the event than Bigelow's. It is important to note that Angelton mentioned the priest Krunoslav Draganović (and no one else by name) in connection with the transport of the gold. Intelligence agents repeatedly mentioned Draganović in connection with the gold, as we will see in this chapter and subsequent ones. Emerson Bigelow did not get his information about the gold from Angelton's report because the latter merely states that the gold was contained in two boxes and did not assign any monetary value to it.[8] Furthermore, Bigelow's 1946 report could not have had any connection with Angelton's earlier report because Angelton spoke of two *boxes*, whereas Bigelow-Gowen spoke of ten *truckloads*. Of course, we may be dealing with two shipments to Rome that took place at separate times and independently of each other. But on the face of it, two boxes seem more credible than ten truckloads. The Ustaša priest, Draganović, is named in connection with both shipments.

As the months passed in 1946, intelligence agents tracked the Ustaša, a rogue government during the war and an illegal movement after the war, and the gold various Croat fascists had at their disposal. In October, the same month of the Bigelow dispatch, British authorities arrested the Ustaša's General Moskov in Venice and "confiscated 3,200 gold coins and 75 diamonds."[9] Gold coins and loose diamonds equates unmistakably with victim loot. We may deduce, further, from the arrest in Venice that when the Ustaši fled Croatia they divided up the gold among them. But whether this was the same cache of gold as that of the priest Draganović cannot be said.

The Tripartite Commission

Germany stole or seized so much state and looted gold during the war that afterward the United States, France, and Great Britain set up a commission, called the Tripartite Commission for the Restitution of Monetary Gold, in an effort to return national treasuries to their rightful states. Much of the ill-begotten gold had flowed from Germany through Swiss banks and on to Spain and Portugal to pay for the wolfram ore or tungsten that Germany needed to produce steel for modern armaments. Salazar had purchased millions in foreign currencies with the gold Portugal realized from exports to Germany. Clearly, these transactions amounted to multiple millions of dollars, indeed billions in today's currencies. The small quantities of precious metal Croatian fascists stole from their countrymen and their nation were part of these transactions. Yugoslavia, a state once again after the war, if not a nation-state, claimed the Ustaša loot, and its Communist dictator, Josip Tito, wanted the gold returned.

In May 1947, almost two years to the day after the Ustaša regime fled, Yugoslavia brought its claim to the Tripartite Commission, alleging that the Croatian fascists had stolen over 117 kilograms of fine gold that was worth $176,250 in 1940 currency. The presumed theft had occurred in 1941, at the time of the collapse of Yugoslavia. In addition, the Yugoslavs claimed that "the Croatian bank purchased gold looted by the Ustasha from Serbs, Jews and others or took it from their corpses. Several hundreds of thousand were killed by Ante Pavelich."[10] This gold, the claimants limply pleaded, must have been handed over to the Germans or to Allied authorities because of its weight. Does this claim imply that the plundered gold went north to Germany instead of south to Rome? The question has obvious implications for the U.S. State Department's challenge to the Vatican. If ten truckloads of stolen Yugoslav gold were delivered from Switzerland to Rome in 1946, as Bigelow claimed and Gowen recalled, why did Tito not ask the Tripartite Commission to investigate such an immense stash of gold instead of the minute (in comparison) 117 kilograms in German hands?

Basing his opinion on records of the German Reichsbank, U.S. army officer William G. Brey asserted in October 1947 that the Yugoslav claim could not be substantiated.[11] Nevertheless, the Tripartite Commission decided to hear the case that year. Attempting to bolster its suit, in 1948 Yugoslavia produced a witness to the theft. Mato Crnek, a bank official, saw the gold being taken from the bank, or so the Yugoslavs claimed. The story had to be changed later when it became known that Crnek was in the service throughout the war and not in the bank. Crnek mustered out of the army on April 30, 1945, and headed northward toward Austria on May 8. This is what Crnek said he witnessed:

> I saw a lorry being driven by Vutuc [a Ustaša officer] himself. . . . Vutuc pro-
> voked often incidents on the way being awfully rude, he was menacing with
> a revolver in his hand everywhere. At a crossing not far from our frontier,
> the column stopped and the driver said to me that Vutuc [had] provoked
> an incident again. Being inquisitive, I went forward and at that moment I
> saw that four German officers (or noncommissioned officers) [his emphasis]
> were aiming at Vutuc with their revolvers and forced him to turn aside from
> the road into a meadow. I continued on my way further.[12]

There, out of Crnek's sight in the meadow, the Germans supposedly relieved Vutuc of the Ustaša's gold.

Yugoslavia's claim before the Tripartite Commission totaled 117.55623 kilograms consisting of 84.80352 kilograms of fine gold, 28.63436 kilograms of sundry gold coins, and 4.11475 kilograms of gold scrap and shavings. The commission accepted Crnek's testimony, not because of his alleged banking past but because as an army veteran he would have known the difference between the uniforms of the Allies and the Germans: "Furthermore," the commission wrote in its final statement, "Mr. Mato Crnek who, since 10 April, 1941, must have been subjected to the German and Italian military administration . . . and must have been familiar with the uniforms of the Axis armies, stated, on oath, that they were four German officers" who had detained Vutuc and relieved him of the gold.[13] Of the 117-plus kilograms of gold, the commission decided that 109.34773 kilograms undoubtedly belonged to the Yugoslav bank and had been stolen by the illegal Ustaša regime. The remaining 8.20490 kilograms of gold did not belong to the national bank but consisted of gold the Ustaši had looted from its victims and from corpses.

The deliberations of the Tripartite Commission took place after Emerson Bigelow's October 1946 dispatch, but there is no indication that the commission took Bigelow's statement into account in its decision. Since Bigelow's report was made to the Treasury Department, not to the U.S. intelligence service, it may not have been readily available to the commission. If the commission was cognizant of it (and there is no evidence it was), the members would not have seen it as relevant to the removal of the gold on the nights of the 7th and 8th of May 1945 from the vault in the Croatian bank, where the Ustaši had stashed it, presumably in 1941. In other words, the commission did not think in either-or terms—that the gold had gone either to Germany or to Rome. In this they were unquestionably right, because, as we will see, the amount of gold taken to Rome exceeded by far the 117-plus kilograms the German soldiers supposedly seized. Furthermore, as the report of the arrest in Venice of a Ustaša fugitive with a stash of gold and diamonds, the report of the gold taken during the war to Switzerland, and the report of the two boxes of gold in Father Draganović's possession all suggest, a number of different fascist runaways helped themselves to gold, whether in the form of looted coins or bank bars. In a word, the decision of the Tripartite Commission does not invalidate the reliability of the Bigelow dispatch.

Simultaneous with the publication of the State Department's Eizenstat monograph that challenged the Vatican regarding the Ustaša gold, the Croatian Historical Institute in Zagreb published its own account of the stolen gold. State department historians were unaware of the Croat publication, but subsequently one of the department's historians, Ron Neitzke, reviewed it and found reason to be critical of the Eizenstat monograph. "The Bigelow report [contained in the monograph] is at such variance with other credible sources that it must be regarded with extreme skepticism," Neitzke wrote.[14] The well-documented Croat study shows that the Ustaši took 287.710 kilograms of gold in bars and coins, which comes to over 431,550 in 1946 dollars and well over 4 million in today's currency. Neitzke did not question whether the gold was brought to Rome but how much gold was brought there. The 287 kilograms the Croat study reported weighed more than 600 pounds—too much for Agent Angelton's two boxes but a load that would not tax one truck, let alone the ten trucks Bigelow and Gowen reported. Thus, the Croatian study shows that the Ustaši got away with a considerable amount of gold, some of which made its way to Rome.

The Croatian Historical Institute's research reinforces the evidence in the U.S. national archives that various Ustaša personnel dipped into the looted and stolen gold. Two trunks of gold were carried over the

Slovenian-Austrian border, one trunk was broken into near Wolfsberg, Austria, by lower-ranking Ustaša officers, and two trunks went to Rome. In addition, an unknown quantity of gold coins was passed around to a number of Ustaša fascists as they made ready to flee their homeland on May 7, 1945. There is some evidence that British occupational authorities also acquired part of the loot.[15]

The Croatian record backs up the accuracy of Angelton's 1946 report: both identify Krunoslav Draganović as the person who took the gold to Rome. Angelton, however, did not know how much gold Draganović carried away in the two boxes. The Croat study puts the amount at about 45 kilograms, worth a little more than $67,500 dollars (about $697,846 in 2006 dollars). Two boxes or two trunks could easily transport 45 kilograms—99 pounds—of gold. At any rate, 45 kilograms was the amount Draganović had in his possession in Rome. Whether other Ustaša fugitives had additional portions of the 287-plus total kilograms of gold that were taken cannot be said, but it is not unlikely.[16]

Beyond any doubt Ustaša gold came to Rome. What happened to it after it reached Rome? Where was it kept? The Croatian Historical Institute provides the following account. From June 1945 until January 1946, Father Krunoslav Draganović kept the 45 kilograms of gold in his possession in Rome, not at the Vatican and not in the Croatian seminary of St. Jerome's, where almost all of the Ustaša fugitives and refugees had their board and room. Approximately half of what Draganović took out of Croatia was in the form of gold coins, most of which had been looted from Jewish and Serbian victims of the Ustaša terror. During the latter months of 1945, Draganović spent about 10 percent of the gold, whether on himself or to support other Ustaša fugitives is not known. At any rate, in January 1946 Vilko Pečnikar, a former general in the Croatian army, relieved Draganović of the remaining gold at gunpoint.[17]

Looking back, we can see that we have two absurdly different accounts of just how much gold traveled to Rome via the Ustaša exiles. Was it ten truckloads or two boxes? This discrepancy is little cause for wonder when we reflect on the situation in wartime Europe. Faced with the Ustaša treachery, the Yugoslav regime divided up its gold and hid it in a number of locations, some of which we have identified. But was that all of them? Then the Italians stole much of the hidden treasury. But how much? Not all of it, in all likelihood. Evidence indicates that a good many other thefts took place that can no longer be reliably traced, either with regard to where and when the theft occurred or with regard to the eventual whereabouts of the loot. Whatever the Italians had seized, the Germans, in turned, seized from them. This might have been the gold that the Tripartite Commission returned to Yugoslavia. Had ten truck-loads of gold been taken in 1946 from Switzerland to Rome, Tito would surely have demanded the return of this gold first, since it exceeded the value of what the Germans had taken by billions and billions of dollars. In the end, the study of the contemporary Croatian historians is more credible by far than the reports of Bigelow and Gowen. That Vilko Pečnikar might have relieved Draganović of two boxes of gold can easily be imagined; that he took ten truckloads from him cannot.

The supposition here is that Draganović was misusing the gold, which caused Pečnikar to take it from him. The Ustaša removed the gold from Croatia to fund a conspiracy to overthrow Tito. One cannot rule out personal gain, of course, but the dream of a return to glory and power gripped the Ustaša leader, Ante Pavelić, whenever he was in exile. As we will see in the following chapter, Pavelić found a secure hideout in Rome in Vatican properties after the war. There he plotted his dreamed-of triumphant return. It may be supposed that either because he did not agree with how Draganović was using the gold reserve or because he wanted to control it himself, he sent Pečnikar, his son-in-law, to wrest the remaining gold from the priest. Even though Draganović lost hands-on control of the Ustaša loot, he and the Franciscan Dominik Mandić con-tinued to disburse the funds for the immediate needs of the exiled Ustaši living in the St. Jerome seminary and elsewhere in Italy.

Alperin v. Vatican Bank

What did Pečnikar do with the loot? Taking it to an Italian state bank for safekeeping was out of the question. It would have resulted in ques-tioning by Italian and Allied authorities and a report to the Tripartite Commission. Bigelow believed the gold found its way to the Vatican. Whether or not this occurred, the Vatican certainly knew about the gold but failed to report it to the commission. The Vatican's lawyers in *Alperin v. Vatican Bank* argue that the Holy See had no obligation to return the Ustaša loot to Yugoslavia in 1946 because the country was ruled by a hostile Communist regime in the Cold War era.

> The decision by a sovereign instrumentality to give the funds to a foreign anti-Communist political movement rather than to a Communist regime, at the time where the Cold War was beginning in earnest in Europe, is not a "commercial" act; it is *jure imperii*, a deeply sovereign act.[18]

The argument is completely without merit. The Tripartite Commission, which consisted of western non-Communist nationals, accepted Yugoslavia's claim to stolen gold late in 1947, even as the East and West were indeed slipping into the Cold War confrontation. Except for in the mind of Pius XII, no Cold War existed yet in 1946. Retaining stolen gold was not therefore a sovereign act.

There is no reason to doubt that the Ustaša gold ended up as a deposit in the Vatican Bank—not, of course, ten truckloads but something like the much smaller estimate of the Croatian Historical Institute. As the postwar years rolled by, the deposited gold had to be "laundered" or changed into various currencies to finance an evolving sequence of tasks. The immediate need was for upkeep for many dozens of Ustaša exiles. As pressure mounted for war criminals to be expatriated, false identity papers had to be fabricated. As the day when Pavelić would decide the time was ripe to invade Yugoslavia and overthrow Tito became ever more distant, some of the funds from the Vatican bank had to be used for the ratline—paying for passage for war criminals who dared not linger any longer in Europe. *Alperin v. Vatican Bank* alleges that in 1952 Pavelić withdrew 5 million Swiss francs—over $1 million in the currency of the day—from a Vatican Swiss bank account into which the Vatican bank had previously laundered and deposited 2,400 kilograms of the Ustaša's looted gold. Lawyers for the plaintiffs seemed to have pulled this sum out of thin air. It further alleges that the Franciscan who had been managing the Ustaša's funds in Rome, Dominik Mandić, emigrated to the United States. There he settled in Chicago, working out of St. Jerome's parish, which was run by the same branch of Franciscans that had so notoriously tarnished the name of the order during the Ustaša genocide in Croatia. Mandić had ample funds at his disposal that he used to publish ethnically racist literature for the Croat-speaking colony in the United States and for other projects.[19]

The sums of money at the disposal of the exiled Pavelić and Mandić far exceed the modest amount the Croatian historians estimated that the Ustaša took to Rome after the war. On the other hand, they amount to only a small fraction of the ten-truckload report of Bigelow and Gowen. If such an amount ever came into the Vatican bank, today there are still billions of dollars that have not, and probably cannot, be accounted for. As we have seen, significant skepticism surrounds the story of a convoy of trucks laden with gold.

The papal defense team in *Alperin v. Vatican Bank* has not contested the allegation that an immense shipment of gold arrived by truck in Rome in 1946. Vatican lawyers content themselves with the blanket assertion that the plaintiffs' case put forward conclusory "facts"—bald assertions which the court need not credit.[20] This approach considerably weakens the defense, whose principal argument is that there is no evidentiary connection between the losses of the plaintiffs and the gold deposited in the Vatican bank.[21] Losses, such as stolen gold commemorative coins, currency, and jewelry, cannot be traced. Property losses that occurred in wartime well over half a century ago may not be traceable. In *Alperin v. Vatican Bank,* what the plaintiffs lost was not like artwork (identifiable objects of record), nor were they like insurance policies (whose holders are a matter of record). Thus, the Vatican's lawyers would have had a considerable advantage if they had pointed out that besides the alleged ten truckloads of gold, Yugoslav gold ended up in Germany and in the pockets of a good many individual Ustaši. Given this wide dispersion of Yugoslav gold, it would be impossible to demonstrate—and, indeed, impossible for the plaintiffs' lawyers to argue—that the portion that ended up in the Vatican bank originated with their clients rather than with other victims.

If the case against the Holy See were to be decided on the basis of moral law and historical fact, the Vatican would be hard put to it to defend itself. Mass murder and theft on the part of a regime Pius XII favored undeniably took place. A portion of the stolen loot undeniably found its way to Rome. Once there, the pope and other high Vatican persons certainly knew about it but made no effort to see that it was returned to rightful owners or their next of kin. In all probability, the Vatican bank laundered the stolen property and oversaw its dispersion worldwide. But whether or not the Vatican must answer for its actions will be determined not by the reconstruction of historical events or by moral law but by the laws of the United States. In this domain, the Vatican's lawyers may prove to have the upper hand.

The federal court in California may decide to dismiss the *Alperin* case because it does not have jurisdiction over the subject matter. In 1984, President Ronald Reagan recognized the Vatican as a sovereign state. The Holy See therefore falls under the protection of the Foreign Sovereign Immunity Act.[22] On this ground alone, the plaintiffs' case may miscarry. Alternately, the court may decide to hear the case under the commercial activity exception to the Foreign Sovereign Immunity Act. If that happens, the Vatican's lawyers, asserting that the exception is mere use of semantics by the plaintiffs' counsels, will be able to point to a recent court decision that somewhat resembles the *Alperin* case. In March 2006, the Second Federal Court of California used the essence-of-complaint rule in deciding against the plaintiff in *Garb vs. the Republic of Poland.* In that case, the court did not uphold the commercial activity argument as an exception to the Foreign Sovereign Immunity Act.[23] We see here that what is at issue concerns civil, not moral, law. Thus, whether the Holy

See was party to stolen goods is not the question, but rather whether the stolen goods—in this case, liquid assets—constitute "tangible" property according to the commercial activity exception.[24] They do not. In another case similar to *Alperin*, the courts ruled against a "ripple effect," meaning that if illegally obtained liquid assets lead to additional commercial activity at some point down the road, the court will not hear the case. Here, the legal question is not whether the Vatican bank acted to distribute stolen funds but whether the fact that it distributed the funds in 1952 to benefit Mandić's Chicago enterprises six years after the alleged theft constitutes a commercial ripple effect. A final illustration culled from many the lawyers use against the claims of the plaintiffs in *Alperin*: the case has no standing at bar, they say, because the Vatican was only a third party to the plaintiff's injury. Once again, the question here is not whether the Vatican bank facilitated the use of stolen property but only whether according to U.S. law it committed the crime or whether the Ustaša did so.[25]

Clearly, the question of looted gold and the Vatican as it would be decided in the historian's court or in the theologian's court will little resemble whatever is decided in civil court. In view of the fact that European countries opened their World War II bank books for review at the request of the U.S. State Department after the Swiss bank scandal, the Vatican's unwillingness to do so suggests that it has something hide. Ultimately, what the Holy See does not wish to disclose is the disastrous web of mistakes pertaining to Yugoslavia that entrapped Pius XII throughout his papacy. The pope's first entanglement came early in his tenure when he preferred the Nazi puppet state of Croatia over the Yugoslavia the Treaty of Trianon created after World War I, even though the new entity was ruled by a convicted murderer, Ante Pavelić. After receiving the papal blessing in 1941, Pavelić and his Ustaša lieutenants unleashed an unspeakable genocide in their new country. But Pius XII refused to cut his ties with Catholic Croatia and in 1943 once again imparted the papal blessing on Pavelić, who by that time was a genocidal killer. We will never know what words of moderation and caution, if any, the pope imparted to the dictator on that occasion. When the fascists lost World War II, the fascist experiment in Croatia was over. But it was not over for Pope Pius. Compounding his earlier missteps, the pope sheltered Pavelić and other Ustaša war criminals, hoping that they might yet succeed in a triumphal return to the land they had so badly bloodied. Might not the looted gold that the Ustaši brought with them to St. Jerome's Croatian seminary make such a return to glory possible? We turn in the next chapter to Pavelić in hiding in postwar Rome.

10
ANTE PAVELIĆ
WAR CRIMINAL, MURDERER, AND
DEFENDER OF THE FAITH

The goal of Ante Pavelić's life was to establish a religiously and ethnically monolithic Croatian state in place of Yugoslavia. In pursuit of this goal Pavelić murdered King Alexander II of Yugoslavia between World War I and World War II and massacred hundreds of thousands of people during the war. In this manner Ante Pavelić had become one of the world's foremost war criminals by 1945.

Fortunately for the Ustaša dictator, Pius XII distinguished between those who committed political murder and those who murdered for other reasons. This distinction led the pontiff to protect Pavelić in Rome after he had made good his escape from the country he had ruthlessly ravished during the war. Because, like Pavelić, Pope Pius wanted to see a Catholic state in the Balkans in place of Tito's emerging Communist dictatorship, the Ustaša dictator found refuge in Vatican properties in Rome. In the end, Ante Pavelić was never captured and never brought to justice.

After hiding out in Rome, Pavelić made good his escape from Europe to a safe harbor in Argentina through the Vatican's ratline. Many other Ustaša criminals had already emigrated to Argentina through the same ratline before Pavelić did so in 1948. By that time the Cold War was developing rapidly, and the United States reversed its policy and joined in the Vatican's illegal emigration operation, even using the same Vatican ratline. In this way, Pope Pius led the west in an unethical fight against communism. Pope Pius did not hesitate to flout principles of justice in pursuit of a pragmatic goal that was necessary to protect the Catholic Church, or so the pontiff thought. To defeat communism, the pope protected Pavelić; appointed Hudal and, as we will see in the following chapter, Krunoslav Draganović to the Pontifical Commission of Assistance; and sponsored the Italian and Spanish ratlines.

Pavelić's infamy was so great that most of the belligerents of the war wanted to capture him. Russian and Yugoslav spies joined Italian and American intelligence agents in Rome, all trying to corner and seize the Ustaša dictator. But the Vatican refused to obey the call to surrender war criminals. There were and are so many properties scattered around Rome that enjoy Vatican state's privilege of extraterritoriality, meaning that like an embassy they are protected by law from foreign trespass, that Pavelić could hide out virtually indefinitely. Pope Pius probably believed that he was simply exercising the age-old Church privilege of asylum by protecting Pavelić from a Communist kangaroo court, but he knew that the dictator had already been tried and found guilty in democratic France for the murder of King Alexander. The Vatican broke the law by hiding Pavelić, unlike those who sought him. They complied with the law by not intruding into Vatican properties.

Ante Pavelić arrived in Rome in the spring of 1946, one year after the end of World War II. He remained in the Eternal City until close to the end of 1948. This was his choice. He could have emigrated to Argentina at any moment during his stay of nearly three years, but he was determined to return to his homeland to overthrow the government, as he had done, with Nazi help, in 1941. It was this intention, of course, that led Pius XII to shelter him. The pope was still willing to gamble on the creation of a Catholic Croatian state, just has he had gambled, and lost, during the war. Pope Pius would lose a second time, and when it became evident that Pavelić would not be able to return to power, his usefulness to Pius XII's geopolitical hopes dissolved. Then it was time for Pavelić to leave Rome and move on to South America.

Pavelić knew Rome well even before his postwar stopover there. The future dictator of Croatia fled to Italy after killing King Alexander (and the French foreign minister) in 1934 and remained there until he became Hitler's puppet dictator of Croatia in 1941. This layover of seven years came about because the fascist dictator of Italy, Mussolini, refused to extradite fellow fascist Pavelić to France. Thus, when Pavelić had to flee Croatia at the end of the war, he was well acquainted with the lay of the land and with the Vatican. In May 1941, just after becoming dictator of Croatia, Pavelić was received in a private audience by Pope Pius, who imparted the papal blessing on the murderer who was soon to become a genocidal killer.

Between the last months of the war and 1947, reports of the whereabouts of Ante Pavelić were infrequent and unreliable. In May 1945,

Pavelić was determined to hold off Tito's Communist partisans until the Allies liberated Croatia. Instead, by the end of the year the new dictator of the country, Josip Tito, had petitioned for Pavelić's extradition so he could stand trial for mass murder.[1] At the end of the war Pavelić and his entourage made their escape, fleeing north toward Nazi Austria. From there the Croats split up, some going to Munich, some to Paris, and some to Rome. Even though they were apart, they were united for a period of time by their intention to return to their homeland and participate from 1945 to 1948 in the Krizari movement that sought to overthrow Tito. Pavelić, however, seems to have been intercepted by the British, from whom he escaped, or possibly was allowed to escape. Thereafter, until his return to Rome, Pavelić apparently hid out in an Austrian village near the Croatian border.[2]

As Pavelić and other Ustaša members hatched plans for invading Tito's Yugoslavia from their hideouts, the Vatican's relationship with Yugoslavia passed from frosty to frigid.[3] As we have seen, Pius XII grew paranoid about Tito's threat to Italy, but he had reason to be fearful of what the Communist dictator was doing to the Church in Yugoslavia. The Vatican's motivation for harboring Pavelić grew in lockstep with its apprehension about Tito's treatment of the Church. Even though hostility toward Communist Yugoslavia was on the rise in the United States, the U.S. government maintained its intention of finding and extraditing Pavelić because of the enormity of his war crimes. Tito accused the Allies of protecting Croatia's greatest war criminal, but in fact, for months on end he simply could not be found.

In 1946, intelligence agents tried to figure out the whereabouts of Pavelić but got nowhere. Some thought he had escaped to Argentina, others thought he had returned to his hideout in Austria. Those who thought Pavelić was in Rome were not sure where. Some thought he was at the pope's summer residence in Castel Gandolfo, where he was reputed to be in close contact with Under-Secretary of State Montini.[4] Italian intelligence also reported that Pavelić and Montini were in close contact.[5] But others believed that he was in hiding with the dozens of refugees and war criminals in the Croatian San Girolamo degli Illirici, the seminary of St. Jerome, right in Rome. Counter Intelligence Corps agent William Gowen thought the chances of capturing Pavelić were slim unless officers broke the law and entered extraterritorial properties that belonged to the Vatican.[6]

Agent Gowen is of particular interest in the Pavelić case. All intelligence agents involved in the case, regardless of nationality, believed by 1947 that Pavelić had found refuge in a Vatican property or properties.

We can add to this the fact that Agent William Gowen's father, Franklin Gowen, was assigned at that time to the U.S. diplomatic mission to the Vatican. This leads one to suspect, even to conclude, that the twin posting of father and son to Rome could not have been an accident.[7] This implies that U.S. intelligence hoped that the father's inside connection to the Vatican might at last produce exact information for the son about Pavelić's whereabouts that would lead to his extradition to Yugoslavia to stand trial. But, as we will see, it implies much more, because it was precisely in the middle of 1947 that the United States backed off of the Pavelić case. This suggests, in turn, that the American intention to use the family relationship to finger the refugee dictator became reversed: the Vatican used the father-son relationship to induce the United States to forbear. But let us follow the story from its beginning.

A cluster of buildings stands at the top of the road leading up the main street of the Aventine Hill, one of the famed Seven Hills of Rome. One of them, Special Agent Gowen speculated at the beginning of 1947, housed Ante Pavelić. St. Anselmo's, the Benedictine church and seminary, occupied the top of the Aventine. Seminarians from many countries studied there, but of course they were much younger than Pavelić, who would have been about 60 years old by the end of the war. Although the public was allowed to visit the church, other buildings of the complex were off limits to anyone who was not a member of the Benedictine Order.

Adjacent to Saint Anselmo's is Santa Sabina, a Dominican property that commands extraordinary views of the city of Rome below. Here again, the general public could enter only the church, one of the most ancient of the city of Rome. Thus, the monastery afforded a safe hiding place. Certain that war criminal Pavelić hid out in one of the two complexes atop the Aventine, Agent Gowen drew a map of the district for the benefit of his intelligence superiors. In fact, however, the only reason Gowen seemed to have for his conjecture was the existence of a hidden or subterranean passageway (and perhaps more than one) leading from the religious complexes down the side of a steep cliff to the street some 150 feet below, where there was a breach in the wall that separated the church properties from public domain.

What is of interest is not Gowen's cloak-and-dagger guesswork—he even reported fresh footsteps at the hole in the wall—but the conclusion of his report. Pavelić, Gowen noted, has been "dodging around Europe as his own master for about 15 years. It would seem," Gowen continued, "that only direct action against the Via Cavour house, illegal entry into extraterritorial territory or action against such known Pavelic contacts as Draganovic, Krunoslav, can ultimately reveal the hiding place of Pavelic and lead to his apprehension. Observation continues."[8] Clearly the chase was on, but as we will see, Gowen's recommendation would not last the year.

Robert Clayton Mudd, also a Counter Intelligence Corps agent assigned to the Pavelić case, filed a report from Rome headquarters at the same time Gowen filed his report. Since Gowen had already addressed the situation on the Aventine Hill, Mudd provided background on Pavelić's prior terrorist activity and then recommended, like Gowen, that the Croat dictator be brought to justice.

> Pavelic tops the list of those that the state department and foreign office have agreed to hand over to Tito for trial. Recommendation: in view of the fact that this man is a criminal, as well as a political criminal, every effort should be made to apprehend him and ship him back to the Yugoslav government for trial. In doing so not only would the Yugoslav propaganda guns be silenced and the people of Yugoslavia forced to admit that their previous propagandas [sic] was all false, but also a serious threat to security would be removed and the position of the Anglo-americans strengthened with regard to those south Slav elements who were pro-allied before the war.[9]

Mudd's recommendation is of interest not only because he believed that catching and extraditing Pavelić was the right thing to do but also because he did not hesitate to address the issue of policy. The arrest of Pavelić was in principle the right action, he argued, and it also carried sensible foreign affairs gains. We see here that field agents were not automatons. This fact would have a bearing on the Pavelić case as it unfolded in the months ahead in 1947.

While intelligence agents were busy trying to corner Pavelić, the Vatican was busy trying to get Ustaša war criminals off the hook. As we will see in chapter 11, the Vatican's constant pressure on the Allies to relent in the search for Ustaša criminals finally paid off in the middle of 1947. Ante Pavelić was the linchpin in the pope's effort. But up until the middle of the year, the Allies remained firm in their intention to extradite Pavelić. Since the end of the war, Marshal Tito had continually pressed the Allies to capture and extradite Pavelić. Tito's secret agents were searching for him "frantically," according to an American intelligence report, because much of the hope of Tito dissidents within Yugoslavia depended on the return of the former dictator. In 1946, anti-Communist forces in Yugoslavia were heartened when an airplane dropped pamphlets in Croatia signed by Pavelić saying that the Croats should continue fighting against the Tito regime until the final showdown between Pavelić and Tito took place.[10] The Allies had intended to comply with Tito's request for extradition, but, as we have seen, for all of 1945 and 1946 and much of

1947 they did not know in which Vatican property Pavelić was hiding. The Americans and British advised Marshal Tito to apply directly to the Vatican for information about the elusive Pavelić. In 1946, a Yugoslav diplomat, Vladimir Stakic, did just that in an interview with Cardinal Eugène Tisserant, who assured him that neither he nor the Vatican knew where the fugitive Ustaša dictator was.[11] Since the Vatican knew very well that wanted war criminals huddled in the Croatian seminary of St. Jerome's and elsewhere on Vatican properties, it seems likely that when it came to Pavelić's whereabouts a "don't ask, don't tell" policy prevailed between the Holy See and the superiors of the various religious houses concerned.

But it is just as likely that Cardinal Tisserant lied to Stakic. On April 7, 1946, Tisserant was emphatic in his interview with Stakic that the Holy See wanted to see justice done: "You may have my full assurance that we have the list of all the clergymen who participated in these atrocities and we shall punish them at the right time to cleanse our conscience of the stain with which they spotted us."[12] On April 7, Tisserant insisted that the Catholic Church and the Vatican condemned the crimes of the Ustaša regime. Yet one month later, Tisserant pleaded with the Argentine ambassador to allow fugitive Germans to emigrate. "I have been looking after certain compatriots who have retreated from Germany to Italy and are living here in difficult circumstances," he wrote.[13] While pretending to want to see justice done, Tisserant sought to have war criminals elude it.

The hunt continued for Pavelić, who did not materialize atop the elegant Aventine Hill nor far beneath it at the hole in the wall Agent Gowen spotted. Intelligence personnel began to look elsewhere. The search grew even more intense. Two more U.S. intelligence agents were assigned to the case in the spring of 1947. Pavelić, they determined, was not holed up in Vatican properties on the Aventine but in another papal institution on the via Giacomo Veneziano, number 17. The picture grew even more cloudy when the U.S. civil censorship agency intercepted a letter from Argentina to Germany that stated that Pavelić had arrived in that South American country; the letter provided details of his escape, such as the fact that he was dressed as a priest.[14]

Agents Gowen and Mudd did not buy this story. They insisted that Pavelić had no intention of leaving Europe. They were sure that he would never abandon his life's mission to return in triumph to Croatia. By mid-1947 the two agents had determined that Pavelić was indeed residing on the via Giacomo Veneziano. They knew which stairwell led to his quarters and they knew the coded door-knocking routine to gain admittance to his residence. Pavelić now sported a goatee and his hair was cropped short in the style of a German army officer. A contingent of twelve Ustaša fascists acted as his bodyguard. When Pavelić left the property he was transported in an automobile with Vatican plates. Even with all this security, it would certainly be possible to nab the war criminal the moment he stepped off Vatican property. A trap was set by English and U.S. occupational authorities (not Agent Gowen).

What took place next is stunning. In a complete reversal of their recommendation at the beginning of the year, Agent Gowen advised in August 1947 that Pavelić be left alone in the Vatican's protective custody! Only half a year since he had said that Pavelić must be seized and repatriated, Gowen had adopted the Vatican's point of view on the Ustaša dictator. In the eyes of Pius XII, it would not be right to return Pavelić to Yugoslavia, where he would not get a fair trial. The result would be that the forces supporting atheism and aiding communism would be weakened. Pavelić's "crimes of the past," Gowen wrote, mirroring Vatican thinking, "cannot be forgotten, but he can only be tried by Croats representing a Christian and Democratic Government."[15] The Vatican was disregarding the fact that Pavelić had already been tried by France, "a Christian and Democratic Government," but Agent Gowen disregarded that fact. He concluded his report by saying that the United States should appreciate the Vatican's view of Pavelić and not take direct police action against him.

What was going on? Only six months earlier, Gowen and Mudd had recommended that every "effort should be made to apprehend him [Pavelić] and ship him back to the Jugoslav government for trial." Why did Gowen change his mind so radically in the middle of 1947?

Because William Gowen's father, Franklin, worked in the U.S. diplomatic mission to the Vatican, the younger Gowen had access to information that was not available to other intelligence agents. The Vatican may actually have initiated this process. In the summer of 1946, Franklin Gowen had asked Robert Murphy, Truman's political adviser to zonal Germany, about the whereabouts of his son and learned that he was posted in the U.S. zone.[16] Before the end of the year, Agent William Gowen was transferred to Rome. It would be naive to think that the father-son appointments were happenstance. In fact, Agent Mudd said as much when he reflected in August 1947 that his colleague William Gowen worked *inside* the Vatican.[17] Another army officer wrote similarly that Agent Gowen operated in the Vatican.[18]

Everyone in the Vatican knew of Pope Pius's fear of Communist Yugoslavia. Franklin Gowen heard about the pope's concern directly from

Under-Secretary Montini.[19] It appears that Agent William Gowen, whom the Counter Intelligence Corps had reassigned to Rome to worm information from the Vatican regarding Pavelić's whereabouts, fell under the influence of Monsignor Montini and the entourage surrounding him— British minister D'Arcy Osborne and the American diplomats Harold Tittmann and Franklin Gowen—with the result that he changed his recommendation. Instead of advising that Pavelić be arrested, he said that he should be shielded from arrest.[20] At this time the Vatican was urging the United States and Great Britain not to seize Ustaša war criminals hiding out in Rome. The British Foreign Office was unsympathetic, to say the least. D'Arcy Osborne was instructed in February 1947 to let the Vatican know that "the Pope's anti-Communist propaganda would be more convincing if he had a more positive line to show as regards the Nazis and Fascists."[21] But the Holy See, impervious to London's contemptuous tone, wanted to treat Ustaša blacks as innocent grays. By the spring of 1947, the Vatican was putting intense pressure on the United States and Britain not to send these criminals back to Yugoslavia.[22] In Rome, Special Agent Gowen felt the same pressure from inside the Vatican regarding the number one black fugitive, Ante Pavelić.

If, as the national archive's Pavelić file reports, Agent Gowen picked up information from a "high Vatican source," we may assume that the senior Gowen relayed to the junior Gowen whatever information the Holy See, meaning the pope through Monsignor Montini, wished to divulge. Of course, Franklin Gowen would not divulge information that might allow Moscow, Zagreb, or Roman Communists to embarrass the Vatican by exposing its protection of war criminals. But by the middle of 1947 there was no longer any question of that happening. It became increasingly evident that Gowen was obtaining more and more details about the hitherto-elusive Pavelić. Agent Gowen now knew where he was to be found, what he looked like, and how to communicate with him. After Pavelić underwent a serious operation in September, Gowen believed he could actually arrange an interview with the convalescent at a location off Vatican property.[23] Gowen recommended that no action against Pavelić be taken until such an interview could be made. This obviously implies that Gowen had found a way to communicate through Vatican intermediaries with the Ustaša dictator.

At this point, summer and fall of 1947, it remained to be seen whether resistance forces inside and outside Yugoslavia could succeed in unseating Tito. If they succeeded, then Pavelić would have to face up to his past in a court of law to which the Vatican would not object. "The ultimate disposal of Pavelić," agents Gowen and Louis Caniglia wrote in August, "is necessary if the Croat democratic and resistance forces are to ever be recognized by the U.S."[24] Because of his contacts inside the Vatican, Gowen believed that he would be able to verify that British intelligence personnel were protecting Pavelić (in cooperation with the Holy See) in covert disregard of the directives of London's Foreign Office. In the event that a democratic government came to power in Croatia, Agent Gowen reasoned, the British could be forced to arrest and extradite him themselves.[25] Pavelić's fate thus depended on whether the resistance—Vlatko Maćek's Peasant Party—succeeded in Yugoslavia. Of course, this line of reasoning amounted only to pretense. If the Holy See truly cared about justice, Pavelić would have been extradited to France for his murders in Marseilles after World War I. Furthermore, the chance of any new regime—other than Pavelić's Ustaša—replacing Tito's rule was slim to none.

By the middle of 1947, Agent Gowen had become well versed in the Vatican's thinking about Ante Pavelić. He was seen as a militant Catholic who had formerly fought against members of the Orthodox Church (indeed, he had murdered hundreds of thousands of them) and "today is fighting against Communist atheism."[26] This is why the Vatican protected Pavelić, Gowen reported. By September, the intelligence agent was pressing even more resolutely for an appreciation of the Vatican position. Gowen warned that Pavelić's "contacts are so high and his present position is so compromising to the Vatican, that any extradition of subject would be a staggering blow to the Roman Catholic Church."[27]

This report has a dramatic and urgent ring, and it can be misunderstood for that reason. The embarrassment that could befall the Vatican was *not* because of its ratline. The U.S. state department had known about that since the Vincent La Vista report of July. And, of course, Pavelić had not yet fled via the Vatican's ratline to Argentina and may, at this time, have had no intention of doing so. Rather, the embarrassment would have come from Pavelić's trial in Yugoslavia, from which Marshall Tito would wring every drop of anti-West propaganda at the expense of Pius XII and the capitalist system. At the time of Gowen's September memo, not quite one year had elapsed since the trial of Archbishop Stepinać, which, as we have seen, presaged the Cold War. The U.S. government understood that Stepinać's trial posed valid questions of guilt, but popular opinion in the west held that the archbishop's trial did not resolve these questions. A trial of Pavelić, by contrast, would lack the trappings of Stepinać's show trial; there was ample evidence to expose him as a mass murderer. Pius XII had given unofficial recognition to the Ustaša regime, had actually met with Pavelić subsequent to the murder of King Alexander, and had harbored him after the war. The embarrassment to the Vatican in terms of the nascent Cold War would indeed have been "staggering."

Agent Gowen's warning must be understood in the context of the Cold War; it was not meant in the first instance to ward off embarrassment to the Vatican. That, after all, was not what an American intelligence agent was all about. Rather, Agent Gowen wanted to parry a blow against the United States, the leader of the capitalist world whose economic system the Vatican found far superior to that of communism. Again and again over the half-century before 1945, the Vatican had condemned atheistic communism and its prohibition of private property. The Vatican, one of the last monarchical kingdoms with expansive land holdings in aristocratic Europe, became wholly committed to the stock market system of the capitalist world when it was forcefully deprived of its feudal property. As the Cold War began to develop in the second half of 1947, there was no question as to which side the Vatican was on, even though it officially continued to claim neutrality. With the reputation of Pius XII not yet impugned by the Holocaust, Agent Gowen saw that the moral authority of Pope Pius would be bankrupt if Marshal Tito was given the chance to put Ante Pavelić on trial. Gowen moved to preserve the integrity of his country's ally.

Agent Gowen's memo had its intended effect on intelligence policy. At about the time of Gowen's August and September memos, word got to Rome to leave Pavelić alone. This transpired with striking abruptness. Gowen's supervisor, Bernard J. Grennan, who was the Counter Intelligence Corps chief in zone five—Rome—received a message that instructed him to proceed with Pavelić's arrest, but suddenly the plan was halted in its tracks: the bottom of the message read "HANDS OFF!"[28]

Just at this time, the summer of 1947, the United States authorized the Central Intelligence Agency, successor to the Counter Intelligence Corps, to make a distinct change in goals. Now instead of collecting unsavory Nazi scientists for scientific work in the United States (Operation Paperclip), agents were to provide safe harbor for any and all persons the U.S. government felt would serve the national interest (Operation National Interest).[29] As the authors of the Interagency Working Group of the U.S. and Japanese national archives wrote in *U.S. Intelligence and the Nazis*, "there was no compelling reason to begin the postwar era with the assistance of some of those associated with the worst crimes of the war."[30] The Holy See thought otherwise and pressed the Allies explicitly and effectively to join them in ratline activity.

British intelligence, MI-6, and the Central Intelligence Agency got the word to leave Pavelić alone. Regular army and foreign affairs ministries in the United States and Great Britain, who were kept in the dark about the "hands off!" order, could not understand what developed in the ensuing months. In the fall, American and British army personnel pressed each other to arrest Pavelić. Neither was at liberty to do so because both Allied partners were using Ustaša fascists as informers. A plan therefore was hatched whereby the Allies would jointly alert the Italian police when Pavelić left Vatican property and the police would then detain the Croatian dictator as a war criminal. This plan was never enacted. "The Brits," an American officer complained in November 1948, "to this day have not called up to put the plan in effect."[31]

Allied diplomats in the field and at home offices were similarly nonplussed. Myron Taylor continued to be concerned as late as April 1948 about the blacks in Italy. He urged that their cases be adjudicated so that the remaining grays in detention could be released to go home.[32] Ambassador John Moors Cabot complained bitterly in the summer of 1947 that "many Croats are escaping from detention, in Rome evidently, because they are not being properly guarded and these birds are then getting to Argentina."[33] Cabot knew whereof he spoke, as he had just been reassigned from Argentina to Yugoslavia. Blacks were "slipping though our fingers," the ambassador implied, "in spite of our stated support for prosecution of war criminals." The guilty

> for whom irrefutable evidence of guilt exists should be ferreted out and returned to Yugoslavia. I suggest that in addition to taking urgent measures to remedy the above situation, we might ask Vatican in return for information we are transmitting for [a] list of Yugoslavs it is sheltering.[34]

Cabot knew, of course, that if such a list were forthcoming Ante Pavelić's name would be at the top.

By the summer of 1948, the Ustaša resistance movement in Yugoslavia had collapsed. At the trials of those arrested at home or sent back to Yugoslavia as blacks from abroad, Father Krunoslav Draganović and Ante Pavelić were identified as the leaders of the resistance movement against Tito's Communist regime. Once that movement ceased being viable, Pavelić was of no further use to the Vatican. In October 1948, Ante Pavelić, the assassin and mass murderer, boarded the ocean liner *Sistriere* and sailed to Argentina and freedom.[35] In pursuit of its geopolitical vision for a Catholic state neighboring Italy, Pius XII had subverted justice twice by sheltering a bloody and ruthless dictator who had once been the ally of Europe's only other genocidal ruler, Adolf Hitler.

11
THE BIGGEST RATLINE

If a ratline's success is to be measured in terms of the degree of degradation of its clientele, then surely Bishop Hudal's ratline takes the prize. If, however, the number of assisted criminals is the criterion, then the operation of the Ustaša priest Krunoslav Draganović would have to be counted as the number one ratline. The matter of rank is of course ludicrous. In terms of disservice to the cause of humane governance and the cause of improving humanity, Pius XII's two Italian ratlines fed into one degenerate path.

Why bother studying yet another ratline? Although there is no doubt that the pope sponsored the Spanish and Hudal ratlines, Draganović's operation reveals the direct involvement of Pius XII himself. The closest link between a sponsor and an emigration operation belonged not to the Vatican but to the American Joint Distribution Committee. The AJDC helped whites—Jewish refugees—emigrate to Palestine, an illegal movement to be sure, but one which enjoyed widespread international approval because of the Holocaust. The Vatican's ratlines helped blacks—Nazi and Ustaša Holocaust perpetrators—to elude justice. Had these operations been known, they would have elicited widespread international disapproval. Of the two operations, the Vatican's obviously had to be more covert, a circumstance that tended to conceal the link between sponsor and ratline. But as we will discover, the pope's determination to rescue some of Draganović's Ustaša war criminals led him at last to show his hand in a manner that produced documented opposition by the British Foreign Office.

The issue of what motivated ratline sponsors also emerges in the context of Draganović's operation. The motivation of sponsors and agents varied. Ideology—opposition to communism—drove Pope Pius and Bishop Hudal. As the Cold War developed, the complicity of the United States in ratline operations was also ideological. Sympathy for Nazis and other fascists propelled dictator Juan Perón. Draganović worked his ratline first out of nationalistic zeal for Croatia and, when that cause collapsed, out of love of money. But regardless of ideological motives, all roads led to Rome. Until 1946, the ratlines moved blacks, both Nazi and Ustaša, from Rome to the port city of Genoa to set sail for Barcelona. After that, they moved their clients to Argentina.

One final reason for attending to Draganović's misguided but effective work relates to how governments function. Within an executive branch, the left hand does not always know what the right hand is doing. This can be either purposeful or accidental or both, as it was in this case at different periods. U.S. and British intelligence moved well ahead of the curve with regard to Draganović's ratline, while departments of state lagged well behind it. Not until July 1947 did the U.S. State Department's Vincent La Vista produce his very important investigation of illegal emigration from Rome, by which time the United States had already made an executive decision to allow anti-Communist black fascists to walk away from their World War II crimes. La Vista's report, a boon for historians, had no effect on history. Soon after the British foreign ministry advised Pius XII in contemptuous tongue-in-cheek fashion that protecting Ustaša war criminals would not be a good way for him to play Gregory VII (the powerful medieval pope), Ante Pavelić was basking in "hands off" status.[1]

The Vatican's connection to Krunoslav Draganović originally had nothing to do with a ratline. Draganović's impressive backers, Archbishop Stepinać (Zagreb) and Archbishop Sarić (Sarajevo), had opened doors for him at the Vatican before the war. After Draganović finished his studies for the priesthood in Yugoslavia, Sarić sent him to Rome for graduate studies, where the young cleric delved into the ethnology—ominously—of Balkan affairs.[2] When Croatia became a Nazi puppet state during the war, Draganović became a leading figure in the bureau of colonization and used the rationale of his doctoral dissertation as the theoretical basis for forcing Orthodox Serbs to convert to Catholicism.[3] The bureau of colonization took property away from Serbs, redistributing it, and that of murdered Serbs, to Catholic Croatians. Besides his association with ethnic cleansing, Draganović also served as an army chaplain with the rank of lieutenant colonel in the notoriously brutal Jasenovać concentration camp.[4] Although Yugoslavia requested that he be extradited for war crimes after the war, the occupational authorities in Italy never complied, and Tito soon had bigger fish to fry. In 1943, Draganović had a falling out with Eugen Kvaternik, the head of Pavelić's Order and

Security Office and a pathological killer.[5] He returned in the summer of 1943 to Rome, where, as the former personal secretary to Archbishop Sarić, he provided the Vatican with valuable inside information about Croatian church and state affairs. Draganović wasted no time establishing himself in Rome; soon he was the secretary of the Croat embassy in Rome and was hobnobbing frequently with German occupational forces. U.S. agents described him as early as 1945 as "very venal," a trait that would only grow with time and one that American intelligence would come to exploit during the Cold War.[6]

The downturn in Nazi wartime fortunes inevitably doomed the Ustaša regime in Croatia. At some point near the end, Draganović returned to his native country to take some of the ill-begotten Ustaša treasury to Rome and to prepare for dictator Pavelić's eventual arrival in the Eternal City. In Rome, Draganović became known in intelligence circles as the very visible alter ego of the invisible Pavelić. During this time, Draganović also engaged in getting high churchmen who were Ustaša members out of Croatia. Bishop Rozman (or Roxman) of Ljubljana, whom the British considered to be a war criminal, fled to Austria; Archbishop Ivan Sarić, considered a war criminal in Yugoslavia because of his passionate support of Pavelić and the Ustaša, took cover in Vatican property in Rome. A large number of other clerical and lay Ustaša members, many of them war criminals, settled in the Croatian seminary near the Vatican, St. Jerome's. As the war ended, thousands of other ethnic Croatian refugees and fugitives—some black, but mostly gray—were penned up in displaced persons camps in Italy.

The Vatican's Pontifical Commission of Assistance appointed Krunoslav Draganović to help take care of the refugees from Croatia. He was in his element. Still relatively young of age at 32 and very familiar with the Roman scene, the Italian-speaking Draganović made his way as fluidly in American-occupied Rome as he had previously done when the city was occupied by the Germans. The Vatican not only wanted Draganović to care for the thousands of grays, most of whom would return, if possible, to an ethnic Croatian state, but also to find shelter for the Ustaša blacks who were expecting to return to oust Marshal Tito. The scheme had worked once under Ante Pavelić and Pope Pius hoped it would work again. Draganović served the Vatican as the front man in this venture, and, as one intelligence report put it, "in many instances it [was] hard to distinguish the activity of the church from the activity" of Draganović.[7]

With hindsight it is clear that the chances for the re-creation of an ethnic Croatian state were minimal at best. But this was not clear in the immediate postwar years. Pius XII, Bishop Hudal, Jose La Boos in

Spain, and Krunoslav Draganović were united by the expectation of war between the west and the Soviets. Such an event might have created the right circumstances for Pavelić's return to Yugoslavia. But unlike in 1941, when Pavelić enjoyed the patronage of Hitler, Josip Tito held power in the Balkans with Soviet backing. So long as that situation obtained, Ustaša and Vatican prospects were doomed. But the dreams of Pope Pius died hard.

Disunity among the Croatians and the Ustaša hobbled the movement as well. In Yugoslavia, Archbishop Stepinać was reputedly organizing a resistance movement, the Krizari, after Pavelić's abandonment of the government. Draganović helped by recruiting Croats from refugee camps to return to the homeland to muster anti-Tito forces. But the political and military leader of the Krizari movement, Vlatko Maćek, wanted to disassociate the anti-Tito movement from the Ustaša and Pavelić.[8] Maćek, who favored a degree of autonomy for Croatia within Yugoslavia through democratic means, opposed Pavelić's effort to seek autonomy through a bloody revolution.[9]

The refugee Ustaši were also disunited. Two main groups, one in Austria and one in Italy, took their orders from different officers who seemed to lack close coordination. Pavelić understood that a premature return to the homeland would likely fail and sought to restrain restless refugees. Pavelić himself could not play as active a role as he would undoubtedly have liked because of his need to remain hidden in Vatican properties. His son-in-law, Vilko Pečnikar, assumed the leadership, and, as we have seen, relieved Draganović of the looted Ustaša gold. Since no rift between Draganović and Pavelić ever occurred, it is likely that Pečnikar took possession of the gold because of Draganović's venality rather than because of a disagreement between Draganović and Pavelić. But because of Pečnikar's close association with Pavelić and the Ustaša, Maćek's anti-Tito movement within Yugoslavia wanted nothing to do with him. This rift reverberated through the various enclaves of exiled Ustaši, loosening Pečnikar's political control of the Ustaša. Fewer and fewer Ustaši associated with him.[10] "Pecnikar seems more and more alone," a U.S. agent reported. "His stauncher friends have been slowly but steadily abandoning him."[11] The shared desire of Croat refugees to unseat Tito provided a degree of unity, but when it came to action they splintered, some agreeing that the Ustaša should disband and back Maćek's movement and some looking for a return of Pavelić and a revived Ustaša government.[12] Only the expectation of war kept the hopes of all alive to some extent.

While plotters schemed during most of 1945 and 1946, the Ustaša remnant had to be cared for somehow, and those among them who were wanted war criminals needed to be hidden. This became Draganović's work within the Vatican's Croatian refugee support effort, a subunit of the Pontifical Commission of Assistance. Many months before the Vincent La Vista report for the State Department, U.S. intelligence documented Draganović's labor for the refugees and his connection to the Vatican. Most Ustaša fascists holed up in St. Jerome's Croatian seminary. Draganović obtained false identification papers for those who were considered war criminals by international standards, enabling them to escape Allied authorities. Boarding a large number of Ustaša refugees required funding, which Draganović obtained from a number of Vatican sources: donations from Croatian Americans, the gold that Pečnikar took from Draganović, and Vatican funds for information services.[13] There is no documentary evidence that Pečnikar stashed the looted gold in the Vatican bank, but repeated reports that the Holy See funded the operation at St. Jerome's make this seem likely.[14] A Croatian priest, Dominik Mandić (also spelled Mandich in intelligence reports), served with Draganović as the liaison between the Vatican and St. Jerome's. A report Acting U.S. Political Advisor to the Acting Supreme Occupational Commander Joseph N. Greene made to the political advisor of the American ambassador to Italy also indicated Vatican financial support for anti-Tito organizations, both for the Ustaša or for Maček's Peasant Party and the Krizari.[15]

The United States Uncovers the Ustaša Ratline

Draganović's ratline activity began soon after the end of the war, even though most of his efforts during the immediate postwar months centered on providing for gray and black Croat refugees. Prosecution of war criminals was a high priority for occupation authorities, and a number of the Ustaša refugees simply could not risk idling around Rome to see if military action in Europe would begin. Among these was Vjekoslav Vrančić, whom Hitler himself had decorated. Father Mandić, Draganović's Franciscan colleague, arranged the escape of Dinko Šakić, who had run the notorious Jasenovać concentration camp during the last months of the war.[16] Uki Goñi estimates that about 200 Ustaša war criminals escaped to Argentina during 1945 and 1946 using visas that the Argentine dictator Perón had issued to Draganović. Skillfully exploiting Argentine records, Goñi has been able to identify by name many of these individual criminals, the nature of their war crimes, and the manner in which Draganović or Mandić facilitated their emigration.

Counter Intelligence Corps agent Robert C. Mudd, whom we have met in connection with the search for Ante Pavelić, documented the activities of the Vatican and Draganović on behalf of war criminals who resided in St. Jerome's and those who were fleeing to South America. Mudd compiled a list of Ustaši who were being "fed, clothed, and housed" in St. Jerome's. Over 100 of them were trying to get out of Europe via the ratline to Argentina that the Argentine government and the Vatican jointly sponsored.[17] Another intelligence report of Agent Mudd noted that many of the "more prominent Ustaši war criminals and quislings are living in Rome illegally, many of them under false names. Their cells [at St. Jerome's] are maintained, their papers still published, and their intelligence agencies still in operation."[18] Draganović and other agents liaising with the Holy See "travel back and forth from the Vatican several times a week in a Vatican car which cannot be stopped because of diplomatic immunity."[19] The car took them inside St. Jerome's. Mudd concluded that Draganović's "sponsorship of these Croat quislings"

> definitely links him up with the plan of the Vatican to shield these ex-Ustashi nationalists until such time as they are able to procure for themselves the proper documents to enable them to go to South America. The Vatican, undoubtedly banking on the strong anti-communist feelings of these men, is endeavoring to infiltrate them into South America in any way possible to counteract the spread of Red doctrine.[20]

Mudd had the names of several particular "long sought after war criminals" who also lived in St. Jerome's. Draganović naturally denied that the Vatican sponsored the escape of these individuals but Mudd entertained no doubts about the Vatican's auspices.

Clearly, during the two years following the end of the war, U.S. intelligence agents had acquired an accurate picture of what the Ustaša refugees and the Vatican were up to both with regard to the anti-Tito movement and to Draganović's ratline. Diplomats, on the other hand, still did not know what was going on. Had he known of the ratline activity and the Vatican's backing of it, the French ambassador to the Holy See, Jacques Maritain, would have resigned with a loud protest. There is nothing in the papers of Myron Taylor or his assistants, Harold Tittmann and Franklin Gowen, that would indicate that any of them knew. Not, that is, until the summer of 1947, shortly after the State Department received Vincent La Vista's report, when U.S. agent William Gowen changed his mind about arresting Ante Pavelić. This timing was coincidental, however. Pressure on Agent Gowen came from inside the Vatican, certainly not as a result of the La Vista report, to which we now turn.

U.S. diplomat John Moors Cabot was the key player whose memos in June 1947 to the State Department confirmed from non-Italian sources what La Vista had disclosed the previous month. Either by happenstance or, more likely, because of Cabot's suspicions about how and why war criminals were finding their way to Argentina, Cabot moved in 1947 from his diplomatic post in South America to Yugoslavia, the reconstituted state that included the former Nazi puppet state of Croatia. In South America, he had witnessed the influx of fascists, some of whom he had reason to suspect were war criminals. Then, in Yugoslavia, the Tito government showed him evidence of Ustaša war crimes that had been committed by Croats now living in Italy or Austria. The tone of Cabot's message to the State Department about the ratlines gives the impression that he wanted the State Department to investigate: "I must again express to the department my respectful but very serious concern at [the] manner in which Yugoslav Quisling matter is being handled."[21] Cabot was urging state to take action, not confirming what state suspected and was considering investigating. Cabot either did not know about the La Vista report or, if he did know about it, he was urging state to take action on it.[22]

In presenting his concerns to the State Department, Cabot was obviously unaware of all that U.S. intelligence agents knew, and had known for some time, about the ratline from Spain and about Hudal's and Draganović's operations. "Some arrangement," Cabot asserted vaguely, "has been worked out with the Vatican and Argentina by which collaborationist Yugoslavs will be helped to emigrate to Argentina." Cabot bitterly complained to state that the United States was flouting "our own commitments." To Cabot, ratlines constituted a moral issue, a matter of what is right and wrong, not, as the Holy See seemed to think, a matter of emerging international confrontation between east and west. "By our attitude," Cabot wrote with some indignation, we are protecting those "guilty of terrible crimes committed in Yugoslavia."[23] Basing his accusation on materials available at the embassy in Yugoslavia, Cabot assured state that there could be no doubt about his charges; they were, he said, "crystal clear."

Cabot pressed on. Intimating that the United States might be using fascists as informers, he felt his country was not living up to its "commitments and moral obligations." As far as he could ascertain, Cabot wrote, the United States had not taken effective action to curtail the ratlines, had prevented the British and Italians from do so, and was scheming with the Vatican and Argentina in a manner that let blacks escape.[24] Cabot ended with a double warning:

> How can we defend this record before the UN if the Yugoslavs take it there
> I do not know, and there are increasing evidences they will. As I see it we
> may then be forced either to accept a humiliating decision against us or so
> manipulate things as to show that we also consider UN a mere instrument
> of power politics. I also trust [that] the Catholic Church realizes how ex-
> tremely damaging this affair might be to its position in [Yugoslavia].[25]

Cabot was nothing if not insistent. His memos may well have been the
tripwire for state to take action on the La Vista report.

Whereas U.S. intelligence agents were assigned to certain cases, such
as that of Pavelić or Hudal, the State Department wanted La Vista to
frame the whole ratline picture for them, verifying whatever allegations
the department had picked up, including, of course, Cabot's. Consequently, much of what La Vista reported intelligence agents already knew
and had reported themselves, albeit not to state. But there is one very important exception—Dr. Willy Nix, a German double agent whose work
for the Vatican was a cover for his work for his actual paymaster, the
Soviet Union.[26] What this means is that the Vatican's covert ratline operation was all for naught—derailed from the very beginning because Nix
sent Communist agents to South America instead of anti-Communists.
This was one of La Vista's most stunning findings.

Postwar Rome was a city of transients. La Vista could only guess
at their number, which he put at somewhere between 100,000 and 1
million. Almost every East European and Russian nation contributed
to the floating mass of people. An indefinite number of fascists, both
Italian, German, and Austrian, mixed in with other refugees. Unlike
Eastern Europeans who fled because Communists had seized power in
their lands, black fascists fled because of their war crimes. Many Yugoslavs, of course, and some Slovaks fled their countries for both reasons.
Thousands and thousands of Eastern European Jews, Holocaust survivors whose homes gentiles had taken possession of, sought passage from
Italy to Palestine. La Vista encountered this sea of humanity, which was
mostly gray, he knew, but which also included a substantial number of
whites and blacks.[27]

A number of agencies in Rome and other Italian cities attempted
to facilitate the transfer of these hundreds of thousands of transients to
new destinations abroad. Principal emigration agencies were the Pontifical Commission of Assistance, whose agencies made up the largest such
operation in Rome, and, the American Joint Distribution Committee,
the second largest. The AJDC smuggled Jews to Palestine but also helped
thousands emigrate to North and South America, where, ironically, Argentina took in more than any other country. The Pontifical Commission

of Assistance operated on a nationality basis; each country was assigned a priest to deal with refugees from his land. Monsignor Baldelli headed the pontifical commission and reported to Montini in the Vatican secretariat. Altogether there were about twenty of these agencies under Baldelli.[28] Most of the refugees the Red Cross and papal commission helped were heading to the western hemisphere. These agencies obviously provided a much-needed service.

The problem, La Vista determined, lay in the fact that pro-German (which is to say pro-Nazi and pro-Yugoslav, which is to say pro-Croat) personnel had infiltrated the Red Cross operation in Rome. The same situation applied to the Pontifical Commission of Assistance, because pro-Nazi (Hudal) and pro-Ustaši (Draganović) individuals had been appointed by the commission to its national units. Compounding this unfortunate fact was the close cooperation between the Red Cross and the national offices of the papal commission, which gave preference to refugees who were Catholics, or at least pro-church and anti-Communist. Thus, the two agencies' pro-fascist personnel combined their knowledge and resources to feed the ratlines. We have already seen how this combination worked in practice in Bishop Hudal's ratline operation. What transpired there, La Vista determined, constituted the rule. A person applied to the papal commission's office of his nationality, obtained a letter of identification, and took it to a Red Cross office, which routinely issued him their identity card. Neither the papal nor Red Cross offices screened applicants for war criminals. Once in possession of the Red Cross identity card, a person was eligible to apply for a visa. Nazi and Ustaša fascists beat a steady path to Rome to obtain new identities. "In this category," La Vista wrote

> there has been and still are large groups of Nazi-Germans who come into Italy for the sole purpose of obtaining fictitious identity documents, passports, and visas, and leave almost immediately via Genoa and Barcelona for Latin America.

Draganović's ratline also flourished nicely in the cozy relationship between the Red Cross and the papal commission. As La Vista put it, "the Yugoslav movement in this picture is of particular interest since there appear to be altogether too many refugees in Italy who are apparently anti-Tito."[29]

The emigration services of the various agencies could not function without host countries to accept refugees. The pontifical commission was successful because of the ability of the Vatican to put pressure on predominantly Roman Catholic countries in South America to open their doors to anti-Communist displaced persons. We have seen that the Holy See began doing this early on, well before the end of the war, with Argentina, which took in the largest number of refugees, followed by Mexico and Cuba. Other Latin American countries participated as well. La Vista wrote:

> This appeared to be an inexplicable situation but further investigation indicated that in those Latin American countries where the church is a controlling or dominating factor, the Vatican has brought pressure to bear which has resulted in the foreign missions of those countries taking an attitude almost favoring the entry into their country of former Nazi and former fascists or other political groups, so long as they are anti communist. That in fact is the practice in effect in the Latin American consulates and missions in Rome at the present time.[30]

For the most part, the priests who headed up the various national agencies under the Pontifical Commission of Assistance did not misuse their authority to benefit war criminals. The exceptions were Bishop Hudal, who eagerly sought out Nazis, Draganović at St. Jerome's, and the German priest Anton Weber. Father Carlos (or Karl) Bayer, who ran the German office out of the former German embassy and worked as secretary to Monsignor Baldelli, told historian Gitta Sereny that he and others knew that war criminals passed through their agencies, but that it was not possible to check peoples' stories because of the sheer number of refugees.[31] Some priests acted out of naiveté. "Fr. Gallov who runs the Hungarian welfare agency . . . innocently believes any story and issues the bona fide for the person to take to the Red Cross to get a legit passport."[32] One did not have to be in charge of one of the national agencies of the papal commission to benefit from the Vatican's support for indiscriminate refugee assistance. Father Anton Weber, mentioned above in connection with the Spanish ratlines, admitted to Gitta Sereny that he helped SS Nazis emigrate when they applied to his St. Raphael Society's office in Rome. Weber said that Vatican funds were used for this service.[33] Neither Krunoslav Draganović nor Willy Nix headed national agencies affiliated with the Holy See, yet both enjoyed papal support and protection. Intelligence agents were not able to penetrate the ratlines of either Draganović or Nix, but Nix's work came to an abrupt end in the summer of 1947, at which time he mysteriously vanished.

From the moment the Allies occupied Rome late in the war, Willy Nix successfully pulled the wool over the eyes of U.S. intelligence agents. Nix ran the office in Rome of the "Free German Committee," whose phony but lofty avowed purpose was to rid Germany of Nazis and re-educate Germans along peaceful and democratic lines. On a more practical level, Nix promised that he would help the Allies identify German Nazis. Nix told intelligence agents a yarn about his persecution at the hands of the Gestapo, who, he said, took everything from him but his life. He said that he had spent two to three years in Sachsenhausen and other concentration camps before escaping and making his way to Rome, where the Vatican gave him funds to assist Allied soldiers who had fled POW camps. In reality, of course, he used the money to help Nazis escape to South America. U.S. intelligence agents downplayed Nix and his efforts. He was said to have dominated his small association of Germans in Rome like a "little Hitler." Other Germans did not particularly like him.[34] U.S. intelligence agents concluded that "the group does not have much going for it."

Having sold the Allies his cover story and convinced them of his unimportance, Nix managed to help Nazis escape from the end of the war to the summer of 1947. Suddenly, just at the time of La Vista's sojourn in Rome, Nix's luck ran out when it was discovered that

> a number of people escaped from a dp camp in Italy and made their way to the office of Dr. Willy Nix in Rome who is the head of the Free German Committee. Nix then furnished them with id [*sic*] papers even though he knew that they were wanted. They then made contact with others, including Fr. Bayer, who made arrangements for their hiding until time of departure. Further checking suggests that Dr. Nix serves both underground Nazis and Russia in spiriting people out of Europe.[35]

Further investigation showed that the Vatican's emigration network was so sophisticated that it could find jobs in South America for escaped refugees. Based on this information, the Italian government issued warrants for Nix's arrest, but minutes before his capture, he was tipped off and fled to Vatican City. "It has always been thought," La Vista wrote in his memo to state, "that Dr. Nix was operating under the benevolent protection of the Vatican," and his flight there proved it.[36]

This was shocking news for the U.S. State Department. Not only was the Vatican helping suspected war criminals escape, but worse, Soviet agents had infiltrated Nix's operation and had used it to place their people in South American countries. Just how many Russians found their way to the western hemisphere La Vista could not say, but he estimated that as many as 10 percent of all refugees in Italy were Russian. Using his speculation about the number of refugees—100,000 to one million—this would mean as few as 10,000 and as many as 100,000 Russians in Italy, numbers that appear preposterously high. Even making allowance for exaggeration about the numbers, the State Department had reason to be alarmed.

The question of who blew the whistle on Nix has not been answered. Interestingly, La Vista never mentioned Krunoslav Draganović in his rather detailed report, although he was the secretary of the Croat national unit of the Pontifical Commission of Assistant for refugees. Other operatives—Hudal, Bayer, Weber, Gallov—working under the Vatican are mentioned by name. None of them controlled emigration operations that were as well known as Draganović's at St. Jerome's. Add to this the fact that Draganović was a known entity in Rome—known personally even by U.S. intelligence agents—and La Vista's omission seems curious. How did it happen that Nix's career ended precisely at the time of La Vista's stay in Rome? How did La Vista manage to put the finger on Nix when he had eluded any number of intelligence agents? How did it happen that he discovered Nix's Soviet connections when intelligence agents could not? Krunoslav Draganović might be the answer to these questions. The whole purpose of the Vatican's ratline operations was to infiltrate South America with anti-Communists. "Knowing this, and knowing the methods of operation of Catholic agencies which are sponsoring the emigration of anti Communists to these [Central and Latin American] countries, the Communists are using these very agencies for the purpose of sending their own agents to these same countries," La Vista wrote.[37] Draganović's ratline depended on the Vatican's intention to infiltrate Latin America. By catering to Communist agents, Nix sabotaged the Holy See's efforts. It is plausible that Draganović tipped La Vista off to Nix's operation in exchange for being left out of the report that would be sent to the State Department. Unfortunately, no documentary evidence has come to light to substantiate this speculation. And the question of why the Vatican would take Nix in, given the nature of the allegation against him, must somehow find an answer. Attempting to solve the Willy Nix riddle is only an interesting distraction. The important fact is that the Vatican believed that Nix worked the ratline for them and when he got in trouble the Holy See opened its doors to him. Nix stepped inside and disappeared from history.

When Herbert J. Cummings of the U.S. State Department received La Vista's second memo in July 1947, he reacted immediately, calling a large meeting to discuss what the government should do.[38] Before letting the Vatican know that its ratline operation had been exposed, the State Department wanted some verification of the La Vista report and instructed Graham Parsons of the U.S. mission to the Holy See to check into the matter. Parsons confirmed La Vista's facts. "Known or wanted war criminals [have] reached Italy illegally and applied and received these [identity] documents under assumed names and have to date successfully evaded apprehension."[39] Anyone, Parsons wrote, could obtain these documents through the "assistance of persons operating under the protection of the Vatican." All a war criminal had to do was to contact one of the national agencies working "under the protective custody of the Vatican [the Pontifical Commission of Assistance] or Dr. Nix's "Free Austrian Committee."[40] Anyone, Parsons continued,

> can secure a letter of recommendation . . . to any Welfare Group under the protection of the Vatican, stating that his name is so, and his nationality is such, and that he desires an International /Red Cross Identity Document. . . . He may be directed to Father Gallov, [the] Hungarian Catholic priest, in temporary control of welfare units operating under the protection of the Vatican. Fr. Gallov will either direct subject by letter to his personal contact in the International Red Cross or to Dr. Vida . . . stating in effect that he has known subject for some time and assistance will be appreciated . . . to enable him to secure an IRC Identity document. This letter will bear the S an official stamp of the Vatican. UFFICIO ASSISTENZA RELICIOSA PER UNGAREAL IN URBO.[41]

At that point, Parsons explained, the suspected war criminal could remain in Italy without fear of being detained by the police until he received a visa from a South or Central American country.

Next, Parsons checked out the other end of the ratline. At the Panama consulate, he was told that Panama admitted some immigrants as long as they were not Communists. "For this reason persons possessing a fascist background are favorably considered," Parsons wrote.[42] All of the national units under the Vatican processed refugees in this manner, "assisting persons from their native countries to escape prosecution regardless of the country attempting to apprehend these persons." In short, Parsons, verified everything that La Vista had reported and added new details in some instances. Given these assurances, the State Department directed Parsons to bring the matter of the ratlines to the attention of the Holy See and sent him an airgram detailing the substance of the discussion that Cummings had convened.[43]

Given Parsons' assurances of the reliability of La Vista's memo, Cummings relayed the decisions state had reached to Parsons and embassy personnel stationed in Europe and South America. These were to notify the U.S. minister in Bern to contact the European headquarters of the International Red Cross in Bern about the fact that the Rome branch of the Red Cross was issuing bogus passports; second, they were to bring the entire ratline issue to the attention of London; third, they were to call attention of the American Joint Distribution Committee to the matter of their involvement; and finally, they were to notify "our consular officers to beware of the fraudulent practices outlined in the [La Vista] report. In this connection, consideration is also being given to the best means of seeking the cooperation of Latin American governments in preventing persons with fraudulent documents from entering this hemisphere."[44] Parsons was instructed to take the matter up with the Vatican and notify the Italian police.

Any field agent who had been working in U.S. intelligence for the previous two years would have been astonished that the State Department was so out of touch. The data on the Vatican's Spanish and Roman ratlines that intelligence agents had collected over this period of time had never been passed on to the State Department, or, if it had, it had become lost in state's paper shuffle. After the war, U.S. intelligence had been downsized and gone through several reorganizations, from the Office of Secret Service to the Strategic Services Unit to the Central Intelligence Group.[45] Intelligence agents' reports had been duly filed and collected, but the information that startled Cummings in the summer of 1947 had not found its way to his desk before that time. Ambassador Cabot's memo finally woke everyone up, even though, as we have seen, in 1946 memos about the fact that fugitives from justice were emigrating to Argentina had reached the State Department from diplomat Hiram Bingham IV.

The State Department felt that the ratline matter had to be brought immediately to the attention of the British Foreign Office. Ironically, the British had known about Draganović's activity, if not the entire ratline operation, for more than a year. Because Ustaša fugitives were subject to British, not U.S., control, the British evidently saw no need to notify the State Department. State was third man out—the British knew, U.S. intelligence knew, but state did not know.

The Argentine author of *The Real Odessa*, Uki Goñi, understood that the papers of the British Foreign Office would be critical in searching for links between Draganović's ratline and the Vatican and used them extensively in his research.[46] One of the editors of the Vatican's World War II documents, American Jesuit Robert Graham, denied that any such link existed. A second editor of the documents, German Jesuit Burkhart Schneider, emphatically denied that Vatican money was used to help fugitive Nazis when Gitta Sereny pressed him on this point.[47] Graham, Schneider, and the other two editors of *Actes et Documents* left out all of the documents dealing with the origin, development, and operation of the Holy See's emigration work, some of which had taken place during the war years. Uncovering document after document in which the Holy See attempted to protect war criminals from British authorities, Goñi has thwarted these attempts to cover up the operation once and for all.

As a result, two independent sources attest to the Holy See's ratline operations: the reports of 1945 to 1948 of U.S. intelligence agents and the papers of the British Foreign Office.

A standoff between the Vatican and England began soon after the war in August of 1945, when the Holy See asked that the British not extradite the 600 Ustaši being held in a Naples POW camp. Dissatisfied with the reply, the Vatican sent a second message, this time in the name of Pius XII. According to the Vatican secretariat, the Ustaši holed up in St. Jerome's had sent an urgent appeal to the Holy Father on behalf of the detained Croatians, particularly those in POW camp 215.[48] Telling the British Foreign Office that the Croats at St. Jerome's had asked the pope to intercede for them was the Vatican secretariat of state's roundabout way of saying—without actually saying it—that the pope was pleading for the detained Ustaša prisoners. Actually, at this time the voice of the Vatican secretariat of state was the voice of Pope Pius XII himself because he had not appointed anyone to succeed Cardinal Maglione after his death in 1944. Nevertheless, despite the pope's direct appeal, the British refused, telling him that they would not protect war criminals.

Yugoslavia subsequently pressed the Allies to arrest and extradite five Ustaša officers who were hiding out in the Oriental Institute, a Vatican extraterritorial building. Milan Nedić, Hitler's puppet ruler of Serbia, the first area in Europe that had been declared "free of Jews," was among the group.[49] London instructed D'Arcy Osborne to tell Vatican authorities that the likes of Nedić and Pavelić were not Thomas á Beckets (the martyred twelfth-century archbishop of Canterbury).[50] Yugoslavia claimed rightly that by protecting suspected war criminals the Vatican's Pontifical Commission of Assistance was in violation of the United Nations' order to return criminals to the place where their crimes had been committed. Osborne reported to the Foreign Office that there was no way Pope Pius would turn over the war criminals to the Communist Tito. The standoff continued.[51]

The next confrontation came in April 1947. It concerned fifteen Nazi collaborators who were being detained in the Regina Elena prison in Rome. Among the group was General Moskov, whom the British had arrested in Venice, confiscating 3,200 looted gold coins and 75 diamonds from him. In its appeal, the Vatican called the prisoners "humanitarians." Astounded, the British gave Osborne "icy instructions" to let the Vatican secretariat know that those "who worked for the Pavelić Ustaša government were giving their support and approval to a regime which flouted humanitarian principles and which condoned atrocities unsurpassed in any period of human history."[52] While the Holy See appealed to Great Britain, Draganović appealed on behalf of the war criminals to the United States. The Vatican would not let up, and the British Foreign Office was in no mood to give in. Victor Perowne, D'Arcy Osborne's successor at the British mission to the Holy See, felt the Vatican's pressure, but London told Perowne in no uncertain terms that the Ustaša was a "wholly undesirable organization [which] has not only been collectively responsible for vile atrocities on an immense scale during the war but has ever since its inception made use of murder as a normal political weapon."[53] These exchanges between the Vatican and the British Foreign Office clearly establish the fact that Pius XII himself was protecting the fugitives in St. Jerome's. A CIA report indicating the Vatican secretariat's disapproval of Draganović's work was filed in 1952, some years after the standoff between the pope and the British.[54] By this time, the ratline had fulfilled the Holy See's purposes and the Vatican's hopes that Pavelić would overthrow Tito had been dashed. After that failure, Draganović's motivations had become more purely venal.

While all the conflict between the Holy See and the British Foreign Office took place, Draganović, Hudal, and others worked their ratlines. German priest Karl Bayer, who operated the German national refugee office under the pope's Pontifical Commission of Assistance, remembered Draganović well when Gitta Sereny interviewed him decades later. "He was the chief administrator of the Vatican escape route through Genoa," he recalled.[55] U.S. intelligence noted that in 1946 Draganović sent fifty Ustaši to Argentina via Barcelona. After 1946, his fugitives departed from Genoa. The Argentine government's investigation determined that about fifty Ustaša leaders reached their country and that overall possibly 115 did so.[56] But Goñi has found evidence in Argentina that pushes the number of escaped Croatian war criminals much higher. Late in 1946 Draganović received 250 landing permits from the Perón government. Additional immigration papers show that well over 1,000 Croatian refugees, some gray and some black, reached Argentina via the Draganović ratline.[57] At the Genoa port of embarkation, Draganović's fugitives, as well as hundreds of other supposedly anti-Communist fascist or Catholic refugees, were assisted by the archbishop of the city, Giuseppe Siri.[58] The archbishop had created two Church committees, U.S. intelligence determined, whose purpose it was to help refugees, including fugitives. Karl Bayer confirmed this independently: "Yes, it's quite likely that [Draganović] received support from Cardinal Siri who is now archbishop of Genoa; there again, you see, one's obligation was simply to help people who were in need of help."[59] Ante Pavelić himself escaped through the Genoa ratline, as well as other major Ustaša war criminals such as Mile Starčević, Stjepan Hefer, and Vjekoslav Vrančić.[60]

FIGURE 14. Pius XII with Guiseppe Siri, cardinal archbishop of Genoa, in 1954.
Earlier, the pope's Papal Commission of Assistance and the cardinal's National
Committee for Emigration to Argentina had allowed atrocity perpetrators to
emigrate to South America, where they were to combat communism.
Courtesy of Bettmann Archive.

Pope Pius paid for the passage of many of the Ustaša criminals, using
funds that came to him through the NCWC. American bishops became
involved with the Croatian refugee situation in Italy immediately after
the war. An NCWC study found about 40,000 refugees who were afraid
to go back to Yugoslavia. This implies that many of them were actually
refugee fugitives from justice. In March, the Holy See asked Cardinal
Samuel Stritch of Chicago, who was visiting Rome, to press the United
Nations Relief and Rehabilitation Administration to work on behalf of
1,000 refugees in the Eternal City "whose plight is grave."[61] It referred
specifically to the Ustaši holed up in the Croatian seminary in Rome, "San
Girolanio Degli Illirci [*sic*]," St. Jerome's. We now know that "grave"
meant that they were suspected war criminals, but to Stritch the language
meant that they were potential victims of Yugoslav Communists. Shortly
after this, the NCWC began doing the work in South America to ease the
flow of Eastern European refugees into their countries.

In the fall of 1946 Ante Doshen, whose identity as a convicted felon the American bishops had not yet learned, contacted cardinals Francis Spellman and Samuel Stritch to tell them that Croatian refugees in Rome were being sent back to Yugoslavia against their will. This was happening, he said, because "the interpreters with American military government are largely Communists or fellow-travelers."[62] This was the usual pitch to the Americans. That fall also marked the first time that Monsignor Montini contacted the U.S. hierarchy about the Croatian "problem." This likely means that Doshen had a connection to the Ustaši refugees in Rome and the Vatican, because in October the apostolic delegate to the United States informed U.S. bishops that "the Holy See has expressed the desire that the American hierarchy undertake to help these unfortunate victims of the war," among whom, of course, were the Ustaša war criminals.[63]

Pius XII repeatedly asked the British Foreign Office to remove Ustaši war criminals in POW and displaced persons camps and at the Croatian seminary of St. Jerome's from the list of those to be returned to Yugoslavia, as we have seen. While he was pressing the British, Pope Pius enlisted the financial support of U.S. bishops, especially Cardinal Stritch. Why did he single out Stritch? His Chicago diocese was home to one of the largest congregations of Croatians in the United States—St. Jerome's Croatian Catholic Church, located in the city's South Side. The finances of this parish improved so much during the war years that the Franciscan Croatians who staffed the church were able to pay off all its debts.[64] Cardinal Stritch collected funds on his own to add to the funds of the NCWC for the "refugees" in Rome—$5,000 in 1949.[65] These funds were very likely collected annually from 1946 on from Catholics in St. Jerome's parish in Chicago for the Ustaši war criminals holed up in St. Jerome's seminary in Rome. A substantial number of Croatian Americans were Ustaša and Pavelić sympathizers.

The Vatican's Ratlines Set a Precedent

The Holy See and the United States began the postwar era in totally divergent positions regarding fugitive refugees, but by the summer of 1947 they had converged onto the same course. To begin with, the U.S. Congress passed immigration legislation allowing a limited number of refugees to enter the country so long as they were not war criminals. During the postwar period, the Vatican was promoting emigration of any anti-Communists in Spain and Italy regardless of crimes some may have committed during the war. In 1943, the Allies signed the Moscow Declaration, promising to return suspected war criminals to the country where their alleged crimes had been committed to be tried there in a court of justice. The Big Three agreed in Potsdam to try war criminals at Nuremberg, although they were sorely tempted to summarily shoot them by firing squad.[66] A list of some 70,000 suspected war criminals was compiled and as new suspects emerged, they were to be added to the list, which would be updated and circulated among the national authorities of the Allies.[67] Although from the beginning, the United States violated the agreement by harboring Nazi scientists, Operation Paperclip, at times it rejected some whose "usefulness was compromised by their wartime pasts."[68] As a rule, the United States dutifully complied with the Moscow Declaration, as the hunt for Pavelić and other war criminals demonstrated. The Vatican's postwar practice, on the other hand, protected war criminals as fascist anti-Communists, allowing them to hide out in extraterritorial properties in Rome or in Vatican City and helped them escape to South American countries. Thus, at the outset of the postwar era the policies of Pius XII and the Allies regarding war criminals contradicted each other in theory and in practice (for the most part).

But it was difficult for the Allies to enforce the Moscow Declaration to the letter for several reasons. The quality of U.S. intelligence limited the ability of the United States to comply. When an intelligence agent responsible for Hungary was criticized for the low quality of his reports, he shot back to his superior officers saying that they could expect no better when they sent him "Iowa farm boys" who knew nothing of Eastern European politics and could not speak Hungarian.[69] U.S. and British intelligence personnel used refugees to fill the gap. Agent Mudd infiltrated a Croat national into St. Jerome's to collect data on war criminals. Colonel G. F. Blunda, assistant director of intelligence for the Mediterranean theater of operations, used a number of Croat nationals as agents.[70] The British lacked the personnel to guard and administer the huge displaced persons camps in which grays and blacks intermingled, so they employed Croatian nationals as security.[71] Draganović, who helped care for these displaced persons, had easy access to the criminals among them. More important, by 1946 England and the United States were increasingly reluctant to return possible war criminals to countries whose postwar political circumstances practically guaranteed an unfair trial. The U.S. State Department declared that in Yugoslavia, "there is no justice . . . in our sense of the term. Accused often has no access to counsel, courtroom crowd is hostile, judges prejudiced and in attitude indistinguishable from prosecutor, defense prevented from introducing documents or witnesses."[72] Although this analysis resembled the attitude the Holy

See had adopted immediately after the war, the Allies and the Vatican chose different responses. The Americans and British returned Ustaša war criminals whenever Yugoslavia could produce prima facie evidence of guilt. But the Vatican was not swayed even by that kind of evidence.

As we have seen, the Allies did not waver in trying to locate and extradite Pavelić. Not, that is, until the middle of 1947, the point of convergence for the United States and the Holy See regarding refugee war criminals. Pope Pius kept the ratlines going until the dawn of the Cold War, when the United States joined in the effort to use fascists to fight communism. The British, while returning bona fide war criminals to Yugoslavia, used very undiplomatic language to shame the Holy See into releasing those it harbored. This, to no avail. By the end of 1947 the British Foreign Office had given up trying to use moral persuasion to pry loose fugitives being protected by the Holy See. In March 1947, President Harry Truman asked Americans to make a global commitment against communism, a landmark speech that became known as the Truman Doctrine. "The clearest dividing point" marking the beginning of the Cold War, "was [George] Marshall's return from Moscow" to tell President Truman in April that diplomacy would not work with the Soviets.[73] In July 1947, the Central Intelligence Agency came into existence. U.S. intelligence personnel, who were not up to the task of infiltrating Communist countries, began to employ fascists, including Krunoslav Draganović. The mindset of American agents regarding suspected war criminals changed. As one agent put it, "any SOB who was against the Russians was our SOB."[74] In the summer of 1947, the new program code-named National Interest came into existence and Project Paperclip was phased out. The latter had had a narrow focus regarding immigration candidates, but National Interest offered U.S. protection to anyone who was anti-Communist. "Under the protective blanket of Cold War philosophy, no plot or person was too unsavory to bring into the fold," historian Linda Hunt wrote.[75] On July 22, 1947, Secretary of State George Marshall agreed that thirty-six Ustaši, including some accused of deporting Croatian and Serbian Jews to death camps and of "Jew hunting," should be sent from captivity in Italy, where they were awaiting deportation to Yugoslavia, to zonal Germany and the custody of the British and the United States.[76] Not by accident did Ante Pavelić gain "hands off" status in July 1947, the date that marks the year and month of U.S. and papal convergence regarding war criminals.

For the ever-more-venal Draganović, the ensuing years were golden. For each Croat fascist for whom he arranged emigration, he received 25,000 lire from the American Catholic Church through its agency, the NCWC. In 1954, the World Council of Churches gave Draganović 186,000 lire to assist refugees, money which he used only for Croat fascists.[77] He was also in the pay of the CIA, which gave him 1,400 dollars for each emigrant. In this capacity, Draganović arranged for the emigration in 1950 of Klaus Barbie, the "Butcher of Lyons," where he had served as chief of the Gestapo. Barbie ruthlessly deported Jews to their deaths, including, shortly before the liberation of Lyons, forty-one children from the Izieu children's home. Barbie enjoyed more than thirty years of freedom before having to stand trial in France for his World War II crimes.[78]

The cases of Klaus Barbie and Ante Pavelić aptly illustrate the convergence of U.S. and Vatican policy regarding war criminals by the middle of 1947. Pavelić, protected by the Holy See, eventually escaped to Argentina through the complicity of the United States when it suddenly switched to a "hands off" policy for him. Barbie was protected by U.S. intelligence but escaped because of Vatican complicity. Both men escaped through the Holy See's ratline operated by Draganović. The Holy See could claim, of course, that Pope Pius did not know about Barbie's crimes, but would it have mattered? It certainly did not matter in Pavelić's case; Pius was well aware of his crimes. Both Barbie and Pavelić were wanted for murder by France. After Barbie's eventual extradition from Bolivia to face justice in France, the United States finally admitted its guilt in protecting and secreting him out of Europe. In 1983, the United States apologized to the government of France.[79] Neither Pius XII nor his successors have apologized for protecting Pavelić, who, in the eyes of Pius XII "was a militant Catholic who yesterday fought the Orthodox church and today is fighting communist atheism."[80]

12
AN OBSESSION WITH
COMMUNISM

Today interest in Pius XII is high. The question whether he should be canonized has spiked even greater curiosity and divisiveness. Before the question of sainthood arose, some accused Pope Pius of "silence" whereas others argued that he had spoken out about the Holocaust. Revising my own opinion, I have argued here that Pius did speak out in his 1942 Christmas message. After the possibility of sainthood for Eugenio Pacelli became an issue, points of contention about how to view him multiplied. For historians, these amount to no more than small distractions. As Raul Hilberg and Lucy Dawidowitz wrote at the onset of Holocaust history, a collapse of western values and western religion opened the door to the destruction of European Jewry. It was not, in Albert Schweitzer's words, the failure of one man—Pope Pius—but the failure of all Christians. The Protestant and Catholic churches were among the first to grasp this, although it took some time for the German churches to do so. The Catholic Church in its entirety recognized its failure during the Second Vatican Council (1962–1965), when it corrected age-old beliefs about Jewish guilt for deicide and proclaimed that Jews remained God's chosen people. During the war, very few people grasped the significance of what was happening to the Jews, although Jacques Maritain was a notable exception. To go beyond the present-day posturing in the literature of the "Pius Wars" and the debate about the pope's "silence," we need to begin by asking what significance the Holocaust had for Pius XII.

The Supersessionist Perspective

Several situations arose during and after the time of the Holocaust that shed light on the question of Pope Pius and the Holocaust. It became clear in the spring of 1943 to Pius and others at the Vatican that the Jews were being murdered en masse. That was when the Italian priest Pirro Scavizzi told Pius that the murder of the Jews was total—even infants and the elderly were being mercilessly slaughtered. When he heard this, Pius broke down and wept uncontrollably.[1] In April 1943, Pius wrote to the bishop of Berlin, Konrad Preysing, who had been pressing the pope to do more to intervene. Pius, on the defensive, told Preysing that he was doing everything in his power to help Jews, whether they had converted or not. Pius wrote that as Jewish life was coming to an end his fatherly love and fatherly concern went out to them in the greatest measure during their period of hopeless desolation.[2] This was the same time that Pius XII wrote in *Mystici Corporis Christi* (The Mystical Body of Christ) that "our love embraces all people whatever their nationality or race."[3] Thus, clearly, at the immediate time of the Holocaust, at the moment when Pius knew for certain what it meant, he was mindful of the Jewish people. But the pope did not let his emotions dictate his actions. The overwhelming majority of the Roman Jews seized on October 16, 1943, were women and children. Many of the women were elderly. Pius knew that the destiny of these people was exactly what had caused him a few months earlier to weep profusely and to write of his sadness to Bishop Preysing, yet he said nothing, nor did he make a symbolic protest by going to the train station when the Jews, crammed in freight cars, left for Auschwitz.

Immediately after the war, this picture of a pope heartbroken by the murder of European Jews changed. In October 1945, Gerhart Riegner visited the Vatican to ask for help to locate Jewish children who had been hidden by Catholics during the Holocaust. He told Montini that Jews desperately needed to find the children because European Jewry had lost 1.5 million children to the death camps. Montini felt that Riegner was exaggerating the case and took issue with the figure of 1.5 million.[4] This stand rankled Riegner, who later recalled that the appointment with Montini was "one of the most dramatic and unhappy meetings I have had in my life."[5] Riegner spent the next thirty minutes trying to persuade the high-ranking Vatican cleric of the correctness of the statistic before Montini finally conceded the point. "I think that it was only at that moment," Riegner later said, "that he grasped for the first time, the extent of our catastrophe."[6] Montini reported to Pope Pius every day, sometimes twice a day. If Pius had held a different opinion from Montini's about the mortality of Jewish children, Montini would have known it and would not have contested Riegner's figure. Thus, at the time the war ended, the Vatican had not bothered to inform itself about the extent of Jewish lives that had been lost.

Two other prominent Jews met with Pius XII to discuss the problem of hidden Jewish children, Leon Kubowitzki in September 1945 and Rabbi Isaac Halevi Herzog in the spring of 1946. Pius told Kubowitzki that "he knew the sufferings of [Kubowitzki's] people and had followed their fate with great love."[7] This remark seems to square with what Pius had written to Bishop Preysing and with his emotional breakdown upon hearing the news of the murder of Jewish children and elderly Jews. Kubowitzki pleaded for the release of Jewish children still living with Catholic families. Pius, surprised, asked if there were many and requested that Kubowitzki send him a memorandum on the situation of Jewish children which he promised to give his special attention. The audience was very cordial, Pius XII's face marked all the while "by much affection." Kubowitzki wrote that as he took his leave, Pius "smiled broadly as we shook hands when parting but when I looked again I had the impression that there was a note of triumph or irony in his smile, but I may be mistaken."[8] As we will see, he may not have been mistaken.

The highly educated and politically experienced Rabbi Herzog was less awestruck and less differential than Kubowitzki when he met with Pius in March. According to the rabbi's notes, he "called upon [the pope] to repent for the sins of Christianity towards the people of Israel throughout the generations," a proposition that surely raised the pope's hackles.[9] Herzog then praised the Church for rescuing Jews and pleaded for the return of hidden children, each one of whom, he said, was like a thousand to the Jewish community because of their wartime losses. Herzog asked Pope Pius to make a broad appeal for release of the children, but Pius "promised to help me [only] if I ran into difficulties." In summarizing the audience, Rabbi Herzog characterized the pope as a clever politician. By asking Kubowitzki and then Herzog for a memorandum citing the details of the problem, the pope asked Jews to accomplish an impossible task. How does one compose a detailed memorandum on a hidden population?

A decade later, Pius XII met with his envoy to zonal Germany, Archbishop Aloisius Muench. With great delight, the pope told Muench the following joke:

> Hitler died and somehow got into heaven. There, he met the Old Testament prophet Moses. Hitler apologized to Moses for his treatment of the European Jews. Moses replied that such things were forgiven and forgotten here in heaven. Hitler was relieved and said to Moses that he always wished to meet him in order to ask him an important question. Did Moses set fire to the burning bush?

The Holy Father, Muench wrote, "told me the story with a big laugh."[10]

The pope's joke came at the expense of the memory of European Jews. Riegner, Kubowitzki, and Herzog would have perceived it as a mockery of the 6 million who had been killed. Undoubtedly, Pius had told this story to Montini, Tardini, and others. The pope's jest is a clue that the highest personnel of the Vatican had still not internalized the meaning of the Holocaust. Like Montini, unable to accept the figure of 1.5 million dead Jewish children, Pius XII was content to let the murder of the Jews recede into history. How do we make sense of these conflicting responses? First Pius cried uncontrollably upon hearing that many children and the elderly were among those gassed. Then, after the Holocaust, he implied to Jewish leaders that he wanted to help them locate hidden children but in fact did nothing. Finally, years later, he saw what had happened to Europe's Jews as a suitable topic for humor.

It is impossible to reconcile these episodes but not impossible to understand them. For 1900 years, the Catholic Church had saddled itself with a teaching called supersessionism, which teaches that Christianity had supplanted Judaism. Christ's death on the cross rendered the religion of the Jews valueless.[11] According to this teaching, Jews broke their covenant with Yahweh, thereby losing their status as the chosen people.[12] God withdrew the affectionate bond that had been given to the Jews and bestowed it with much greater abundance on the Christian people and their church because of the grace the betrayed Messiah purchased for them with the crucifixion. Their only salvation, according to supersessionist teaching, was through conversion to the church.

In June 1943, the height of the Holocaust, a time when the pope knew about mass murder in gas chambers, Pius, whose seminary education steeped him in supersessionism, released *Mystici Corporis Christi*. The encyclical was published at the same time as Pius's June 1943 address in which, as we have seen, he minimized what was happening to European Jews when he said that they were "sometimes dying" (see chapter 4). As the Jews were being physically eliminated by asphyxiation in occupied Poland, the spiritual leader of the Catholic world eliminated them theologically in Rome. In *Mystici Corporis Christi* Pius wrote that all men regardless of race were united in the Church—if they converted.[13] If Jews did not convert, their destiny lay out of the reach of the Church because they had broken the covenant.

That does not mean that when Pius heard that Jewish children and elderly Jews were being murdered he did not feel sorry for them. In

Mystici Corporis Christi he wrote that God expects Christians to love all people regardless of their race.[14] Thus, it was not contradictory for Pius, profoundly moved, to have wept upon hearing the dreadful news. But that was then—the middle of 1943. Fourteen years later, when Pope Pius told the dreadful joke relating to the Holocaust to his trusted nuncio, that emotional moment had long since faded away. What remained was the traditional Catholic supersessionist teaching. Because the Jews had crucified their messiah, they had fashioned their own dismal future as homeless earthly wanderers whom Hitler had set upon. We see then that because of supersessionism, Pius XII assigned the murder of European Jews an altogether different significance than Christians do today. For Pope Pius, Hitler was not killing God's chosen people, for the Jews had long since given up their birthright. That distinction notwithstanding, Pius deplored the murder of the Jews.

Supersessionism allowed Pius XII to lapse into callousness when he secretly protected war criminals even as Jews praised him for what he had done to spare them during the Holocaust. The pope basked after the war in accolades from Jewish leaders around the world for his humane efforts during the Nazi era. Frequently during the war, the leaders of the World Jewish Congress, individual Jews, and prominent national or local Jewish spokespersons had sought the pope's help in rescue work. In doing so, they invariably praised him for past efforts. The following from President Roosevelt's War Refugee Board is illustrative:

> We know his Holiness has been sorely grieved by the wave of hate which has engulfed Europe and the consequent mass enslavement, persecution, deportation and slaughter of helpless men, women and children. His Holiness, we also know, has labored unceasingly to reinculcate a decent regard for the dignity of man activated by great compassion for the sufferings of a large portion of mankind. The tireless efforts of his Holiness to alleviate the lot of the persecuted, the hunted and the outcast are also known to us.[15]

On another occasion the War Refugee Board alluded to the "tireless efforts of his Holiness to alleviate the lot of the persecuted, the hunted and the outcast."[16] When it encouraged Spain to help rescue Jews, the Board referred "to the intervention of the Holy See whose humanitarian efforts have contributed to saving millions of persecuted refugees in Europe."[17] In his futile effort to convince Pope Pius to make a radio address to save Jews in Hungary, Alex Easterman of the World Jewish Congress referred to the pope's "deep sympathies for persecuted people."[18] Of course it made sense to flatter the pope when favors were being asked of him. After the war there were additional reasons for such flattery—asking the pope to mitigate antisemitism in Eastern Europe or, as we have just seen, asking his help in finding rescued children. Nevertheless, praise for Pius XII from the World Jewish Congress, the American Joint Distribution Committee, and the chief rabbi of Palestine was sincere. Individual groups of Jews came to Rome to thank the pope for rescuing them.

This is all very understandable. Who else, after all, could they thank? The countless Catholics who had individually or in groups rescued Jews were often unknown. Most would remain unknown and it would require some years before institutions like convents and monasteries could be identified for their rescue work and gratefully recognized. So Jewish leaders did the obvious—they thanked Pius XII and in thanking him they were expressing their thanks to all of those in the Church who had acted heroically or humanely. Individual Jews who were actually on the scene during the Holocaust—Gerhart Riegner, Settimio Sorani, and Reuben Resnik—knew quite well that it was not the pope who deserved the gratitude, but they realized that such thanks deflected from him to lower clergy, to nuns, and to men and women in the pews.

Pope Pius reveled in the spotlight of praise that shone on him. The Vatican's newspapers promoted the image of the pope as a humanitarian rescuer who had opposed the Nazis. Resnik recalled that after his and Kubowitz's audience with Pius, a big story about it was published in *L'Osservatore Romano* that was picked up by the media around the world.[19] Now that the war was over, Pius wanted the world to know that he had been stalwart in his opposition to Hitler. Just as the war in Europe ended, Pope Pius broadcast that "we never ceased throughout the war . . . to refute the ruinous and relentless demands of National Socialist doctrine, which use[d] refined scientific methods in order to torture or liquidate people who were often innocent." Pius continued, saying that his words of opposition to National Socialism were taught to the German people who studied them in parish circles.[20] It would be surprising, to say the least, for the Gestapo to have tolerated such study groups, and no documentary evidence of them has ever turned up. As to the pope's assertion that he had "never ceased" to refute Nazi racism, Tittmann told German resistance operative Josef Müller that he "had heard rather widespread criticism of the pope in connection with his latest speech, because he had waited until Germany had been defeated before attacking the Nazis in public."[21] Indeed, the pope's claim contradicts the understanding that the Vatican had reached with the German Church during the war that he would leave criticism of the Nazi regime to the German bishops. According to Josef Müller, the recommendation of Catholic resistance in Germany was that the pope should stand aside while the German hierarchy carried on the struggle against the Nazis inside Germany. Müller said that the pope had followed this advice throughout the war.[22]

Pope Pius's claim to the contrary sought to convince the world that he had bravely stood up to Hitler year in and year out.

While soaking up the adulation of Jewish leaders around the world, Pius failed to share the limelight with those whom he knew to be the authentic rescuers—men and women such as Margit Slachta and Padre Benedetto in Rome. Indeed, the Vatican denied permission for French Jesuit Pierre Chaillet to travel to New York, where he was to be honored by B'nai B'rith for his rescue work during the war.[23] Similarly, Pius failed to share center stage with those who had actually confronted the Nazis—churchmen such as Johannes de Jong and Bernhard Lichtenberg in Berlin.[24] What was worse than this self-aggrandizement was the fact that while posing as the grand rescuer and perennial Nazi opponent, Pius XII's ratline operation was allowing the very Nazis who had persecuted and murdered the Jews to escape. The pope's postwar posturing and his "burning bush" joke give the appearance of brazen cynicism. Was Pius conscious of this—of being disingenuous and hypocritical? Was Leon Kubowitzki perceptive when he took a second farewell look at Pope Pius and saw "irony in his smile?"

It would be a mistake to interpret supersessionism as meaning that Pope Pius could be unconcerned about Hitler's murderous rampage against Jews as it took place. Bound by the Augustinian precept, Pope Pius could not have shut a blind eye to the murder of the Jews, nor could he have wished it.[25] Supersessionism can account for the pope's 1942 Christmas address opposing genocide if he meant to include Jews among the victims, and he wrote to Bishop Preysing in Berlin saying that he did include them—in fact, meant exactly them. We do not actually know what motivated the pope to give the 1942 Christmas address. Did he do it to protest the killing or did he do it primarily to uphold his moral authority? The two purposes are not, after all, mutually exclusive. It does not seem likely that Pius thought his words would actually stop the trains to Auschwitz, although he may have thought that at least Pavelić in Croatia would heed them. If he had intended to make a determined effort to stop Germany's onslaught, he would have encouraged the Dutch, German, and French bishops to protest. But in 1943, the Vatican did not answer the Dutch appeal for a papal condemnation of the Holocaust and he did not support Bishop Preysing in his forceful attempt to induce the German hierarchy to do so that same year, nor did he encourage the French Vichy bishops to continue their criticisms of Nazi antisemitism in 1943. Thus, the Christian tradition of supersessionism allowed the pope to regret the Holocaust as it took place while at the same time allowing him to concentrate on preserving the Church that had inherited the Jews' birthright. Supersessionism cannot be used to argue that Pius XII kept silent about the Holocaust. Rather, it left Pius XII free not to dwell on the disaster and to move on to preserve the treasure given to the new chosen people, about whom he wrote so explicitly in *Mystici Corporis Christi* while the Holocaust was under way.

Preserving the treasure given to the new chosen people meant one thing to Pope Pius—protecting the Church from communism. The apparent cynicism of Pius was a by-product of the fact that the pope provided passage to Nazi and Ustaša fugitives, not the incentive for it. Such was his fear of communism that he believed fascist fugitives would battle it in South America. Throughout his tenure as the cardinal secretary of state and as pope, Pius XII remained glued to this effort. Some contemporaries, who did not perceive this steadfastness, believed Pius to be an indecisive person. His papal successor, Angelo Roncalli, said Pius could not act decisively "unless he was absolutely sure of himself."[26] Myron Taylor wrote in 1941 that Pius could not speak out about atrocities in Poland "largely because of the indecision in his mind as a result of extreme discouragement and depression."[27] Later, in 1945, Harold Tittmann wrote that "by temperament important decisions do not come easy to Pius XII."[28] One suspects that those who thought Pius indecisive took this view because the pope did not make the decisions they hoped he would make. For a more correct view of Pope Pius, Taylor might have reflected on what Cardinal Pacelli told him in 1936—namely, that the Soviet Union was the greatest threat looming over the future of the west.[29] True, Pius was prone to second-guessing himself and vacillating on issues that did not seem absolutely central to him. One of the pope's closest collaborators, Domenico Tardini, noted this characteristic:

> [Pope Pius] did not like to make up his mind immediately. . . . He was not only slow in finding a solution but, when it came to formulating the solution, he seemed to have difficulty even in choosing his words. . . . In the end he was still not satisfied and sometimes by telephone, he would give a completely different solution.[30]

Tardini's characterization was, no doubt, often dependable, but when it came to a certain few issues, communism above all, Pius was far from indecisive.[31]

Cold War Paranoia

Pius XII's obsession with communism is the key to understanding his papacy. We can proceed with this line of thinking with some confidence. The fear that moved Pope Pius during and after the war was the same fear that dominated the Vatican during the interwar years, when Pacelli was the secretary of state. For the interwar years we are able to speak with certainty because the Vatican's records for those years are open. Thus, what seems to be the most likely motivation of Pius XII during the war is based on *incomplete but substantial* data that are in accord with what we know to be the case before the war based on *complete* data.

Two scholars, Gerhard Besier and Peter Godman, one a German and the other a New Zealander, have independently studied the newly released interwar documents of the Holy See. On the matter of the Vatican's anticommunism their interpretations show exceptional agreement. As we have discussed in chapter 5, the Congregation of the Holy Office (now called the Congregation for the Doctrine of the Faith) carefully reviewed Nazi racism in the middle of the 1930s. This congregation carried great importance because it deliberated over matters of faith and morals about which the First Vatican Council had pronounced the pope to be infallible. By the fall of 1936, the Holy Office had thoroughly considered contemporary dangers to the faith and prioritized them. Leading the list was the racist state, second came hypernationalism, and only then came communism.[32] Pacelli agreed about the danger of racism. As we saw in chapter 3, he wrote that the Nazi "message of a new materialism of race" contradicted the "joyous news of Christ's teaching."[33]

Nevertheless, Pius XI and his secretary of state, Cardinal Pacelli, disregarded the work of the Holy Office. The pope closely followed the Holy Office's wording in strongly condemning communism in *Ubi Arcano* but quite clearly watered down its wording in *Mit brennender Sorge* so that the Nazi racist state would not nullify the concordat.[34] Pacelli's office of the secretariat, which was in charge of diplomacy, overruled the Congregation of the Holy Office, which was in charge of faith and morals. As Besier has found, the Vatican ignored the vast fund of knowledge at its disposal about racism, totalitarianism, and Nazism when it came to making decisions in the political sphere. "An inner connection between theological reflection and political action cannot be found," Besier wrote.[35] Quite independently, Godman concluded identically that "politics [came] first and doctrine second" in establishing the Church's order of priorities.[36]

That Pacelli and Pius XI did not follow the advice of their own in-house experts is surprising; that they feared communism more than National Socialism is not. As we saw in chapter 6, the Holy See's opposition to communism reached back into the nineteenth century and was reinforced by every pope down to and including Pius XI. Even before Hitler came to power, the Vatican favored National Socialism simply because the alternative was communism.[37] During Germany's internal political struggles after the 1929 depression, Secretary of State Pacelli did not like it when members of the Catholic Center Party formed alliances with the left-of-center Social Democrats as a way to deter the National Socialist party. Pius XI and his secretary of state firmly set the Vatican on the path of anticommunism, a path from which Pius XII would never stray. After the war, Pius repeated the strictures against Italian Catholics forming the political alliances with socialists that, as Cardinal Pacelli, he had disliked among German Catholic politicians between the wars.

Before, during, and after World War II, Pius hewed unswervingly to an anti-Communist path. Pius XII's drive to keep the Soviets out of Catholic Eastern Europe during the war is quite understandable. Here his mistrust of communism worked hand in glove with his diplomatic bent. Some contemporaries—German Jesuits Gustav Gundlach and Robert Leiber; D'Arcy Osborne; and, above all, Domenico Tardini—thought that it was this diplomatic consciousness that kept Pope Pius from speaking out about the Holocaust.[38] They thought that Pius was afraid to speak out lest he disqualify himself in Germany's eyes as a peace negotiator. This is nearly accurate. Not speaking out about the Holocaust after 1942 can to some extent be explained by the pope's hope that he could be the mediator of a peace that would separate the Soviets from Western Europe. During the war he never completely abandoned his aspiration to be a mediator of peace. Amazingly, at the beginning of the war, he cooperated with the German resistance to remove Hitler and settle differences between Germany and the west. Even after the Allies' Casablanca declaration in 1943 dashed the pope's hopes for a diplomatic role in a negotiated peace, he refused to relinquish his ambition. What a negotiated peace meant to Pius was a restored Germany without the Nazi regime—a bulwark against Soviet communism. It astounded historian Saul Friedlander that Pius would still be hoping for a negotiated peace in 1943, accepting in the balance the corollary that this would mean continuance of the Nazi slaughter of the Jews.[39] Supersessionism—the Church comes first—dictated this priority to Pope Pius. In the latter months of the war, the pope's mistrust of Stalin mandated that instead of coming to an understanding with the Soviets as the Allies wished, Pius dug in his heels, convinced beyond persuasion that a modus vivendi with communism could not be achieved.

Before the Cold War, Pope Pius was at war with communism. It was no accident that a standoff between communism and the Church became the hallmark of the early Cold War. Before the west tensed up because of the Berlin Airlift, Archbishop Stepinać's trial in Yugoslavia made headlines worldwide, as did Cardinal Mindszenty's trial in Hungary soon thereafter. Had the Communist-Socialist bloc won the 1948 elections in Italy, Rome would have become the scene of another standoff: Pope Pius would have refused to step foot outside of Vatican City and thousands of tourist-pilgrims would have descended on the city to rally around him.

The years immediately after the end of the war marked the zenith of Pius XII's obsession with communism. Aggression characterized his demeanor.[40] Without an army, he looked to the United States to do his soldiering. Envoy Graham Parsons reported from the Vatican that Pius thought of the "power, wealth and influence of the U.S. as the only chance to put down communism."[41] The president's envoys, Taylor and Tittmann, were taken aback by his aggressiveness. As the first Cold War warrior, Pius XII anticipated the hard line against the Soviets well before former prime minister Churchill's Iron Curtain speech of 1946 and before the Truman Doctrine of the following year. Jacques Maritain, the French ambassador to the Vatican after the war, saw that Pope Pius was mentally and emotionally fixated on communism and realized that he would not be able to divert the pope from the realm of politics and from the practical to the spiritual realm.[42] With keen insight Maritain wrote in 1948 that

> Pius XII thinks that it is his mission to save the western civilization from communism. Thus his head is taken up more and more with matters political. . . . One is tempted to say that this attention to the political is too much considering the essential role of the church.[43]

Displeased with Pius, the French ambassador resigned his post in 1948.

Nothing other than Pius XII's obsession with communism can explain the Vatican's ratlines. Pius XII's absolution of Germans for Nazi guilt, his refusal to extradite German nationals, the clemency he sought for condemned murderers (and later for all convicted war criminals), and his implementation of escape routes for fascist fugitives from justice are all of a piece. All had the single purpose of halting the expansion of Communist ideology. In retrospect, the pope's frantic anxiety about Italian politics immediately after the war may strike us as understandable but, as Maritain perceived, as too single minded. The ratlines, however, carried the obsession with communism well beyond the limit of moderation and rationality. By today's standards, the ratlines were clearly unethical. Today most contemporaries of the North Atlantic communities have jettisoned the supersessionist mentality, either because they are secularists or because they are Christians who have learned better. With popular papal figures like John XXIII and John Paul II in our memory, it is difficult for us to conceive of a pope who would provide hideaways and "getaways" for Nazi war criminals just because a supersessionist belief left him free to obsess about the danger communism posed for the Church. The life of the Church had greater importance than allowing those who had killed the Jews to be tried for their crimes. Somehow, fighting communism justified the ratlines in the pope's mind and in his code of ethics.

Had they known about the ratlines, would Pius XII's contemporaries, still carrying supersessionist baggage, have been able sanction his actions? Not at all. Except in Germany itself, North Atlantic society's first postwar concern was to bring atrocity perpetrators to justice—hence the Nuremberg Trials and subsequent zonal army trials. The ratlines, which defeated this very objective, would have shocked non-Catholics and even most Catholics of the pope's day. Evidence of the ratlines was scant because they were hidden within the immense postwar refugee emigration work carried on by the Pontifical Commission of Assistance and other agencies. Few outsiders knew about Pius XII's efforts to save war criminals, and those who did know had no idea of how extensive they were. When Pope Pius asked the British Foreign Office to free Ustaša war criminals, he met with indignation, rejection, and insult of a very undiplomatic tenor. Outrage would have been the public's reaction had the ratlines been discovered. Pope Pius seemingly did not grasp that abetting the escape of the very criminals who had implemented the Holocaust would have been judged profoundly unethical by contemporary society. Or, alternately, he assumed that all would be forgiven when the western world came to understand the monstrous threat communism posed. The assumption proved to be accurate. By the time that the U.S. State Department and British Foreign Office realized what Pope Pius was up to, the Cold War had prompted executive orders that stopped them from interfering with his clandestine efforts on behalf of fugitives from justice.

The Vatican's Nazi ratlines came into being and functioned because of the Vatican's privacy and secrecy in its operations. These traits had been acquired over many centuries. In the Middle Ages and again during the Renaissance, the Vatican had played a major role in European politics. Its power declined in early modern times but, as David Kertzer has written, the Holy See clung tenaciously to its temporal kingdom and fought for decades to regain it after 1870. For a time during the nineteenth century, its intelligence service surpassed that of European secular states, as David Alvarez has shown. The Roman curia accustomed itself over time to the operational style of a temporal power. Unfortunately, so did the papal office, to a greater or lesser extent. Collegiality suffered as a consequence, as the bitter experience of Polish bishops during and after the war demonstrated. The German bishops did not want a concordat with Hitler in 1933; they told Pius XI in 1935 that the concordat "serves to send the message to the masses to sleep and separates them more easily, imperceptibly, and gradually from the church's forms of organization," and in 1937, they told the pope and Cardinal Pacelli that the concordat was a dead letter.[44] Their opinions were brushed aside then and again after the war, when they had no enthusiasm for a renewal of the concordat with a post-Hitler state. For Pius XI and Pius XII, concordats were the "linchpin of political reality."[45]

Pius XII's ratlines emerged in the context of the Vatican's operational mode of secrecy. The covert exercise of temporal political power suited Pope Pius, who listened every night at 11:15 to the BBC radio newscast without fail.[46] Rather than speak out against the German aggression that caused World War II, he worked behind the scenes with the underground resistance in Germany. He told Tittmann not to tell anyone about his New York bank account and not to mention the visit between the two of them in his apartment. He wanted the transfer of the Vatican's gold reserves to the United States to be kept quiet. The Vatican's worldwide financial investments were and are a closed book. Although the Vatican is politically a neutral state, Pius XII secretly encouraged the United States to arm Italy after World War II. The ratlines fit easily into the Vatican's accustomed clandestine mode of operation. American Catholics bankrolled the Vatican's emigration work, but church leaders were never told that fugitives from justice were among the beneficiaries. Not many American Catholics would have dropped their dollars into collection baskets at Mass had they known in 1945 and 1946 that they were paying for the escape of Nazis and other war criminals.

Pius XII was the next-to-the-last pope to live through the era of all of the great "isms" of modern Europe: liberalism, socialism, communism, and fascism.[47] Except for fascism, the Church saw all of them as its enemy. Doing battle against the evils of modernity became endemic to the Vatican. Pope Pius XII took up the battle against communism as his special mission. It defined his papacy. As Jacques Maritain perceived, Pius believed his mission in life was to save western civilization from communism. After World War II, the struggle between religion and communism took on the magnitude of a final showdown in the pope's eyes. It became the purpose of the Catholic religion to do battle with communism. Like Maritain, the British and American envoys recognized this. The pope confided to them that his choice of canonizations aimed to bring "about a rebirth of faith and thus buttress the Catholic world against communism."[48] In Pius XII's eyes, communism constituted an insidious enemy that had fifth columns all over the world, through which it achieved power "through unrelenting singleness of purpose and tactics shrewdly adapted everywhere to the need of the time and place."[49] The pope, Parsons reported to the U.S. secretary of state, "spoke from a background *of constant preoccupation* with the world-wide struggle between Christian morality and Atheist communism" (emphasis added).[50]

To a considerable extent, Pius XII isolated ethical considerations from the decision-making process. This divorce of practice from theory took place across the board, from diplomacy to finance to politics, and resulted in a misalignment of the Vatican's ethical compass. We first took note of this during the interwar period when Cardinal Pacelli and Pius XI decided to take a strong position against communism rather than against Nazi racism, although the Holy Office had advised to the contrary. This inconsistency points to a fault line in papal governance. It may be that the frequent turnover of the papal office causes some amount of dysfunction in Vatican administration. But it seems just as likely that papal preoccupation with politics after the loss of the patrimony of St. Peter in 1870 led both Pius XI and Pius XII to give inordinate importance to the office of the Vatican secretariat.

The same fissure between theory and practice came into play in economic decision making. As John Pollard has demonstrated, Pius XI had no regard for the teaching of his predecessor Leo XIII or, for that matter, his own pronouncements when it came to investing Vatican funds. Pius XII continued to isolate money matters from everyday life, which meant, unfortunately, isolation from the reality of war and the Holocaust. Pope Pius evidently had no second thoughts about buying a blacklisted banking chain during the war that was run by fascists and catered to fascists, or, as seems likely, investing in tungsten, a high-tech war material. Even though Pius XI and Cardinal Pacelli had told German Catholics in 1933 to "alleviate the suffering of German Jews,"[51] Pacelli as Pius XII did not divest Vatican funds in major Italian insurance companies that cheated Jews by not allowing them to cash in their policies or, as we now know, refusing to pay inheritors of the Holocaust victims life insurance benefits. These investments resulted from the popes' nonfeasance; they were not in the habit of checking their investment choices against their teachings on capitalism. But when Roman Jews thought they could buy their way out of the grasp of the Nazi death machine, the best Pius XII could do was to offer them a loan. This was not a case of nonfeasance; Pope Pius made a conscious decision.

The divorce of theory from practice typified Vatican diplomacy during the Holocaust. In the eyes of Harold Tittmann, the Holy See's secretariat of state differed from foreign affairs departments of other states in that in "its correspondence with Vatican diplomats abroad, its main concern was the religious life of the faithful rather than international politics."[52] Historian John Morley found that in theory there was more to the secretariat's mission than Tittmann's observations could make out. Roman pontiffs wanted their office for diplomatic affairs to be a model for other nations so as to realize the ideal of the "brotherhood of men."[53] The goal of Vatican diplomacy should be to strive to assure the "principles of justice and charity." Toward this end, the Holy See sent envoys to nations to "defend the rights and to serve the needs of the people."

The reality of the Vatican's diplomacy during the Holocaust did not resemble what Tittmann observed or the actual purpose of the secretariat's mission as the Holy See thought of it. To paraphrase historian Besier, because the Church concentrates on the administration of the sacraments, it must be watchful to protect this function under all circumstances.[54] Protection of that function constituted the rationale of the papacy's policy of concordats. By allowing the Germans to disrupt the sacramental life of Polish Catholics without a public outcry in order to protect its concordat with Germany (in the hope that that country would prevail against Soviet Communists), Pius XII seriously wronged the Polish people and failed to see his error in sealing a concordat with a lawless state. In this instance, Tittmann's analysis was incorrect. Pius XII's main concern was *not* the religious life of the Polish faithful; rather, it was international politics.

Of course, papal diplomacy failed Europe's Jews as well as Polish Catholics. Historian John Morley found that the aim of Vatican diplomacy during the Holocaust was "to avoid offense to any nation." To this end, reserve and prudence characterized papal diplomacy to such an extent that the Vatican ruled out humanitarian concern for the Jews.[55] Under Pope Pius, the secretariat made little attempt, Morley concluded, to work toward the ideals of justice and brotherhood and other similarly exalted goals.[56] Pius XII caused Vatican diplomacy to fail "because in neglecting the needs of the Jews, and pursuing a goal of reserve rather than humanitarian concern, it betrayed the ideals that it had set for itself."[57]

Reserve and prudence did not at all characterize Vatican diplomacy when the question of bombing Rome came into play. During 1942 and 1943, the Vatican became downright confrontational regarding this issue, threatening more than once to protest publicly should Rome be bombed. We have discovered the reason for this—namely, that in the mind of Pope Pius, destroying Vatican City would also destroy the faith of Catholics worldwide. What Pius thought Communists had been trying to do over years and decades—destroy the Church—bombing would do with swift finality. In the matter of the possible bombing of Rome, therefore, the Vatican took an aggressively proactive course that contrasts sharply with its reserved, passively active demeanor regarding Jews. In both threats—bombing and communism—Pope Pius, in the words of Harold Tittmann, "was always thinking in terms of the church's future centuries."[58] This long-term view availed European Jews and Polish Catholics little.

Pius XII's decision to allow war criminals to evade the bar of justice was closely related to the conduct of diplomatic affairs but clearly on the wrong side of the ethical borderline. Beginning with Ante Pavelić, the Vatican knew the identity of many of the individuals it harbored and assisted and knew that they had committed multiple murders. Others were not known by name to the Holy See but were known by name to Hudal and Draganović, whom the Vatican had engaged to operate its emigration programs. Virtually everyone in the western world knew of the multiple crimes Germans had committed during the war. Pius himself had no doubt about this. As we have noted, the Holy See kept a list of Croatian clerics believed to have engaged in atrocities. But since the war had ended as it had with the Soviet Union on the doorstep of the west, Pius made a purely political decision to shelter the guilty from the courts of justice.

In so doing, Pope Pius defied the movement toward international accountability of states toward individuals and other nations. European countries had jointly held Napoleon Bonaparte responsible for France's aggression, and the Treaty of Versailles after World War I a century later held Germany and the Kaiser responsible for their actions. The movement toward accountability gathered some momentum during the interwar era with the founding of the League of Nations and signing of the Kellogg-Briand Pact in 1928 that attempted, albeit feebly, to end national aggression.[59] Building on these steps, the Allies signed the Moscow Declaration in 1943, which stated in part that Germans who committed crimes against combatants or civilians would be "brought back to the scene of their crimes and judged on the spot by the peoples they have outraged."[60] The discovery of the intact Majdanek concentration-death camp with its gas chamber and crematory—which *New York Times* correspondent W. H. Lawrence described as "the most terrible place on the face of the earth"—and then of other death camps and concentration camps horrified the civilized world and solidified opinion that those responsible for atrocities had to be held responsible for their actions.[61] In August 1943, the Allies pointedly told the Vatican that it should not harbor war criminals. In view of the possibility

that Mussolini and other prominent Fascists and persons guilty of war
crimes may attempt to take refuge in neutral territory, His Majesty's Government feel obliged to call upon all neutral countries to refuse asylum to
any such persons; and to declare that they will regard any shelter, assistance
or protection given to such persons as a violation of principles for which
the United Nations are fighting.[62]

By harboring suspected war criminals and harnessing the Church's international hierarchy to provide them with passage to countries beyond
Europe, Pius XII moved directly against the current of international
accountability, violated the Moscow Declaration, and undermined the
Nuremberg Trials that were even then under way.

Not wishing to hold Germany or the Kaiser responsible for aggression in World War I for fear of sparking a Communist revolution in that
country, President Woodrow Wilson remarked "Had you rather have the
Kaiser or the Bolsheviks?"[63] This was the position Pope Pius took after
World War II, except that, of course, the pope acted in secret because of
the disgrace to which he and the Church would have been exposed had
his ratlines become known. Like President Wilson, Pius XII was invoking
a purely political decision. What moved him to do so? Why did Pius XII
subject religion and the Church to a political end? It was not his love of
Nazis but his fear of Communists that led Pius to foster unethical ratlines
for fascist war criminals.

In Richard Hofstadter's essay about the politics of paranoia, he
wrote that it was characteristic of the Cold War era to conceive of the
conflict between Christianity and communism as a war to death in which
"Christianity is set forth as the only adequate counterpoise to the communist credo." Two events in 1917—the Bolshevist revolution in Russia
and the apparition of Our Lady of Fatima in faraway Portugal—fixed the
battle lines of the twentieth century in the mind of Eugenio Pacelli. After
World War II, Pius XII pioneered the politics of paranoia, clinging to a
"Manichean conception of life as a struggle between absolute good and
absolute evil and the idea of an irresistible Armageddon."[64] Choose, Pope
Pius warned Italian voters as he mobilized them against communism in
1948, "the solid rock of Christianity" or life "without God."[65]

NOTES

Preface

1. Domenico Cardinal Tardini, *Memories of Pius XII,* trans. Rosemary Goldie (Westminister, Md.: Newman Press, 1961), 73. This characterization of the pope misses the mark completely for the postwar period.

2. Harold H. Tittmann, Jr., *Inside the Vatican of Pius XII: The Memoir of an American Diplomat during World War II,* ed. Harold H. Tittmann, III (New York: Doubleday, 2004), 96. Tittmann's title was Assistant to the Personal Representative of the President to His Holiness Pope Pius XII.

Introduction

1. David Alvarez, *Spies in the Vatican: Espionage and Intrigue from Napoleon to the Holocaust* (Lawrence: University Press of Kansas, 2002), 297.

2. David I. Kertzer, *Prisoner of the Vatican* (Boston: Houghton Mifflin, 2004), and *The Popes against the Jews: The Vatican's Role in the Rise of Modern Anti-Semitism* (New York: Alfred A. Knopf, 2001); Peter Godman, *Hitler and the Vatican* (New York: Free Press, 2004); Gerhard Besier, *Der Heilige Stuhl und Hitler-Deutschland. Die Faszination des Totalitären* (Munich: Verlagsgruppe Random House, 2004); Alvarez, *Spies in the Vatican*; and, John Pollard, *Money and the Rise of the Modern Papacy: Financing the Vatican, 1850–1950* (Cambridge: Cambridge University Press, 2005).

3. Susan Zuccotti, *Under His Very Windows: The Vatican and the Holocaust in Italy* (New Haven, Conn.: Yale University Press, 2000); Robert Katz, *The Battle for Rome: The Germans, the Allies, the Partisans, and the Pope, September 1943–June 1944* (New York: Simon & Schuster, 2004); Paul Damian O'Shea, "Confiteor. Eugenio Pacelli, the Catholic Church and the Jews. An Examination of the Responsibility of Pope Pius XII and the Holocaust, 1917–1943" (Ph.D. diss., Macquarie University, 2004); Gerald D. Feldman, *Allianz and the German Insurance Business, 1933–1945* (Cambridge: Cambridge University Press, 2001); Christopher R. Browning with contributions by Jürgen Matthäus, *The Origins of the Final Solution: The Evolution of Nazi Jewish Policy, September 1939–March 1942* (Lincoln: University of Nebraska Press, 2004).

4. Richard Breitman, Norman J. W. Goda, Timothy Naftali, and Robert Wolfe, *U.S. Intelligence and the Nazis* (Washington, D.C.: National Archives Trust Fund Board for the Nazi War Crimes and Japanese Imperial Government Records Inter-agency Working Groups, 2004).

5. Uki Goñi, *The Real Odessa: Smuggling the Nazis to Perón's Argentina* (London: Granta, 2002). The second edition contains an afterword that is critical for linking Pius XII to the ratlines. See also Breitman, Goda, Naftali, and Wolfe, *U.S. Intelligence and the Nazis.*

1. Eugenio Pacelli

1. Jürgen Zimmerer, "Krieg, KZ und Völkermord in Südwestafrika. Der erste deutsche Genoczid," in *Völkermord in Deutsche-Südwestafrika. Der Kolonialkrieg (1904–1908) in Namibia und seine Folgen,* ed. Jürgen Zimmerer and Joachin Zeller (Berlin: Links, 2003), 50.

2. Zimmerer, "Krieg, KZ und Völkermord in Südwestafrika," 52 and 57.

3. In a presentation at Georgetown University on April 14, 2004, Prof. Wendy Lower discussed possible connections between the genocides Germany perpetrated in Southwest Africa and during World War II.

4. Jürgen Zimmerer, "The German War of Extermination in South-West Africa (1904–1908) and the Global History of Mass Violence," paper presented at the conference Lessons and Legacies VIII, Brown University, Providence, R.I., November 4–7, 2004.

5. Quoted in Zimmerer, "Krieg, KZ und Völkermord in Südwestafrika," 45.

6. Ibid., 60.

7. Robert G. Weisbord, "The King, the Cardinal and the Pope: Leopold II's Genocide in the Congo and the Vatican," *Journal of Genocide Research* 5, no. 1 (2003): 35–45.

8. Ibid., 36.

9. Ibid., 38–39.

10. Quoted in ibid., 39.

11. Quoted in ibid., 42.

12. Ibid., 40.

13. See chapter 3 of David Alvarez, *Spies in the Vatican: Espionage and Intrigue from Napoleon to the Holocaust* (Lawrence: University of Kansas Press, 2002).

14. Paul Damian O'Shea, "Confiteor. Eugenio Pacelli, the Catholic Church and the Jews. An Examination of the Responsibility of Pope Pius XII and the Holocaust, 1917–1943" (Ph.D. diss., Macquarie University, 2004), 167. O'Shea kindly informed me that his sources for the papal letter were Herbert Jedin and John Patrick Dolan, eds., *The History of the Church* (New York: Crossroad, 1979), 10:38–39; and *New York Times,* November 10, 1915.

15. Ibid.

16. John Pollard, *Money and the Rise of the Modern Papacy: Financing the Vatican, 1850–1950* (Cambridge: Cambridge University Press, 2005), 115.

17. Ibid.

18. Thomas M. Coffey, *Lion by the Tail: The Story of the Italian-Ethiopian War* (New York: Coffey, 1974), 115–116.

19. Pollard, *Money and the Rise of the Modern Papacy,* 177–178.

20. Peter Godman, *Hitler and the Vatican* (New York: Free Press, 2004), 16.

21. Quoted in Coffey, *Lion by the Tail,* 127.

22. Quoted in ibid.

23. Ibid., 128.

24. Hilarius Breitinger to Cardinal Michael Faulhaber, "Meine Internierung in Polen," October 9, 1939, Records of the Reichssicherheitshauptamt, Reel 8, Center for Advanced Holocaust Studies, U.S. Holocaust Memorial Museum, Washington, D.C. (Hereafter CAHS-USHMM.)

25. Ibid.

26. Report of August Rauhut, Posen, to Cardinal Michael Faulhaber, January 29, 1940, Records of the Reichssicherheitshauptamt, Reel 8, CAHS-USHMM.

27. (Author unknown), "La Persecution Religieuse en Pologne," October 1942, Entry 210, Box 375, Folder 413, RG 226, location 250/64/28/07, National Archives and Records Administration (hereafter NARA).

28. Breitinger to Faulhaber, October 9, 1939.

29. Ibid.

30. Robert Leiber, S.J., Rome, to Bishop Konrad Preysing, October 28, 1945, V/16-4, Preysing Papers, Diocesan Archives, Berlin.

31. OSS, Foreign Nationalities Branch, information from Mr. Fotitch, whom the writer had interviewed on May 11, 1942. Fotitch was the exiled minister of Yugoslavia who was living in New York. Entry 210, Box 413, RG 226, location 250/64/29/5, NARA.

32. Norman J. W. Goda, "The Ustaša: Murder and Espionage," in *U.S. Intelligence and the Nazis,* ed. Richard Breitman, Norman J. W. Goda, Timothy Naftali, and Robert Wolfe (Washington, D.C.: National Archives Trust Fund Board for the Nazi War Crimes and Japanese Imperial Government Records Interagency Working Groups, 2004), 208.

33. Cardinal Tisserant, interview with Vladimir Stakic, Rome, April 7, 1946, Entry 1069, Box 28, RG 59, location 250/48/29/05, NARA.

34. OSS memo, n.p., May 24, 1943, Entry 214, Box 7, RG 226, location 250/64/33/07, NARA.

35. Tittmann, Vatican City, to Secretary of State James F. Byrnes, airgram, November 27, 1945, in *Service Oecuménique de Presse et Informations,* June 1943, number 22, Entry 1073, Box 32, RG 59, location 250/48/29/05, NARA.

36. "Air Service Command Puts All into Combat," *New York Times,* July 8, 1943, 10.

37. Goda, "The Ustaša: Murder and Espionage," 206ff.

38. Ibid., 207–208.

39. Ibid., 207.

40. Ibid., 210.

41. I am dubious about U.S. Holocaust Memorial Museum historian Peter Black's claim that Stepinać urged the Vatican to recognize Pavelić's government after his murderous campaign began. Stepinać preferred a Maček government for Croatia in place of Pavelić. See Peter R. Black, "Report on Archbishop Alojzije Stepinac," Center for Advanced Holocaust Studies occasional paper, October 2, 1998.

42. Tony Judt, *Postwar: A History of Europe since 1945* (New York: Penguin Press, 2005), 49.

43. For particulars, see my *The Catholic Church and the Holocaust, 1930–1965* (Bloomington: Indiana University Press, 2000), chapter 3.

2. The Genocides of Polish Catholics and Polish Jews

1. Gerhard Besier, *Der Heilige Stuhl und Hitler-Deutschland. Die Faszination des Totalitären* (Munich: Verlagsgruppe Random House, 2004), 297.

2. Ibid., 72ff.

3. Before World War II, Pacelli favored the German position in border disputes with Poland over Danzig and Silesia; see ibid., 75–76 and 95. After the war, Pius XII continued along the same path, favoring Germany in the Oder-Neisse border dispute; see below, chapter 6.

4. Not a direct quote; taken from the diary of a high-ranking officer. See Christopher R. Browning with contributions by Jürgen Matthäus, *The Origins of the Final Solution: The Evolution of Nazi Jewish Policy, September 1939–March 1942* (Lincoln: University of Nebraska Press, 2004), 17.

5. Richard C. Lukas, *The Forgotten Holocaust: The Poles under German Occupation, 1939–1944* (Lexington: University Press of Kentucky, 1985), 1–3.

6. Götz Aly, Belinda Cooper, and Allison Brown, *"Final Solution": Nazi Population Policy and the Murder of the European Jews,* trans. Belinda Cooper and Allison Brown (New York: Oxford University Press, 1999), 23.

7. Chapter 2 of Browning's *The Origins of the Final Solution* is titled "Poland, the Laboratory of Racial Policy."

8. Aly, Cooper, and Brown *"Final Solution,"* 5.

9. Ibid., 17.

10. Bohdan Wytwycky, *The Other Holocaust: Many Circles of Hell—A Brief Account of 9–10 Million Persons Who Died with the 6 Million Jews under Nazi Racism* (Washington D.C.: Novak Report, 1982), 51.

11. Aly, Cooper, and Brown *"Final Solution,"* 34.

12. Browning, *Origins of the Final Solution,* 107.

13. Aly, Cooper, and Brown *"Final Solution,"* 137–138.

14. Browning, *Origins of the Final Solution,* 109.

15. Quoted in Aly, Cooper, and Brown *"Final Solution,"* 38.

16. Ibid., 43.

17. Quoted in Browning, *Origins of the Final Solution,* 44.

18. Aly, Cooper, and Brown *"Final Solution,"* 51.

19. Browning, *Origins of the Final Solution,* 62 and passim.

20. Ibid., 68.

21. Aly provides examples of Polish evasiveness in his first three chapters.

22. Aly, Cooper, and Brown *"Final Solution,"* 62.

23. Jean Dingell, "Property Seizures from Poles and Jews: The Activities of the Haupttreuhandstelle Ost," in Center for Advanced Holocaust Studies, *Confiscation of Jewish Property in Europe, 1933–1945: New Sources and Perspectives* (Washington, D.C.: Center for Advanced Holocaust Studies, U.S. Holocaust Memorial Museum, 2003), 34–35.

24. From Martin Bormann's notes; not a direct quote. See Browning, *Origins of the Final Solution,* 98.

25. Aly, Cooper, and Brown *"Final Solution,"* 40, 43, 47, and passim.

26. Report on conditions in Poland sent to Pope Pius XII, Records of the Reichssicherheitshauptamt, Reel 38, CAHS-USHMM.

27. Browning, *Origins of the Final Solution,* 176–177.

28. John Delaney, whose doctoral dissertation dealt with Polish forced labor, kindly responded on March 17, 2006, by e-mail to my request for information about the number of Poles forced into exile as laborers. He estimates that 1.7 million exiled Poles is a conservative figure.

29. Aly, Cooper, and Brown *"Final Solution,"* 23.

30. Browning, *Origins of the Final Solution,* 16.

31. Report on conditions in Poland, February 2, 1940, Records of the Reichssicherheitshauptamt, Reel 38, CAHS-USHMM.

32. Ibid.

33. Ibid.

34. Browning, *Origins of the Final Solution,* 32.

35. Wytwycky, *Other Holocaust,* 41.

36. Ibid., 51.

37. Anonymous, *La Persécution Religieuse en Pologne,* October 1942, Entry 210, Box 375, Folder 413, RG 226, location 250/64/28/07, NARA. The document seems to have been written in French for foreign consumption; the author was very well acquainted with information bearing on the Polish Church.

38. Harold H. Tittmann, Vatican City, to U.S. State Department, March 29, 1946, Entry 1068, Box 14, RG 59, location 250/48/29/30, NARA.

39. A thorough consideration of this policy may be found in Bernhard Stasiewski, "Nationalsozialistische Kirchenpolitik im Warthegau," *Viertaljahresschrift für Zeitgeschichte* 7 (1959): 46–75.

40. Heydrich, Berlin, to Stuckardt, February 28, 1940, Records of the Reichssicherheitshauptamt, Reel 38, CAHS-USHMM.

41. The RHSA approved of these measures on March 22, 1940; see Records of the Reichssicherheitshauptamt, Gau Danzig, West Preussen, Reel 38, CAHS-USHMM. See also Verordnung über die Erhebung von Beiträgen durch religiöse Vereiningungen und Religionsgesellschaften, March 14, 1940, Records of the Reichssicherheitshauptamt, Reel 38, CAHS-USHMM.

42. Himmler, Berlin, to Bormann, March 11, 1940, Records of the Reichssicherheitshauptamt, Reel 38, CAHS-USHMM. The documents in this file confirm what Stasiewski suspected in 1959, namely, that Martin Bormann was the force behind the radical disestablishment of the churches in the Warthegau.

43. Dr. Paech to an SS officer, n.d., n.p., Records of the Reichssicherheitshauptamt, Reel 38, CAHS-USHMM.

44. Dominicus Bednarz [O.F.M.], Posen, report on the condition of the church in Posen to the head of the Sicherheitspolizei in Berlin, November 9, 1939, Records of the Reichssicherheitshauptamt, Reel 38, CAHS-USHMM. Bednarz claims that the information in his report is either first hand or comes from absolutely reliable sources.

45. Stasiewski, "Nationalsozialistische Kirchenpolitik im Warthegau," 65–75.

46. Browning, *Origins of the Final Solution,* 189.

47. For a more detailed study, see Michael Phayer, "Pius XII and the Genocides of Polish Catholics and Polish Jews," *Kirchliche Zeitgeschichte* 15, no. 1 (2002): 238–262.

48. *La Persécution Religieuse en Pologne.*

49. Ibid.

50. August Hlond, *The Persecution of the Catholic Church in German-Occupied Poland. Reports presented by H. E. Cardinal Hlond, Primate of Poland,*

to Pope Pius XII, Vatican Broadcasts and Other Reliable Evidence, preface by H. E. A. Cardinal Hinsley, Archbishop of Westminster (New York: Longmans Green, 1941), 115–117. German intentions to deport the Jews were reported by the Times ("Himmler to Direct Reich Repatriation," October 24, 1939, 5); see Aly, Cooper, and Brown "Final Solution," 18.

51. Besier, Der Heilige Stuhl und Hitler-Deutschland, 314.

52. I have addressed this issue in Phayer, The Catholic Church and the Holocaust, 1930–1965 (Bloomington: Indiana University Press, 2006), 25–26. Leon Papeleux wrote that the threat of physical destruction came to the Vatican via Germany's ambassador to Chile. Papeleux provides no documentation, a vexing but not unusual practice of French-writing authors. Until the Vatican archives are opened, we will not have a final answer to this question, barring a chance discovery in some archive elsewhere.

53. Pierre Blet, S.J., Angelo Martini, S.J., Burkhart Schneider, S.J., and Robert Graham, S.J., eds., Actes et Documents du Saint Siège Relatifs á la Seconde Guerre Mondiale (Vatican City: Liberia Editrice Vaticana, 1965–1967), 3:489–491. (Hereafter ADSS.)

54. Orsenigo to Maglione, August 17, 1940, ADSS, 3:426.

55. ADSS, 2:489–491.

56. Hilarius Breitinger, Als Deutscher Seelsorger in Posen und im Warthegau, 1934–35, Veröffentlichungen der Kommission für Zeitgeschichte bei der Katholischen Akademie in Bayern (Mainz: Grünewald, 1984), 36:130.

57. Adam Sapieha, Cracow, to Luigi Maglione, February 2, 1942; ADSS, 3: 528–529.

58. Breitinger, Posen, to Pius XII, July 28, 1942; ADSS, 3:608–615.

59. Ibid.

60. Manfred Clauss, Die Beziehungen des Vatikans zu Polen während des II Weltkrieges (Cologne: Böhlau, 1979), 179.

61. Report by the Polish ambassador to the Holy See on the situation in German-occupied Poland, memorandum no. 79, May 29, 1942, Myron Taylor Papers, Decimal File 1940–1944, File 866A.001/103, RG 59, NARA, Washington, D.C.

62. Ibid.

63. ADSS, 3:46.

64. Peter Kent, The Lonely Cold War of Pius XII (Montreal: McGill-Queen's University Press, 2002), 37.

65. Karol Radonski to Luigi Maglione, London, September 14, 1942; ADSS, 3:633–636.

66. David Engel, Facing a Holocaust: The Polish Government-in-Exile and the Jews, 1943–1945 (Chapel Hill: University of North Carolina Press, 1993), 22.

67. Engel, Facing a Holocaust, 41–42.

68. Breitinger, Posen, to Pius XII, November 23, 1942; ADSS, 3:681–684.

69. Breitinger, Posen, to Pius XII, March 4, 1943; ADSS, 3:735.

70. See the draft of Pius's letter to Adam Sapieha in ADSS, 3:798ff., dated May 31, 1943.

71. ADSS, editors' introduction to volume 3.

72. Browning, Origins of the Final Solution, 113. In the following account of the origin and development of the Holocaust, I am condensing material from Browning, chapters 6 through 9. Those interested in following the fascinating details of the buildup to genocide and its implementation can find them in Browning.

73. Here I am following the account of Browning, *Origins of the Final Solution,* chapter 4, "The Polish Ghettos."

74. Ibid., 154.

75. Ibid., 240.

76. See the chapter by Jürgen Matthäus, "Operation Barbarossa and the Onset of the Holocaust, June–December 1941," in Browning, *Origins of the Final Solution,* esp. 244.

77. Browning, *Origins of the Final Solution,* 309.

78. Ibid., 314.

79. Ibid., 372.

80. Ibid.

81. Browning, *Origins of the Final Solution,* 416–423.

82. Christopher Browning, *Nazi Policy, Jewish Workers, German Killers* (New York: Cambridge University Press, 2000), 62.

83. Browning, *Nazi Policy,* 86.

84. See Greiser's statement in Entry 144, Box 91, File 1146, RG 153, NARA.

85. Browning, *Nazi Policy,* 78.

86. Quoted in Susan Zuccotti, *Under His Very Windows: The Vatican and the Holocaust in Italy* (New Haven, Conn.: Yale University Press, 2000), 104, from *ADSS,* 8:665–666.

87. Montini's title was Secretary of the Section for Ordinary Ecclesiastical Affairs within the Office of the Secretariat of State.

88. Lukas, *Forgotten Holocaust,* 25.

89. In *The Catholic Church and the Holocaust,* I wrote that it was the loss of the battle of Stalingrad that led to the reversal of German treatment of Poles. That may have been partially true, as the earlier skirmishes leading up to the battle of Stalingrad began in 1942. Nevertheless, the key to understanding the change of the Poles' fortunes under German occupation was the order to employ them in place of the Jews.

90. Browning, *Origins of the Final Solution,* 382.

91. Raul Hilberg, *The Destruction of European Jews* (New York: Holmes & Meier, 1985), 1:219.

92. Tardini's title was Secretary of the Section for Extraordinary Ecclesiastical Affairs in the Office of the Secretariat of State.

93. Harold H. Tittmann, Jr., *Inside the Vatican of Pius XII: The Memoir of an American Diplomat during World War II,* ed. Harold H. Tittmann, III (New York: Doubleday, 2004), 60–61.

94. Ibid., 56ff.

95. Gerald Fogarty, *The Vatican and the American Hierarchy, 1870–1965* (Wilmington, Del.: Michael Glazier, 1985), 273ff.

96. Harold H. Tittmann to U.S. State Department, summer 1942, paraphrased by Leland Harrison, American Ministry Legation, Bern, RG 84, location 350/68/25/02, Box 23, NARA.

97. Pope Pius said explicitly after the war that he had resisted German pressure to call Operation Barbarossa a crusade; see J. G. Parsons's memo of a conversation between him and Maritain, July 15, 1947, Box 15, entry 1068, RG 59, location 250/48/29/01-05, NARA.

98. James Dunn, assistant to Myron Taylor, to Secretary of State George Marshall, July 15, 1947, Entry 1071 Box 30, RG 59, location 250/48/29/05, NARA.

99. For a more detailed discussion of this, see Phayer, *The Catholic Church and the Holocaust,* 58ff.

100. Tittmann, *Inside the Vatican of Pius XII,* 37.

3. Pius XII's 1942 Christmas Message

1. Pierre Blet, S.J., Angelo Martini, S.J., Burkhart Schneider, S.J., and Robert Graham, S.J., eds., *Actes et Documents du Saint Siège Relatifs á la Seconde Guerre Mondiale,* 11 vols. (Vatican City, 1965–1967).

2. Leonidas E. Hill, III, "The Vatican Embassy of Ernst von Weizsaecker," *Journal of Modern History* 39, no. 2 (1967): 138–159; Owen Chadwick, "Weizsaecker, the Vatican, and the Jews of Rome," *Journal of Ecclesiastical History* 28, no. 2 (April 1977): 179–199.

3. Walter Laqueur, *The Terrible Secret: Suppression of the Truth about Hitler's "Final Solution"* (New York: Little Brown, 1980). Laqueur does, however, discuss the United Nations' declaration on genocide of December 17, 1942.

4. The Center for Advanced Holocaust Studies at the United States Holocaust Memorial Museum has obtained a microfilm copy of the newly released Vatican records from the period 1922 to 1939. The index for the records has now been prepared by Suzanne Brown-Fleming, the center's senior programs officer for university programs.

5. Because the Christmas address did not actually lead to the curtailment of murder or to a public outcry against murder, historical surveys of the Holocaust often do not even mention it. See, for example, the excellent study of Leni Yehil, *The Holocaust* (New York: Oxford, 1991). In my own work, *The Catholic Church and the Holocaust, 1930–1965* (Bloomington: Indiana University Press, 2001), I dismissed the 1942 Christmas address in cursory fashion on page 49.

6. Henry Friedlander, *Pius XII and the Holocaust: A Documentation* (New York: HarperCollins, 1966), 142.

7. Peter Godman, *Hitler and the Vatican* (New York: Free Press, 2004), chapter 6, esp. 66–67.

8. Ibid., 86.

9. Ibid., 92.

10. Ibid., 72.

11. Laqueur, *The Terrible Secret,* 55.

12. David Alvarez, *Spies in the Vatican: Espionage and Intrigue from Napoleon to the Holocaust* (Lawrence: University of Kansas Press, 2002), 285–291.

13. Paul Damian O'Shea, "Confiteor: Eugenio Pacelli, the Catholic Church and the Jews. An Examination of the Responsibility of Pope Pius XII and the Holocaust, 1917–1943" (Ph.D. diss., Macquarie University, 2004).

14. John F. Morley, *Vatican Diplomacy and the Jews during the Holocaust, 1939–1943* (New York: Ktav, 1980); Susan Zuccotti, *Under His Very Windows: The Vatican and the Holocaust in Italy* (New Haven, Conn.: Yale University Press, 2000); and Phayer, *The Catholic Church and the Holocaust.*

15. Outgoing telegrams to U.S. Department of State, September 4, 1942, Entry 1071, Box 29, RG 59, location 250/48/29/05, NARA. This box contains a notepad summary of the telegrams.

16. Morley, *Vatican Diplomacy and the Jews during the Holocaust,* 87.

17. Phayer, *The Catholic Church and the Holocaust,* 48–49. Historian Susan Zuccotti has very competently detailed the varied sources of numerous atrocity accounts that reached Pope Pius in *Under His Very Windows,* chapter 7.

18. Laqueur, *The Terrible Secret,* 226–227.

19. Ibid., 227. On January 3, 1942, all of the nations at war with the Axis powers signed a nonbinding agreement that said that none would seek peace independently. Although this alliance was referred to as the United Nations, it should not be confused with the world body that was formed in 1945. Prior to 1945, "United Nations" refers specifically to the multinational alliance against Germany during World War II. "War Pact Is Signed," *New York Times,* 3 January 1942, 1.

20. Christopher Browning has vouched for Riegner's accuracy; see C. R. Browning, "A Hitler Decision for the 'Final Solution'? The Riegner Telegram Reconsidered," *Holocaust and Genocide Studies* 10, no. 1 (Spring 1996): 3–10.

21. Gerhart Riegner, "A Warning of the World Jewish Congress to Mobilize the Christian Churches against the Final Solution," Stephen S. Wise Inaugural Lecture, Hebrew Union College, Cincinnati, Ohio, 1983, 7–8.

22. Harold H. Tittmann, Vatican City, to Secretary of State Edward Stettinius, June 16, 1942, Decimal File 1940–1944, Box 5689, File 866A.001/103, RG 59, NARA.

23. Harold H. Tittmann to U.S. State Department, memorandum no. 114, September 15, 1942, Myron C. Taylor Papers, Decimal File 1940–1944, Box 5689, File 866A.001/103, RG 59, NARA.

24. Tittmann, Vatican City, to Secretary of State Cordell Hull, October 6, 1942, in U.S. State Department, *Foreign Relations of the United States 1942* (Washington, D.C.: U.S. Government Printing Office, 1961), 3:777.

25. Diomedes Arias Schreiber to his government, November 24, 1942, Entry 210, Box 419, RG 226, location 250/64/29/06, NARA.

26. Owen Chadwick, *Britain and the Vatican during the Second World War* (Cambridge: Cambridge University Press, 1986), 213. For a summary of data the Vatican received regarding the murder of the Jews, see Phayer, *The Catholic Church and the Holocaust,* 47–48.

27. Ibid., 213. Ledokowski was called the "black pope" because as a Jesuit he wore a black soutane, whereas the pope wore white.

28. Harold H. Tittmann, Vatican City, to Secretary of State Cordell Hull, December 19, 1942, Decimal File 1940–1944, File 866A.001/103, RG 59, NARA.

29. D. J. R. to Mr. Huddle, U.S. State Department, memorandum, December 11, 1942, Entry 2113L, Box 23, RG 84, location 350/68/25/02, NARA. The origin of the information was a French bishop who had just returned from seeing the pope.

30. *ADSS,* 8:755.

31. "11 Allies Condemn Nazi War on Jews: United Nations Issue Joint Declaration of Protest on 'Cold-Blooded Extermination,'" *New York Times,* December 18, 1942, 1.

32. Laqueur, *The Terrible Secret,* 229–237; Thomas E. Woods, *Karski: How One Man Tried to Stop the Holocaust,* foreword by Elie Wiesel (New York: J. Wiley, 1994).

33. Laqueur, *The Terrible Secret,* 225–227.

34. Gerhart Besier, *Der Heilige Stuhl und Hitler-Deutschland. Die Faszination des Totalitären* (Munich: Verlagsgruppe Random House, 2004), 314.

35. Ibid., 193–194.

36. Gerhart Besier argues that if Germany had broken the concordat, it would have seriously diminished Pacelli's papal prospects, for it was his consummate accomplishment; see *Der Heilige Stuhl und Hitler-Deutschland,* 293–294.

37. D. J. R. to Huddle, December 11, 1942.

38. "Text of Pope Pius XII's Christmas Message Broadcast from Vatican to the World," *New York Times,* December 25, 1942, 10.

39. See Michael Phayer, "Pius XII and the Genocides of Polish Catholics and Polish Jews," *Kirchliche Zeitgeschichte* 15, no. 1 (2002): 252ff.

40. O'Shea, "Confiteor," 219–220.

41. Besier, *Der Heilige Stuhl und Hitler-Deutschland,* 263. The Supreme Congregation of the Holy Office was at the very top of the Vatican bureaucracy; see Godman, *Hitler and the Vatican,* 23–24.

42. Harold H. Tittmann to U.S. State Department, December 10, 1942, paraphrased by Leland Harrison, Entry 2113L, Box 23, RG 84, location 350/68/25/02, NARA.

43. Pope Pius explicitly said after the war that he had resisted German pressure to call Operation Barbarossa a crusade against atheistic Bolsheviks; see J. G. Parsons's memo of his conversation with Maritain, July 15, 1947, Box 15, entry 1068, RG 59, location 250/48/29/01-05, NARA.

44. Susan Zuccotti. "*L'Osservatore Romano* and the Holocaust, 1930–1945," *Holocaust and Genocide Studies* 17, no. 2 (Fall 2003): 249–277.

45. Myron C. Taylor, Rome, telegram to Franklin D. Roosevelt, March 27, 1941, Box 151, Folder 4, Sumner Welles Papers, Franklin D. Roosevelt Presidential Library and Museum.

46. Besier, *Der Heilige Stuhl und Hitler-Deutschland,* 28.

47. Office of Myron Taylor to U.S. State Department, Box 5689, RG 59, location 250/34/11/1, NARA.

48. Tittmann to Secretary of State Cordell Hull, December 30, 1942, Entry 1071, Box 29, RG 59, location 250/48/29/05, NARA.

49. Tittmann to Department of State Cordell Hull, January 7, 1943, Entry 1071, Box 29, RG 59, location 250/48/29/05, NARA.

50. Harold H. Tittmann, *Inside the Vatican of Pius XII: The Memoir of an American Diplomat During World War II,* ed. Harold H. Tittmann, III (New York: Doubleday, 2004), 123–124.

51. After his service at the Vatican during and after the war, Tittmann was rewarded with an ambassadorship. But he felt that his Vatican post was the high point of his career.

52. *Baltimore Sun,* December 26, 1942, 9; *Chicago Tribune,* December 25, 1942, 7; *Washington Evening Star,* December 25, 1942, 10. The microfilm copy of the London *Times* in the Library of Congress shows that no editions of the newspaper were published on the dates mentioned. Perhaps the editors thought that the papal message was old news by the twenty-eighth.

53. "Christian Personalism and Peace," *Commonweal* 37, no. 2 (January 8, 1943): 291.

54. John LaFarge, "Small Business Supply Post-War Jobs?" *America* 68, no. 15 (January 16, 1943): 405.

55. Ibid.

56. Riegner. "Warning of the World Jewish Congress," 16.

57. Pius XII, Vatican City, to Preysing, April 30, 1943, Korrespondenz V/16-4, Diocesan Archives, Berlin.

58. Kazimierz Papée, the Polish ambassador to the Holy See, wanted the pope to single out the Nazis as perpetrators; see Box 5689, RG 59, location 250/34/11/1, NARA.

59. J. M. Snoek, *Nederlandse Kerken en de Joden, 1940–1945* (Kampen: J. H. Kok, 1990), 139.

60. Ibid., 75.

61. J. Presser, *Ashes in the Wind: The Destruction of Dutch Jewry,* trans. Arnold Pomerans (Detroit, Mich.: Wayne State University Press, 1988), 147.

62. See the excellent account of Stein's letter in Godman, *Hitler and the Vatican,* 34–35.

63. Presser, *Ashes in the Wind,* 147ff.

64. The "Pastoral Letter of the Dutch Church" may be found in *The Catholic Mind* (1943): 58–60.

65. I discussed the case of the Dutch Church's protest in March 2004 at a conference on The Netherlands and the Holocaust at the Toronto University Graduate School, March 2004. Michael Marrus, dean of the graduate school, sponsored the conference.

66. In 1938, Schuster protested the Nazi pogrom in Germany; see O'Shea, "Confiteor," 276. In 1943, the OSS reported that Schuster forbade Catholics to aid Nazis or fascists under pain of excommunication; Reel 6, RG 226, location 190/10/12/06, NARA. The BBC reported this, as did the *New York Times* ("Milan's Cardinal Hits Aid to Nazis," October 17, 1943, 43).

67. Phayer, *The Catholic Church and the Holocaust,* 91ff.

68. See ibid., 129. I have discussed the question of why French church leaders did not continue to speak out against the treatment of Jews after the 1942 Christmas address with Michael Marrus. A solution eluded us. I think it is likely that a document that is missing or not yet found explains the silence of the French Church. It is true that by 1943, Vichy France had become part of occupied France, but German occupation had not kept the Dutch Church from speaking out. For more on the French Church, see Michael R. Marrus and Robert O. Paxton, *Vichy France and the Jews* (New York: Basic Books, 1981).

69. Richard Breitman and Raffaella Luciani, "Pilgrim's Progress: A Look inside the Vatican during World War II," unpublished manuscript used with permission of the authors.

70. Several OSS reports allege that Pius XII prompted French bishops to protest in 1942; see for example Entry 2113L, Box 23, RG 84, location 350/68/25/02, NARA. This seems unlikely, as there is no corroborating document in *ADSS.* It seems clear that if the pope had prodded the French bishops in 1942 they would have had enough sense to speak out in 1943 after the Christmas address.

71. Jacques Duquesne, *Les Catholiques français sous l'Occupation,* new ed. (Paris: Grasset, 1996), 312. Journet wanted to publish an article in 1943 condemning the deportation of Jews from France, but his bishop would not allow it on the grounds that it would jeopardize the security of Switzerland. For more on Journet, see Urs Altermatt, *Katholizismus und Antisemitismus: Mentalitäten, Kontiuitäten, Ambivalenzen; zur Kulturgeschichte der Schweiz, 1918–1945* (Frauenwald: Verlag Huber, 1999).

72. Duquesne, *Les Catholiques français sous l'Occupation,* 296.

73. Ibid., 315.

74. Mr. F. A. Dolbeare to Col. David Bruce, November 13, 1944, "Special Black Report," Entry 210, Box 375, File "Blackie," RG 226, location 250/64/28/07, NARA.

75. Ibid.

76. The *service du travail obligatoire* provoked the French regarding German aggression more than anything else; see Robert Zaretsky, "What Was Left Unsaid: The Word and Deeds of Bishop Jean Girbeau of Nîmes, 1939–1945," 5–6, paper presented at the 2001 conference of the German Studies Association, Washington, D.C.

Although the OSS was delighted to have an agent who had direct and close contact with the pope, they had no way to check on his reports. It would have been highly unusual for a pope to vent his criticism of a cardinal to an ordinary low-ranking priest, one who, in this case, was under severe reprimand from his Dominican superior in the United States.

77. Quoted in Roman Bleistein, S.J., "Katholische Bischoefe und der Widerstand Gegen den Nationalsozialismus," *Stimmen der Zeit* 207 (1989): 582.

78. Phayer, *The Catholic Church and the Holocaust,* 71–77.

79. Zuccotti, *Under His Very Windows,* chapters 16 through 19.

80. Louis de Jong, *The Netherlands and Nazi Germany* (Cambridge, Mass.: Harvard University Press, 1990), 1–22.

81. David Engel, *Facing a Holocaust: The Polish Government-in-Exile and the Jews, 1943–1945* (Chapel Hill: University of North Carolina Press, 1993), 22–43.

82. The office of the U.S. envoy at the Vatican noted the Polish ambassador's reaction in its report to state; Box 5689, RG 59, location 250/34/11/1, NARA.

83. Friedlander, *Pius XII and the Third Reich,* 175–176.

84. Leonidas E. Hill, *Die Weizsäcker Papiere 1933–1950* (Frankfurt, 1974), 363.

4. 1943

1. *Acta Apostolicae Sedis* 35 (1943): 165–171. The Italian reads "*destinati talora, anche senza propria colpa, a costrizioni sterminatrici*" (167). This message was given in February; the June address is discussed below. The February message was not public and was not picked up by the press.

2. *ADSS,* 9:274. The date was May 5, 1943. Maglione, in speaking about the gassing of the Jews, referred to them vaguely as "persons."

3. *ADSS,* 9:291.

4. *ADSS,* 9:287–289.

5. Ibid.

6. Ibid.

7. Ibid.

8. Owen Chadwick, *Britain and the Vatican during the Second World War* (Cambridge: Cambridge University Press, 1986), 213.

9. On the central role of Tardini in shaping the pope's policies, see Peter Godman, *Hitler and the Vatican* (New York: Free Press, 2004), 96 and passim.

10. Paul O'Shea referred to the encyclical in "Confiteor. Eugenio Pacelli, the Catholic Church and the Jews. An Examination of the Responsibility of Pope Pius XII and the Holocaust, 1917–1943" (Ph.D. diss., Macquarie University, January 2004), 76.

11. According to Richard Rubenstein's cognitive dissonance theory, Pope Pius did indeed *wish* for the death of the Jews; see Richard L. Rubenstein and John K. Roth, *Approaches to Auschwitz*, rev. ed. (Louisville, Ky.: Westminster Press, 2003), 339. For a theological explanation of *Mystici Corporis Christi* that emphasizes the nonracist character of the encyclical, see Robert A. Krieg, *Catholic Theologians in Nazi Germany* (New York: Continuum, 2004), 168–170.

12. "Pope Bids Nations Obey Laws of War," *New York Times*, June 3, 1943, 5. The *Times* gave this story greater play than it had done earlier for the pope's Christmas address. The pope's emphasis in the June address was not on the murder of Poles "and others" but on the hostage situation. Regarding the phrase "people sometimes dying," see Zuccotti, "*L'Osservatore Romano* and the Holocaust, 1930–1945," *Holocaust and Genocide Studies* 17, no. 2 (2003): 265.

13. Harold H. Tittmann to U.S. State Department, paraphrased by Leland Harrison, Box 23, RG 84, location 350/68/25/02, NARA.

14. Zuccotti, *Under His Very Windows*, see chapter 10.

15. Ibid., 150–152.

16. Chadwick, "Weizsaecker, the Vatican, and the Jews of Rome," 186. During this time, fall 1943, the only conflict between the Vatican and Ambassador Weizsäcker occurred when Under-Secretary of State Montini came to believe that 6,000 Italians were to be taken as hostages and killed because six Germans had been executed. The hostage report turned out to have no basis in fact and, in any event, did not concern Jews.

17. Robert Katz, *The Battle for Rome: The Germans, the Allies, the Partisans, and the Pope, September 1943–June 1944* (New York: Simon & Schuster, 2003), 106.

18. Louis P. Lochner, ed., *The Goebbels Diaries, 1942–1943*, translated and introduced by the editor (Garden City, N.Y.: Doubleday, 1948); see the entry for July 27, 1943.

19. Pasqualina Lehnert, *Ich dürfte Ihm Dienen* (Würzburg, 1983), 121.

20. Tittmann, Vatican City, to State Department, October 28, 1943, Decimal File 740.0011, M982, Reel 164, RG 59, NARA.

21. "Abroad: Italy Has Become Hitler's Last Scapegoat," *New York Times*, September 11, 1943, 12.

22. Records of the Reichssicherheitshauptamt, September 26, 1943, reel 37, CAHS-USHMM.

23. Leonidas E. Hill, III, "The Vatican Embassy of Ernst von Weizsäcker, 1943–1945," *Journal of Modern History* 39, no. 2 (June 1967): 146.

24. Ibid., 147. Hill's source for this information is the affidavit of K. G. Wollemweber, book 9, unpublished materials prepared by the defense, Weizsäcker's trial, "U.S. Military Tribunal, IV (IVa), Nürnberg, case no. 11, U.S. vs. Ernst Weizsäcker et al," IMT Documents, Blue Set.

25. Hill, "The Vatican Embassy of Ernst von Weizsäcker," 147.

26. Albrecht von Kassel, "The Pope and the Jews," in *Storm over "The Deputy,"* ed. Eric Bentley (New York: Grove Press, 1964), 74.

27. Katz, *The Battle for Rome*, 63.

28. David Kertzer, *The Popes against the Jews: The Vatican's Role in the Rise of Modern Anti-Semitism* (New York: Alfred A. Knopf, 2001).

29. David S. Wyman, *The Abandonment of the Jews: America and the Holocaust, 1941–1945* (New York: Pantheon Books, 1984), 238.

30. Zuccotti thinks this route would have been effective; see *Under His Very Windows*, 157.

31. Ibid., 181ff.

32. Zuccotti disagrees with this analysis and concludes that the Vatican "took no initiatives" to help. Ibid., 187.

33. Richard Breitman, "New Sources on the Holocaust in Italy," *Holocaust and Genocide Studies* 16, no. 3 (2002): 402–414. It is difficult to explain Kappler's reference to the Vatican's assistance to Jews. He did not mean Roman Jews because they remained in their homes, too unconcerned about danger, prior to the *razzia*. Kappler may have said this (as Breitman speculates in reference to something else) to dissuade Berlin from going ahead with the *razzia*.

34. Katz, *The Battle for Rome*, 76.

35. See the "Fool's Gold" section of the following chapter. U.S. intelligence was aware of the shipment of the Jews' gold to Kaltenbrunner; see OSS report to Donovan, October 5, 1943, Entry 210, Box 304, RG 226, location 250/64/27/04, NARA. Kappler imagined that his 50-kilogram "gift" would help Germany's balance-of-payments problem; see Entry 122, decoded messages from Rome, decode 7256, RG 226, NARA.

36. Breitman, "New Sources on the Holocaust in Italy," 404. Breitman notes that the newly available decodes neither affirm nor deny that Kappler opposed the roundup of Jews.

37. OSS report, n.d., Box 440, RG 84, location 250/64/25/05-06, NARA.

38. Kaltenbrunner to Kappler, October 11, 1943, Entry 122, decoded messages from Rome, decode 7458, October 11, 1943, RG 226, NARA.

39. Kappler distrusted von Kessel and nearly arrested him on charges of treason, but this does not seem to have had anything to do with the Roman Jews; see Albrecht von Kessel, *Verborgene Saat. Aufzeichnungen aus dem Widerstand 1933 bis 1945,* ed. Peter Steinbach (Berlin: Ullstein, 1992), 274.

40. Breitman, "New Sources on the Holocaust in Italy," 405.

41. Katz, *The Battle for Rome*, 80.

42. Ibid.

43. Kappler did not cooperate with the German diplomats in their efforts to protect the Jews.

44. Katz, *The Battle for Rome*, 83.

45. Zuccotti, *Under His Very Window*, 155. The best accounts of the events of October 16 may be found in Zuccotti, chapter 11, "The Rome Roundup"; and Katz, *The Battle for Rome,* chapter 7, "Under His Very Eyes."

46. Quoted in Katz, *The Battle for Rome*, 107.

47. *ADSS*, 9:509–510.

48. See von Kessel, "The Pope and the Jews," 72. Von Kessel was sympathetic to Pope Pius and therefore had not reason to lie about the letter.

49. Ibid.

50. In later years, Bishop Hudal claimed that he wrote the letter, which is true only in the sense that it was he who put pen to paper.

51. See Peter Godman, *Hitler and the Vatican* (New York: Free Press, 2004), 125. I discuss Hudal's machinations more thoroughly in chapter 6.

52. For the text of the telegram, see Katz, *The Battle for Rome*, 107.

53. See Zuccotti, *Under His Very Window*, 165.

54. Ibid., 162.

55. On many occasions both before and after October 16, Pope Pius spoke with German ambassadors von Bergen and Weizsäcker but never brought up the subject of the murder of the Jews, even during the *razzia*. Pius declined to see Weizsäcker. See Hill, *Die Weizsäcker Papiere*.

56. The most remarkable aspect of Harold Tittmann's memoir, *Inside the Vatican of Pius XII*, is his silence about the events of October 16 and the days thereafter. The reason for the omission is that when he contacted former Delasem head Settimio Sorani to provide details of the Vatican's assistance to the Jews of Rome, he learned from Sorani that such details did not exist. See the next chapter.

57. On this point, Robert Katz, Leonidas Hill, Owen Chadwick, Susan Zuccotti, Paul O'Shea, John Morley, and I are all in agreement. Sanchez concedes that the Vatican's documents put the Holy See in a negative light, but he is unable or does not wish to come to judgment; see José M. Sanchez, *Pius XII and the Holocaust: Understanding the Controversy* (Washington, D.C.: Catholic University of America Press, 2002), 146. John Morley discussed the Weizsäcker-Maglione meeting in detail in *Vatican Diplomacy and the Jews during the Holocaust* (New York: Ktav Publishing House, 1980), 180–181, and gives the entire text of Maglione's minute. He concluded that the meeting did not constitute a protest.

58. Jane Scrivener, *Inside Rome with the Germans* (New York: Macmillan, 1945). A few months later, when *L'Osservatore Romano* criticized the seizure of additional Jews, Scrivener took special note of it.

59. Zuccotti, "L'Osservatore Romano," 26.

60. Entry 122, decoded messages from Rome, decode 7672, 17/10/43, RG 226, NARA.

61. Breitman, "New Sources on the Holocaust in Italy."

62. Hill, *Weizsäcker Papiere*, 355. Katz sees Weizsäcker's night letter of October 17 confirming the Hudal letter as "a direct challenge" of the Vatican to Berlin. I disagree with this; Weizsäcker's intent was to portray the pope as the best pontiff Berlin could hope for. This is why Jesuit Robert Graham condemned Weizsäcker's letter, saying that it ruined Pius XII's reputation. I am puzzled by Katz's interpretation as it does not seem to fit the context of chapter 7, "Under His Very Eyes" in his *The Battle for Rome*.

63. *ADSS*, 9:505.

64. Original in *ADSS*, 9:505–506. Here I am using Robert Katz's translation; see Katz, *The Battle for Rome*, 104–105.

65. Katz, *The Battle for Rome*, 105.

66. Diomedes Arias Schreiber to his government, November 24, 1942, Entry 210, Box 419, RG 226, location 250/64/29/06, NARA.

67. Most of this correspondence may be found in Boxes 2433–2435, 2439, 2441, 2448–2449, 2151–2154, 2457–2458, 2461–2463, 2465, 2469, and 2470–2777, RG 59, NARA. Additional correspondence would be found in London, although English intransigence about responding to the pope's entreaties not to bomb Rome led Pius to work through the Americans.

68. Tittmann, *Inside the Vatican of Pius XII*, 65–66.

69. Harold H. Tittmann to Secretary of State Cordell Hull, December 31, 1942, Entry 1071, Box 29, location 250/48/29/05, NARA.

70. Apostolic Delegate Cicognani, Washington, D.C., to Myron Taylor, June 15, 1943, Decimal File 740.0011, M982, Reel 164, RG 59, NARA.

71. James Dunn to Harold H. Tittmann, June 24, 1943, Entry 1071, Box 29, location 250/48/29/05, NARA.

72. President Franklin D. Roosevelt to Secretary of State Cordell Hull, June 24, 1943, Entry 1071, Box 29, location 250/48/29/05, NARA.

73. Secretary of State Cordell Hull, Washington, D.C., to Apostolic Delegate Cicognani, June 29, 1943, Entry 1071, Box 29, location 250/48/29/05, NARA.

74. Pius to F. D. Roosevelt, September 6, 1943, Decimal File 740.0011, M982, Reel 164, RG 59, NARA.

75. Tittmann, *Inside the Vatican of Pius XII,* 167.

76. Major General Harry H. Johnson, U.S. Army, Rome, to Harold H. Tittmann, June 25, 1944, Entry 1069, Box 28, RG 59, location 250/48/29/05, NARA.

77. Katz, *The Battle for Rome,* 147.

78. Harold H. Tittmann to Secretary of State Cordell Hull, December 18, 1942, Entry 1071, Box 29, RG 59, location 250/48/29/05, NARA.

79. Hill, *Weizsäcker Papiere,* 374.

80. Diomedes Arias Schreiber to his government, December 9, 1942 (copy), Entry 210, Box 419, RG 226, location 250/64/29/06, NARA.

81. Cicognani to Taylor, June 15, 1943.

82. Hill, *Weizsäcker Papiere,* 374.

83. Memo of the British legation to the Holy See, May 31, 1945, Entry 1068, Box 7, RG 59, location 250/48/29/01, NARA.

84. OSS report of October 19, 1943, Entry 210, Box 65, RG 226, location 250/64/22/04, NARA.

85. Maglione to British minister Osborne, October 12, 1943, Decimal File 740.0011, M982, Reel 164, RG 59, NARA.

86. Susan Zuccotti, *The Italians and the Holocaust: Persecution, Rescue, and Survival* (New York: Basic Books, 1987), 133.

87. OSS report of February 21, 1944, Entry 210, Box 327, RG 226, location 250/64/27/07, NARA.

88. Foreign service posts of U.S. State Department, post of May 4, 1944, Entry 3220, Box 23, RG 84, location 350/68/25/03, NARA.

89. Katz, *The Battle for Rome,* 136.

90. Ibid., chapter 16, especially 258–260.

91. OSS report, no date, Entry 210, Box 440, RG 84, location 250/64/25/05-06, NARA.

92. Ibid.

93. OSS report, October 29, 1943, Box 65, RG 226, location 250/64/22/04, NARA.

94. Zuccotti, *Under His Very Windows,* 195.

95. Myron C. Taylor, Vatican City, to Secretary of State Edward Stettinius, March 26, 1945, Box 32, Entry 1073, RG 59, location 250/48/29/05, NARA.

96. See Zuccotti, *Under His Very Windows,* chapter 13.

97. Eugene J. Fisher, director of Catholic-Jewish Relations for the Secretariat for Ecumenical and Interreligious Affairs of the National Conference of Catholic

Bishops, wrote that Weizsäcker (whom Fisher mistakenly identified as Catholic) communicated Maglione's protest "gently and encouragingly" to Berlin. Fisher assumed incorrectly that this put a stop to the roundups; see "Who Was Pius XII?" in *The Holocaust and the Christian World*, ed. Carol Rittner, Stephen D. Smith, and Irena Steinfeldt (London: Kuperard, 2000), 130–132.

98. Tittmann telegram of January 4, 1944, Decimal File 740.0011, M982, Reel 164, RG 59, NARA.

99. Hill, "Vatican Embassy of Ernst von Weizsäcker," 147.

100. Anonymous Foreign Service Post, Box 47 General Records, 1944: 840.4-848 Balkans, RG 84, NARA.

101. Pius XII, Vatican City, to Preysing, March 21, 1944, Korrespondenz 1944–1945, BAB V/16-4, Diocesan Archives, Berlin.

102. Anonymous telegram to J. W. Jones, U.S. State Department, October 19, 1943, Decimal File 740.0011, M982, Reel 164, RG 59, NARA.

103. Maglione to Osborne, October 12, 1943.

104. Gerhart M. Riegner, *Niemals Verzweifeln*, trans. Michael von Killisch-Horn (Gerlingen: Psychosozial-Verlag, 2001), 164.

105. Hill, *Weizsäcker Papiere*, 353.

106. Pius XII to Preysing, March 21, 1944. Copies of Preysing's letters to Pius are missing from the Berlin diocesan archives except for the one dated March 1943.

107. Records of the U.S. Foreign Office; see U.S. State Department, *Foreign Relations of the United States 1944* (Washington, D.C.: U.S. Government Printing Office, 1966), 1:1123.

108. Phayer, *The Catholic Church and the Holocaust*, 104–109.

109. Endre Hamvas to Justinian Serédy, May 11, 1944, RG 52.009.01*1, CAHS-USHMM.

110. For the remainder of Hamvas's protest, see Phayer, *The Catholic Church and the Holocaust*, 107.

111. Moshe Y. Herczl, *Christianity and the Holocaust of Hungarian Jewry*, trans. Joel Lerner (New York: New York University Press, 1993), 206.

112. Robert Rozett, "International Intervention: The Role of Diplomats in Attempts to Rescue Jews in Hungary," *The Nazis' Last Victims. The Holocaust in Hungary*, ed. Randolph L. Braham (Detroit, Mich.: Wayne State University Press, 1998), 138.

113. Ibid., 139.

114. Raul Hilberg, *The Destruction of European Jews* (New York: Holmes and Meier, 1988), 2:838.

115. Randolph L. Braham, *The Politics of Genocide* (New York: Columbia University Press, 1981), 2:1085.

116. Randolph L. Braham, *Studies on the Holocaust* (Boulder: Rosenthal Institute for Holocaust Studies of the City University of New York and Social Science Monographs of the University of Colorado, 2000), 33–35.

117. Rozett, "International Intervention," 143.

118. David Kranzler, "The Swiss Press Campaign that Halted Deportations to Auschwitz and the Role of the Vatican, the Swiss and the Hungarian Churches," in *Remembering for the Future* (Oxford: Pergamon, 1988), 1:162.

119. Braham, *Studies on the Holocaust*, 57.

120. O'Shea, "Confiteor," 345.

121. Hilberg, *The Destruction of European Jews,* 388.

122. U.S. Representative to the Advisory Council for Italy A. Kirk to Myron C. Taylor, Rome, October 10, 1944, Entry 1069, Box 4, RG 59, NARA.

123. John. F. Morley, "Vatican Diplomacy and the Jews of Hungary during the Holocaust: October 15, 1944, to the End," paper presented at the Second International Holocaust Conference, Berlin, 1994.

124. Myron C. Taylor, note verbale to the Vatican Secretariat of State, RG 59, Entry 1069, Box 4, NARA.

125. A. Kirk to Myron C. Taylor, October 18, 1944, RG 84, location 250/64/25/05-06, Entry 1069, Box 59, NARA.

126. Morley, "Vatican Diplomacy," 5.

127. Ibid., 5–6.

128. Phayer, *The Catholic Church and the Holocaust,* 106–107.

129. Morley, "Vatican Diplomacy," 6.

130. War Refugee Board to Acting Secretary of State Stettinius, October 25, 1944, Box 441, RG 84, location 250/64/25/05, NARA.

131. F. C. Gowen, Vatican City, to Myron C. Taylor, November 7, 1944, Entry 1069, Box 4, RG 59, location 250/48/29/05, NARA.

132. Morley, "Vatican Diplomacy," 10.

133. Ibid., 18.

134. Ibid., 25.

135. Ibid., 20.

5. Papal Capitalism during World War II

1. J. E. Hoover, Washington, D.C., to Assistant Secretary of State Adolf A. Berle, Jr., September 22, 1941, Decimal File 1940–44, Box 5689, File 866A.001/103, RG 59, NARA.

2. Harold H. Tittmann, Jr., *Inside the Vatican of Pius XII: The Memoir of an American Diplomat during World War II,* ed. Harold Tittmann, III (New York: Doubleday, 2004), 42ff.

3. David I. Kertzer, *The Popes against the Jews: The Vatican's Role in the Rise of Modern Anti-Semitism* (New York: Alfred A. Knopf, 2001), 80.

4. Ibid., chapter 5.

5. For details, see ibid., chapter 1.

6. David Kertzer describes a last-ditch effort during World War I; see *Prisoners of the Vatican* (Boston: Houghton Mifflin, 2004), 241–242.

7. In his excellent study of papal finances, *Money and the Rise of the Modern Papacy: Financing the Vatican, 1850–1950* (Cambridge: Cambridge University Press, 2005), John F. Pollard emphasizes the financial aspect of the pilgrimages, whereas Kertzer emphasizes the diplomatic tension that resulted from them; see *The Popes against the Jews,* 252 and passim.

8. Pollard, *Money and the Rise of the Modern Papacy,* 64.

9. Ibid., 62. "Black" here means Catholic, not to be confused with black refugees, with whom I deal below, who were fascist war criminals.

10. Ron Chernow, *The House of Morgan* (New York: Atlantic Monthly Press, 1990), 285.

11. For details, see Pollard, *Money and the Rise of the Modern Papacy,* 139ff.

12. For Ernesto Pacelli, see ibid., 70ff.; and for Francesco Pacelli, see 139.

13. "Imperial papacy" is Pollard's phrase; see ibid., 153.

14. Ibid., 144.

15. Ibid., 145. The Dawes Plan helped stabilize Germany's postwar economy by rationalizing its indemnity payment schedule.

16. Amministrazione Speciale per la Santa Sede, created under the Lateran Treaty.

17. Pollard, *Money and the Rise of the Modern Papacy,* 144. The name of the Vatican bank is Instituto per la Opera di Religione. Nogara's title was Delegate of the Special Administration.

18. Harold S. Tittmann, Vatican City, to Col. William Wedemeyer, Rome Area Allied Command, May 11, 1945, Entry 1068, Box 3, RG 59, location 250/48/29/01, NARA.

19. Pollard remarks that there is no biography of Nogara; see *Money and the Rise of the Modern Papacy,* 143–147.

20. See the monetary table in ibid., xiii.

21. See ibid., 159ff., which has excellent details about these transactions.

22. Ibid. See the chart on page 162.

23. Ibid., 171.

24. Ibid., 172. This fact should give pause to Vatican apologists who, grasping at straws, have argued that the Vatican had to soft-pedal its dealings with the Axis powers or Mussolini would have shut off the pope's water.

25. Ibid., 173. Pollard states unequivocally that Nogara was the most important financier ever to be associated with the modern papacy; see page 143.

26. Ibid., passim.

27. Diary of Joseph Patrick Hurley, Personal Files, Loose Notes, 1938–1940, Cabinet 6, Drawer, 1, Hurley Administration Records, Archives of the Diocese of St. Augustine, Florida (hereafter Hurley Diary). Hurley's diary is unpaginated. I am most grateful to Dr. Charles Gallagher for providing me with sections of the diary.

28. A Mass stipend is an offering for the celebration of the Eucharist for a special intention. It is a traditional means of supporting the clergy. Canon law, however, forbids priests from refusing requests from the poor. A Mass stipend offering is usually a small amount—five or more dollars. In 1944, the Holy See received about $130,000 for mass intentions; see Foreign Funds Control Subject Files, Box 487, File marked "Vatican City Funds in the U.S., Transfer of," RG 131, location 230/38/32/5, NARA.

29. Hurley Diary.

30. Quoted in Pollard, *Money and the Rise of the Modern Papacy,* 48.

31. Hurley Diary.

32. All quotes are from the Hurley Diary.

33. Pollard, *Money and the Rise of the Modern Papacy,* 138. Regarding the gift, see Gerald Fogarty, *The Vatican and the American Hierarchy, 1870–1965* (Wilmington, Del.: Michael Glazier, 1985), 230.

34. "Global South Will Shape the Future of the Catholic Church," *National Catholic Reporter,* October 7, 2005, 20.

35. John Pollard, who has reviewed Nogara's diary, found it a treasure trove of information; see *Money and the Rise of the Modern Papacy,* 17.

36. Regarding Germany, see ibid., 187.

37. Myron C. Taylor, Rome, to Franklin D. Roosevelt, May 17, 1940, Box 5690, RG 59, location 50/34/11/1, NARA.

38. Pollard, *Money and the Rise of the Modern Papacy,* 187.

39. The Vatican, of course, could have done its banking directly from Switzerland, but that would have necessitated moving gold reserves to that country. The Vatican probably did not want to risk putting its gold reserves where Hitler could get hands on them.

40. Tittmann, Rome, to Secretary of State Cordell Hull, July 28, 1941, Box 487, RG 131, location 230/38/32/5, NARA.

41. See the letters of J. W. Pehle of April 21 and 23, 1942, to Henry Morgenthau, Foreign Funds Control Subject Files, Box 487, File marked "Vatican City Funds in the U.S., Transfer of," RG 131, location 230/38/32/5, NARA.

42. Memorandum to the U.S. Treasury Department on the transfer of sums from U.S. currency into the currency of European countries, Box 5690, RG 59, location 250/34/11/1, NARA.

43. See also Pollard, *Money and the Rise of the Modern Papacy,* 187–188.

44. Ibid., 169.

45. Chernow, *The House of Morgan,* 286.

46. Gerald Feldman, *Allianz and the German Insurance Business, 1933–1945* (Cambridge: Cambridge University Press, 2001).

47. Credit Suisse credited the Vatican bank's account with 6,407.50 francs on order of the Reichsbank on November 12, 1944. "Violations and Compliances of Swiss Banks, 1942–1960," Box 457, RG 131, NARA. At the end of the war, Nogara's Special Administration held the following accounts in Germany:

44,100 rm at 4.5 percent interest from 1939 and 92,600 rm at 4.5 percent interest from 1940

415,730 rm deposited in a Vorzugssperrkonto in December 1943 (about $60,000)

7, 913 deposited in the Handelssperrkonto on September 21, 1944 (about $1,000)

64 rm in another account

21,603 rm in the former German-Italian clearing account (about $2,700)

See Entry 1069, Box 287, RG 59, location 250/48/29/05, NARA.

48. Walter Shiles, American Consul General, Basel, Switzerland, to Leland Harrison, American Minister, Bern, January 14, 1946, Entry 3228 (Switzerland), Box 13, File 851, RG 84, location 350/68/32/1, NARA.

49. Ibid.

50. Prior to this time the United States had not blocked Vatican accounts, as it had done with Italian accounts. By the middle of 1941, the Vatican had notified the United States that funds available for use on the continent, meaning Swiss francs, were running out and that it would have to use its Chase bank account. See File 840.51 (Frozen Credits) for letter of April 17, 1942, requesting transfer of money into Swiss francs; letter of June 20, 1941, of the apostolic delegate informing the Vatican that the United States would not freeze its assets; telegram of July 28, 1941, from the cardinal secretary of state saying that because of steady depletion of other available resources, the Vatican would soon be obliged to draw on its funds in the United States. All in Box 5690, RG 59, location 250/34/11/1, NARA.

51. J. E. Hoover to Assistant Secretary of State Adolf A. Berle, Jr., May 22, 1942, Box 5690, RG 59, location 50/34/11/1, NARA.

52. J. E. Hoover, Washington, D.C., to Assistant Secretary of State Adolf A. Berle, September 30, 1941, Box 5690, RG 59, location 50/34/11/1, NARA.

53. Reich Security Main Office Report, August 1941[?], Records of the Reichssicherheitshauptamt, Reel 36, Frame 37, CAHS-USHMM.

54. Harold H. Tittmann, Washington, D.C., to Mr. Willis, September 2, 1964, Foreign Funds Control, Subject Files, Box 487, File marked "Vatican City Funds in the U.S., Transfer of," RG 131, 230/38/32/5, NARA.

55. Harold H. Tittmann to U.S. State Department, telegram, August 29, 1942 (surely misdated—the date was 1943), Decimal File 1945–1949, File 740.0011 E.W./1-2145, Box 3489, RG 59, NARA.

56. Tittmann to Willis, September 2, 1964.

57. The documents in the national archives pertaining to Sudameris are quite numerous, originating from many different federal agencies. The issues surrounding the transfer of controlling interest first to Milan and then to the Vatican were many and complex. For this reason the Economic Warfare Section of the War Division of the U.S. Department of Justice authorized one of its employees, Virginia Marino, to draw up a composite account of this banking enterprise. See "Report of Recent Activities of the Banque Francaise et Italienne pour L'Amerique du Sud (Sudameris)," May 9, 1944, Entry 16, Box 850, File 70712, RG 226, location 190/2/28/6, NARA. (Hereafter "Marino Report.")

58. "Marino Report," 10.

59. Ibid., 4.

60. See ibid., 10, for the "Axis bank" designation. For the notification to the U.S. State Department, see Norman Armour, Buenos Aires, Argentina, to Secretary of State Cordell Hull, February 23, 1942, Boxes 99–100, RG 60, location 230/31/2/4, NARA.

61. Several different records at the National Archives deal with the Vatican's purchase; the particulars vary from record to record. The information here comes from a Safehaven report: Entry 210, Box 168A, RG 226, location 190/4/16/2, NARA.

62. "Marino Report," 12.

63. The United States continued to hold this view throughout the war; see U.S. State Department, Washington, D.C., to Myron C. Taylor, May 4, 1945, Box 34, Entry 1073, RG 59, location 250/48/29/06, NARA.

64. Pollard, *Money and the Rise of the Modern Papacy,* 170.

65. Copy of a report from the U.S. State Department to the officer in charge of the American mission, London, March 27, 1944, Box 201, File 711.3, RG 59, location 350/62/3/07, NARA.

66. Ibid.; the following was quoted from a memorandum of a conversation between Mattioli and Mr. Cuccia regarding possible German takeover of the Banca Commerciale Italiana, March 27, 1945, Box 201, File 711.3, RG 84, location 350/62/3/07, NARA.

67. Memo for the ambassador from WDR, November 1943, Box 142, RG 84, location 350/48/18/4, NARA.

68. Harold H. Tittmann to U.S. State Department, June 1942, Box 23, RG 84, location 350/68/25/02, NARA.

69. It is not clear just exactly when Tittmann did this; the first mention I found

does not come until 1943. But it makes no sense to assume that Tittmann warned Maglione *after* the Vatican had purchased the bank. See the memo from J. H. M., October 11, 1943, Box 142, RG 84, location 350/48/18/04, NARA. When Maglione told British minister Osborne that Sudameris had been bought without his knowledge or consent, Maglione must have been referring to when the decision to do so came about. This makes sense because Nogara did not answer Maglione. See Harold H. Tittmann, Vatican City, to Secretary of State Cordell Hull, April 13, 1943, Box 99, RG 60, location 230/31/2/4, NARA.

70. "Marino Report," 8–9.

71. British embassy, Buenos Aires, June 18, 1943, to the Enemy Transactions Department, Box 141, RG 84, location 350/48/18/04, NARA.

72. Giovanni F. Malagodi, Buenos Aires, to Raffaele Mattioli, chairman of Banque Française et Italienne, January 24, 1945, Box 201, File 711.3, RG 84, location 350/62/3/07, NARA.

73. Nogara contacted Harold Tittmann regarding delisting of the bank often and every year from 1942 through 1945; see the Marino Report.

74. Secretary of State Cordell Hull to Myron C. Taylor, August 23, 1944, Entry 1069, Box 28, RG 59, location 259/48/29/5, NARA.

75. Board of Economic Welfare, "Axis Connections of Certain Fire and Marine Insurance Companies Operating in Argentina," April 1943, Entry 157, Box 1, File AH-87, RG 169, location 570/56/24/04, NARA.

76. Malagodi to Mattioli, January 24, 1945.

77. Myron C. Taylor, Rome, to Secretary of State Cordell Hull, August 28, 1944, Box 28, Entry 1069, RG 59, location 250/48/29/5, NARA.

78. "Marino Report," 12. Nogara expressed himself in nearly identical words on other occasions; see Entry 1073, Box 34, location 250/48/29/06, RG 59.

79. Secretary of State Cordell Hull, Washington, D.C., to Myron C. Taylor, September 15, 1944, Entry 1069, Box 28, RG 59, location 250/48/29/5, NARA.

80. On the Marino Report, see note 56 in this chapter.

81. Maura E. Hametz, "The Ambivalence of Italian Anti-Semitism: Fascism, Nationalism, and Racism in Trieste," *Holocaust and Genocide Studies* 16, no. 3 (2002): 376–401.

82. Zuccotti, *Under His Very Windows*, chapter 4 and passim.

83. Kertzer, *The Popes against the Jews*, 221.

84. Phayer, *The Catholic Church and the Holocaust*, 19.

85. Kertzer, *The Popes against the Jews*, chapter 12, esp. 240ff.

86. Kertzer characterizes the distinction as "terribly wrong"; see *Popes against the Jews*, 4.

87. For a complete study of the LaFarge draft, see Georges Passelecq and Bernhard Suchecky, *L'encyclique Cacheé de Pie XI. Une occasion manquée de l'eglise face à antisemitismus* (Paris: La Découverte, 1995). I discussed their work in *The Catholic Church and the Holocaust*, 4.

88. Tittmann told Montini in 1942 that public humiliation of Jews violated Article 1, part 2 of the Lateran Treaty. However, Pope Pius did nothing about it. See Tittmann, *Inside the Vatican*, 120.

89. Gerhard Besier, *Der heilige Stuhl und Hitler-Deutschland. Die Fascination des Totalitären* (Munich: Verlagsgruppe Random House, 2004), 285–286. For a contrary view, see, Zuccotti, *Under His Very Windows*, 49ff.

90. Vrba used this language at a session on intentionalists versus functionalists at the 1988 Holocaust conference at Oxford University.

91. Entry 196, Box 16, File 30, RG 226, location 190/10/9/5, NARA. This file gives background information on foreign insurance companies operating in Italy.

92. Safehaven Report, April 1, 1945, Entry 210, Box 337, RG 226, location 250/64/28/1, NARA. Nogara crossed paths in the business world with Frigessi and Morpurgo in many ways. For example, he sat with the latter on Banca Commerciale in Milan. See Pollard, *The Popes against the Jews,* 173.

93. Report on the Italian insurance industry, n.d., Office of Alien Property, Box 219, RG 131, location 230/38/19/6, NARA. Italian insurance companies were required by law to be separate entities; thus, Fondiaria's life, fire, and accident lines were independent firms. In reality, insurance companies got around this by investing heavily in each other. For example, Fondiaria Life owned 2,231 (or 3,903; the archival source is not clear) shares of Fondiaria Accident.

94. Quoted in Godman, *Hitler and the Vatican,* 33.

95. Phayer, *The Catholic Church and the Holocaust,* 5.

96. Gerald D. Feldman, *Allianz and the German Insurance Business, 1933–1945* (Cambridge: Cambridge University Press, 2001), 395.

97. Entry 16, Box 1411, File 123359, RG 226, location 190/4/5/2, NARA.

98. See the report of Ellery W. Stone to Arpesani, April 24, 1946, Entry 2779, Box 190, File 850.6, RG 84, location 350/62/3/5, NARA.

99. See Feldman, *Allianz and the German Insurance Business,* chapter 7 and passim.

100. Report on the Italian insurance industry, n.d., Office of Alien Property, Box 219, RG 131, location 230/38/19/6, NARA.

101. Feldman, *Allianz and the German Insurance Business,* 400 and passim.

102. For a lucid history of how the business community and the Holocaust became bedfellows, see Peter Hayes, *Industry and Ideology: IG Farben in the Nazi Era* (Cambridge: Cambridge University Press, 1987).

103. Before the publication of his *From Cooperation to Complicity: Degussa in the Third Reich* (Cambridge: Cambridge University Press, 2004), Peter Hayes gave a bone-chilling lecture at the German Historical Institute in 2001 in which he referred to the odor of gold fillings that had been extracted from corpses at death camps upon their arrival at the Degussa firm in Germany.

104. Entry 16, Box 1411, File 103884, RG 226, NARA.

105. In all, 400 companies shared the 40,000,000-franc liability of the Printemps fire; see Alfred Manes, "The Re-insurance Industry," July 31, 1942, Entry 285B, Box 95, RG 60, location 230/31/2/4, NARA.

106. Safehaven investigation of all Italian insurance companies, April 1945, COI/OSS Central Files, Entry 92, Box 502, File 8, RG 226, location 190/6/1/4, NARA.

107. Board of Economic Warfare report, June 15, 1943, Entry 285B, Box 64, RG 60, location 230/31/1/6, NARA.

108. Feldman, *Allianz and the German Insurance Business,* 258.

109. Ibid., 235.

110. Quoted in ibid., 320.

111. Pollard, *Money and the Rise of the Modern Papacy,* 171.

112. For a good survey of Catholic economic and social thought, see Paul Misner, *Social Catholicism in Europe* (New York: Crossroad Publishing Company, 1991).

113. See Pollard, *Money and the Rise of the Modern Papacy,* 163–165.

114. Vatican radio protested the despoilment of the Warthegau population, as we saw in chapter 2. This protest was short lived.

115. Richard Breitman, "New Sources on the Holocaust in Italy," *Holocaust and Genocide Studies* 16, no. 3 (2002): 404.

116. An excellent account of the cruel exercise may be found in Zuccotti, *Under His Very Windows,* 153ff.

117. See Raphael Levy, n.p., to Bruce Chapman, December 10, 1947, AR 4554 #1050, Archives of the American Joint Distribution Committee, New York, New York. The money came from the United Jewish Appeal, of which the Joint Distribution Committee was a constituent member.

118. Delasem is an acronym for Delgazione Assistenza Emigranti Ebrei.

119. Settimio Sorani, memorandum describing his conversation with Heathcote Smith, Chief of the International Government Committee of Refugees, no date or place, Entry 1069, Box 4, RG 59, location 250/48/29/5, NARA.

120. The Home Office authorized the transmission of the money to the finance office of the Foreign Office: "We have authorized the expenditure of H.M. Minister at the Vatican of the Lira equivalent of $20,000 for this charitable relief work." Telegram to U.S. State Department [?], March 6, 1944, Entry 3220, Box 32, RG 84, location 350/68/25 /03, NARA.

121. Harold H. Tittmann, Rome, to Secretary of State Cordell Hull, August 2, 1944, Box 28, RG 59, location 250/48/29/5, NARA.

122. Zuccotti, *Under His Very Windows,* 184.

123. Tittmann, Washington, D.C., to Abba P. Schwartz, n.d., AR 33/44, File 716 (Reports on the Situation of Jews in Italy, 1943–1945 and 1961–1962), Archives of the American Joint Distribution Committee.

124. Ibid.

125. Harold H. Tittmann to Moses A. Leavitt, January 6, 1962, AR 33/44, File 716, Archives of the Joint Distribution Committee.

126. Sandy Mendel, Rome, to Moses A. Leavitt, January 23, 1962, AR 33/44, File 716, Archives of the Joint Distribution Committee.

127. Settimio Sorani, Florence, to Harold H. Tittmann, January 22, 1962, translated by the Joint Distribution Committee in Italy and forwarded to Tittmann, AR 33/44, File 716, Archives of the Joint Distribution Committee.

128. Roswell D. McClelland to Tittmann, Bern, May 24, 1943, Entry 1068, Box 4, RG 59, location 250/48/29/01, NARA.

129. Sorani to Tittmann, January 22, 1962.

130. Zuccotti, *Under His Very Windows,* 184.

131. Resnik's statement is in the Archives of the American Joint Distribution Committee.

132. Reuben B. Resnik, "Efforts in Relief, Rescue and Resettlement during World War II," presentation to the Detroit Jewish Historical Society, June 12, 1988. Copy in the Archives of the Joint Distribution Committee.

133. OSS report, n.p., n.d. [February 1944], Box 440, RG 84, location 250/64/25/ 05, NARA.

134. Switzerland, an arms producer, must have bought some tungsten from the peninsular countries, but I have not found data specifying the amount.

135. William Norton Medlicott, *The Economic Blockade* (London: Longmans, Green, 1959), 2:560.

136. Stuart Eizenstat, *U.S. and Allied Wartime and Postwar Relations and Nego-*

tiations with Argentina, Portugal, Spain, Sweden, and Turkey on Looted Gold and German External Assets and U.S. Concerns about the Fate of the Wartime Ustasha Treasury (Washington, D.C.: n.p., 1998), see section on Portugal.

137. Entry 369B, Box 3, RG 59, location 250/64/25/05, NARA. These amounts may have been later revised, but only marginally.

138. Eizenstat, *U.S. and Allied Wartime and Postwar Relations and Negotiations with Argentina, Portugal, Spain, Sweden, and Turkey,* see section on Spain.

139. Antonio Louça and Ansgar Schaefer, "Portugal and the Nazi Gold: The 'Lisbon Connection' in the Sales of Looted Gold by the Third Reich," *Yad Vashem Studies* XXVI (2004): 111–112.

140. These were described as "transactions involving protection of principal, reinvestments, and transfers of principal"; G. F. Fletcher to W. S. Surry, December 6, 1946, Entry 369B, Box 3, RG 59, NARA.

141. Medlicott, *The Economic Blockade,* 1:532.

142. E. S. Crocker, Charge d'Affaires, Embassy, Lisbon, Portugal, annual economic review to Secretary of State James F. Byrnes, October 28, 1946, Entry 3127, Box 15, File 850, RG 84, location 350/67/12/04, NARA.

143. Medlicott, *The Economic Blockade,* 1:524.

144. Telegram to U.S. State Department, October 6, 1943, Box 5690, RG 59, location 50/34/11/1, NARA. I found no record of Spanish or Portuguese ships being challenged in this way. Shipments to neutral countries in or near Axis territory required a license, or navicert, in order to pass through Allied blockades.

145. Naval intelligence report, 1940–1946, C-10-F, Box 159, RG 38, NARA.

146. J. E. Hoover, Washington, D.C., to A. A. Berle, Jr., November 8, 1941, Box 5690, File 840.51 (Frozen Credits), RG 59, NARA. In December 1942, a Vatican official flew from Rome to Lisbon, taking with him under diplomatic immunity excess baggage of about 1,000 pounds. The contents of the pouch may have been for additional deposits in Portugal; see the December 23, 1941, OSS report in Box 65, location 250/84/22/04, RG 226, NARA.

147. Pollard, *Money and the Rise of the Modern Papacy,* 145.

148. Ibid., 147.

149. Bernstein, U.S. Treasury Department, to Plakia, memorandum, February 3, 1943, Box 5690, RG 59, location 250/34/11/1, NARA.

150. Ibid. The identity of "FF" is not known.

151. November 16, 1944, Entry 210, Box 436, RG 226, NARA.

152. Louça and Schaefer, "Portugal and the Nazi Gold," 113.

153. Ibid., 115. See also Entry 369B, Box 3, RG 59, location 250/45/35/7, NARA.

154. E. S. Crocker to Secretary of State James F. Byrnes, annual economic review, October 28, 1946, Entry 3127, Box 15, File 850, RG 84, location 350/67/12/04, NARA.

155. "Portugal Plans Inflation Loan," *New York Times,* May 1, 1943.

156. Louça and Schaefer, "Portugal and the Nazi Gold," 118–122. I found the wording of the quote in a paper at the Center for Advanced Holocaust Studies at CAHS-USHMM that is no longer available. The argument of Louça and Schaefer in their *Yad Vashem Studies* article varies only slightly from the paper I saw.

157. Pollard, *Money and the Rise of the Modern Papacy,* 177–179.

158. R. H. Tawney, *Religion and the Rise of Capitalism* (New York: New American Library, 1955), 235.

159. Pollard, *Money and the Rise of the Modern Papacy,* 163. Chernow also states that Pius XI put no restrictions on Nogara; see *The House of Morgan,* 286.

160. Pollard, *Money and the Rise of the Modern Papacy,* 115.

161. *ADSS,* 10:506.

162. See the letter to Maglione and Montini reproduced in "The Truth Emerges," *Inside the Vatican* (February 2003): 14.

163. In 1944, after the Allied occupation of Rome, relief funds from the western hemisphere poured into Rome, to which the Vatican contributed 5 million lira. See F. Gowen to Secretary of State Cordell Hull, telegram, November 2, 1944, Entry 1071, Box 29, RG 59, location 250/48/29/05, NARA. There are other isolated instances of Vatican donations during the war. Radio reports in September 1943 credited the Vatican with donating 500,000 Finnmarks to Finland for POWs and Finnish children and 100,000 levas for those suffering in Bulgaria because of the war; see Box 65, RG 226, location 250/64/22/04, NARA. These scattered reports do not provide enough information to afford anything like a general picture of Vatican largesse during the war.

6. The First Cold War Warrior

1. James Dunn to Secretary of State Dean Acheson, February 9, 1949; quoted in Peter C. Kent, *The Lonely Cold War of Pius XII* (Montreal: McGill-Queen's University Press, 2002), 239.

2. Earl Brennan, Chief, Italian Section SI, report on all intelligence for Italy/Albania, September 1945, Entry 210, Box 319, RG 226, location 250/62/28/02, NARA.

3. OSS intelligence report, Rome, July 24, 1946, Entry 211, Box 48, RG 226, location 250/64/33/4, NARA. Father Schiltz was the liaison between the Jesuit mother house and the Vatican. From October 1944 to the end of 1945, the dispatches of the OSS were extremely compromised by a phony "plant" who fed intelligence agents with information that supposedly came from high Vatican sources. As historian David Alvarez has written, the Americans fell for these reports hook, line, and sinker. By October 1945, envoy Taylor knew that the fabricated information came from the duped OSS agent Angelton. He told the State Department the leaked information was "plausible inventions fabricated by unauthorized persons with a view to peddling them around to various foreign missions at Rome." See Myron C. Taylor, Vatican City, to Secretary of State James F. Byrnes, October 19, 1945, Entry 1073, Box 33, RG 59, location 250/48/29/06, NARA. I have adopted the policy of using OSS reports only if the information in them conforms to information from other sources. See David Alvarez, *Spies in the Vatican: Espionage and Intrigue from Napoleon to the Holocaust* (Lawrence: University Press of Kansas, 2002), 248ff.

4. Ibid.

5. Earl Brennan, Chief, Italian Section, SI, to W. H. H. Shepardson, Chief, SI, December 20, 1944, (OSS report), Entry 210, Box 485, RG 226, location 250/64/2/01, NARA.

6. Frank J. Coppa, "Pope Pius XII and the Cold War: The Post-War Confrontation between Catholicism and Communism," in *Religion and the Cold War,* ed. Dianne Kirby (New York: Palgrave, 2003), 62.

7. Ibid. This is not a direct quote but Pius's words as recalled by Father Schiltz. Box 48, location 250/64/33/4, RG 226, NARA.

8. Again, not a direct quote.

9. Tony Judt, *Postwar: A History of Europe since 1945* (New York: Penguin Press, 2005), 109.

10. Vera Bücker, *Die Schulddiskussion im deutschen Katholizismus nach 1945* (Bochum: Studienverlag Brockmeyer, 1989), 15–18.

11. Owen Chadwick, "Weizsaecker, the Vatican, and the Jews of Rome," *Journal of Ecclesiastical History* 28, no. 2 (April 1977): 216.

12. Leonidas Hill, ed., *Die Weizsäcker Papiere, 1933–1950.* (Frankfurt: Propyläen Verlag, 1974), 343.

13. Paul Damian O'Shea, "Confiteor. Eugenio Pacelli, the Catholic Church and the Jews. An Examination of the Responsibility of Pope Pius XII and the Holocaust, 1917–1943" (Ph.D. diss., Macquarie University, 2004), 349.

14. Ibid., 350.

15. Harold H. Tittmann, Jr., *Inside the Vatican of Pius XII: The Memoir of an American Diplomat during World War II,* ed. Harold Tittmann, III (New York: Doubleday, 2004), 180.

16. Hill, *Die Weizsäcker Papiere,* 379–381.

17. OSS report on papal announcement called the Judah Report, n.d., Entry 210, Box 423, location 250/64/29/07, RG 226, NARA.

18. The British legation to the Vatican reviewed the issue of the open city at the end of May 1945. Rome had been bombed only twice, once in July and once in August 1943. It was asserted, unflatteringly, that the city had been saved from further bombing not because of the pope's pleas but because of the speed with which the Allies entered Rome. In fact, the Allies did not take the city nearly as quickly as they might have after their landing at Anzio beach in January 1945. See the memo of the British Legation to the Holy See, May 31, 1945, Entry 1068, Box 7, RG 59, location 250/48/29/01, NARA.

19. David I. Kertzer, *Prisoner of the Vatican* (Boston: Houghton Mifflin, 2004).

20. Susan Zuccotti, *Under His Very Windows: The Vatican and the Holocaust in Italy* (New Haven, Conn.: Yale University Press, 2000), 17.

21. Peter C. Kent, *The Pope and the Duce: The International Impact of the Lateran Agreements* (New York: St. Martin's Press, 1981), 97.

22. Ibid., 112.

23. *Dilectissima Nobis* (1936) and *Divini Redemptoris* (1937).

24. Dianne Kirby, "Harry Truman's Religious Legacy: The Holy Alliance, Containment, and the Cold War," in *Religion and the Cold War,* ed. Dianne Kirby (New York: Palgrave, 2003), 86.

25. Kent, *The Pope and the Duce,* 154 and 180.

26. Both Peter Godman and Gerhard Besier extensively discuss how the Vatican studied this issue; see Peter Godman, *Hitler and the Vatican* (New York: Free Press, 2004), and Gerhard Besier, *Der Heilige Stuhl und Hitler-Deutschland. Die Faszination des Totalitären* (Munich: Verlagsgruppe Random House, 2004).

27. "Oggi, Al Compiersi," September 1, 1944 (papal statement).

28. Kent, *The Pope and the Duce,* 157.

29. "C'est un Geste," July 10, 1946, letter to Charles Flory, president of the Semainse Sociales de France.

30. J. Graham Parsons, Foreign Service Officer, Vatican City, to Secretary of

State George Marshall, November 29, 1947, Entry 1068, Box 18, RG 59, location 250/48/29/01-05, NARA.

31. *Mit dem Gefuehl,* September 4, 1949 (to German bishops for 1949 Katholikentag meeting).

32. *Que hermoso espectaculo,* March 11, 1951 (to Spanish workers).

33. *Carissimis Russiae populis,* July 5, 1952.

34. Dispatch from George Kennan, Moscow, January 10–11, 1946, on January 10, 1946 article in *Pravda,* Entry 2799, Box 122, RG 84, location 350/62/10/5, NARA.

35. Cordell Hull to Harold H. Tittmann, January 22, 1944, Decimal File 740.0011, M982, Reel 164, RG 59, NARA.

36. Ambassador Weizsäcker noted this; see Hill, *Die Weizsäcker Papiere,* 363ff.

37. Brennan to Shepardson, December 20, 1944. See Peter C. Kent, *The Lonely Cold War of Pope Pius XII: The Roman Catholic Church and the Division of Europe, 1943–1950* (Montreal: McGill-Queen's University Press, 2002), 29, for Sturzo's quotation in the *New York Times.*

38. M23376-31669, Reel 126, RG 226, NARA.

39. OSS report on the condemnation of the Christian leftist party, January 6, 1945, Entry 210, Box 423, RG 226, location 250/64/29/07, NARA.

40. See Kent, *The Lonely Cold War of Pope Pius XII,* 28ff.

41. Myron Taylor, Vatican City, to Secretary of State Edward Stettinius, May 11, 1945, Entry 1068, Box 8, RG 59, location 250/48/29/01, NARA.

42. Judt, *Postwar: A History of Europe since 1945,* 48.

43. Myron C. Taylor to Secretary of State Edward Stettinius, April 20, 1945, Entry 1071, Box 29, RG 59, location 250/48/29/05, NARA.

44. Myron C. Taylor to Secretary of State Edward Stettinius, February 6, 1945, Entry 1071, Box 29, RG 59, location 250/48/29/05, NARA.

45. Franklin Gowen to U.S. State Department, memo, January 24, 1946, Entry 1069, Box 28, RG 59, location 250/48/29/5, NARA.

46. Undersecretary of State Montini quoted the pope in Entry 1069, Box 28, RG 59, location 250/48/29/5, NARA.

47. Franklin Gowen to Secretary of State James F. Byrnes, probably sent in July 1946, Entry 1071, Box 30, RG 59, location 250/48/29/05, NARA.

48. James Dunn to Secretary of State James F. Byrnes, November 19, 1946, Entry 1071, Box 30, RG 59, location 250/48/29/05, NARA.

49. J. G. Parsons, memo of a conversation with Montini, September 16–17, 1947, Entry 1068, Box 15, RG 59, location 250/48/29/01-05, NARA. Montini did not mention the pope, but it may be assumed that Montini reflected the pope's concern.

50. J. G. Parsons, memo of a conversation with Maritain, July 15, 1947, Entry 1068, Box 15, RG 59, location 250/48/29/01-05, NARA.

51. See J. G. Parsons, memos of conversations with Montini and Tardini, November 21, and 25 and December 10, 1947, Entry 1068, Box 15, RG 59, location 250/48/29/01-05, NARA.

52. Dunn to Secretary of State Marshall, November 19, 1948, Entry 1071, Box 30, RG 59, 250/48/29/05, NARA.

53. J. G. Parsons to Secretary of State George Marshall, February 13, 1948, Entry 1071, Box 30, RG 59, location 250/48/29/05, NARA.

54. Judt, *Postwar: A History of Europe since 1945,* 147.

55. Patrick McNamara, *A Catholic Cold War: Edmund A. Walsh, S.J., and the Politics of American Anticommunism* (New York: Fordham University Press, 2005), 152.

56. Harold H. Tittmann to Secretary of State James F. Byrnes, telegram, December 14, 1945, Entry 1073, Box 31, RG 59, location 250/48/29/05, NARA.

57. OSS report, Rome, July 24, 1946, Entry 211, Box 48, RG 226, location 250/64/33/4, NARA. See also Kent, *The Lonely Cold War of Pope Pius XII*, 136–137.

58. J. G. Parsons, memo of a conversation with Maritain, July 25, 1947, Entry 1068, Box 15, RG 59, location 250/48/29/01-05, NARA.

59. The vacillation found an echo in a conversation between J. G. Parsons and Mr. Cianfarra of the New York Times bureau in Rome. Cianfarra found "Tardini very very pessimistic . . . war inevitable. Russia will not compromise but Cianfarra found Montini to be a person of 'great vision' and balance. Tardini is impulsive and dynamic. Tardini is forceful, energetic, uncompromising. Montini is logical, skillful in dealing with adversary." J. G. Parsons, memo of a conversation with Mr. Cianfarra, August 15, 1947, Entry 1071, Box 30, RG 59, location 250/48/29/05, NARA.

60. James Dunn to Secretary of State James F. Byrnes, July 15, 1947, Entry 1071, Box 30, RG 59, location 250/48/29/05, NARA.

61. J. G. Parsons, memo of a conversation with Montini, November 7, 1947, Entry 1068, Box 15, RG 59, location 250/48/29/01-05, NARA. For more details on the significance of the Marshall Plan and the pope's enthusiastic response to it, see Kent, *The Lonely Cold War of Pope Pius XII*, 191ff.

62. Letter of J. Graham Parsons to "Red" (Walter C. Dowling, Division of Southern European Affairs, U.S. State Department), March 9, 1948, Entry 1068, Box 21, RG 59, location 250/48/2901-05, NARA.

63. Judt, *Postwar: A History of Europe since 1945*, 289.

64. Luciano Segreto, "A New Social and Economic Order in Italy?" in *The Postwar Challenge, 1945–1958,* ed. Dominik Geppert (New York: Oxford University Press, 2003), 132.

65. John Pollard, "The Vatican, Italy, and the Cold War," in *Religion and the Cold War,* ed. Dianne Kirby (New York: Palgrave, 2003), 108.

66. Secretary of State George Marshall to envoy, February 6, 1948, Entry 1073, Box 32, RG 59, location 250/48/29/05, NARA.

67. J. G. Parsons to Secretary of State George Marshall, March 26, 1948, Entry 1071, Box 30, RG 59, location 250/48/29/05, NARA.

68. Quoted in Kent, *The Lonely Cold War of Pope Pius XII*, 196.

69. A. Tarnowski to Monsignor Howard J. Carroll, director, National Catholic Welfare Conference, Rome, December 3, 1948, 10/25/7, American Catholic History Center and University Archives, Catholic University of America. (Hereafter ACUA.)

70. J. G. Parsons, memo of a conversation with Joseph P. Walshe, January 14, 1948, Entry 1068, Box 15, RG 59, location 250/48/29/01-05, NARA.

71. See chapter 8.

72. Pollard, "The Vatican, Italy, and the Cold War," 109.

73. Linda Hunt, *Secret Agenda: The United States Government, Nazi Scientists, and Project Paperclip, 1945–1980* (New York: St. Martin's Press, 1991), 158.

74. Judt, *Postwar: A History of Europe since 1945*, 142. Trieste was occupied by Allied forces and declared a Free City by the United Nations in 1947. In 1954 it was awarded to Italy.

75. See Judt, *Postwar: A History of Europe since 1945*, chapter 5, "The Coming of the Cold War."

76. Myron C. Taylor to Secretary of State Edward Stettinius, February 28, 1945, Entry 1071, Box 29, RG 59, location 250/48/29/05, NARA.

77. Office of Myron C. Taylor, Vatican City, to U.S. State Department, April 26, 1945, Entry 1073, Box 34, RG 59, location 250/48/29/06, NARA.

78. Myron C. Taylor to Secretary of State Edward Stettinius , April 7, 1945, Entry 1071, Box 29, RG 59, location 250/48/29/05, NARA.

79. Charles R. Gallagher, "Patriot Bishop: The Public Career of Archbishop Joseph P. Hurley, 1937–1967" (Ph.D. diss., Marquette University, 1998).

80. Judt, *Postwar: A History of Europe since 1945,* 140.

81. Gowen to Secretary of State James F. Byrnes, January 8, 1946, Entry 2799, Box 122, RG 84, location 350/62/10/5, NARA.

82. Charles R. Gallagher, "The United States and the Vatican in Yugoslavia, 1945–1950," in *Religion and the Cold War,* ed. Dianne Kirby (New York: Palgrave, 2003), 120.

83. Harold H. Tittmann to Secretary of State James F. Byrnes, March 28, 1946, Entry 1071, Box 30, RG 59, location 250/48/29/05, NARA.

84. Kent, *The Lonely Cold War of Pope Pius XII,* 106.

85. Ibid.

86. Ibid., 162.

87. Ibid., 163.

88. Caserta memo to Harold H. Tittmann, July 22, 1945, Entry 1069 Box 28, RG 59, location 250/48/29/5, NARA.

89. Kent, *The Lonely Cold War of Pope Pius XII,* 164.

90. Gallagher, "The United States and the Vatican in Yugoslavia," 132.

91. See chapter 11.

92. Norman J. W. Goda, "The Ustaša: Murder and Espionage," in *U.S. Intelligence and the Nazis,* ed. Richard Breitman, Norman J. W. Goda, Timothy Naftali, and Robert Wolfe (Washington, D.C.: National Archives Trust Fund Board for the Nazi War Crimes and Japanese Imperial Government Records Interagency Working Groups, 2004), 206–208.

93. U.S. Strategic Services Unit dispatch of June 22, 1946, from Angelton, Entry 210, Box 457, RG 226, location 250/64/30/04, NARA.

94. Franklin C. Gowen, Vatican City, to Secretary of State James F. Byrnes, January 14, 1946, Box 187, RG 84, location 350/62/3/5, NARA.

95. U.S. Strategic Services Unit dispatch, January 22, 1946, Entry 217, Box 6, RG 226, location 250/64/34/2, NARA.

96. Gallagher, "The United States and the Vatican in Yugoslavia," 126–127.

97. Phayer, *The Catholic Church and the Holocaust,* 37–40.

98. Myron C. Taylor, Vatican City, to U.S. State Department, June 30, 1948, Box 4012, RG 59, NARA.

99. J. G. Parsons, memo of a conversation with Sir Victor Perowne, British Minister to the Holy See, December 10, 1947, Box 15, Entry 1068, RG 59, location 250/48/29/01-05, NARA.

100. Peter C. Kent, "Toward the Reconstruction of Christian Europe: The War Aims of the Papacy, 1938–1945," in *FDR, the Vatican, and the Roman Catholic Church in America, 1933–1945,* ed. David B. Woolner and Richard G. Kurial (New York: Palgrave Macmillan, 2003), 169.

101. Ibid., 169–170.

102. OSS report, December 7, 1944, Box 369, Entry 210, RG 226, location 250/64/28/06, NARA.

103. OSS memo, Caserta, Italy, November 25, 1944, Box 469, Entry 210, RG 226, location 250/64/30/6, NARA.

104. Undated OSS report, Box 236, Entry 210, File 3, RG 226, location 250/64/26/01, NARA.

105. See "Italy Delays Action on Yugoslav Claims," *New York Times,* April 19, 1945, 8.

106. Foreign Service posts of the State Department, "Top Secret" file 1944–47, 822–844, Box 5, RG 84, NARA.

107. In time, the economy of the German Democratic Republic faltered so badly that the regime had to tolerate the institutional Church because of the economic resources Catholics in the Federal Republic of Germany extended to their co-religionists in the east. See the masterful study of Bernd Schäfer, *Staat und katholische Kirche in der DDR* (Cologne: Böhlau Verlag, 1998), 25–31.

108. Many Germans had joined the Nazi party opportunistically. True fascist ideologues remained enemies of Communists.

109. Schäfer, *Staat und katholische Kirche in der DDR,* 30–38.

110. See John Cornwell, *Hitler's Pope: The Secret History of Pius XII* (London: Viking, 1999). Peter Kent wrote, quite mistakenly, that I am in agreement with Cornwell; see Kent, *The Lonely Cold War of Pope Pius XII,* 9.

111. Memo of a conversation between J. G. Parsons and John O. Riedl, chief, Catholic Affairs Section, Educational and Religious Affairs Branch, Office of Military Government U.S., October 30, 1947, Box 15, Entry 1068, RG 59, location 250/48/29/01-05, NARA.

112. Schäfer, *Staat und katholische Kirche in der DDR,* 57ff.

113. Kirby, "Harry Truman's Religious Legacy," 84.

114. Pollard, "The Vatican, Italy, and the Cold War," 115. There is disagreement as to whether the decree of excommunication was intended for "home consumption," as Pollard writes, or was meant as a broad manifesto against communism; see Kent, *The Lonely Cold War of Pope Pius XII,* 242ff.

115. Schäfer, *Staat und Katholische Kirche in der DDR,* 66.

116. Ibid., 25–31.

117. Ibid., 69–70.

118. Bishop Muench recorded Pius XII's words after an audience with him on June 7, 1951; Muench Diary XI, May 20, 1951, to September 13, 1951, Papers of Cardinal Aloisius Muench, ACUA.

119. Wienken's title was Director of the Commissariat of the Fulda Bishops Conference.

120. Schäfer, *Staat und katholische Kirche in der DDR,* 74–75. After the death of Bishop Preysing, the Vatican allowed Wienken and the other bishops in the Communist sector to pursue the modus vivendi— a "live and let live" approach to life under Communist rule.

121. Muench was the Apostolic Visitor, later the regent, in zonal Germany before becoming nuncio in 1951.

122. Entry for July 12, 1946, Muench Diary I, June 19, 1946, to October 23, 1946, Papers of Cardinal Aloisius Muench, ACUA.

123. Entry for February 18, 1947, Muench Diary II, October 24, 1946, to April

9, 1947, Papers of Cardinal Aloisius Muench, ACUA. Probably close to the pope's exact words.

124. Entry for October 13, 1948, Muench Diary VI, October 9, 1948, to May 16, 1949, Papers of Cardinal Aloisius Muench, ACUA.

125. Entry for October 25, 1949, Muench Diary VIII, October 16, 1949, to November 29, 1949, Papers of Cardinal Aloisius Muench, ACUA.

126. Entry between July 12 and July 25, 1946, Muench Diary I, June 19, 1946, to October 23, 1946, Papers of Cardinal Aloisius Muench, ACUA.

127. Entry for February 28, 1947, Muench Diary II, October 24, 1946, to April 9, 1947, Papers of Cardinal Aloisius Muench, ACUA.

128. Josef Frings, bishop of Cologne, was also made a cardinal in 1946, as Cologne was traditionally awarded a cardinal.

129. Werner Blessing, "Deutschland in Not, wir in Glauben. Kirche und Kirchenvolk in einer katholischen Region 1933–1949," in *Von Stalingrad zur Währungsreform,* ed. Martin Broszat, Klaus-Dietmar Henke, and Hans Woller (Munich: R. Oldenbourg, 1988), 68.

130. "Pope Pressures Germans," *New York Times,* November 20, 1945, 5.

131. Record of conversation with President Hoover, February 14, 1947, Muench Diary II, October 24, 1946 to April 9, 1947, Papers of Cardinal Aloisius Muench, ACUA.

132. Gowen to Secretary of State James F. Byrnes, Vatican, January 9, 1946, Entry 1068, Box 13, RG 59, location 250/48/29/01-05, NARA.

133. For a very coherent analysis of these forces, see Frank M. Buscher, *The U.S. War Crimes Trial Program in Germany, 1946–1945* (New York: Greenwood Press, 1989).

134. James Dunn to Secretary of State George Marshall, October 29, 1948; Box 30, Entry 1071, RG 59, location 250/48/29/05, NARA.

135. Buscher, *The U. S. War Crimes Trial Program in Germany,* 94.

136. Phayer, *The Catholic Church and the Holocaust,* 163.

137. Quoted in Suzanne Brown-Fleming, *The Holocaust and the Catholic Conscience* (Notre Dame, Ind.: University of Notre Dame Press, 2005), 80–81.

138. Dunn to Secretary of State Marshall, October 29, 1948.

139. Brown-Fleming, *The Holocaust and the Catholic Conscience,* 82.

140. Ibid., 83–84.

141. Ibid., 93. See also Phayer, *The Catholic Church and the Holocaust,* 142.

142. See chapters 7 and 11.

143. Brown-Fleming, *The Holocaust and the Catholic Conscience,* 98.

144. Ibid., 90.

145. J. Graham Parsons, Vatican City, to Secretary of State George Marshall, March 10, 1948, Entry 1068, Box 20, RG 59, location 250/48/2901-05, NARA.

146. Buscher, *The U. S. War Crimes Trial Program in Germany,* 176.

147. Clemens August Graf von Galen, *Rechtsbewusstsein und Rechtsunsicherheit* (Rome, 1946), printed as a manuscript. It was undoubtedly printed in Italy because Allied authorities would have suppressed it in zonal Germany.

148. Buscher, *The U. S. War Crimes Trial Program in Germany,* 93.

149. Quoted in Brown-Fleming, *The Holocaust and the Catholic Conscience,* 90. I assume that Muench meant the Landsberg prisoners who had been found guilty and sentenced at the Dachau army trials. On Neuhäusler, see Buscher, *The U.S. War Crimes Trial Program in Germany,* 93ff.

150. Buscher, *The U. S. War Crimes Trial Program in Germany*, 93.

151. Ibid., 71 and 85.

152. Ibid., chapter 6.

153. Brown-Fleming, *The Holocaust and the Catholic Conscience*, 94–98. See also Phayer, *The Catholic Church and the Holocaust*, 162–165.

154. Of the seventeen mobile killing squad members convicted at Dachau, fourteen were sentenced to death but five were later granted clemency; see Buscher, *The U. S. War Crimes Trial Program in Germany*, 177.

155. Ibid., 152–153.

156. Judt, *Postwar: A History of Europe since 1945*, 244.

157. OSS report on the Vatican's view of Eastern Europe, October 1945, Entry 210 Box 358, RG 226, location 250/64/28/04, NARA.

158. Secretary of State George Marshall to envoy, February 6, 1948, Entry 1073, Box 32, RG 59, location 250/48/29/05, NARA.

159. Kent, *The Lonely Cold War of Pope Pius XII*, 98.

160. Telegram sent to Washington and from there to Harold H. Tittmann, October 4, 1945, Entry 1071, Box 29, RG 59, location 250/48/29/05, NARA. The telegram's information originated with the Italian ambassador to Poland, Reale.

161. OSS report 187, Entry 210, Box 236, RG 226, location 250/64/26/01, NARA.

162. Translation of an article in *L'Osservatore Romano* regarding the Polish concordat, September 26, 1945, Entry 1069, Box 28, RG 59, location 250/48/29/05, NARA. Tittmann sent the translation to the State Department.

163. Telegram from Harold H. Tittmann, October 4, 1945, Entry 1071, Box 29, RG 59, location 250/48/29/05, NARA.

164. Judt, *Postwar: A History of Europe since 1945*, 27.

165. Report from Prince Hubertus zu Loewenstein, Press Department of Caritas Bremen, dated 1947, 10/197/5, ACUA.

166. The Oder and the Neisse rivers formed the new boundary line between Germany and Poland.

167. Kent, *The Lonely Cold War of Pope Pius XII*, 123.

168. Ibid., 163.

169. See Phayer, *The Catholic Church and the Holocaust*, 180–181; and Kent, *The Lonely Cold War of Pope Pius XII*, 126–127 for details.

170. Bernstein to General J. T. McNarney, September 14, 1964, Entry 1069, Box 28, RG 59, NARA.

171. Kent, *The Lonely Cold War of Pope Pius XII*, 187–190.

172. Ibid., 205.

173. Myron C. Taylor to Secretary of State Edward Stettinius, March 21, 1945, Entry 1071, Box 29, RG 59, location 250/48/29/05, NARA.

174. Secretary of State James Byrnes to envoy, February 15, 1946, Entry 1073, Box 32, RG 59, location 250/48/29/05, NARA; Myron C. Taylor to Secretary of State James Byrnes, June 1946, Entry 1073, Box 32, RG 59, location 250/48/29/05, NARA.

175. The chapters that follow take up the subject of Vatican-sponsored assistance to fugitives.

176. Kent, *The Lonely Cold War of Pope Pius XII*, 128.

177. John Lewis Gaddis, *The United States and the End of the Cold War* (New York: Oxford University Press, 1992), 64.

178. Melvyn P. Leffler, *A Preponderance of Power* (Stanford, Calif.: Stanford University Press, 1992), 13.

179. For their complicity, see chapter 11.

180. Leffler, *A Preponderance of Power*, 20.

181. Judt, *Postwar: A History of Europe since 1945*, 103.

182. Ibid., 126–128.

183. Ibid., 128.

184. Gaddis, *The United States and the End of the Cold War*, 61.

185. Ibid., 62.

186. OSS report of March 7, 1945, Donovan microfilm A3304, Reel 5, Entry 180, RG 226, NARA.

187. Schäfer, *Staat und katholische Kirche in der DDR*, 247.

188. Judt, *Postwar: A History of Europe since 1945*, 585ff. Compare Gaddis, *The United States and the End of the Cold War*, 164; and Kent, *The Lonely Cold War of Pope Pius XII*, 261. For an opposite view, see Coppa, "Pope Pius XII and the Cold War," 63. On vast differences of opinion between Judt and Gaddis, see Judt's review of Gaddis's *The Cold War: A New History* in *The New York Review of Books* 53, no. 5 (March 2006): 11–15.

189. Judt, *Postwar: A History of Europe since 1945*, 590.

7. The Origin of the Vatican Ratlines

1. Peter Godman, *Hitler and the Vatican* (New York: Free Press, 2004), chapter 5, especially 50ff.

2. Kevin P. Spicer, *Resisting the Third Reich: The Catholic Clergy in Hitler's Berlin* (Dekalb, Ill.: Northern Illinois University Press, 2004), chapter 2.

3. Godman, *Hitler and the Vatican*, 104. The Holy Office is the Congregation for the Doctrine of the Faith.

4. Ibid., chapter 11, esp. 120–122. Hudal published *Deutsches Volk und christliches Abendland* in 1935 and *Die Grundlagen des Nationalsozialismus* in 1937.

5. Peter C. Kent, *The Lonely Cold War of Pope Pius XII: The Roman Catholic Church and the Division of Europe, 1943–1950* (Montreal: McGill-Queen's University Press, 2002), 144–145, points out that the Vatican did not initially favor Italian intervention in Spain.

6. See Michael Phayer, *The Catholic Church and the Holocaust* (Bloomington: Indiana University Press, 2000), 231n85.

7. Godman, *Hitler and the Vatican*, 131–132.

8. Gerhart Besier, zusammenarbeit mit Francesca Piombo, *Der Heilige Stuhl und Hitler-Deutschland. Die Faszination des Totalitären* (Munich: Verlagsgruppe Random House, 2004), 263.

9. For a brief account of the doomed encyclical, see Phayer, *The Catholic Church and the Holocaust*, 3–4; for a complete account, see the excellent study of Georges Passelecq and Bernard Suchecky, *L'encyclique cachée de Pie XI. Une occasion manquée de l'eglise face à antisemitismus* (Paris: La Découverte, 1995).

10. As quoted in Paul Damian O'Shea, "Confiteor. Eugenio Pacelli, the Catholic Church and the Jews. An Examination of the Responsibility of Pope Pius XII and the Holocaust, 1917–1943" (Ph.D. diss., Macquarie University, 2004), 237. Peter

Godman, while admitting Pius XI's emotional personality, does not think that *Humani Generis* would have been a sharp rebuke; see Godman, *Hitler and the Vatican*, 165–166. Most commentators are in agreement with Godman, but O'Shea's argument cannot be overlooked.

11. Hansjakob Stehle, *Geheimdiplomatie im Vatikan. Die Päpste und die Kommunisten* (Zurich: Benziger, 1993), 198.

12. J. G. Parsons, memo of a conversation with Maritain, July 15, 1947, Entry 1068, Box 15, RG 59, location 250/48/29/01-05, NARA.

13. As a graduate student at the University of Munich, I was able to meet Dr. Josef Müller. At that time, Holocaust studies did not exist and I was engaged in social history. Dr. Müller patiently answered whatever questions I put to him, thinking, no doubt, that they were completely inane. For my part, it was an opportunity of a lifetime, a lost opportunity of a lifetime.

14. Klemens von Klemperer, *German Resistance against Hitler: The Search for Allies Abroad, 1938–1945* (Oxford: Oxford University Press, 1992). 172.

15. David Alvarez and Robert A. Graham, S.J., *Nothing Sacred: Nazi Espionage against the Vatican* (London: F. Cass, 1997), 24ff.

16. Harold H. Tittmann, Jr., *Inside the Vatican of Pius XII: The Memoir of an American Diplomat during World War II*, ed. Harold H. Tittmann, III (New York: Palgrave, 2004), 37.

17. Ibid., 60–61.

18. Michael Phayer, "The Genocides of Polish Catholics and Polish Jews," *Kirchliche Zeitgeschichte* 15, no. 1(2002): 238–262. On the Vatican's exaggerations, see Susan Zuccotti, "*L'Osservatore Romano* and the Holocaust, 1930–1945," *Holocaust and Genocide Studies* 17, no. 2 (2003): 15–16.

19. Stehle, *Geheimdiplomatie im Vatikan,* 201.

20. Harold H. Tittmann to state, Vatican City, June 1942, Box 23, RG 84, location 350/68/25/02, NARA.

21. In his memo to state, Tittmann reported that Francis Osborne believed that Pius was preparing the ground for a peace initiative; Harold H. Tittmann, Vatican City, to state, July 11, 1942, Box 23, RG 84, location 350/68/25/02, NARA.

22. Uki Goñi, *The Real Odessa: Smuggling the Nazis to Perón's Argentina* (London: Granta, 2002), chapter 1, "War Games."

23. See the pope's speech in *Catholic Mind*: "The Social Question in the New Order," 39, no. 923 (June 8, 1941): 1–16.

24. Ambassador Llobet to Ruiz Guiñazú, October 6, 1942, Guerra Europea, File 1, vol. 4, Cable 1272, Archives of the Foreign Minister of Argentina. I am indebted to Uki Goñi for forwarding the contents of the cable to me.

25. OSS report, December 23, 1942, Reel 6, Italy—Vatican City, RG 226, location 190/10/12/06, NARA.

26. Goñi, *The Real Odessa*, chapter 2, "Perón Leaps to Power."

27. OSS intercept of Argentine correspondence, April 7, 1943, Entry 210, Box 419, RG 226, location 250/64/29/06, NARA. The Vatican disapproved, of course, of Catholic Chile's relations with the Soviet Union; see the OSS report of January 10, 1945, Entry 134, Box 219, File 1372, RG 226, location 190/7/32/2, NARA.

28. Papal Nuncio, La Paz, to Vatican Secretariat of State, January 30, 1942, Entry 16, File 12103, Reel 39, RG 226, NARA.

29. Goñi, *The Real Odessa,* 13.

30. Signed statement of Schellenberg, February 7, 1946, Entry 1088, Box 25, RG 226, location 250/48/30/07, NARA.

31. R. Henry Norweb, Lisbon, to state, January 28, 1944, Box 92, File 851, RG 84, location 350/68/17/7, NARA. W. Butterworth of the U.S. embassy in Madrid sent a copy of Franco's speech of May 13, 1944, which expressed the "two wars" notion, to the U.S. State Department; see Entry 3162 Box 38, File 800, RG 84, location 350/67/27/01, NARA. See also Goñi, *The Real Odessa,* chapter 7, "Cardinal Recommendations."

32. OSS report, Entry 210, Box 236, RG 226, location 250/64/26/01, NARA.

33. Intelligence report on the Falange, 3 Entry 451B, Box 16, File 4, RG 59, location 250/46/9, NARA.

34. Bernard Baruch, Lisbon, to U.S. State Department, August 13, 1945, Box 6, Class #112, File #01-237, RG 65, location 230/86/17/4, NARA.

35. OSS report, October 1944, Entry 451B, Box 16, RG 59, location 250/46/9/3, NARA.

36. Earl Brennan, Chief, Italian Section Office of Special Investigation, report on all intelligence for Italy/Albania by Office of Special Investigation, September 1945, Entry 210 Box 319, RG 226, location 250/62/28/02, NARA.

37. Caffery to U.S. State Department, May 8, 1945, Entry 1069, Box 28, RG 59, location 250/48/29/5, NARA.

38. Madrid, August 22, 1944, Entry 3162, Box 37, File 711, RG 84, location 350/67/27/04, NARA.

39. For more on Lesca and Daye, see Goñi, *The Real Odessa,* chapter 6, "The Nazi Escape Begins."

40. Ibid., 93.

41. Ibid., 96.

42. OSS report on the Miranda de Ebro POW camp, Entry 210, Box 35, RG 226, location 250/64/21/06 NARA.

43. "Neutrals Warned on Asylum Access," *New York Times,* August 1, 1943, 12.

44. E. L. Padberg, Legal Attaché, U.S. Embassy, Portugal, to J. J. Wagner, Lisbon, April 10, 1946, Box 4080, RG 59, location 250/36/29/02, NARA.

45. James F. Byrnes to Robert Murphy, January 2, 1946, in U.S. State Department, *Foreign Relations of the United States 1946* (Washington, D.C.: U.S. Government Printing Office, 1969), 5:794.

46. Ambassador, the Argentine embassy, Rome, June 13, 1946, to Juan A. Bramuglia, Minister for Exterior Relations, AMRECIC Political Division, Holy See 2/1946, National Archives, Argentina.

47. Michael Marrus, *The Unwanted: European Refugees in the Twentieth Century* (New York: Oxford University Press, 1985), 323.

48. Report of Monsignor O'Grady, July 1, 1947, 10/37/8, ACUA.

49. Ibid.

50. Comparative budget statement of War Relief Services-NCWC for February 1, 1948–January 31, 1949, 10/3/5, Records of the National Catholic Welfare Council, ACUA. (Hereafter NCWC Records.) Other contributions for emigration are to be found among the NCWC Records, but I found no cumulative record.

51. Pius XII to John T. McNicholas, archbishop of Cincinnati and chairman of the NCWC, December 24, 1948, 10/37/6, ACUA.

52. File papers in 10/37/14, ACUA.

53. File notes pertaining to the setting up of the National Catholic Resettlement Council, December 1947, 10/37/10, ACUA.

54. See below, chapters 9 and 10.

55. Report of Captain Henry R. Nigrelli, June 5, 1946, Entry 212, Box 5, RG 226, location 250/64/33/5, NARA. Nigrelli's source was a person whom Father Torrazza had contacted to participate in the program.

56. Ibid.

57. Interdivisional Area Committee on Latin America, November 13, 1944, Entry 451B, Box 9, RG 59, location 250/46/9/3, NARA.

58. On the anticommunism of the American Church, see especially Kent, *The Lonely Cold War of Pope Pius XII*, 55 and passim.

59. Address by Rt. Rev. John J. O'Grady, executive secretary, NCWC, January 10, 1948, 10/37/10, ACUA.

60. Nigrelli report, June 5, 1946, Entry 212, Box 5, RG 226, NARA.

61. Ibid.

62. Intelligence report, Entry 210, Box 35, RG 226, location 250/64/21/06, NARA.

63. W. Bonsal, charge d'affaires, American embassy, Madrid, Barcelona, November 21, 1946, to Richard Ford, American consul general, copies to U.S. State Department, Entry 127, Box 8, File 74, RG 226, location 190/7/21/1, NARA.

64. Vincent La Vista to Herbert J. Cummings, filed May 15, 1947, Box 4080, RG 59, location 250/36/29/02, NARA.

65. J. Graham Parsons, Vatican City, to Walter "Red" Dowling, August 13, 1947, Box 4080, RG 59, location 250/36/29/02, NARA.

66. See chapter 11.

67. OSS report, Madrid, to state, May 29, 1947, Entry 127, Box 8, File 74, RG 226, location 190/7/21/1, NARA.

68. Ibid.

69. See chapter 8. There is no record of a meeting between Hudal and Boos, however.

70. OSS intelligence report of January 29, 1947, Entry 127, Box 8, File 74, RG 226, location 190/7/21/1, NARA.

71. OSS report of May 29, 1947, Entry 127, Box 8, File 74, RG 226, location 190/7/21/1, NARA.

72. OSS report of February 17, 1947, Entry 127, Box 8, File 74, RG 226, location 190/7/21/1, NARA.

73. OSS report of February 13, 1947, Entry 210, Box 35, RG 226, location 250/64/21/06, NARA.

74. OSS report of February 3, 1947, Entry 210, Box 35, RG 226, location 250/64/21/06, NARA.

75. Ibid.

76. Embassy report of February 13, 1947, Entry 127, Box 8, RG 226, File 74, location 190/7/21/1, NARA.

77. Monsignor Montini's letter to Father Karl Sauer is mentioned by W. O. Taites of the Madrid Embassy in a communication to Mr. Culbertson. See Entry 127, Box 8, File 74, RG 226, location 190/7/21/1, NARA.

78. Circular letter no. 5 to all American consular offices in Spain, Madrid, February 3, 1948, Entry 210, Box 35, RG 226, location 250/64/21/06, NARA.

79. Ibid.

80. Ibid.

81. W. O. Taitus to Mr. Culbertson, March 4, 1948, Entry 127, Box 8, File 74, RG 226, location 190/7/21/1, NARA.

82. John Moors Cabot, Belgrade, to U.S. State Department, June 11, 1947, Box 3623, RG 59, location 250/36/19/6, NARA. In his memo, Cabot says that the United States was involved in the Vatican-Argentine ratline, a fact he deplored. This is in fact the case. We will deal with the Cabot memo in detail in the chapter 11 below on Krunoslav Draganović.

83. See the obituary of Bingham in the *Washington Post*, May 25, 2006, A27.

8. Bishop Hudal's Ratline

1. Alois C. Hudal, *Römische Tagebücher. Lebensbeicht eines alten Bischofs* (Graz, 1976), 21.

2. Ibid., 298.

3. Ibid., 294–295. One hardly knows whether or not to believe Hudal's story about the misaddressed envelope, although the bishop repeated it twice in his memoir.

4. OSS interviews of August 24, 1944; June 24, 1944; and September 18, 1944, Entry 210, Box 259, RG 226, location 250/64/25/04, NARA.

5. Entry 210, Box 236, File 4, RG 226, location 250/64/26/01, NARA. The report, unfortunately, does not give a date for the visit to the seminary, but it is clear from the context that it took place sometime in the early fall of 1944.

6. OSS account of the first meeting of the Austrians in Rome, July 2, 1944, Entry 210, Box 259, RG 226, location 250/64/25/04, NARA.

7. Ibid.

8. Ibid.

9. Report of Oliver Rockhill and Lt. Frederic Burkhardt, Rome, June 10 and 20, 1944, Entry 210, Box 259, RG 226, location 250/64/25/04, NARA.

10. RG 226 Entry 210, Box 236, location 250/64/26/01, NARA.

11. OSS reports of June and September 1944 provide the links to the Vatican and Argentina; see Entry 210, Box 259, RG 226, location 250/64/25/04, NARA.

12. Hudal, *Römische Tagebücher*, 201.

13. La Vista report, May 15, 1947, Box 4080, RG 59, location 250/36/29/02, NARA.

14. Uki Goñi, *The Real Odessa: Smuggling the Nazis to Perón's Argentina* (London: Granta, 2002), 249.

15. Gitta Sereny, *Into That Darkness* (New York: Simon and Schuster, 1983), 315.

16. Goñi, *The Real Odessa*, 230–231. CEANA stands for Comisión de Esclarecimiento de Actividades Nazis en la Argentina, a commission set up by the government to investigate Argentina's ties to war criminals in 1997.

17. Juan Maler, *Frieden, Krieg, und "Frieden"* (printed in Europe: self published, 1987), 321ff.

18. Ibid., 322.

19. Ibid., 326.

20. Goñi, *The Real Odessa*, 231.

21. Maler, *Frieden, Krieg, und "Frieden,"* 327.

22. Ibid., 328.

23. The source for this information is the Hudal archive at the Santa Maria dell'Anima in Rome. CEANA was given permission to research the Hudal papers. See Goñi, *The Real Odessa*, chapter 10, "Criminal Ways." The information, valuable as it is, is nevertheless incomplete. CEANA used the services of Professor Matteo Sanfilippo, an Argentine teaching at an Italian university, to do the research of the Hudal papers. Uki Goñi suspects, with reason, that Sanfilippo could not have exhausted the material in the archive since he is not a specialist in the questions posed by postwar emigration and the ratline. I learned of Sanfilippo's limitations from Goñi, with whom I corresponded on January 13, 2005.

24. Francis Kalnay, Chief X-2 branch, report on the Austrians in Rome, September 26, 1944, Entry 210, Box 259, location 250/64/25/04, RG 226.

25. Goñi, *The Real Odessa*, 284–285.

26. Ibid., chapter 10.

27. Sereny, *Into That Darkness*, 289.

28. Goñi, unpublished portions of chapter 16, "A Roman Sanctuary," of *Into That Darkness*.

29. Hansjakob Stehle, *Geheimdiplomatie im Vatikan. Die Päpste und die Kommunisten* (Zurich: Benzig, 1993). 198.

30. Goñi, *The Real Odessa*, 328, based on records found by Seanna.

31. Hudal, *Römische Tagebücher.*

32. Stehle, *Geheimdiplomatie im Vatikan*, 203.

9. Looted Gold and the Vatican

1. Office of Military Government U.S. financial records, file on Yugoslavian gold, Box 442, RG 226, location 390/35/13/7, NARA.

2. Briefs of the plaintiff's lawyers in *Emil Alperin, et al. v. the Instituto per le Opere di Religione* [Institute of Religious Works, aka the Vatican Bank] *and the Order of the Friars Minor,* Case 3:99-cr-o4941-MMC, Document 262, filed 02/14/06 at U.S. District Court, Northern District of California. This case is hereafter referred to as *Alperin v. Vatican Bank.*

3. Ibid.

4. Stuart Eizenstat, *U.S. and Allied Wartime and Postwar Relations and Negotiations with Argentina, Portugal, Spain, Sweden, and Turkey on Looted Gold and German External Assets and U.S. Concerns about the Fate of the Wartime Ustasha Treasury* (Washington, D.C.: n.p., 1998). William Slany, assisted by a team of researchers, wrote the report, which was published in house in the State Department under the name of Eizenstat, who was undersecretary of state for economic, business, and agricultural affairs in 1998. In a briefing, Eizenstat said that the State Department had asked the Vatican to open its records. Vatican officials, Eizenstat said, were "open in their discussions with him" but that they lacked the personnel to produce the bank data.

5. Bigelow, n.p., to Glasser, July 19, 1946, Entry 183, Box 27, RG 226, location 190/9/22/05, NARA. This gold has nothing to do with the gold that Bigelow later reported going to Rome.

6. *Alperin v. Vatican Bank,* document 262, 24–25.

7. Eizenstat, *U.S. and Allied Wartime and Postwar Relations and Negotiations.* The quote in the paragraph is from page x of the preliminary report.

8. U.S. Strategic Services Unit report of James Angelton, January 22, 1946, Entry 210, Box 6, RG 226, location 250/64/28/02, NARA. Agent Angelton would later become the victim of a hoax which led him to file fraudulent reports. These concerned internal Vatican affairs and only those. There is no reason to doubt the authenticity of Angelton's other reports in general and of this one in particular.

9. Goñi, *The Real Odessa,* see the afterword; source for the information is Foreign Office 371/67398 R2394 and Foreign Office 371/67376 R5965, Public Record Office, National Archives, London (hereafter PRO).

10. National Bank of Yugoslavia, Belgrade, to the Tripartite Commission for Restitution of Monetary Funds [*sic*], September 29, 1947, Entry 2113L, Box 7, RG 84, location 350/49/265/7, NARA.

11. See Brey's report based on records of the Precious Metals Department and the Reichsbank, October 9, 1947, Office of Military Government, U.S. Finance Division, Box 442, RG 226, location 390/35/13/7, NARA.

12. Department of State, Office of Financial Operations, Records Relating to the Tripartite Commission for the Restitution of Monetary Gold, Entry 1068, Box 14, File 840.4; and NN3-59-96-59, Lot 62DD115, Box 13, RG 59, location 250/48/29/30, NARA.

13. Source for the quote is NN3-59-96-59, Lot 62DD115, Box 13, RG 59, location 250/48/29/30, NARA.

14. Ron Neitzke, Office of the Historian, Department of State, "Ustasha Gold: Sources, Amount, and Disposition. U.S. and Allied Wartime and Postwar Relations and Negotiations With Argentina, Portugal, Spain, Sweden and Turkey on Looted Gold and German External Assets and U.S. Concerns About the Fate of the Wartime Ustasha Treasury," unpublished paper in author's possession, April 1999, 2. Neitzke relied on the Croatian publication by Zlato I. Novac, *Nezavisne Drzave Hrvatske izneseni u inozemstvo 1944 i 1945* (Gold and Money of the Independent State of Croatia Moved Abroad 1944 and 1945) (Zagreb: Croatian Historical Institute, 1997).

15. Neitzke, "Ustasha Gold," 4–6.

16. For a different account of how the Ustaša secured the gold and then divided it, see Goñi, *The Real Odessa,* 209. Goñi's source in endnote 347 is to Box 107, File ZF010183 IRR case files, Impersonal Files, RG 319, location 270/84/22/03, NARA, which holds no pertinent data on the Ustaša gold question. His other reference is to John Loftus and Mark Aarons, *Unholy Trinity: How the Vatican's Nazi Networks Betrayed Western Intelligence to the Soviets* (New York: St. Martin's Press, 1997), no page cited. *Unholy Trinity* is not a reliable account in many instances. Goñi's account and mine agree about the detail that Draganović took two boxes of gold to Rome.

17. Neitzke, "Ustasha Gold," 3.

18. Brief of the defendant's lawyers in *Alperin v. Vatican Bank,* document 272-1, filed 02/20/06 at U.S. District Court, Northern District of California.

19. In Chicago, Mandić founded the Croatian Publishing House and the Croatian Historical Institute with funds that originated with the looted Ustaša treasury.

20. *Alperin v. Vatican Bank,* document 272-1, 4, 34, and 45.

21. Ibid., 47.

22. Ibid., 4.

23. Ibid., 11–12.

24. Ibid., 18.
25. Ibid., 32.

10. Ante Pavelić

1. Office of Secret Service report, May 11, 1945, Entry 21, L series, Box 443, File 56469, RG 226, location 190/4/32/7, NARA.

2. When American intelligence agents became intensely active in their search for Pavelić in 1947, they attempted from time to time to piece together where he had been prior to his arrival in Rome. The reports vary in their particulars, although all agree that the dictator's flight took him to Austria. One intelligence report said that Pavelić had been arrested by the British, who planned to return him to Yugoslavia to stand trial and recommended that the case be closed! See U.S. Army Counter Intelligence Corps report, August 25, 1945, Box 173, File IRR XE001109 Pavelic, RG 319, location 270/84/1/4, NARA, College Park, Maryland.

3. For an excellent distillation of Vatican policy in Eastern Europe, including Yugoslavia, see Peter C. Kent, *The Lonely Cold War of Pope Pius XII* (Montreal: McGill-Queen's University Press, 2002).

4. Uki Goñi, *The Real Odessa: Smuggling the Nazis to Peron's Argentina* (London: Granta, 2002), 327ff.

5. Lt. Col. G. F. Blunda, Headquarters, Mediterranean Theater of Operations, to Col. Carl Fritzsche, Assistant Deputy Director of Intelligence, November 8, 1947, Box 173, File IRR XE001109 Pavelić, RG 319, location 270/84/1/4, NARA.

6. Ibid.

7. William Gowen graciously permitted me to interview him in 1999 in New York. Subsequently, we corresponded on several occasions regarding the Ustaša fascists in Rome. During the interview, former agent Gowen adamantly refused to discuss any connection between him and his father with reference to either the Pavelić case in particular or the Ustaša in general.

8. Box 173, File IRR XE001109 Pavelić, RG 319, location 270/84/1/4, NARA. This box is the principal source on Pavelić. Many documents in it are anonymous U.S. intelligence reports.

9. Ibid.

10. Agents William Gowen and Louis Caniglia, Counter Intelligence Corps Rome, August 29, 1947, sent presumably to their commanding officer, Box 173, File IRR XE001109 Pavelić, RG 319, location 270/84/1/4, NARA.

11. Cardinal Eugène Tisserant, interview with Vladimir Stakic, April 7, 1946, Entry 1069, Box 28, File marked 1947, RG 59, NARA.

12. Ibid.

13. The source for Goñi's assertion in *The Real Odessa*, 99, is Tisserant's letter, which he found in the archives of the Argentine embassy, Rome.

14. Intercepted letter from Antonio E. Vucetich, El Socorro, Argentina, to Olga Vucetich-Radic, May 6, 1947, Entry 1068, Box 17, Folder marked "Political General 1947," RG 59, location 250/48/29/01-05, NARA.

15. Gowen and Caniglia to their commanding officer, August 29, 1947.

16. File papers note Franklin Gowen's action; see Entry 1073, Box 32, RG 59, location 250/48/29/05, NARA.

17. Blunda to Fritzsche, November 8, 1947.

18. Ibid.

19. F. Gowen to Secretary of State James Byrnes, October 14, 1946, Entry 1071, Box 30, RG 59, location 250/48/29/05, NARA.

20. Jacques Maritain was also frequently with this clique, but it is unthinkable that as France's ambassador to the Holy See he would countenance talk of giving Pavelić his freedom. That is because a French court of justice had condemned Pavelić to death. Evidently, when Maritain was present, the Pavelić situation was not brought up.

21. Dianne Kirby, "Harry Truman's Religious Legacy: The Holy Alliance, Containment, and the Cold War," in *Religion and the Cold War*, ed. Dianne Kirby (New York: Palgrave, 2003), 79.

22. Goñi, *The Real Odessa*, 329ff. For more detail, see chapter 11.

23. Memorandum of William Gowen, Special Counter Intelligence Corps Agent, to Counter Intelligence Corps [Headquarters] Rome, September 12, 1947, Box 173, File IRR XE001109 Pavelić, RG 319, location 270/84/1/4, NARA.

24. Ibid.

25. Ibid.

26. Gowen and Caniglia to their commanding officer, August 29, 1947.

27. Gowen to Counter Intelligence Corps [Headquarters] Rome, September 12, 1947.

28. Bernard J. Grennan, Special Counter Intelligence Corps Agent, Mediterranean Theater Chief of Operations, to Supervising Counter Intelligence Corps Agent of Zone 5, undated memorandum, Box 173, File IRR XE001109 Pavelić, RG 319, location 270/84/1/4, NARA.

29. Linda Hunt, *Secret Agenda: The United States Government, Nazi Scientists, and Project Paperclip, 1945–1980* (New York: St. Martin's Press, 1991), 125.

30. Richard Breitman, Norman J. W. Goda, Timothy Naftali, and Robert Wolfe, eds., *U.S. Intelligence and the Nazis* (Washington, D.C.: National Archives Trust Fund Board for the Nazi War Crimes and Japanese Imperial Government Records Interagency Working Groups, 2004), 7.

31. Blunda to Fritzsche, November 8, 1947.

32. Myron C. Taylor, memorandum to James Dunn, April 14, 1948, Entry 1068, Box 21, RG 59, location 250/48/2901-05, NARA.

33. Ambassador John Moors Cabot, Belgrade, to Secretary of State George Marshall, June 25, 1947, Box 3623, RG 59, location 250/36/19/6, NARA.

34. Ibid.

35. Goñi, *The Real Odessa*, 223–224, gives the particulars of Pavelić's flight.

11. The Biggest Ratline

1. Uki Goñi, *The Real Odessa: Smuggling the Nazis to Perón's Argentina* (London: Granta, 2002), Afterword.

2. U.S. Army Counter Intelligence Corps report on Draganović, February 12, 1947, Entry A1-86, Box 12, RG 262, NARA.

3. Norman J. W. Goda, "The Ustaša: Murder and Espionage," in *U.S. Intelligence and the Nazis,* ed. Richard Breitman, Norman J. W. Goda, Timothy Naftali, and Robert Wolfe (Washington, D. C.: National Archives Trust Fund Board for the

Nazi War Crimes and Japanese Imperial Government Records Interagency Working Groups, 2004), 211.

4. Ibid.

5. Goñi, *The Real Odessa,* 203–204.

6. Intelligence report, May 10, 1945, Entry A1-86, Box 12, RG 262 NARA. This box contains a collection of memos compiled by CIA forerunners.

7. U.S. Army Counter Intelligence Corps report on Draganović, February 12, 1947.

8. U.S. Strategic Services Unit dispatch of June 22, 1946, signed by Agent Angelton, Entry 210, Box 457, RG 226, location 250/64/30/04, NARA.

9. Goda, "The Ustaša: Murder and Espionage," 206–208.

10. U.S. intelligence report, n.d., n.p., Entry 211, Box 48, RG 226, location 250/64/33/4, NARA.

11. Ibid.

12. Report of Joseph N. Greene, political advisor, Trieste, to Alexander C. Kirk, political advisor, U.S. embassy in Rome, April 22, 1946, Entry 2799, Box 109, RG 84, location 350/62/10/3, NARA.

13. Intelligence reports of February and October 1946, Entry A1-86, Box 12, RG 262, NARA.

14. The Bigelow report, discussed above, suggests that the gold reached the Vatican but does not say that Pečnikar delivered it there.

15. Greene to Kirk, April 22, 1946, Entry 2799, Box 109, RG 84, location 350/62/10/3, NARA.

16. Goñi, *The Real Odessa,* 214–219.

17. Report of Special Agent Robert C. Mudd, September 5, 1947, Entry 134B, RG 319, NARA.

18. Report of Special Agent Robert C. Mudd, n.d., n.p. Entry A1-86, Box 12, RG 262, NARA.

19. Ibid.

20. Ibid. See Goda, "The Ustaša: Murder and Espionage," 212, for a more detailed account of Agent Mudd's activity. Goda notes that the CIA was unable to penetrate Draganović's operation sufficiently to identify all of the war criminals who escaped to Argentina. Through his work with Argentine documents, Uki Goñi has filled in this gap in the record.

21. John Moors Cabot to U.S. State Department, June 11, 1947, Box 3623, RG 59, location 250/36/19/6, NARA.

22. La Vista's first report on the Vatican ratlines came in May 1947 and did not seem to elicit much response from state. Cabot filed his report in June. La Vista then filed a second report to the department of state in July, which jolted department officials to action.

23. Cabot to State Department, June 11, 1947.

24. England was in charge of postwar matters relating to Yugoslavia; hence, Ustaša war criminals were its responsibility.

25. Cabot to State Department, June 11, 1947.

26. The first writers to exploit the La Vista report were John Loftus and Mark Aarons in *Unholy Trinity,* in 1992. Only Loftus had access to the La Vista papers. Their book was shocking to say the least, especially the disclosure that Dr. Nix was a double agent. But because no one could verify their account and because of the authors' exaggerations and sensationalism, their work found a mostly general, not

scholarly, audience. A number of years passed before the La Vista papers became available for general use at the National Archives and Records Administration in College Park. It is now evident that beneath their sensational account, Loftus and Aaron told a tale that was mostly accurate.

27. La Vista, report titled "Illegal Emigration Movements in and through Italy" to Herbert J. Cummings, July 14, 1947, Box 4080, RG 59, location 250/36/29/2, NARA. The May 15 memo, also to Cummings, carries the same title and is also located in Box 4080, RG 59, location 250/36/29/02, NARA.

28. In one account (La Vista to Cummings, July 14, 1947), La Vista put the number at sixteen agencies, but in the other account (La Vista to Cummings, May 15, 1947), he said it was twenty-two. Monsignor Baldelli is identified in a memo of J. Graham Parsons, May 12, 1948 (presumably to the State Department, regarding the La Vista investigation), Entry 1068 or 1069, Box 22, RG 59, location 250/48/29/05, NARA.

29. Parsons to State Department[?], May 12, 1948.

30. Ibid.

31. Gitta Sereny, *Into That Darkness* (New York: Simon and Schuster, 1983), 310–315.

32. La Vista to Cummings, July 14, 1947 and May 15, 1947.

33. Sereny, *Into That Darkness*, 320.

34. OSS report on the German group in Rome, July 12, 1944, Entry 210, Box 217, RG 226, location 250/64/25/04, NARA.

35. La Vista to Cummings, July 14, 1947 and May 15, 1947.

36. Ibid.

37. Ibid.

38. U.S. State Department, Washington, D. C., to J. Graham Parsons, July 28, 1947, Entry 1068, Box 17, Folder marked "Political General 1947," RG 59, location 250/48/29/01-05, NARA.

39. J. Graham Parsons, Vatican City, to Walter Red Dowling, August 13, 1947, Box 4080, RG 59, location 250/36/29/02, NARA.

40. Actually, the Free German Committee.

41. Parsons to Dowling, August 13, 1947. "Ungareal" is the Latin for Hungary, the native country of Father Gallov. In this document, Parsons was actually retrieving information from a document that could have been written as early as December 1946. Parson's document, like the earlier of the two La Vista reports, floated around State Department offices without triggering a response.

42. Ibid.

43. The airgram is missing from boxes 31–32 of Entry 1072, RG 59, location 250/48/29/6, NARA, which is where it should be. I have not found any response from Parsons to state giving the results of his discussion of Draganović's work with Vatican officials.

44. U.S. State Department, outgoing airgram A-392, July 25, 1947, to embassy, Rome, Box 4072, Central Files 1945–49, 800.012817-2547 top secret, RG 59, location 250/36/29/1, NARA.

45. The General Accounting Office reported to Congress that "the fear that was generated by General Clay's March 1948 'war is imminent' telegram was due in large part to the lack of intelligence the U.S. had on Soviet intentions"; see Comptroller General of the United States, *Nazis and Axis Collaborators Were Used to Further*

U.S. Anti-Communist Objectives in Europe—Some Immigrated to the U.S. (Washington, D.C.: General Accounting Office, 1985). It seems likely that intelligence was collected but was not passed on to the executive branch of government, as it should have been.

46. After the publication of the first edition of *The Real Odessa,* the well-known British Catholic journal *The Tablet* praised Goñi's work but felt that he had exaggerated the Vatican's connection to Draganović's ratline. This criticism spurred Goñi to return to the British archives and painstakingly work through them to find the essential links. See Goñi, *The Real Odessa,* 326.

47. Sereny, *Into That Darkness,* 315ff.

48. Goñi, *The Real Odessa,* 329, based on WO 204/11333, folios 51 and 51D, PRO.

49. On Nedić, see Christopher R. Browning with Jürgen Matthäus, *The Origins of the Final Solution: The Evolution of Nazi Jewish Policy, September 1939–March 1942* (Lincoln: University of Nebraska Press, 2004), 336–337. Serbia's Jews were murdered by an Austrian regiment serving in Hitler's army; see Walter Manoschek, *Serbien ist Judenfrei* (Munich: Oldenburg, 1993).

50. Goñi, *The Real Odessa,* 331.

51. Ibid., based on Foreign Office 371/67371 R1769, PRO.

52. The Vatican appeal may be found in Foreign Office 371/67376 R6058, PRO. The British rejection of the appeal is found in WO 204/11133. There is a misprint in Goñi, *The Real Odessa,* 336, where the final "3" is omitted from 11133.

53. Goñi, *The Real Odessa,* 339.

54. See Goda, "The Ustaša: Murder and Espionage," 216. Draganović's storied career took several more intriguing twists. According to a CIA report, his eventual kidnapping by Yugoslav agents was actually set up by the Vatican; see Goda, 216ff.

55. Sereny, *Into That Darkness,* 309.

56. Goda, "The Ustaša: Murder and Espionage," 211.

57. Goñi, *The Real Odessa,* 213–214.

58. Ibid., 235.

59. Sereny, *Into That Darkness,* 309.

60. Goñi, *The Real Odessa,* 214. In the final chapter of the second edition of *The Real Odessa,* Goñi identifies many Ustaša war criminals by name.

61. General secretary of NCWC to Monsignor Patrick A. O'Boyle of WRS of the NCWC, March 15, 1946, 10/36/34, NCWC Records, ACUA.

62. John F. Cronin, S.S., to Monsignor Carroll, November 13, 1946, NCWC interoffice memo, 10/36/35, NCWC Records, ACUA.

63. Apostolic Delegate to the United States Cicognani to Francis Cardinal Spellman, October 23, 1946, 10/36/35, NCWC Records, ACUA.

64. See the Web site of the St. Jerome Croatian Catholic Church of Chicago at www.stjeromecroatian.org.

65. NCWC bishops' war emergency and relief fund statement of disbursements from October 16, 1949 to April 15, 1950, 10/3/6, NCWC Records, ACUA.

66. Michael R. Marrus, *The Nuremberg War Crimes Trial, 1945–1946: A Documentary History* (Boston: Bedford Books, 1997), 23–24.

67. Comptroller General, *Nazis and Axis Collaborators,* chapter 2.

68. Ibid., 23.

69. This exchange was extracted from a document by national archives archivist

Greg Bradsher in his compilation of NARA records: "Holocaust-Era Assets: A Finding Aid to Records at the National Archives at College Park," National Archives and Records Administration, 1999.

70. Lt. Col. G. F. Blunda, Headquarters, Mediterranean Theater of Operations, to Col. Carl Fritzsche, Assistant Deputy Director of Intelligence, November 8, 1947, Box 173, File IRR XE001109 Pavelić, RG 319, location 270/84/1/4, NARA.

71. U.S. Strategic Services Unit report, Rome, February 28, 1946, Entry 210, Box 457, RG 226, location 20/64/30/04, NARA.

72. Comptroller General, *Nazis and Axis Collaborators*, 12.

73. David McCullough, *Truman* (New York: Simon and Schuster, 1992), 582.

74. Comptroller General, *Nazis and Axis Collaborators*, chapter 2.

75. Linda Hunt, *Secret Agenda: The United States Government, Nazi Scientists, and Project Paperclip, 1945–1980* (New York: St. Martin's Press, 1991), 125 and 264.

76. Outgoing airgram from Secretary of State George Marshall, Washington, D.C., July 27, 1947, Box 3623, RG 59, location 250/36/19/6, NARA.

77. Counter Intelligence Corps report filed by Agent Robert Mudd, September 5, 1949, Dossier AA766849WJ, RG 319, NARA.

78. Norman J. W. Goda, "Manhunts: The Official Search for Notorious Nazis," in *U.S. Intelligence and the Nazis,* ed. Richard Breitman, Norman J. W. Goda, Timothy Naftali, and Robert Wolfe (Washington, D.C.: National Archives Trust Fund Board for the Nazi War Crimes and Japanese Imperial Government Records Interagency Working Groups, 2004), 426–430.

79. Ibid., 430.

80. Agents William Gowen and Louis Caniglia, Rome, memo for the officer in charge, August 29, 1947, Entry 134B, Box 173, RG 319, NARA.

12. An Obsession with Communism

1. Hansjakob Stehle, *Geheimdiplomatie im Vatikan. Die Päpste und die Kommunisten* (Zurich: Benziger, 1993), 205. Stehle's source for this is *ADSS*, 8:669, which does not indicate the pope's tearful reaction. Susan Zuccotti, *Under His Very Windows: The Vatican and the Holocaust in Italy* (New Haven, Conn.: Yale University Press, 2000), 105, also reports on Scavizzi but does not mention the pope's reaction.

2. Pius, Rome, to Preysing, April 30, 1943, V/16-4 Korrespondenz 1944–1945, Diocesan Archives, Berlin. This is a rather awkward sentence, written in German, which I have tried to translate as literally as possible while retaining the sense.

3. *Mystici Corporis Christi,* paragraph 6, available online at http://www.vatican.va/holy_father/pius_xii/encyclicals/documents/hf_p-xii_enc_29061943_mystici-corporis-christi_en.html.

4. John T. Pawlikowski, "The Vatican and the Holocaust: Unresolved Issues," in *Jewish-Christian Encounters over the Centuries: Symbiosis, Prejudice, Holocaust, Dialogue,* ed. Marvin Perry and F. M. Schweitzer (New York: P. Lang, 1994), 301.

5. Quoted in Michael Marrus, "To Whom Did They Belong? The Vatican and the Custody of Jewish Child Survivors after the Holocaust," *Holocaust and Genocide Studies,* in press.

6. Ibid.

7. Quoted in ibid.

8. Quoted in ibid.

9. Quoted in ibid.

10. Suzanne Brown-Fleming, *The Holocaust and Catholic Conscience: Cardinal Aloisius Muench and the Guilt Question in Germany* (Notre Dame, Ind.: University of Notre Dame, 2006), 1. Muench related the pope's story to a stateside clerical acquaintance.

11. In his doctoral dissertation, Paul Damien O'Shea explained the relationship between the encyclical and the Holocaust; see "Confiteor. Eugenio Pacelli, the Catholic Church and the Jews. An Examination of the Responsibility of Pope Pius XII and the Holocaust, 1917–1943" (Ph.D. diss., Macquarie University, 2004), 339ff.

12. Ibid., 339.

13. *Mystici Corporis Christi,* paragraph 5.

14. *Mystici Corporis Christi,* paragraph 6.

15. War Refugee Board to Secretary Maglione, June 24, 1944, Box 441, RG 84, location 250/64/25/05 and 06, NARA.

16. Secretary of State Cordell Hull to Harold H. Tittmann, May 26, 1944, Entry 1073, Box 31, RG 59, location 250/48/29/05, NARA.

17. Harold H. Tittmann to Secretary of State Maglione, May 1, 1944, Entry 1069, Box 4, RG 59, location 250/48/29/05, NARA.

18. F. C. Gowen to Myron C. Taylor, November 7, 1944, Entry 1069, Box 4, RG 59, location 250/48/29/05, NARA.

19. See Reuben Reznik, "Efforts in Relief, Rescue and Resettlement during World War II," talk presented to the Detroit Jewish Historical Society, June 12, 1988, Reznik Papers, Archives of the American Joint Distribution Committee, New York, New York.

20. Allocution of Pius XII, June 2, 1945, quoted in O'Shea, "Confiteor," 35.

21. Memo of Harold H. Tittmann "for the ambassador," June 4, 1945, Entry 1069, Box 28, RG 59, location 250/48/29/5, NARA.

22. Interview of Harold H. Tittmann with Dr. Josef Müller, June 4, 1945, Entry 1069, Box 28, RG 59, location 250/48/29/05, NARA.

23. Thomas F. O'Meara, "A French Resistance Hero," *America* 176, no. 18 (May 1997): 12–16.

24. Father Bernard Lichtenberg (1875–1943) was an outspoken opponent of the Nazis, especially regarding the Jews. He died in a cattle car en route to the Dachau concentration camp.

25. There is a concordance between O'Shea's emphasis on supersessionism as the key to Pius XII's silence about the Holocaust and Richard Rubenstein's theory of cognitive dissonance. O'Shea argues that the supersessionist mentality held Pius XII back from speaking out, and Rubenstein believes that dissonance reduction led Pius to *wish* for the destruction of the Jews. See my discussion of these views in "'It's Not Easy to Help the Jews': Vatican Holocaust Policy—Continuity or Change?" *Holocaust and Genocide Studies,* in press.

26. Memo, Paris, to U.S. State Department, July 19, 1949, Box 49, Papers of Myron C. Taylor, Harry S. Truman Presidential Museum and Library, Independence, Missouri.

27. Myron C. Taylor, Rome, telegram to Franklin D. Roosevelt, March 27,

1941, Box 151, Folder 4, Sumner Welles Papers, Franklin D. Roosevelt Presidential Library and Museum.

28. See the folder marked "Vatican Matters," 1945, Entry 1073, Box 34, Myron C. Taylor Papers, RG 59 NARA.

29. Dianne Kirby, "Harry Truman's Religious Legacy: The Holy Alliance, Containment, and the Cold War," in *Religion and the Cold War*, ed. Dianne Kirby (New York: Palgrave, 2003), 86.

30. Domenico Cardinal Tardini, *Memories of Pius XII*, trans. Rosemary Goldie (Westminister, Md.: Newman Press, 1961), 51.

31. Susan Zuccotti found a hodgepodge of contradictory characterizations of Pius XII; see Zuccotti, *Under His Very Windows*, 60–61.

32. Peter Godman, *Hitler and the Vatican* (New York: Free Press, 2004), 147.

33. Ibid., 73.

34. Gerhart Besier, zusammenarbeit mit Francesca Piombo, *Der Heilige Stuhl und Hitler-Deutschland. Die Faszination des Totalitären* (Munich: Verlagsgruppe Random House, 2004), 263.

35. Ibid., 317.

36. Godman, *Hitler and the Vatican*, 130; see also 146–147.

37. Besier, *Der Heilige Stuhl und Hitler-Deutschland*, 159.

38. Tardini made this point in general, not in connection specifically with the Holocaust. Pius, he wrote, "was by temperament mild and rather shy. He was not made to be a fighter." Similarly, he noted that Pius tended to "avoid rather than to face the battles of life." Tardini meant by this that the pope preferred diplomacy to strong outbursts of criticism. Diplomacy was his way, Tardini believed, of solving difficulties by "patience and perseverence, avoiding strong words, harsh phrases, abrupt gestures." See Tardini, *Memories of Pius XII*, 39 and passim.

39. Michael Phayer, *The Catholic Church and the Holocaust* (Bloomington: Indiana University Press, 2000), 60.

40. Pius XII's aggressive demeanor in the years immediately following the war do not at all fit Tardini's characterization of the pope as "mild . . . shy . . . not meant to be a fighter." See Tardini, *Memories of Pius XII*, 73.

41. Dianne Kirby, "Harry Truman's Religious Legacy: The Holy Alliance, Containment, and the Cold War," in *Religion and the Cold War*, ed. Dianne Kirby (New York: Palgrave, 2003), 88.

42. Phayer, *The Catholic Church and the Holocaust*, 182.

43. Cahiers Jacques Maritain, 4, L'Ambassade au Vatican (1945–1948), Maritain archives, Kolbsheim, France. Maritain wrote these words because he wanted to set down his thoughts before resigning. He began by saying that "in general it can be said that the Vatican governs little and administers a lot especially in the sense of regulations."

44. Godman, *Hitler and the Vatican*, 75 and 139.

45. Ibid., 164.

46. J. G. Parsons, memo of a conversation with Monsignor Tardini, July 30, 1947, Entry 1068, Box 15, RG 59, location 250/48/29/01-05, NARA.

47. The last was Pope John XXIII, born in 1881.

48. J. G. Parsons, memo of a conversation with J. Victor Perowne and Monsignor Francis J. Brennan, Entry 1068, Box 15, RG 59, location 250/48/29/01-05, NARA.

49. J. G. Parsons, memo of a conversation with H. V. Kaltenborn, August 6, 1947, Entry 1068 Box 15, RG 59, location 250/48/29/01-05, NARA.

50. J. G. Parsons, Vatican City, to Secretary of State George Marshall, June 3, 1948, Entry 1068, Box 21, RG 59, location 250/48/2901-05, NARA.

51. Godman, *Hitler and the Vatican,* 33.

52. Harold H. Tittmann, Jr., *Inside the Vatican of Pius XII: The Memoir of an American Diplomat during World War II,* ed. Harold Tittmann, III (New York: Doubleday, 2004), 95–96.

53. John F. Morley, *Vatican Diplomacy and the Jews during the Holocaust, 1939–1943* (New York: Ktav Publishing House, 1980), 12.

54. Besier, *Der Heilige Stuhl und Hitler-Deutschland,* 314.

55. Morley, *Vatican Diplomacy,* 209.

56. Ibid.

57. Ibid.

58. Tittmann, *Inside the Vatican,* 95.

59. See the introductory chapter of Michael Marrus, *The Nuremberg War Crimes Trial, 1945–1946: A Documentary History* (Boston: Bedford Books, 1997).

60. Quoted in Marrus, *Nuremberg War Crimes Trial,* 21.

61. Frank M. Buscher, *The U.S. War Crimes Trial Program in Germany, 1946–1955* (New York: Greenwood Press, 1989), 15.

62. Foreign Office, London, to Osborne for the Vatican, August 4, 1943, *ADSS,* 7:539.

63. Marrus, *Nuremberg War Crimes Trial,* 3.

64. Richard Hofstadter, *The Paranoid Style in American Politics and Other Essays* (New York: Knopf, 1965), 74.

65. OSS report, Rome, July 26, 1946, RG 266, Entry 24, Box 48, NARA.

BIBLIOGRAPHY

Archival Sources

Archives of the Catholic University of America

This archive holds the valuable papers of Bishop Aloisius Muench, which I used extensively in *The Catholic Church and the Holocaust* (see bibliography) and to a lesser extent in this book. Catholic University also houses the extensive papers of the National Catholic Welfare Conference, which set up committees such as the War Relief and Emergency Committee and War Relief Services. These entities worked for and in conjunction with the Vatican's Pontifical Commission for Assistance. Numerous files in groups 10/3, 10/25, 10/36, 10/37, 10/141, and 10/158 document the close association the American bishops had with the Vatican's emigration work.

National Archives and Records Administration—College Park

The papers of the Department of State, Record Group 59 in the national archives, contain the correspondence of President Roosevelt's personal representative to the Holy See and his assistants, even though this staff did not answer to the State Department. These records continue through the Truman administration. Since their correspondence touches on all matters the Holy See wished to bring to the attention of the president and all matters that the president wished to bring to the attention of the Holy Father, these files are voluminous and indispensable. Because Myron Taylor, the president's envoy to the Vatican, was often absent from Rome, a large proportion of the correspondence came from his able assistant, Harold Tittmann. After retiring from State Department service, Tittmann wanted to write a memoir of his years at the Vatican, but he died before he completed the task. His son then took over the assignment, producing an engaging account of the war years as seen from Rome (Harold H. Tittmann, Jr., *Inside the Vatican of Pius XII: The Memoir of an American Diplomat during World War II*, edited by Harold H. Tittmann, III.) Unfortunately, the memoir is not an accurate reflection of the actual Tittmann documents in Record Group 59 or Microfilm 982 in Decimal File 740.0011 of Record Group 59, which should also be consulted. Finally, in this category of information the foreign service posts of the State Department, Record Group 84, are quite useful.

The reports of U.S. intelligence agents in Record Group 226 were equally indispensable, although not as voluminous as those of state. For the historian, the postings of these agents are fascinating because of the contrast they reveal between their awareness of people and events and that of State Department personnel. In this sense, the 226 records are both a complement and a necessary corrective to State Department records. For the purposes of this study, Record Group 226 provided essential information about the Catholic church in Poland (see especially *La Persécution Religieuse en Pologne*, anonymous, October 1942, Entry 210, Box 375, Folder 413, location 250/64/28/07, about the events associated with the October *razzia* in Rome (together with decryptions that have hitherto been unavailable) and, of course, the ratlines. With regard to the latter, Record Group 65 (FBI) and Record Group 319 (army staff) are important, although they are not as comprehensive as the 226 group.

Some of the files in 226 must be used cautiously. The OSS was ecstatic when it managed to place agent "Blackie," Felix Morlion, O.P., at the Vatican because of his supposedly close relationship with Pius XII. Blackie did indeed provide enticing glimpses of Pope Pius. He reported that the pope was

> exceptionally high in his motives and judgments. But he is of extreme sensibility and, although very humble, is very prone to be offended by people who do not approach him the right way and to have deep affection for people who do. (Entry 210, Box 375, location 250/64/28/07)

Intriguing, yes, but reliable? Blackie also reported that the German ambassador to the Holy See, Ernst von Weizsäcker, gave him three official Berlin "white books" detailing German crimes in Poland. That Weizsäcker would have done such a thing is unthinkable, and no more about the books was ever heard.

Since no information about the pope's finances is available at the Vatican, Record Group 131 (Office of Alien Property) is a another valuable and indispensable source. Here transactions of the Vatican bank may be found, although only a fraction of them. Vatican financial dealings with the U.S. treasury may be reviewed in this group; for example, in stack area 230, row 38, compartment 32, shelf 5, Foreign Funds Control Subject Files, Box 487, Folder marked "Vatican City Funds in the U.S. Transfer of." Many documents in this group concern the Italian and German insurance industries. Finding records of the Vatican's venture into this investment field turned out to be like looking for a needle in a haystack. Record Group 131 also holds data on the movement of gold in Europe during the war and files dealing with the work of the Tripartite Commission for the Restitution of Monetary Gold. Much of the archive's data on the Vatican's South American bank, Sudameris, may be found in Record Group 84. Useful financial information may also be found in Record Group 169, the Office of Economic Warfare.

Center for Advanced Holocaust Studies— U.S. Holocaust Memorial Museum

The Center for Advanced Holocaust Studies has been combing Europe for a number of years collecting microfilm of documents in a number of national collections. This offers researchers an enormous advantage. Many of the center's acquisitions relate to Eastern European countries with heavily Catholic populations. These records are a boon for historians interested in the church and the Holocaust. A few examples: RG 15.007, reel 8, contains a valuable report on conditions of the church in Poland soon after the German occupation that was sent to Pope Pius XII; the same reel contains the Verordnung über die Erhebung von Beiträgen durch religiöse Vereiningungen und Religionsgesellschaften (Regulation over the Levy of Contributions by Religious Organizations and Religious Societies) for German-occupied Poland. RG 52.009.01*1 has letters to and from Cardinal Justinian Serédi that relate to the seizure of Jews in Hungary late in the war.

Recently the center has obtained a microfilm copy of the newly released Vatican records from the period 1922 to 1939. The index for the records has now been prepared by Suzanne Brown-Fleming, the center's senior programs officer for university programs. These documents are available for public use. The center acquires new documentary material so regularly that researchers will want to check its inventory for themselves.

Newspapers and Journals

America
Baltimore Sun
Chicago Tribune
Commonweal
National Catholic Reporter
New York Times
Washington Evening Star

Printed and Edited Documents

Acta Apostolicae Sedis, 1909–1970.
Blet, Pierre, S.J., Angelo Martini, S.J., Burkhart Schneider, S.J., and Robert Graham, S.J., eds. Actes et Documents du Saint Siège Relatifs á la Seconde Guerre Mondiale (Acts and Documents of the Holy See Relative to the Second World War). Vatican City: Liberia Editrice Vaticana, 1965–1967.
Hill, Leonidas, ed. Die Weizsäcker Papiere, 1933–1950. Frankfurt: Allstein, 1974.
Lochner, Louis P., ed. The Goebbels Diaries, 1942–1943. Translated and introduced by Louis P. Lochner. Garden City, N.Y.: Doubleday, 1948.

Memoirs

Breitinger, Hilarius. Als Deutscher Seelsorger in Posen und im Warthegau, 1934–35, Veröffentlichungen der Kommission für Zeitgeschichte bei der Katholischen Akademie in Bayern. Mainz: Grünewald, 1973–1998.
Hudal, Alois C. Römische Tagebücher. Lebensbeicht eines alten Bischofs. Graz: Stocker, 1976.
Maler, Juan. Frieden, Krieg, und "Frieden." N.p.: Published by the author, 1987.
Steinbach, Peter, ed. Albrecht von Kessel, Verborgene Saat. Aufzeichnungen aus dem Widerstand 1933 bis 1945 (Albrecht von Kessel, Hidden Seed: Notes from the Resistance). Berlin: Ullstein, 1992.
Tittmann, Harold H., Jr. Inside the Vatican of Pius XII: The Memoir of an American Diplomat during World War II. Ed. Harold Tittmann, III. New York: Doubleday, 2004.

Secondary Sources

(I have omitted some works that I have used but which were cited in the bibliography of The Catholic Church and the Holocaust.)
Altermatt, Urs. Katholizismus und Antisemitismus: Mentalitäten, Kontiuitäten, Ambivalenzen; zur Kulturgeschichte der Schweiz, 1918–1945. Frauenwald: Verlag Huber, 1999.

Alvarez, David. *Spies in the Vatican: Espionage and Intrigue from Napoleon to the Holocaust.* Lawrence: University Press of Kansas, 2002.

———, and Robert A. Graham, S.J. *Nothing Sacred: Nazi Espionage against the Vatican.* London: F. Cass, 1997.

Aly, Götz, Belinda Cooper, and Allison Brown. *"Final Solution": Nazi Population Policy and the Murder of the European Jews.* Trans. Belinda Cooper and Allison Brown. New York: Oxford University Press, 1999.

Besier, Gerhart, zusammenarbeit mit Francesca Piombo. *Der Heilige Stuhl und Hitler-Deutschland. Die Faszination des Totalitären.* Munich: Verlagsgruppe Random House, 2004.

Breitman, Richard. "New Sources on the Holocaust in Italy." *Holocaust and Genocide Studies* 16, no. 3 (Winter 2002): 401–414.

———, Norman J. W. Goda, Timothy Naftali, and Robert Wolfe, eds. *U.S. Intelligence and the Nazis.* Washington, D.C.: National Archives Trust Fund Board for the Nazi War Crimes and Japanese Imperial Government Records Interagency Working Groups, 2004.

Brown-Fleming, Suzanne. *The Holocaust and the Catholic Conscience.* Notre Dame, Ind.: University of Notre Dame Press, 2005.

Browning, Christopher R. *Nazi Policy, Jewish Workers, German Killers.* New York: Cambridge University Press, 2000.

———, with contributions by Jürgen Matthäus. *The Origins of the Final Solution: The Evolution of Nazi Jewish Policy, September 1939–March 1942.* Lincoln: University of Nebraska Press, 2004.

Buscher, Frank M. *The U.S. War Crimes Trial Program in Germany, 1946–1945.* New York: Greenwood Press, 1989.

Chadwick, Owen. "Weizsaecker, the Vatican, and the Jews of Rome." *Journal of Ecclesiastical History* 28, no. 2 (April 1977): 179–199.

Chernow, Ron. *The House of Morgan.* New York: Atlantic Monthly Press, 1990.

Coffey, Thomas M. *Lion by the Tail: The Story of the Italian-Ethiopian War.* New York: Coffey, 1974.

Comptroller General of the United States. *Nazis and Axis Collaborators Were Used to Further U.S. Anti-Communist Objectives in Europe—Some Immigrated to the U.S.* 1985. Washington, D.C.: General Accounting Office, 1985.

Coppa, Frank J., ed. *Controversial Concordats: The Vatican's Relations with Napoleon, Mussolini, and Hitler.* Washington, D.C.: U.S. General Accounting Office, 1999.

Dingell, Jean. "Property Seizures from Poles and Jews: The Activities of the Haupttreuhandstelle Ost." In *Confiscation of Jewish Property in Europe, 1933–1945. New Sources and Perspectives.* Washington, D.C.: Center for Advanced Holocaust Studies, U.S. Holocaust Memorial Museum, 2003.

Duquesne, Jacques. *Les Catholiques français sous l'Occupation.* New ed. Paris: Grasset, 1996.

Eizenstat, Stuart. *U.S. and Allied Wartime and Postwar Relations and Negotiations with Argentina, Portugal, Spain, Sweden, and Turkey on Looted Gold and German External Assets and U.S. Concerns About the Fate of the Wartime Ustasha Treasury.* Washington, D.C.: U.S. Government Printing Office, 1998.

Engel, David. *Facing a Holocaust: The Polish Government-in-Exile and the Jews, 1943–1945.* Chapel Hill: University of North Carolina Press, 1993.

Feldman, Gerald D. *Allianz and the German Insurance Business, 1933–1945.* Cambridge: Cambridge University Press, 2001.

Fogarty, Gerald. *The Vatican and the American Hierarchy, 1870–1965.* Wilmington, Del.: Michael Glazier, 1985.

Gaddis, John Lewis. *The United States and the End of the Cold War.* New York: Oxford University Press, 1992.

Gallagher, Charles R. "Patriot Bishop: The Public Career of Archbishop Joseph P. Hurley, 1937–1967." Ph.D. diss., Marquette University, 1998.

———. "The United States and the Vatican in Yugoslavia, 1945–1950." In *Religion and the Cold War,* ed. Dianne Kirby, 118–144. New York: Palgrave, 2003.

Goda, Norman J. W. "Manhunts: The Official Search for Notorious Nazis." In *U.S. Intelligence and the Nazis,* ed. Richard Breitman, Norman J. W. Goda, Timothy Naftali, and Robert Wolfe, 419–442. Washington, D.C.: National Archives Trust Fund Board for the Nazi War Crimes and Japanese Imperial Government Records Interagency Working Groups, 2004.

———. "The Ustaša: Murder and Espionage." In *U.S. Intelligence and the Nazis,* ed. Richard Breitman, Norman J. W. Goda, Timothy Naftali, and Robert Wolfe, 203–226. Washington, D.C.: National Archives Trust Fund Board for the Nazi War Crimes and Japanese Imperial Government Records Interagency Working Groups, 2004.

Godman, Peter. *Hitler and the Vatican.* New York: Free Press, 2004.

Goñi, Uki. *The Real Odessa: Smuggling the Nazis to Perón's Argentina.* London: Granta, 2002.

Hametz, Maura E. "The Ambivalence of Italian Anti-Semitism: Fascism, Nationalism, and Racism in Trieste." *Holocaust and Genocide Studies* 16, no. 3 (Winter 2002): 376–401.

Hayes, Peter. *From Cooperation to Complicity: Degussa in the Third Reich.* Cambridge: Cambridge University Press, 2004.

———. *Industry and Ideology: IG Farben in the Nazi Era.* Cambridge: Cambridge University Press, 1987.

Hill, Leonidas E., III. "The Vatican Embassy of Ernst von Weizsaecker." *Journal of Modern History* 39, no. 2 (1967): 138–159.

Hofstadter, Richard. *The Paranoid Style in American Politics and Other Essays.* New York: Knopf, 1965.

Hunt, Linda. *Secret Agenda: The United States Government, Nazi Scientists, and Project Paperclip, 1945–1980.* New York: St. Martin's Press, 1991.

Jong, Louis de. *The Netherlands and Nazi Germany.* Cambridge, Mass.: Harvard University Press, 1990.

Judt, Tony. *Postwar: A History of Europe since 1945.* New York: Penguin Press, 2005.

Katz, Robert. *The Battle for Rome: The Germans, the Allies, the Partisans, and the Pope, September 1943–June 1944.* New York: Simon & Schuster, 2004.

Kent, Peter C. *The Lonely Cold War of Pope Pius XII: The Roman Catholic Church and the Division of Europe, 1943–1950.* Montreal: McGill-Queen's University Press, 2002.

———. *The Pope and the Duce: The International Impact of the Lateran Agreements.* New York: St. Martin's Press, 1981.

Kertzer, David I. *The Popes against the Jews: The Vatican's Role in the Rise of Modern Anti-Semitism.* New York: Alfred A. Knopf, 2001.

———. *Prisoner of the Vatican.* Boston: Houghton Mifflin, 2004.

Kirby, Dianne, ed. "Harry Truman's Religious Legacy: The Holy Alliance, Containment, and the Cold War." In *Religion and the Cold War,* ed. Dianne Kirby, 77–102. New York: Palgrave, 2003.

———. *Religion and the Cold War.* New York: Palgrave, 2003.

Laqueur, Walter. *The Terrible Secret: Suppression of the Truth about Hitler's "Final Solution."* New York: Little, Brown, 1980.

Leffler, Melvyn P. *A Preponderance of Power.* Stanford, Calif.: Stanford University Press, 1992.

Louça, Antonio, and Ansgar Schaefer. "Portugal and the Nazi Gold: The 'Lisbon Connection' in the Sales of Looted Gold by the Third Reich." *Yad Vashem Studies* XXVI (2004): 27, 1–20.

Marrus, Michael. *The Nuremberg War Crimes Trial, 1945–1946: A Documentary History.* Boston: Bedford Books, 1997.

———. *The Unwanted: European Refugees in the Twentieth Century.* New York: Oxford University Press, 1985.

———. "To Whom Did They Belong? The Vatican and the Custody of Jewish Child Survivors after the Holocaust." In *Holocaust and Genocide Studies,* in press.

McNamara, Patrick. *A Catholic Cold War: Edmund A. Walsh, S.J., and the Politics of American Anticommunism.* New York: Fordham University Press, 2005.

Misner, Paul. *Social Catholicism in Europe.* New York: Crossroad, 1991.

Morley, John F. "Vatican Diplomacy and the Jews of Hungary during the Holocaust: October 15, 1944 to the End." Paper presented at the Second International Holocaust Conference, Berlin.

———. *Vatican Diplomacy and the Jews during the Holocaust, 1939–1943.* New York: Ktav Publishing House, 1980.

O'Shea, Paul Damian. "Confiteor. Eugenio Pacelli, the Catholic Church and the Jews. An Examination of the Responsibility of Pope Pius XII and the Holocaust, 1917–1943." Ph.D. diss., Macquarie University, 2004.

Pawlikowski, John T. "The Vatican and the Holocaust: Unresolved Issues." In *Jewish-Christian Encounters over the Centuries: Symbiosis, Prejudice, Holocaust, Dialogue,* ed. Marvin Perry and F. M. Schweitzer, 294–310. New York: P. Lang, 1994.

Phayer, Michael. *The Catholic Church and the Holocaust, 1930–1965.* Bloomington: Indiana University Press, 2000.

———. "'It's Not Easy to Help the Jews': Vatican Holocaust Policy—Continuity or Change?" In *Holocaust and Genocide Studies,* in press.

———. "Pius XII and the Genocides of Polish Catholics and Polish Jews." *Kirchliche Zeitgeschichte* 15, no. 1 (2002): 238–262.

Pollard, John. *Money and the Rise of the Modern Papacy: Financing the Vatican, 1850–1950.* Cambridge: Cambridge University Press, 2005.

———. "The Vatican, Italy, and the Cold War." in *Religion and the Cold War,* ed. Dianne Kirby, 103–117. New York: Palgrave, 2003.

Reese, Thomas J. *Inside the Vatican: The Politics and Organization of the Catholic Church.* Cambridge, Mass.: Harvard University Press, 1996.

Riegner, Gerhart. "A Warning of the World Jewish Congress to Mobilize the Christian Churches against the Final Solution." Stephen S. Wise Inaugural Lecture, Stephen S. Wise Temple, Cincinnati, Ohio, 1983.

————. *Niemals Verzweifeln.* Trans. Michael von Killisch-Horn. Gerlingen: Bleicher, 2001.

Roth, John, and Richard L. Rubenstein. *Approaches to Auschwitz: The Holocaust and Its Legacy.* Rev. ed. Louisville, Ky.: Westminster John Knox Press, 2003.

Sereny, Gitta. *Into That Darkness.* New York: Simon and Schuster, 1983.

Snoek, J. M. *Nederlandse Kerken en de Joden 1940–1945.* Kampen: J. H. Kok, 1990.

Spicer, Kevin P. *Resisting the Third Reich: The Catholic Clergy in Hitler's Berlin.* Dekalb, Ill.: Northern Illinois University Press, 2004.

Stasiewski, Bernhard. "Nationalsozialistische Kirchenpolitik im Warthegau." *Vierteljahresschrift für Zeitgeschichte* 7 (1959): 46–75.

Stehle, Hansjakob. *Geheimdiplomatie im Vatikan. Die Päpste und die Kommunisten.* Zurich: Benziger, 1993.

Weisbord, Robert G. "The King, the Cardinal and the Pope: Leopold II's Genocide in the Congo and the Vatican." *Journal of Genocide Research* 5, no. 1(2003): 35–45.

Wyman, David S. *The Abandonment of the Jews: America and the Holocaust, 1941–1945.* New York: Pantheon Books, 1984.

Zimmerer, Jürgen. "The German War of Extermination in South-West Africa (1904–1908) and the Global History of Mass Violence." Paper presented at the conference Lessons and Legacies VIII, Brown University, Providence, R.I., November 4–7, 2004.

————. "Krieg, KZ und Völkermord in Südwestafrika. Der erste deutsche Genoczid." In *Völkermord in Deutsche-Südwestafrika. Der Kolonialkrieg (1904–1908) in Namibia und seine Folgen,* ed. Jürgen Zimmerer and Joachin Zeller, 45–63. Berlin, 2003.

Zuccotti, Susan. "*L'Osservatore Romano* and the Holocaust, 1930–1945." *Holocaust and Genocide Studies* 17, no. 2 (2003): 248–278.

————. *Under His Very Windows: The Vatican and the Holocaust in Italy.* New Haven, Conn.: Yale University Press, 2000.

INDEX

A Holocaust scholar and educator, **Michael Phayer** has lectured throughout the United States. He is a recognized authority on how the Catholic Church and Catholics reacted to the killing of the Jews and how the Holocaust became the occasion for the Church's revision of its teaching about the Chosen People. He is Emeritus Professor of History at Marquette University and the Ida E. King Distinguished Visiting Scholar of Holocaust Studies at the Richard Stockton College of New Jersey. He is author of *The Catholic Church and the Holocaust, 1930–1965* (Indiana University Press, 2000) and *Protestant and Catholic Women in Nazi Germany* and co-author of *Cries in the Night: Women Who Challenged the Holocaust.* His e-mail address is michael.phayer@marquette.edu.